THE RIVALS

James Naughtie presents the *Today* programme on BBC Radio 4 and is former chief political correspondent of the *Guardian*. He also presents *Bookclub* on Radio 4 and music and opera on BBC radio and television. He has been Laurence Stern fellow on the *Washington Post* and Sony Radio Personality of the Year. James Naughtie and his family live in London.

THE RIVALS

*The Intimate Story of a
Political Marriage*

James Naughtie

FOURTH ESTATE · *London*

This paperback revised edition published in 2002
First published in Great Britain in 2001 by
Fourth Estate
A Division of HarperCollins*Publishers*
77–85 Fulham Palace Road
London w6 8jb
www.4thestate.com

A catalogue record for this book is available from
the British Library

ISBN 1-84115-474-1

Typeset by Rowland Phototypesetting Ltd,
Bury St Edmunds, Suffolk
Printed in Great Britain by Clays Ltd, St Ives plc

For Ellie
with love

Acknowledgements

Many people have helped me to try to understand Tony Blair and Gordon Brown, and I am grateful to friends and acquaintances inside and outside politics for their help in describing the absorbing and puzzling phenomenon of their relationship. In revising this book, midway through the first year of their second term, I was reinforced in my view of the ambiguities of their partnership. Events were not persuading them to change the way they worked together, but seemed to be dramatising the tensions and the unspoken rivalries of their political lives going back many years and I owe a debt to those of their friends and colleagues who were willing to share their thoughts with me, especially those who did so despite having been encouraged not to.

I have drawn on conversations going back many years since I first watched the young Blair and Brown arrive in the House of Commons. Naturally these include past conversations with them, but I did not ask them for cooperation in this book and readers can be assured that it is unauthorized. I hope that helps to give it an authentic flavour, catching some of the genuine spirit of their dealings with each other and thereby explaining how they came to achieve and maintain such dominance.

Cabinet ministers and civil servants are inevitably constrained in what they can say publicly about each other, so I have had to accept that many whose words and views are quoted here have to remain anonymous. This did lead to a happy decision about footnotes: there are none. The phrase 'private information' littering the pages would, in any case, have been infuriating for everyone. I hope it appears to make sense. In any case, this is a portrait rather than a conventional biography (Rentoul, Routledge and Macintyre having served us very well in that form already) and I have tried to write about these political lives in a different way. I hope their characters take on some shape, and that their backgrounds and instincts are illuminated. Writing as the government wrestled with its political problems of early 2002, and as the prospect of another phase of the 'war against terrorism' promised a testing time for Blair, I became even more convinced that much of the truth about their style and attitude at challenging moments, and the truth about their political ideas, lies under the surface. In politics, everyone has a past and it tells you everything. This is the story of that history.

Some particular friends have been generous with their thoughts. I have spent long nights puzzling over the subjects of this book with Peter Riddell, Peter Hennessy, and Martin Kettle among many others and have drunk liberally from the Westminster well. All my colleagues on *Today* have been cheerily supportive, and Stephen Mitchell at the BBC stalwart and straight. My other principal debts are to Felicity Bryan, my agent, and to the long-suffering Clive Priddle, a brilliant editor at Fourth Estate, who now has engraved on his heart James Cameron's motto for all journalists: 'There's always another quarter of an hour.' Richard Collins has been a meticulous copy editor and my *Today* colleague and friend Nick Sutton, a writer's dream researcher. Most of all, I thank Ellie for her support and incisiveness, and promise Andrew, Catherine and Flora that we can get back some of the time we have lost.

JN
March 2002

Contents

Introduction: Two Into One

No pair of politicians in our modern history has wielded so much power together as Tony Blair and Gordon Brown. They met when the Labour Party was weak and writhing in agony and then single-mindedly, with the help of the accidents that often shape politics, they were able to create a single political personality for their party and themselves that dominated the affairs of the country at the end of the century. We have seen nothing like it before.

This creation was a phenomenon that seemed to spring from nowhere. Their party was exhausted, angry and divided when they arrived at Westminster and they had to learn their parliamentary politics deep in the shadow of Margaret Thatcher, in the force field of her ideological challenge. Yet when they were only in their mid-forties they were commanding a government with a bigger majority than any one party had known since the Great Reform Act was passed in the days of their great-great-grandfathers. They began their second term in 2001 with seemingly untrammelled power in government, a Prime Minister and Chancellor who had turned politics to their own purposes and whose style was imprinted on their era.

But this power has pain flowing through it. In building a partnership which in its closeness has no modern parallel, Blair and Brown have lived with an intimacy which has caused each of them intense anxiety and anger as well as bringing them the luscious fruits of power. They still live in a political embrace which neither has been able to escape. Each knows that without it he would not have been able to flourish alone. That union has given them everything, including the despair. Neither enjoys the description of their relationship as a marriage, but it is the one that their colleagues in government most often use because they can find no other way of explaining the deep mystery of how their moments of political intimacy are often disturbed by tensions and arguments that seem to well up from a history in the partnership that only the two of them can feel fully or understand. One of their ministers in the Lords – a woman – was trying to explain it to an outsider who wondered how this strange Downing Street relationship worked, and put it like this: 'When you're with them together, you find them finishing each other's sentences.'

Even the weary veterans of the Westminster village, gathering to gossip at the well, find it impossible to rake up a comparison. No Prime Minister and Chancellor in the modern era have operated like this. None of Thatcher's three Chancellors – not even her cherished Nigel Lawson – had a relationship like the one that binds Blair and Brown together. A distance always remained, and when Lawson resigned after their falling-out the Prime Minister tried to carry on as if this was just another of the sad squalls of politics that pass away. None of us who have seen Brown and Blair grow together from their early days and who observe them now in power believe that a parting could be anything less than an earthquake in politics, a shock that would disturb the deepest foundations of their government and their party. And for one of them at least it would be bound to be a tragedy.

Politics doesn't have to be like this. Chancellors of the Exchequer can pass across the landscape without leaving many footprints, and Prime Ministers can appear to command governments alone, taking seriously the title of First Lord of the Treasury engraved on the letter box of Number 10 Downing Street. Their names aren't always coupled together. Heath is Heath, without Barber. Early Wilson is usually not Wilson–Callaghan. Macmillan is Macmillan without the forgotten Heathcoat Amory or Selwyn Lloyd or Maudling. And are the closing years of the eighties thought of as Thatcher–Major? Blair and Brown are different and we can't think of them as characters with separate existences. Their party, dominating the Commons with 419 seats out of 659 in 1997 and 413 out of 659 in 2001, thinks of them as a duopoly, and when Labour MPs try to envisage a government that is not constructed on the Blair–Brown axis they find it hard. They seem to have managed to put a psychological spell on their party. Everyone talks about what life would be like if one or other of them were not there, but no one finds it easy to conceive. In Downing Street and the Treasury they speak of that distant day with an awful fascination. How and when will it come? The knowledge that one day the pattern is bound to be broken is infused with a frisson of fear, because this Prime Minister and Chancellor have expended great energy in persuading their party of their own indispensability. Blair giving way to Brown? An unexpected political cataclysm that destroys one and preserves the other? The decision of one to go off to lead a different life? These are the delicious fantasies of Whitehall, chewed over in the tapas bars of Westminster as enthusiastically as once the strategy and gossip of empire was traded across the tables of the gentlemen's clubs of St James's. Anyone with a foothold in politics in any party knows that it is the obsession of our time and they know why. Like two wrestlers locked in a complicated clinch in the middle of the ring, this Prime Minister and Chancellor twitch and strain but remain nervous of the big thrust to break free. They're absorbed in the complexity of their entanglement.

To watch them over the last twenty years has been to see a friendship develop, turn into a political alliance and, through a fiery clash of ambitions, end up as a mesmerizing and dominant public spectacle. No one who has followed their political careers as an observer now wants to miss the raised eyebrow or the whispered aside or the piece of telling body language because, between these two, nothing is neutral or without significance any more. Everything carries a weight of meaning which they may regret but can no longer wish away.

In the early days they exuded a relish for the games of politics which has been disciplined by their own arguments and by power. Blair was much the more innocent of the two, plunging into Westminster like a youngster pushed off a high diving board by an unseen hand. Meeting him the year before he became an MP when he was fruitlessly canvassing the dedicated Conservatives of Beaconsfield in Buckinghamshire in the by-election of 1982 was to encounter a picture of unsullied vivacity. He had nothing to lose. Indeed as you did the rounds of the villages and lanes, you felt a certain sympathy for this underdog candidate not only facing a Conservative majority of the sort that used to be weighed rather than counted after the polls closed, but having to deal with a rampant Prime Minister raucously rallying her troops to the sound of Falklands war drums. None of us spotted it at the time, but the whole experience sharpened Blair's political enthusiasm and helped him discover that he wanted more. Within a year he was engaged on a quick blitz in County Durham to win the Sedgefield nomination, throwing himself into it as if he had to do a barrister's all-night swot before court in the morning.

Brown's innocence had long gone by this time, and in Scotland he was carrying a political history with him while Blair was getting his first thrills. The student politician and radical intellectual was a fixture in Edinburgh. When you visited his book-strewn flat you were part of a kind of downbeat political salon. The oxygen of politics in Scotland was devolution and Brown was of a generation that felt it had lived half a lifetime in a few wild years. In the seventies, reasonably sane people used to stand in pubs in Edinburgh and talk about what was going to happen when devolution or independence came – next month? next year? – and there was a Parliament and the trappings of a state and even an Embassy Row where ambassadors would come to observe the New Scotland. This is the kind of inflated nonsense that was in the air, and it was known by (almost) everyone to be nonsense. Yet it gave Scottish politics an undeniable surge of energy to which no one objected, and an edge which everyone enjoyed. In this world, everyone knew Gordon Brown. To those of us who travelled home regularly from Westminster and pored over the political map, his tracks were already clear.

The story that began to unfold when the two met at Westminster in 1983 became an absorbing one almost at once. Such was the despair of their generation, in which power seemed nothing more substantial than a flickering mirage on a far distant horizon, they could fling themselves into reform in a way that wouldn't have been possible if they had arrived at a different moment and found themselves constrained by the disciplines of seniority and proper form. Instead, their party was lawless, rudderless, a blank piece of paper. It represented a delicious opportunity for young, inventive minds prepared to create a new identity for Labour.

The mid-1980s were dominated, of course, by Margaret Thatcher. The shrewder young Labour MPs understood that they should use this time to make their own politics. They knew they were probably out of power for the decade, and so Brown and Blair began to scheme their schemes. They were good company in those days round a Commons dining table or in one of the bars, gossiping, plotting tactics for the next day's Employment Bill or just lounging on the Commons terrace on a sultry summer night wondering if their party was ever going to be able to climb out of the pit. They were invigorated by involvement with Peter Mandelson, which changed their lives, and started the clambering of the greasy pole in the shadow Cabinet elections after Labour's 1987 defeat. Even then they seemed to have a plan with a controlled narrative, every chapter pointing to the next.

Their sense of obligation to each other comes from the years they spent together in the parliamentary desert. Their main difficulty, and the principal cause of the cold shaft that often divides them, is the leadership argument of 1994 that only came about because they were so close. The privacy that they insist on preserving for their own negotiations on policy and strategy is the consequence of the intensity that they cultivated when they were free to revel in youthful self-promotion in opposition. Everything is explained by their past.

Explained, but not necessarily made easy. Blair and Brown are a complicated pair. Civil servants puzzle over the contradictions they throw up – the modernizers who want less open discussion in Cabinet; the devolvers who want a stronger Downing Street sec-retariat; the Prime Minister and Chancellor who boast of decisiveness and let the euro argument float from their grasp; the friends whose supporting gangs fight in the street and fill the air with gossip. Labour MPs wonder if the tensions will destroy them; but ask them what comes next, after Blair and Brown have exploded or departed, and you'll wait a long time for an answer.

They engender mystery. For all the obvious power that flows from the huge majority and their public insistence that they'll stick together, the very consciousness of their pact is nerve-racking for the government. Their colleagues don't know what deals they have made, and find it hard to think themselves into a world that has its emotional boundaries policed by Peter Mandelson and Alastair Campbell. Even in government, most of the Cabinet feel outsiders. They find it difficult to get the measure of the pulse in Downing Street. You can feel it beating, but it comes and goes and always seems dangerously elusive.

Ministers, civil servants and journalists are fellow conspirators in their mystery, trying to unravel the enigmatic relationship. Even those of us who watched from the ringside some of the fine feuds and love affairs of power under previous governments find this one hypnotic. Government has not been so concentrated in modern times. Only the neighbours in Downing Street seem to count. If they are as one, nothing can intervene. If the word seeps out that there's a row, or that one of them is on the warpath, the Whitehall air starts to stir and preparations are made for a storm. Everyone is always ready with the defences against that battering, because they think about the relationship all the time.

People who deal with ministers – civil servants, journalists, backbenchers, businessmen – want to know how the land lies. They have to be able to take a reading on relations between Number 10 and Number 11 at any moment. A piece of gossip does the rounds, an inspired leak or a piece of poison over a lunch table spawns a new tale, some unexpected political event flares in the sky, and suddenly there is another question about the central relationship in the government. They have built their administration on that partnership, and the power it commands, and they are stuck with it.

If it were not for the scale of the electoral success of 1997, everyone around Westminster imagines that this way of running a government could not have survived. The most important strength of Blair and Brown together is that they have never been put to that test. The advantages given to them by the majorities of 1997 and 2001 are immense. These reduced the Conservatives to a number of seats well below the 209 that Michael Foot took back to the Commons in 1983, Labour's year of disaster. The strength of their relationship is not only a consequence of their own histories, but of the way that the collapse of a weary Conservative Party after eighteen draining years in power gave them a Parliament that they were tempted to treat as a poodle. Watch Blair at the despatch box on a Wednesday afternoon and you see a Prime Minister who would often rather be back in the office. He enjoys the stage, but the parliamentary audience is not his choice.

The centre of his world is not the cockpit of the Commons, nor even his seat at the centre of the Cabinet table. It is the small room at the back of Number 10 where he and Brown do their deals. From the start of their life in government they operated as they had done in opposition – privately. Blair's colleagues believed it was a secretive system devised to assuage Brown's hurt at the subordinate role he had to occupy after Blair became leader, but the habit also predated that crisis in their relationship, and was the result of the intensity with which they lived their political lives in the eighties. In government, that past was the genetic map that determined how they behaved.

Whether in strategic economic questions, or crisis in the countryside or Kosovo, or trouble from a Labour infatuation with the rich, or from the press, the central relationship was the lightning rod to which everything was automatically attracted. No serious problem in government could be solved without these two laying hands on it, and the thought that it might be otherwise seemed never to have been seriously considered. That fact gave the government its personality, and many of its problems.

The pact which they use to run affairs does give their government strength, but it is strangely vulnerable because it depends on emotions that run deep in each of them. When those emotions are under control, theirs is a partnership of political power unrivalled in the democratic world. Together they're greater than the sum of their parts, and they have succeeded in dominating the middle ground of British politics as a result. But ambition for power and togetherness are not natural bedfellows. For all their instinctive sympathy and old loyalty to each other, their relationship in power is at the mercy of events and the stray personalities of politics who cluster round the throne.

One of the great historians of modern politics and workings of Whitehall, Professor Peter Hennessy, observes that they have changed the rules of power fundamentally. 'A contemporary historian isn't what you need for this subject. You need a medievalist. This is a court. All the assumptions we've made about politics in this country since Lloyd George – that decisions are rational, collective, and conform to a recognizable machinery – have to be thrown aside. They operate quite differently.'

Blair's government generates a running commentary on itself with a gusto which outsiders would find astonishing, and unravelling it is like delving into a pile of eels in a basket. Everything slips and slithers from your grasp, and that elusive quality is one of the reasons for the fascination of ministers and officials with the Blair–Brown partnership. They glimpse it at work for a moment – an agreed new phraseology on Europe, a coordinated series of speeches on the New Deal, even a cheery joint appearance on a radio phone-in – and then it is gone, lost in a flurry of competing briefings from the camp-followers around Whitehall who pass on the whispers from the ante-rooms of power. 'Gordon chewed the carpet.' Or: 'Tony was livid with him.' Or 'Cherie is incandescent. In-can-descent.' The truth is never absolute: another interpretation comes along in a moment. No statement can be made about these two without a qualification or a contradiction coming fast on its heels. Tam Dalyell, the Labour MP who became the longest-serving member of the Commons and Father of the House after the 2001 election, says, with a typically eccentric touch, that the best guide to the government is not some Labour Party pamphlet or manifesto, nor an academic study of The Third Way, but the eighteenth-century memoirs of the Duc de Saint-Simon which he was urged to read at school as a guide to the world of politics.

Saint-Simon's *Memoirs* are the story of the court of Louis XIV at Versailles, observed from the inside. Courtiers cluster round the throne, and jostle for a place near the king at his *levées* and *couchées*, the monarch's flickering eye follows the comings and goings of those who wish him well and those who don't, the spies and tale-tellers feed the court with its lifeblood of gossip. It is the picture of a world of power driven by intrigue and vanity. Dalyell says simply of his party in power: 'It is a court.'

With the passage of time in power, that tendency waxed and did not wane. Blair's first crisis of the second term, away from the Afghan battlefield, was a household affair, about special advisers and civil servants, the raw exercise of political muscle and a minister who appeared not to be telling the truth. The government found that the Stephen Byers affair became in the public mind a dramatization of its own inner character, and as so often in politics a chance series of seemingly unrelated events – the attack on the World Trade Center, the death of Princess Margaret, the battle between a spin doctor and her boss and the crisis on the railways – turned into a gripping public spectacle. They did so because of the particular way this government has dealt with power and because of its own troubled personality.

The Rivals is a story of character and power. They are indivisible. This is not a dual biography but a picture of parallel lives which have reshaped an era. Ours is an age in which personality and celebrity have became the dominant cultural forces and Blair and Brown have ridden that tide. Together they have built a political personality that is all-powerful. This is the story of how they did it, how it works, and how it often threatens to consume them.

PART ONE

"'ERE COMES A TOFF ... 'EAVE A BRICK AT 'IM."

1

The Thespian and the Flanker

Tony Blair and Gordon Brown were closer than they knew, before either of them had any thought of politics. In Edinburgh in the winter of 1967 they were only a couple of miles from each other, doing what they would enjoy most in their teenage years. Brown was submerging himself in the quiet excitements of Edinburgh University library, discovering history. Blair was wrapping himself into a toga to take to the stage at Fettes College as Mark Antony in *Julius Caesar*.

Tempting though it would be to imagine a hazy spring day in the mid sixties with two familiar figures, young and scrawny and mud-streaked, cavorting on rugby fields on either side of the Firth of Forth, one in the deep pink of Fettes and the other in the navy and gold hoops of Kirkcaldy High School, it almost certainly never happened. That particular image of teenage doppelgängers, playing out the first stages of their destiny almost within sight of each other, would be rather too easy and very misleading.

They were not peas from the same pod. When they did arrive in Edinburgh it was from different ways of life and they were set on separate paths. Blair's school years under the Gormenghast-like turrets and pillars of Fettes were programmed by rigid rules that were still self-consciously drawn from the traditions of the English public school – all houses and dorms and sporting spirit.

Blair's father, Leo, had chosen Fettes because it was said to be the finest public school in Edinburgh, the city in which his son had been born in 1953. A pupil from the age of eight at The Chorister School, Durham Cathedral, near the family home, Fettes was a natural progression for Blair. The great central spire of the college seems to command a kind of island on the northern side of Edinburgh, a vast building surrounded by its own trees and grounds. In Blair's day it was its own world, a deeply conservative institution that would start to indulge in tentative change only during his time there. Fettes was for the sons of empire, a place for training administrators and men of affairs, a school in which the pursuit of excellence was often assumed to encompass public success. Leo Blair had lectured in law at Edinburgh University at an earlier stage in his career and was now practising as a barrister on the Newcastle-upon-Tyne circuit, so the Blairs were a comfortable middle-class family, well able to afford the fees at Fettes for their two sons, William and Tony. Going to Fettes was not an act of social climbing. To Blair's father, who held Conservative views, it was a sensible way of making the most of the rewards from his professional achievements.

It would have been odd if Gordon Brown had not become a student in Scotland. The grip of the four ancient universities, all founded before the end of the sixteenth century, was strong. St Andrews, Glasgow, Aberdeen and Edinburgh were *the* places of learning. Only after the new universities began to spring up in the mid-sixties was the old pattern broken. Until then, any student who ventured south of the border was an exotic bird indeed, and the Scottish tradition was for Oxford and Cambridge to be places for a second degree if they were to be contemplated at all. Only in a few schools were they seen as natural options for the high achiever. They were very distant places. And Brown came from a background which was rooted deep in Scottish soil. Growing up in Scotland in the 1950s was to be aware of the weight of tradition. All of us were influenced by the generation that passed on the Victorian values of school, church and self-reliance. Children like Brown, brought up in the manse or the schoolhouse, still the twin pillars of the village or town, were taught that self-improvement was an obligation and so was a commitment to the community around. Whatever the family's party politics, this was overwhelmingly a conservative society in which decency and proper form had to be respected. Radicalism and scepticism were important forces too, but they operated in a context that seemed unchanging, the echo of a settled society.

The label 'son of the manse' often feels like a burden to those who wear it. Images of black-clad ministers glowering from high pulpits, and church elders prodding worshippers out of their homes on Sunday mornings, have proved hard to dispel. The Church of Scotland in which Brown grew up was certainly an institution that clung to many old ways, but it was a world away from the caricature that places so many Scots in the same grim category as the 'Wee Free' Presbyterians in their tiny sect. Dr John Brown brought up his three sons, John, Gordon and Andrew, in quite a different atmosphere. The pressure on them came not so much from a strictness in the home, but from the natural difficulty that anyone has in growing up the son of a highly respected member of the community. They grew up with a father who was considered a saintly man.

Dr Brown was a striking figure, noted for the power of his personality and for his preaching. Theology and social concern were inseparable. His first two children were born in Glasgow, when he was a parish minister in Govan on the southern banks of the Clyde, and in 1954 the family moved to Kirkcaldy when Gordon was three. The town sits on the northern shore of the Firth of Forth within sight of Edinburgh across the water and in an area which Brown has never left. His constituency begins a few miles to the west. He lives on the Forth. His education was completed within twenty miles of his family home. The boys grew up in a manse which was teeming with local life, more of an advice centre and a place of refuge than a grand house. Sunday after Sunday Brown heard his father preach and has often spoken of the effect his words had. 'He taught me to treat everyone equally, and that is something I have not forgotten,' he said in 1995.

At about that time, when his father had just turned eighty, Brown and his two brothers collected a number of his sermons, many of them dating back to their childhood, and had them bound and presented to him. A senior Whitehall civil servant (a Scot) suggested to Brown, who was shadow Chancellor at the time, that the Conservative Lord Chancellor, Lord Mackay of Clashfern, might like to have a copy since he would be interested in those sermons. James Mackay was a member of the strict Free Presbyterian Church (with whom he eventually fell out for the 'sin' of attending a requiem mass). He was indeed struck by Dr Brown's sermons, and wrote to him about one in particular. The two men had never met, but the retired minister was touched to receive the letter. When his son next met the thoughtful civil servant, the shadow Chancellor put his arm round his shoulder in a rare physical gesture of intimacy to thank him for a thought which had given his father such pleasure, and was clearly very moved. Such feelings run strong in Brown, though to outsiders the surface offers few clues to what lies beneath. The ties to his family and his background are exceptionally strong.

That background meant that education was important. Scots of Brown's generation were still reared on the inherited assumption that nothing should interfere with schooling. It was a duty of self-improvement that couldn't be put aside. In his case, it involved starting nursery school at four and ending up at the local secondary school, Kirkcaldy High. In Edinburgh and Glasgow education was a more complicated business, with an expanding private sector and all the jostling and jealousy that it customarily involves, but in places like Kirkcaldy things were straightforward. He would progress down the usual path and, of course, go on to university.

By the time he was sitting his leaving exams in the senior school, he was a natural recruit for a scheme which had intrigued the headmaster, Robert Adam, and which was being taken up by quite a number of Scottish schools. There would be a fast track for pupils who might benefit from an earlier start at university. Brown was academically gifted, a fact obvious to all his teachers from the start, so he was a natural candidate. And off he went to Edinburgh to study history in the autumn of 1967. There appears to have been no concern at school that he might be too young. Any relish, however, was tinged with anxiety and some anger.

As a schoolboy, Brown had been limbering up for student politics by dabbling in embryonic journalism, putting together a crude newspaper with his older brother (which they sold to neighbours for pocket money). He was racing ahead, but the speed disturbed him.

One of his biographers, Paul Routledge, later winkled out a fascinating unpublished essay in which Brown revealed his feelings about the system that had sent him on his way so quickly. Many of his friends had been pushed too fast for their own good and were then confronted with what seemed to them to be failure. Brown wrote: 'Surely it is better for children to succeed at school, and leave with some qualification for work, rather than endure failure, ignominy, rejection and at the least, strain, for the ironic reason of averting failure at university?' The words reek of self-consciousness at his own success, perhaps even of some guilt that he was one of those singled out for glory. Certainly there is evidence of some sense of awkwardness at being set apart so soon from those with whom he'd played rugby and football and watched Raith Rovers, the local Kirkcaldy football team.

He became a student with that feeling of injustice done to friends evidently running strongly in his mind. On top of all that, his arrival in Edinburgh coincided with a crisis of a sort he had never confronted before. At school, he was keen on sport. In his last term he took his place as a flanker in the school XV playing against the old boys and in the course of the game he took a bang on the head. Months later he realized that it had caused a problem with his sight. In the very week that he started as an Edinburgh University student he went into the Royal Infirmary for an examination that led to a period of some terror. The retina of one eye was detached in such a way that the sight of it could not be saved, and there was a scare about the other eye. It might go the same way. He listened to recordings of books made specially for the blind. His first term was sacrificed to the consequences of that moment on the rugby field and there were regular interruptions to his university life, during which he had three more operations. He took a general arts degree in this period, going on to take an honours degree in history after the operations were over, and staying on at the university to study for a Ph.D in Scottish Labour history, a passion that would remain.

His first years in Edinburgh were gruelling. The ban on reading after his operations would have been a handicap and a frustration to anyone: to someone already bookish and intellectually muscular it was a nightmare. Everyone who knows him well recognizes that his single-mindedness and relentless determination must in part be attributed to that trial in his late teens. For them, it explains elements of his character which sometimes seem impenetrable to outsiders.

That first year in Edinburgh, therefore, wasn't for Brown quite the invigorating introduction to student life that the age was promising to be for others. *Les événements* in Paris in the early summer of 1968 were having their effect across Europe, even in Edinburgh, though there were no bonfires or water cannon in the streets. In the piles of paving stones and behind the barricades was the stirring of a radicalism that began to transform campuses (although that term didn't yet apply) for a generation that knew its own music but hadn't yet discovered its own politics. Optimism was in the air. Sometimes it was angry, sometimes it was complacent, but it was there. Around Edinburgh University, student politics was beginning to bubble. Brown's brother John, two years older, was making his name as president of the Students' Representative Council (SRC) – the established student body – and others were starting to find political footholds. One was a notably eloquent young man with red hair. His name was Robin Cook and, five years older than Brown, he was finishing his honours degree in English when the sixteen-year-old arrived from Kirkcaldy. People knew of Cook. He had political ambitions.

Across the city, on the other side of the Georgian New Town, life at Fettes College went on more sedately. While Brown found the world opening up for him at the university, Tony Blair was settling into an institution which would frustrate him and turn him into something of an early rebel, though his irritations had no formal political character. When he became a boarder in the summer of 1966, having just turned thirteen, the regime controlled by the headmaster, Dr Ian McIntosh, was one that would have been familiar to generations long gone. Junior boys could be caned by prefects, apparently with relish. The remnants of a 'fagging' system were still in place, with the young boys acting as valets for their elders, some prefects still enjoying the consequences of the discovery of an inadequately polished shoe or a burnt piece of toast. Blair was beaten more than once. The boys led a life that was cut off. They saw little of the city which surrounded the school. Richard Lambert, later editor of the *Financial Times*, who preceded Blair at Fettes, says: 'It's extraordinary to think that we lived in one of Europe's great cities for six or seven years and hardly saw it. We didn't know Edinburgh at all.' Blair seldom talks of Fettes, but Oxford friends recall unflattering descriptions of his life there.

Blair was lucky that unlike those who had preceded him – they included future acquaintances like Lord Woolf, who became Lord Chief Justice in 2000, and the head of the weapons decommissioning body for Northern Ireland, General John de Chastelain – his generation began to see changes. In particular, Blair came under the influence of Dr Eric Anderson, who was in charge of a new house – Arniston – which opened in his second year at Fettes. Arniston, nowadays populated entirely by girls, became a haven for relaxation, at least by Fettes standards. By the time Blair left for Oxford in 1972, girls had been admitted to the sixth form (to the sound of the gnashing of Old Fettesian teeth worldwide).

The reports of Blair from fellow pupils and staff over the years have been of a boy who always enjoyed attention. From the start, that was the Blair story. He is the first Fettesian to become Prime Minister – in the sixties the Conservative Cabinet heavyweights Selwyn Lloyd and Iain Macleod were the most celebrated old boy politicians – and on the eve of his election in 1997 a former member of staff was happy to ponder his suitability for high office, gesturing towards the school theatre and saying: 'That, of course, is where he was happiest.'

His first outing was as Mark Antony in a house play but he graduated to starring roles in the annual school play, which was taken very seriously, and by the time he was a senior boy he was very much the thespian Blair. Eric Anderson was largely responsible for this enthusiasm. He considered Blair a natural actor who had an ability to think himself into parts: when he was on the stage he believed in his character and meant what he said. His stage activities were combined with regular trips – some illicit, according to contemporaries – into the outside world of Edinburgh, which were the cause of some consternation, as was the length of his hair. He was frequently disciplined and it is clear that by the end of his time at Fettes he was very happy to be away. Although Fettes admitted its first girl in his last year (as a favour to a governor of the school), for someone such as Blair who preferred to listen to Led Zeppelin and had no interest in beating the thirteen-year-old boys being lined up as prospective fags, the place was fairly grim. It changed markedly in the decade or so afterwards, and now takes pride in the description 'progressive' which in Blair's day most of the masters would have taken as an insult.

Inescapably, those Edinburgh years are etched on Brown and Blair. The future Prime Minister never lived there again and it has always been obvious that, although Blair is proud of his Scottish connections (occasionally making time on awkward party conference trips to Glasgow to visit old relations), the school years don't glimmer fondly in his mind. In conversation, the happier times at Oxford always take precedence. Partly, this may be because Blair has never felt part of the kind of establishment whose sons he came to know at school.

As a Conservative, Blair's father, Leo, had harboured hopes of a parliamentary candidacy at one stage, and the pattern of his education was cast in an unsurprising mould, his older brother having gone to Fettes before him. Blair's evident unease as he grew up had less to do with some burning political radicalism – he has always acknowledged that he had no such feelings – than with an instinctive irritation at the rules and the expected form of behaviour.

By the time Blair headed south at the age of nineteen in the summer of 1972 in the hope of greater excitement at Oxford, life in Edinburgh for Gordon Brown had already become more adventurous. The university was on the boil, and the students were discovering the joys of rebelliousness. They were blessed in this enterprise by a principal and vice-chancellor, Michael Swann, who played into their hands. The more they demanded 'democratization' and greater representation on the university's governing bodies, the more he resisted. As a result, the leaders of the students got what they wanted: trouble. A typical incident was the sacking of the editor of the campus newspaper, *Student*, by the university because it had published an article about LSD. Swann announced that he had sent a copy of the paper to the Home Office. There was a minor riot. The editor was reinstated and they waited for the next explosion.

Brown arrived at Edinburgh young and shy, and within three years had turned into a student politician who was becoming adept at using the campus newspaper to make mischief. By the time he finished his history degree and embarked on research for his Ph.D he was stirring it up whenever he could. It was hardly revolutionary stuff, but this was the first phase of student radicalism in Britain, and the university authorities found that they were under siege. Students wanted power in the institutions and at every turn they were happy to bash the vice-chancellors and governing bodies. The student newspapers of the time paint pictures of universities as bastions of stuffiness and reaction, ripe for reform. Brown was in the thick of it.

Like all trainee-radical students of the time, he was helped by South Africa. The Springboks' rugby tour of Britain attracted huge demonstrations across the country in 1970, and universities across Britain vied with each other to get the most protesters on the streets and disrupt the games most effectively. In Edinburgh, there was another spicy ingredient. From somewhere in the university administration came the leak of a list of the investments it held, showing that it had valuable shareholdings in some of the companies which were the pillars of the apartheid regime. The list found its way to Brown and his friends. At the time, this was the kind of political 'crime' which could spark a demonstration, or the occupation of some university office. A special-edition of *Student* was printed and Swann found himself surveying a campus in revolt. It was an embarrassing revelation for him personally, because, like many middle-of-the-road public figures, he was prominently associated with the anti-apartheid movement. The leaked information was used by the students to make the university hierarchy seem hypocritical and secretive, a charge to which it had no convincing reply.

Those of us of the same generation elsewhere in Scotland heard of these antics with predictable interest and envy. Edinburgh was alive. The episode was a humiliation for an institution nominally devoted to academic freedom and the principles of the eighteenth-century Enlightenment which had been one of Edinburgh's glories. It was also embarrassing for a university justifiably proud of its Commonwealth links and its internationalism to be accused of double standards. A substantial number of students were determined to be unforgiving. The place was in ferment, and in Swann the likes of Brown realized they had found a soft target. Copies of *Student* from 1970 have an air of simmering expectation. The authorities were on the defensive.

Within a year students were able to force on the university a change which was resisted and deeply resented by traditionalists in the administration and the academic body: they elected a student rector. In Scottish universities, the post of rector is a remnant of a nineteenth-century concept of symbolic student representation in the government of the institution. The rector was obliged under university statute to be the voice of the student body. It was never a position of real political power, more an emblem of the student presence, but rectors are still elected every few years by the students to sit on the university's highest council, the court. Indeed, they have the traditional right to chair it. In practice, rectorial elections were carnivals at all the universities, with serious candidates outnumbered by eccentrics and oddball figures from stage and screen (although unlikely figures such as John Cleese and Clement Freud have both served as hard-working rectors in St Andrews and Dundee). In sixties' Scotland there were exceptions, like the Liberal leader, Jo Grimond, who was an active rector in Edinburgh and, later, in Aberdeen. From time to time a figure of real distinction was elected. But the idea of a student as rector was generally still too daring.

Brown's first rector was the journalist and sage Malcolm Muggeridge, who in 1968 was engaged in a moral repudiation of his earlier leftism and was an eloquent assailant of all that sixties liberalization represented. He chose Edinburgh for one of his most famous blasts, which he delivered from the pulpit of St Giles Cathedral. The High Kirk of St Giles on the Royal Mile is one of the city's most potent historical buildings, the place where John Knox and his followers hatched the sixteenth-century Reformation against the Catholic hierarchy. Muggeridge took to the pulpit to denounce student immorality and in particular the arrival of the contraceptive pill which, as a rigorous convert to Catholicism, he abhorred. Students in Edinburgh were slothful and self-indulgent. Instead of carrying the torch for progress into a glorious future they were leading spiritually impoverished lives demanding 'pot and pills, for the most tenth-rate form of escapism and self-indulgence known to man'. Muggeridge resigned as rector. It was an electric event in the university's life, dramatizing the widening gap between the lives of most students and the old order. For those who wanted change, Muggeridge's theatrical and tortured outburst was a gift. In *Student*, he was lampooned as a comic figure who had become a sour absurdity.

The temperature was high and the paper was lively. Brown gravitated naturally to it, and became editor in his second year. The tone of the paper was propagandist: student rents . . . university secrecy . . . censorship – they were the staple diet of the editorial. There were, however, distractions. Almost every issue had on its front page, as if by statute, a picture of some pouting female student, usually lying on a grassy bank or lounging on Georgian steps. This was the kind of appeal turned into a populist art form by the tabloids in the seventies, and excoriated by the Labour Party for it, but it seemed to cause Brown no agony at all in his student days. He encouraged it. Young women spread themselves across the page, usually displaying a generous thigh or two, and gave the paper a louche spirit that was obviously intended. One of the pictures inside during Brown's editorship carried the caption 'Marguerite de Roumanie', on the occasion of her election to the SRC. This was Princess Marguerite of Romania, a contemporary of Brown's with whom he was having a relationship. Many years later it led to barbed jokes from Cabinet colleagues about the relative merits of the chancellorship and the throne of Romania.

There are other poignant pictures. In October 1969 the president of the National Union of Students came north to Edinburgh to try to persuade the recalcitrant Scottish Union of Students to merge with it, a sensitive question among student politicians in Scotland (although no one else) at the time. He can be seen on the front page, haranguing the crowd in Edinburgh, all hair, black-rimmed glasses and waving arms. It is Jack Straw. He remembers two things about that visit: 'We won. And the next morning I had the worst hangover of my life.'

Most students cared nothing for the world of trainee politics, but it was fertile ground for those who did. Tremors ran through university administrations across the country and for Brown's generation the prospect of causing more tremors was a nice counterpoint to the ritual scorn which every self-respecting student politician of the left had to pour on the Labour government of the day for its various 'betrayals'. Harold Wilson might have abandoned radicalism; they hadn't.

In such an atmosphere as Edinburgh, it was inevitable that there should be talk of trying to elect a student rector. Within two or three years the idea had become serious enough to produce a candidate who might win. That candidate was Jonathan Wills, a geography student with a shaggy beard and an irrepressible urge for self-promotion, and in late 1971 he beat the satirical cartoonist and journalist Willie Rushton to become the students' representative on the university court. Brown was the chairman of the Labour Club, and Wills was their candidate. This was a symbolic change, in the sense that no one expected the university to be different on the day after the election, but a different kind of political era had indeed begun. Wills was on the court for a year before he resigned. He had been a successful irritant and little more. Brown was the candidate to replace him and in a contest in November 1972 with the future industrialist (later Sir) Fred Catherwood, effectively the Conservative candidate, he won by a huge margin in a campaign which wasn't entirely high-minded – his campaign posters had him promoted by girls called 'Brown's Sugars' (after 'Brown Sugar' by the Rolling Stones from the 1971 album *Sticky Fingers*). *Student* was ecstatic, in the manner of such publications, celebrating the election of one of its own. His margin of victory, it announced cheerily and ridiculously, was 'the equivalent of President Nixon's landslide'.

Brown was now established. As a badge of his election he enjoyed the fact that Michael Swann was sufficiently irritated by it to refuse to attend the formal announcement of the result. From the start they were at war, and the engagement didn't last long. At the end of the year, Swann announced that he would be leaving Edinburgh to become chairman of the BBC, where he thought he would find relative peace. He had no appetite for the struggles that were obviously about to begin. For three years or so, the university establishment had been flinching uncomfortably. Brown turned the rectorship into a campaigning pedestal. He chaired the court, and issued press releases as if they were statements from the court as a whole, which they were not. When one was torn up by the university before it could be issued he announced in *Student* that it was 'political censorship of the lowest and most dreadful sort'. The whole posture was of a democrat pitched against the forces of reaction. His hair was long now, his crowd of supporters were starting to have the feel of a claque, and he was honing a polemical style in his column in the paper. Some of his colleagues from those days – notably Colin Currie and Murray Elder, who had gone to school in Kirkcaldy with him – would remain in the tight inner circle nearly thirty years later.

None of this would be a surprise to colleagues who came to know him in his political career. Already, certain characteristics were obvious. He attracted supporters, who understood the rule that loyalty was expected. He was single-minded. He was fascinated by the power of the printed word in pursuit of a campaign. And he was delving into Scottish Labour history of the twenties for his academic research, work which was pulling him sharply leftwards. He was impatient with the party he had started supporting as a teenager, following his father's example. Like many ministers in the Kirk, Dr Brown was a Labour voter.

Young left-wingers in Scotland had a cause. 'Red Clydeside' was a phrase that had found its way back into politics. The sit-in at Upper Clyde shipbuilders in 1971 had a galvanizing effect on the left, pitting the Scottish unions against Edward Heath's Tory government elected a year earlier. Somehow the tone in Scottish politics changed, with events on the Clyde polarizing opinion. None of the principal objectives of the sit-in were achieved – the decline in shipbuilding and the loss of jobs went on when the tumult had died down – but for Brown and young Labour people of his generation it had a profound effect, allowing them to forget their frustrations with the Labour government of the late sixties. They enjoyed seeing the politics of the street and the shipyard return. Direct action was invigorating. It was no long-term answer, much more a burst of radicalism that passed away quickly, but it charged the atmosphere. For an ambitious young politician it was a good time. There was the smell of cordite in the shipyards, huge demonstrations in the streets and on the campus a university court to be challenged and harried. Brown celebrated Swann's imminent departure with a victory against the university in the High Court in a judgement on the powers of the rector in mid-1973 and demonstrated that at the age of twenty-two he had learned how to use political muscle.

Blair missed it all at Fettes. He was two years younger, marooned at school. The clandestine trips over the wall into Edinburgh, which the boys regarded as something like an escape from Colditz, and arguments with masters about the length of their hair were about as exciting as it got. One of Blair's fellow pupils in Arniston, William Primrose, remembers the atmosphere as quite intimidating: 'In those days the school was quite oppressive, with quite a bit of peer-group pressure to conform. Those who were not conventional in a public school way tended to be mocked.' Blair escaped that mockery, not least because his exploits on the stage gave him a certain profile in the school, and because his rebelliousness appeared to have a certain style to it. It was obvious that schools like Fettes would have to change – the old rules and attitudes would repel the next generation of prospective parents – but change was slow to arrive. Blair was frustrated. In his last term, indeed, he left the school to live at the home of Lord Mackenzie-Stuart, a distinguished Scottish judge (and an Old Fettesian), whose daughter Amanda was the first girl to be accepted by Fettes. It was a deliberate manoeuvre by Blair's housemaster, to keep a rebellious spirit in check. He was frustrated and unhappy and anxious to be away.

At Oxford, Blair was no student politician, and never tried to be one. He took no formal position in the set-piece left–right student struggles of the day. After he arrived at St John's College to read law in 1972 there was an occupation of the Examination Schools building, at the heart of the university which was a *cause célèbre* on the left, a repetition of a famous late sixties episode which Oxford had thought of as its answer to the Paris revolution. The demonstration was a passionate affair for those involved, and the object of curiosity for many others who visited the scene of the action like interested tourists, but for most students it was a distant political event which hardly touched them. Blair's college did have its political cliques, but the ritual elections for the committee of the student body, the Junior Common Room, were not always very serious. One of Blair's closest friends, David Fursdon, recalls finding himself unexpectedly listed on both the right-wing and the left-wing slate in one JCR election. The group around Blair was neither involved in the activity on the left, which was fierce in a teenage sort of way, nor in the High Tory japes of the playboys who clustered round outfits like the Archery Club.

Yet there were glimmerings of Blair's style. One postgraduate student who arrived soon after Blair, Robert Watt, noticed him early on. 'I clearly recall my first sight of him. Someone in the student common room after dinner said "That's Tony Blair over there." When I said "Who's he?" or "So what?", he replied in some awe "He's in a rock band." I've always remembered this – since long before Blair became famous.

'He had an aura about him even then; people noticed him; he stood out. There must have been fifty people in the room but he was the one who got the attention. That may well have been the point of being in the band. In other words, he was already deploying the sorts of assets – trendiness and charm – which have been in evidence ever since.'

The band was Ugly Rumours, a name taken from the cover of a Grateful Dead album which was in vogue at the time. Blair – who used to be listed in the Fettes school choir at Founder's Day concerts as a tenor – was lead singer. According to students in and around St John's at the time, it would be misleading to think of the band as a sensational outfit with much of a following. It was a more modest ensemble. Furzdon recalls being at parties where Ugly Rumours might have been playing in the corner, but no more than that. No one expected that they might one day try to remember where they were when they first heard them play. Did they play at the Beggar's Banquet in St John's in 1974, the alternative College Ball? Quite a few people who were there have no recollection. Yet it helped to give Blair a style. He had no interest in the parliamentary kindergarten of the Oxford Union, whose doorstep he appears hardly ever to have darkened, and never mixed with the radicals who were running the Broad Left group of student politicians at the time. It may be symptomatic of that Oxford atmosphere of the day that none of the campus figures on the left in Blair's time went on to make important careers in mainstream politics. It was a strange atmosphere. Melanie Phillips, the *Sunday Times* columnist, was a left-wing student at St Anne's. 'The sixties generation had gone. We were an in-between generation. The only fashionable place to be political was in the IS [the International Socialists, later to become the Socialist Workers Party]. Anyone who was in the Labour [Party] was regarded by everyone else as an appalling lickspittle and creep just looking for a career.'

Like many – probably most – students, Blair let politics go its own way. He never flirted with the far left, and made no effort to connect with the mainstream parties. Robert Watt says that one of the college catchphrases was 'He's far too intense', used of people who showed enthusiasm for something, particularly politics. Blair was never accused of being too intense.

But he did work hard. David Fursdon says: 'You'd be at a party . . . and you'd turn round at about one o'clock and find that Tony had gone. He'd slipped away quietly a couple of hours before. You'd find that he was getting up at five o'clock to finish an essay or to read something that had to be read. He was popular and gregarious but he was always careful and determined with his work.' It was, however, an application which his friends thought would lead to the law and nothing else.

The other side of Blair that emerged at St John's was spiritual. He has often cited his discovery of the Scottish philosopher John

Macmurray as a turning point in his life, but perhaps more important is the character who turned him towards Macmurray in the first place, a priest with an exceptionally powerful personality called Peter Thomson. Thomson is an Australian with the gift of directness and hypnotic eyes, and he made an impression on Blair that lasts to this day. His forthright character is summed up in an incident that took place at Buckingham Palace in the 1990s.

Peter Thomson had known the Prince of Wales at school in Australia in the sixties and he found himself, more than twenty years later, at an informal lunch with Palace aides discussing, among other things, the standing of the royal family. Asked about the Prince, Thomson recalls with glee that he told his fellow-lunchers that he thought the future king was performing perfectly well and was 'a good bloke'. It was a pity, though, that in public 'he always looks as if he has a carrot stuck up his arse'. Thomson much enjoyed the long silence that followed.

The irreverent reverend imparted a Christian commitment to Blair, an Anglo-Catholic approach which was in keeping with the practices he'd learned as a boy at The Chorister School (but which at Fettes had seemed of little importance to him). Thomson had read Macmurray at theological college and considered him one of the most important British philosophers of the century. The part of Macmurray's philosophy which Blair absorbed was the simple dichotomy which was claimed between 'society' and 'community', a distinction which he has adapted for his political purposes. Community, in Macmurray's definition, is something based on friendship. He rejects the Marxist thinking that has influenced so many mainstream Labour figures that sees conflict as an integral part of any human system. For Blair the combination of a belief in communities built on partnerships and trust between individuals, and the obligation of the Christian to 'love thy neighbour as thyself' was potent. At that stage in his life it was a substitute for formal politics, and the attitudes he developed at Oxford have never left him. Macmurray's deeper thoughts about the need to remove all aggression from society – which made him in the end a Quaker – sprang in part from his rejection of organized politics, and Blair has never followed the argument through. But the celebration of 'community' which was held to be something wider and deeper than any particular kind of organized society was one that attracted him, and stayed with him. Macmurray's ideas have attracted a good deal of ridicule, because they appear to rest on a belief in everyone's capacity for good: communities worked when people were nice to each other. The significance of Blair's interest is that it reveals how much more he has always been attracted to theories of personal responsibility than to political ideology.

Contrast this with Gordon Brown's political journey in Edinburgh. While Blair was completing his second year at Oxford with the college president, Sir Richard Southern, noting in his end-of-year assessment that he seemed 'quite extraordinarily happy', Brown was quite extraordinarily angry. He was already a political figure of substance, and deep in the arguments which had been stirred up with the election of first seven and then eleven Scottish National Party MPs in the two elections of 1974. The politics of Scotland was alive again.

In the Labour Party, the established leaders were solidly resisting any concessions to the SNP by way of devolution. That constituted appeasement. Led by the schoolmasterly figure of the Scottish Secretary Willie Ross, the party establishment's attitude was one of utter antagonism to nationalism and to any kind of elected assembly. But there were some Labour MPs, and a growing number of younger activists in Scotland, who believed that the policy was not only doomed but wrong. They began to plan for a Scottish Parliament, to fulfil the pledge that Keir Hardie had given when he founded the Labour Party in 1899.

Gordon Brown's response to the exhilarating mood was to produce, in 1975, *The Red Paper on Scotland*, a collection of essays which was meant to be the socialist prospectus for a new Scotland. Brown's introduction, entitled 'The Socialist Challenge', gives a vivid picture of his political mind at that moment, and one which is startling to anyone who knows only Chancellor Brown. In it he wrote:

Political power will become a synthesis of – not a substitute for – community and industrial life. This requires from the Labour Movement in Scotland today a positive commitment to creating a socialist society, a coherent strategy with rhythm and modality to each reform to cancel the logic of capitalism and a programme of immediate aims which leads out of one social order into another. Such a social reorganization – a phased extension of public control under workers' self-management and the prioritizing of social needs set by the communities themselves – if sustained and enlarged, would in E. P. Thompson's words lead to 'a crisis not of despair and disintegration but a crisis in which the necessity for a peaceful revolutionary transition to an alternative socialist logic became daily more evident'.

The turgid style is characteristic of leftist pamphlets of the time and *The Red Paper* was a classic of the genre. It was fat, badly printed and bound, with tiny type, but it was stuffed with thinkers and their thoughts. All over Scotland (and in every political party) the serious argument about devolution was boiling. What kind of Scotland should it be? The thought that there might never be a Scottish Parliament was withering away. Margaret Thatcher, elected Conservative leader in 1975, was even having difficulty with the Scottish Tories, quite a number of whom were committed to change. Michael Ancram was appointed party chairman in Scotland (he'd sat in the Commons for Berwick and East Lothian between the February and October elections in 1974) and was having difficulty explaining to her what was going on in Scotland. At one meeting she saw him to the door with the memorable words: 'Michael, I am an English nationalist and never you forget it.' But it was in the Labour Party that the real agony came.

Part of the problem was that a majority of its MPs were anti-devolution. They loathed the SNP – the 'Tartan Tories' they called them disparagingly – and were in no mind to give ground to them. But when Harold Wilson resigned as Prime Minister in March 1976 he bequeathed to his successor, Jim Callaghan, a government without a majority. As well as the informal Lib-Lab pact concluded with the Liberal leader David Steel in 1977, Callaghan had to neutralize the eleven nationalists who might bring him down. So a devolution bill – covering both Scotland and Wales – was born. It was a disaster. The Welsh Labour MPs objected to it even more than the Scots and it fell. Its successors were two separate bills, each setting up an elected Assembly. The story of the three years of the Callaghan government looked at from Scotland was the story of devolution.

During the mid-1970s Brown progressed from student rebel, to *Red Paper* editor, to Labour troublemaker. Once he had finished his Ph.D he began to teach politics at Glasgow College of Technology (though still living in Edinburgh) and began to rise. Older MPs had marked him down as an awkward whippersnapper from the start and when he went on to become chairman of the party's devolution committee in Scotland in 1978 at the age of twenty-seven there was real rage among those of the old guard at Westminster who were fervently opposed to devolution. But the government had to lurch on. Without the SNP and the Liberals, both devoted to the idea of devolution, it could not survive. Though many of its Scottish MPs did not believe in it, the devolution minister in the Cabinet Office, John Smith, finally secured the bill, at the price of a referendum. Again, there was much moaning among old party lags. Away from Westminster, in Scotland, Brown was devolution's leading advocate. It did not make him popular with some of the MPs who trundled back home from London on the night sleeper on a Thursday night. You did not have to spend long in the all-night bar rattling north before you heard the phrase 'that bastard Brown'.

Although it cost him some friends and made him enemies, it was the making of Brown. Robin Cook, the student politician when Brown arrived at university, had been elected MP for Edinburgh Central in 1974 and was convinced that the devolution policy was wrong. But Brown organized students to work on Cook's campaign. Despite their differences on devolution, the personal hostility between them came later. Like Tam Dalyell, MP for West Lothian, who saw himself as the Cassandra of the devolution years, complete with the gift of seeing into the future and the curse of never being believed, Cook campaigned across Scotland against devolution.

When the government was forced to concede the referendum to get the bill through, it was with a built-in high hurdle inserted by the anti-devolutionists which meant that 40 per cent of all those *entitled* to vote had to vote 'Yes' for an Assembly to be established in Edinburgh. The campaign was a disaster for the government, revealing Labour's splits and the lack of enthusiasm for the scheme among some of those who were meant to be its strongest advocates. The vote was lost, on the 40 per cent rule, because the bare majority that voted 'Yes' wasn't big enough, and Callaghan was therefore obliged under the legislation to introduce a Commons order repealing the Scotland Act and stopping the Assembly. He played for time but the SNP deserted him. They tabled a vote of no confidence, the Conservatives seized their moment, and on 29 March 1979 the government lost a vote of confidence by one vote. Mrs Thatcher was elected Prime Minister five weeks later.

The agonies of the Callaghan government quickly matured Brown and a generation of young Scottish politicians. While in England Labour was starting to sink into the rows and splits of the Bennite years and the rise of Militant, Scotland was still gripped by a real constitutional argument over devolution. Brown fought Edinburgh South in the 1979 election but was beaten by Michael Ancram. He began to work in current affairs for Scottish Television in Glasgow, but no one doubted that he would soon find a safe seat.

In fact, he had some difficulty. It was late in the day, just before the 1983 election itself, that he managed to find enough support – much of it on the union left – to give him a chance at Dunfermline East. He won the selection conference easily, but even six months before it had seemed that he might find it hard to be selected anywhere. Anti-devolution figures resented him; the old guard in the party still considered him an upstart; he'd been ruffling feathers for years. When finally Brown was chosen by the voters of Dunfermline it was hardly a happy election night for new Labour MPs. They watched their party sink to its lowest share of the vote for more than sixty years – 27.6 per cent and 209 seats.

On that same night, 9 June 1983, Tony Blair watched the results in Sedgefield, County Durham. His arrival at Sedgefield was as late as Brown's although for different reasons. After he left Oxford his political education was slow and his interest patchy. He went to London to train as a barrister, coming under the magisterial influence of Alexander 'Derry' Irvine in chambers which also produced Cherie Booth, and married her in 1979 with Irvine present as a beaming matchmaker. Only then did politics start to grip him, and his marriage was part of the change. His wife was a budding candidate and had an appetite for party battles that was still undeveloped in Blair himself. Years later he would cheerily admit: 'It was late before I had any politics at all.' His enthusiasm for politics was certainly kindled by his wife. Before he came to London in the mid-seventies he had indulged in no political activity. With his barrister friend Charlie Falconer he began to attend Labour meetings and joined the party. With his wife trying unsuccessfully to win the Labour nomination in Crosby (for the by-election won by Shirley Williams for the SDP) and going on to fight Thanet North in 1983 their household was becoming, surprisingly for him, a political one. By 1982 he wanted to have a trial run for Westminster. He would be the Labour candidate in the hopeless (staunchly Conservative) seat of Beaconsfield in Buckinghamshire, a place of copper beeches, the chalky Chiltern Hills, and not far from the Prime Minister's country home, Chequers.

The by-election was widely covered, not because any of the candidates was particularly interesting or promising, but because it came at a time when the Labour Party was riven by fratricide, appearing determined to destroy itself in set-piece battles between right and left which weakened the leadership of Michael Foot to the point where it appeared beyond rescuing. To top it all, Blair fought the last week of the campaign to the sound of rejoicing from Downing Street as British troops landed in the Falklands to take the fight to General Galtieri, whose Argentine forces had seized them on 2 April. The Prime Minister was rampant and Labour was struggling to stem the tide of defections to the newly constituted Social Democratic Party: the landscape was bleak.

Blair's start was unspectacular, though he had some new advantages. Irvine, an ever-present father figure throughout this period, had introduced him to his old university friend from Glasgow, John Smith. Smith and Irvine were a pair of gossiping, hard-drinking cronies with a happy lawyerly cynicism about politics mingled with an old-fashioned Labour loyalty. Irvine delivered Blair to the Commons one night for his introduction to Smith. The two spent much of the night boozing happily and a friendship was struck which saw Blair through his first parliamentary decade. Without it he would have begun as a much slighter figure.

So just as Brown was closing in on Dunfermline East, calling in favours from the Transport and General Workers Union to try to scupper the local opposition, Blair was engaged in a similar operation. He had decided he wanted a seat that he could win. When he went to Sedgefield to try to win selection, the election of 1983 was all but under way. In a blitz which later became famous as an example of his blend of charm and ruthlessness he won it. With his agent John Burton, who thought he was the most likely of the hopefuls who were chasing the candidacy, he put together a gang of supporters (the 'Famous Five', including Burton, were Phil Wilson, Paul Trippett, Peter Brookes and Simon Hoban) who saw him through. Even in 1983 the seat was as safe for Labour as Beaconsfield had been for the Tories, and Blair was in.

Brown and Blair had arrived at Westminster by different routes which meandered through quite distinct and separate worlds. One was the product of a political machine which he had understood and manipulated and, in the end, mastered with ease. The other was a wide-eyed amateur at politics. His political ambition began to simmer late. One was ideological by nature; the other was intensely distrustful of ideology and had spent long nights arguing himself into an approach to politics which put attitudes and instinct above historical analysis. But perhaps the greatest significance in the long term was that when they took their seats in 1983 for the first time, it was as MPs who belonged to a party which looked as if it might disintegrate before their eyes.

2

The Room with No Windows

'This party has about eighteen months left.' The words were Blair's, heard by all of us, and it was a sentence that he uttered frequently in the months after the election that brought him to the Commons as the youngest member of the Labour opposition, to sit in a party that was the sullen remnant of a routed army. It was angry, divided and confused. Michael Foot's leadership had disintegrated in acrimony and humiliation and Blair found that the exhilaration of election was shot through with despair.

In the long summer nights of 1983 he and Brown discovered that they shared a deep pessimism about Labour's future. Blair, with none of Brown's background on the left, was the less inclined of the two to think of it in a historical context and exuded a simple sense of alarm. He was splenetic about the manifesto on which he had just fought. On Europe, defence and nationalization he had campaigned on party promises in which he – like many other candidates – didn't believe. To judge by his conversations at that time, the prospect of life at Westminster seemed intolerable unless his party changed. Labour in 1983 was the party that said: 'We will negotiate withdrawal from the EEC which has drained our natural resources and destroyed jobs', a view which the government he eventually led would associate with those in the political outback. He would sit in the darkness of the Commons terrace overlooking the Thames after some late night vote and talk with journalists and colleagues in apocalyptic terms about Labour. The constant refrain was: 'We haven't got long.' Knowing Blair then was knowing an MP whose obvious ambition was tempered by a fear that he might have landed in a party in terminal decline. Visits to the leader's office in those days were extraordinary. Michael Foot would be reading a new biography of Swift, or revisiting an edition of Byron's letters, in what seemed a conscious effort to forget what was going on around him. Across the Thames in County Hall, Ken Livingstone was running the Greater London Council and not only taunting the Conservative government with his policies. He was taunting Foot too, by pursuing a leftist agenda that the leader was trying to disown. Foot's agony was palpable. For young MPs like Blair it verged on pathos.

His first days at Westminster involved a slightly comic period of cohabitation in a room with the Militant-supporting Dave Nellist, an arrangement thought at the time to be a typical whips' office joke in making a relatively smooth public schoolboy share a desk with the party's most obvious outsider (genial though the gangly, bearded Nellist usually was). It didn't last, and by the time the summer recess came, six weeks after the election, Blair and Brown had already decided to become room-mates, crammed into a windowless, airless office just off the main committee corridor of the Commons. They had the advantage of a niche near the main thoroughfare of Parliament in the thick of things, where gossip fills the air. But it was little more than a cupboard with desks.

Brown commanded most of the space in the office with his piles of paper and dog-eared books. Colleagues would compare him to a street-dweller whose every possession was dragged around in a moving pile. Towers of paper leaned into every corner, toppling over now and then to reveal forgotten coffee cups and their furry dregs. When you were invited in you struggled to find a place to perch. Blair seemed the organized intruder in this chaos, complete with barrister's briefcase embossed with his initials. From the start they were a pair that seemed interesting more for their contrasts than for their similarities.

Brown was already an operator, blooded in those Scottish battles and with a mind always tuned to political strategy. Blair was an innocent by comparison. His experience in Sedgefield had left no scars; Brown was covered in them. Blair was a relative unknown when he came to Westminster. He was wide-eyed. The other new MPs recognized the relationship for what it was. Martin O'Neill, a constituency neighbour of Brown's, says that everyone watched Blair acquire his political education. 'Gordon was in charge . . . and Tony was happy with that. It's how he learnt everything.' Brown had networks, in the unions and in Scotland, which provided 20 per cent of the Labour MPs in the 1983 Parliament. He opened that maze of contacts and political folklore to Blair when they came together.

Brown's reaction to the catastrophic election defeat of 1983 – the worst for Labour since 1922 – was different from Blair's. Characteristically, Brown began to make allies and to plan. He never talked about the disintegration of Labour, only about political strategies for survival. He was still gripped by the story of Labour in the twenties and knew that, although his party's position was grim, there was nothing new under the sun.

The difference in their outlook is obvious in their maiden speeches, both made in July. Brown's was a detailed assault on government economic policy, with the hailstorm of statistics that would become his parliamentary trademark, and a claim that mass unemployment would produce mass poverty in his constituency and others like it. Blair had spoken three weeks earlier on 6 July, also about unemployment, but even at this stage in the political kindergarten he was drawing a distinction between his hopes and past Labour thinking. He took the trouble to say that he called himself a socialist 'not through a textbook that has caught my intellectual fancy, nor through unthinking tradition' but because he preferred cooperation to confrontation. From the start, socialism was a word with which he was very careful. He was sparing with it, and almost sounded as if he was grappling for some new way of describing what he was. Even in that first parliamentary outing there are glimpses of the impatience with his party's old ways, and a reluctance to use the old language.

Labour was a churning pot of impatience all summer. Thatcherism was at its high point and new Labour MPs were realizing that it would be a long time before they had a chance to sit on the other side of the Commons. They were right, of course: it would take fourteen years. In the shadow Cabinet, Gerald Kaufman, a veteran operator from the vanished world of Wilson and Callaghan, called the 1983 manifesto 'the longest suicide note in history' and that was the view of many in the parliamentary party, maybe a majority. When Tony Benn (who had lost his seat in Bristol) claimed that the election had been something of a victory for Labour because nearly eight and a half million people had voted for a socialist programme, he was engulfed in a tide of venom. John Smith, who had more personal affection for Benn than most of his front bench colleagues, having worked with him in the Department of Energy, would say simply, 'The man's mad.' He would shake his head in despair.

Foot's inevitable resignation announcement came quickly, and the leadership election that rolled through the summer turned into an orgy of breast-beating about the past. Change there had to be, though there was no agreement about which policies should go and which party rules should be rewritten. That would take years to settle. For the moment, Neil Kinnock and Roy Hattersley represented between them a commitment to some sort of modernization. They had many policy differences – Kinnock was still a fervent unilateralist and wanted to pull out of Europe and Hattersley thought the opposite – but they engineered an informal pact through their campaign managers, Robin Cook and John Smith, to sell themselves as a team. The so-called 'dream ticket' for leader and deputy leader duly scooped up more than two-thirds of the votes in the electoral college. Their dream wasn't that they might find a way of agreeing on policy in a few weeks, simply that they'd save the Labour Party from itself.

Neil Kinnock told the party conference where he was elected that the response to the election disaster must be 'never again', but he discovered quickly that among the unions especially there was little appetite for party reform. Moreover, his own loyalty to Foot, whose leadership campaign he had managed in 1980, meant that on his part there could be no sudden break with the past. Reinventing the party was going to be slow.

It is hard to exaggerate the depth of despair in the Labour Party of 1983. In the General Election campaign the Social Democrats and the Liberals, who together came within three-quarters of a million votes of Labour out of thirty-one million cast, were issuing grandiose predictions that they would supplant Labour as the natural opposition – claims that seemed ludicrously inflated even to some of those making them, since they had only twenty-three seats in the Commons, but which helped nonetheless to make the natural story of politics the sickness of Labour and to prompt the whispered question, 'Is it terminal?' In addition, the Social Democrats, founded only two years earlier, were eating into Labour's middle-class support and a series of disastrous by-elections had sapped it of any self-confidence. Warrington, Hillhead (where Roy Jenkins was elected for the SDP), Bermondsey and Darlington were names to make Labour shiver. Margaret Thatcher, Falklands victor, was in command in the Commons with a majority of 144 and the Labour opposition was doomed to turn in on itself, in an orgy of policy rewriting and organizational reform, before it could imagine presenting itself to the country as a credible alternative government.

For younger MPs the only hope was that, in the phrase that Blair was to use as opposition leader way in the future, things could only get better. Kinnock was promising a new era, and that at least gave a pinprick of hope to those younger MPs who had concluded that it was pointless to wait for Thatcherism to explode and for lost Labour votes automatically to come flooding back. It wasn't going to happen like that. The sense of the era as a transitional one was sharpened by the event that hobbled Kinnock's leadership at the start. In retrospect it would be seen as part of the change that Blair, and Brown to a lesser extent, felt must come.

The miners' strike began in March 1984 and lasted for twelve weary months. Kinnock took a battering. Labour's heart was on the picket lines, but for a good many members of the parliamentary party the picture of Arthur Scargill leading the miners to what most of those around Kinnock believed was certain defeat was a nightmare vision brought to life. Kinnock described him with deliberate cruelty as a First World War general, whose troops were being slaughtered. Brown was one of many who was painfully caught. His was a mining constituency, and his maiden speech had been devoted in large part to the survival of the pits and the prosperity of the families around them. But like most Labour MPs he found Scargill's opposition to a strike ballot impossible to defend: in private he would talk of the strike as a disastrous mistake, and admitted afterwards that it had been doomed from the start. The strike prolonged Labour's agony: the unhappy entanglement with Scargill lasted a full year.

Backbenchers were walking through a valley of despair. Many of their constituency parties were sunk in poisonous combat between factions and they could scarcely believe that theirs was a party that had been in government only four years earlier. MPs were bitter about the reselection rules which had been introduced by the party conference as part of the Bennite response to the 1979 defeat, and many of them found themselves condemned to be parliamentarians whose relations with the activists in their own party in the country were hostile and sour. No one at Westminster, even oldies who had taken part in the struggles between left and right in the fifties, could remember an atmosphere quite like it. The prospect of government seemed to exist only beyond a very distant horizon.

Meanwhile, Margaret Thatcher's Conservatives were relishing their political struggle with the unions, the battle which she had long expected and for which she had prepared. Around her there were those who had doubts – no one could talk privately for more than five minutes to her deputy, Willie Whitelaw, without sensing the depth of his unease and the passion with which he roared his favourite word 'Trouble!' – but she was determined to resist any settlement that didn't give the government a clear victory in the miners' strike. She saw it as the latest test of her resolve.

When she spoke to her backbenchers in July 1984 just before the summer recess, the Prime Minister chose to put the strike in the context of the 1982 Falklands War: 'We had to fight an enemy without in the Falklands. We always have to be aware of the enemy within, which is more difficult to fight and more dangerous to liberty.' She said that the striking miners were 'a scar across the face of the country' and spoke of the threat of tyranny. This was redolent of a remarkable speech she had made at Cheltenham Racecourse just after the Falklands when she declared that Britain had 'found herself again in the South Atlantic' and said: 'We have ceased to be a nation in retreat. We have instead a new-found confidence – born in the economic battles at home and tested and found true 8,000 miles away.' Politics was being played out on the high wire, in an atmosphere of exhilaration and danger. The autumn of 1984, when the IRA bombed the Thatcher Cabinet in the Grand Hotel, Brighton, seemed to bring proof that this was an age in which the unimaginable might always happen. To stand on the seafront on that October morning and gaze at the ruined façade was to sense that this was a momentous political era. It was bizarre to talk to Cabinet ministers streaked with dust and watch the plaster fall from the walls. Everything seemed infected by the event. They were fevered times.

So the early parliamentary years of Brown and Blair – in those days the names were always in that order – were lived in a political hothouse. Their party was still shuddering with the consequences of defeat, and engaged in a messy civil war that forced dozens of MPs to expend most of their energy in battles in their own backyards. The Liberals and the SDP were digging themselves in as a serious political force, goading Labour on its policies on defence, Europe and the economy, and the government was engaged in economic reforms and changes to trade union law which many Labour MPs realized would change the rules of politics for ever. The clock was running too fast to be turned back. It was therefore a happier time for younger MPs than for the old warhorses who wandered round the Commons shellshocked by the pace of change. For the newcomers, the only way was up.

Blair was the first to get a front bench job, as a junior Employment spokesman. He was surprised but grabbed it. John Smith had passed word to Kinnock's office that young Blair, as Derry Irvine called him, was a likely talent. Blair was called to the leader's office where he was ushered in by Kinnock's chief of staff, the beaming Falstaffian figure of Charles Clarke, whom he scarcely knew. It was Clarke who seemed in charge; Blair didn't know why he was there. Seventeen years later, Clarke would join Blair's Cabinet and become party chairman. The employment role was Blair's chance to exploit his barrister's training in employment law and, more importantly for his future, it opened a door to the unions. From the beginning his relationship with them had its ups and downs, because he was privately less outraged by some of the Thatcher reforms than the union leaders with whom he dealt, but he had the chance at last to make himself known.

Gordon Brown played a canny hand with Kinnock, turning down his first offer of a job in the shadow Scottish team. He had enough sense to realize that he risked disappearing into the familiar but confined pastures of Scottish Office politics, which have been known to have a suffocating effect on a promising career. His decision was revealing. With his background in Scotland, he was a natural recruit as a Scottish Office spokesman, but he was already surveying a wider and more inviting landscape and ambition led him away from Scotland. His second chance was the one he wanted, joining John Smith's Trade and Industry team in 1985.

They continued to share their room, and started to enjoy opposition as front benchers. But around them their party was still in a terrible state. Those left-wingers who had abandoned the Bennite causes of the early eighties were beginning to assemble in what became known as the 'soft left' and quite a few were going through the miserable and embarrassing process of shedding their past. Everyone, it seemed, wanted to be in the Tribune Group. Instead of being the dissident voice of old, it now turned into the voice of the leadership. If you were a Kinnockite you were in Tribune, so Brown didn't find it difficult to take Blair along in 1985, although he would never share the affection of the likes of Brown and Cook for the history of the left that they still cherished. It was because of Brown that Blair joined Tribune. His mentor John Smith, part of the Hattersley camp that kept a deliberate distance from the left, would never have suggested it.

In those days Tribune was like some kind of rolling revivalist meeting, marked by personal confessions and recantations. Kinnock was disposing of many of the policies that Labour had put before the electorate in 1983 – European membership wouldn't be renegotiated and defence policy was beginning slowly to turn towards multilateralism – and it was obvious that he wanted to reverse some of the organizational changes championed by the Bennite left, though it would only be after Kinnock was long gone as leader that something approaching a one-member-one-vote system of party democracy would arrive, and even then in a form that gave the unions a powerful collective voice in the electoral college. Yet by 1985 things were on the move. Party conferences saw fewer combat jackets and more suits, and the modernization banner was the one to march behind if you wanted to progress in Kinnock's party.

For most Labour MPs, the event that lifted the sullen mood of defensiveness and promised better things to come was Kinnock's speech to the 1985 conference in Bournemouth, always a town in which Labour seemed slightly uncomfortable. Perhaps it was the right place, well away from the traditional party pleasure garden of Blackpool, to signal a turning point. Kinnock's assault on Militant and all its works – dramatized by his contemptuous attack on the Militant-controlled Labour council in Liverpool – was the lancing of a boil. No leader had attacked a section of his own party in such terms for a generation and more, and the sight of Kinnock vibrating with anger on the platform sent most of his MPs into a state of modest ecstasy. Brown and Blair were among those MPs who thought it was the boldest and most welcome display of leadership they had experienced. Some were appalled, of course. Eric Heffer stomped off from his national executive seat on the platform to denounce Kinnock as a traitor to his party. But the overwhelming reaction was one of light-headed relief. For MPs like Brown and Blair, it promised to be the beginning of the end of the nightmare. Many MPs believed that week in Bournemouth marked the end of Labour's lost years, although the momentary optimism was misleading too, lending a false feeling of recovery when long years in opposition still lay ahead. Both Brown and Blair regarded Kinnock's speech with relief. Neither had a Militant problem in his constituency, but they thought that until Labour was seen to reject the far left outright it would remain unelectable. They both supported the subsequent party purge of Militant members, denounced by the hard left as a witchhunt but enthusiastically promoted by the Kinnockites in Tribune.

In the midst of all this, Labour made a decision which had a profound effect on them. The first impact was wholly pleasurable, and helpful to their careers, but in time it would seem a moment that also created between them a bond from which they couldn't escape and which at times appeared able to suffocate them. In September 1985 Peter Mandelson was appointed director of communications for the party.

Mandelson was an exotic creature even then. The clinching interview with Kinnock and Hattersley was – they thought – dazzling, but afterwards Kinnock confessed privately that he wasn't entirely comfortable with Mandelson's style. He'd noticed that he was wearing lurid socks and showing them off. 'I know he's . . . that way,' said Kinnock, a little agitated, to Hattersley, 'but why does he have to flaunt it?' There is a dispute about the colour of the socks. Hattersley thinks they were pink, Mandelson blue. The effect was the same. This was before gay lifestyles were widely accepted, least of all in politics, and although Mandelson wore his sexuality relatively discreetly at this stage he never saw much reason to disguise it among friends and acquaintances. He was going to bring a different style to the leader's office.

He displayed a blend of Labour loyalism and irreverence. The loyalism was a family inheritance. As the grandson of Herbert Morrison, Foreign Secretary and leader of the Commons in Attlee's post-war government, Mandelson had been aware of the party since he could walk. He played with Harold Wilson's children as a boy. So after Oxford and a typical phase of student leftism it was natural that he should end up as a Labour councillor in Lambeth in south London, and equally natural that he should resist the blandishments of the Social Democrats when they broke away in 1981. A number of his friends who were struggling with the hard left on Lambeth council did leave – notably Roger Liddle, who would return to play a Downing Street role in years to come – but although on many policy matters and in his attitude to the left he agreed with them, he stayed within the Labour fold. But for his family ties, friends believe he might have defected. He was close to several who did, and does not seem to have expended much energy dissuading them.

But he could not make the final break. Alongside that visceral sense of belonging, however, ran a streak of iconoclasm towards the Labour Party. He has always been impatient with it.

As director of communications, Mandelson began in a characteristic way. Even before he occupied his office, he recruited Philip Gould, a thirty-four-year-old advertising man of earnest disposition who had set up his own agency, whom Mandelson had met only a couple of weeks before. The first Gould memo, which was delivered within days and ran to sixty-four pages – they were still landing on Tony Blair's desk in Downing Street seventeen years later – and sketched out assumptions which would underpin Mandelson's work and the policy reforms of the late eighties. Labour, he said, was seen as a collection of minorities and not a party that represented the majority; it appeared to be more interested in its own activists than in the voters. Gould's remedy was simple. Campaigns should have one purpose – to influence electoral opinion. A strangely obvious conclusion, it was one that led to a period of more than five years of troubled change in the Labour Party.

Early on, Mandelson found Brown and Blair and they found him. In his three years at London Weekend Television, he had been aware of them, and when he had worked as a research assistant in the shadow Cabinet after 1979 (he had worked for Roy Hattersley's leadership campaign in 1983) he knew of Brown in Scotland, but this was the real start of their relationship. He needed talent to push towards television and radio editors to speak for the party, new faces unassociated with the traumas of the past. Within a year the three were operating as a team. Brown would sit in his Edinburgh flat at weekends talking to Mandelson for what seemed hours; and in Blair, Mandelson found a spirit as restless as his own. Tabloid articles began to pop up signed by one or the other. All of us who had these conversations in Mandelson's ceaseless round knew they were supposed to be the two golden boys. The daily line was: 'They are the future.'

At first he spent more time with Brown. Mandelson found in him a rich source of material for the press. Brown had privately cultivated a number of Whitehall contacts from where he would produce regular leaks to embarrass the government, something ministers find deeply irritating, as he would discover in later life. By the time the 1987 General Election came along, Mandelson was established as the conduit for what the Kinnockites called 'progressive thinking'. In turn, that meant that he also began to be hated by elements of the traditional left who had already decided that Mandelson represented the enemy. They were right.

A year after Blair's deadline for the party to review or perish had passed, reform had become more interesting than thoughts of disaster. The poky Commons room had become a little powerhouse. The air was thick with plans, and with ambition. Mandelson was a regular visitor and as the 1987 election approached the three were beginning to be a force in the party that couldn't be ignored by the senior members of the shadow Cabinet. John Prescott, in particular, was finding Mandelson, as he would put it frequently, 'a pain in the backside'. He would joke at shadow Cabinet meetings about what he thought was the absurdity of the new red rose emblem for the party (which Mandelson was championing, though the idea was an advertiser's and not his) and the concentration – obsession, Prescott called it – with advertising techniques and voter research as the bedrock of the campaign.

That campaign was a failure for Labour: the Conservatives returned with a majority of more than a hundred. But despite the fact that the result tossed Kinnock into a period of deep gloom from which it took him months to emerge, Brown, Blair and Mandelson saw it as the first vindication of their approach. If policy could be modernized still further – burying the non-nuclear defence policy which had proved a serious handicap – they believed that the party, for the first time since the 1983 election, might become electable. Neither Brown nor Blair had expected to win in 1987, and they weren't surprised at the scale of the defeat. Rather, they were reassured that a pattern was beginning to emerge for the future.

In particular, Mandelson cherished the memory of a Hugh Hudson film on Kinnock which had run as a much-hyped Labour party political broadcast. It had failed, in the sense that it didn't persuade vast numbers of voters to support Labour, but it set a tone that Mandelson was happy to commend to the party. The joke around Westminster was that the film should have been subtitled 'Jonathan Livingston Kinnock', a reference to the syrupy and vacuous American book and film (*Jonathan Livingston Seagull*) about a bird which had a brief moment of fame in the mid-eighties. In the party machine it was considered a triumph.

Mandelson was particularly proud of the way it had revealed the real Kinnock responding to direct questions about his integrity, capacity and convictions. They had worked hard to get Kinnock in the right mood, throwing question after question at him to get him to rise to the bait and deliberately provoking a passion audible in his responses. The questions did not feature in the broadcast – only Kinnock's replies. The Fleet Street interrogator recruited to draw the best out of the leader was the *Daily Mirror*'s political editor, Alastair Campbell.

It was in this period, Brown and Blair's second Parliament, that a pattern of relationships was established which would condition much of Labour's internal arguments and style for the next decade. Promotions followed quickly: Brown was elected to the shadow Cabinet in 1987, and topped the poll the following year, when Blair joined him. Labour was visibly starting to change at the top. Some of the older warriors were eased aside, and anyone whose convictions ran counter to the new orthodoxy – as with Bryan Gould on Europe – was heading for demotion. With the first promotions and the perceptible stirring of ambition the shared office was abandoned in favour of separate domains – still tiny – on the shadow Cabinet corridor.

Brown and Blair were no longer a pair of juniors, backing up their bosses in the shadow Cabinet and deferring to the leadership. They were making their own way, and with Mandelson egging them on and advising them on how to sharpen their public faces they started to carve out separate careers. The three were still a gang – around Westminster you seldom saw one without one of the others nearby – but they were beginning to build up their own teams of advisers. Blair, for example, turned in 1988 to Anji Hunter, whom he had first met while he was at Fettes, who joined his office and ran his parliamentary life.

The shadow Cabinet as a whole was taking on a new character. Robin Cook was on the rise, and eyeing an important economic portfolio, with any luck at the expense of Brown. John Prescott was nursing grudges against Mandelson (who he believed had tried to marginalize him in the 1987 campaign, as indeed he had) and also against Roy Hattersley, whom he thought an ineffective deputy to Kinnock. He was persuaded to back down from an open challenge to Hattersley by Kinnock, an operation that he regarded as humiliating because it opened him to criticism for alleged disloyalty. From then on Prescott revelled in his natural disposition to distrust the architects of 'modernized Labour'.

Naturally, much revolved around John Smith, now shadow Chancellor. Brown, Smith's deputy, was pitched directly against the Conservative Treasury Chief Secretary, John Major. It provided him with the chance, eagerly seized, to make his reputation as a formidable force in the Commons, but it was also the time in which he sowed seeds of doubt among some colleagues about his approach; these he would reap (with regret) when his own leadership ambitions were put to the test.

One particular episode illustrates it well. Nigel Lawson's 1988 Budget revealed that he had money to spend. It was the pre-boom time, when the coming bust was never mentioned. Smith, leading the Labour Treasury team, was trying to devise a strategy for Budget Day. What would they recommend as spending priorities? Brown, whose commitments to social spending and measures to tackle poverty were the political badge he wore with pride, was nonetheless cautious. Even Smith, caution personified, was surprised. And others in the team were surprised to hear Brown, as shadow Chief Secretary, argue for prudence, his watchword of the future.

Brown had already concluded that Labour had to establish a reputation for fiscal probity if it was ever to be elected. A number of colleagues disagreed. One who was present at that meeting, and who came from the left like Brown, said: 'I realised then where Gordon was heading and I knew that I would not be supporting him in the end.'

The significance of such encounters is that they came at a time when Brown was already being talked up as a future leader, a message spread assiduously by Mandelson. Brown's profile was well known and his friends and rivals were lining up, as politics makes them do. Robin Cook, for example, had always resented Brown's capacity to gather round him a band of loyalists – not something that Cook had managed for himself – and believed that on policy he was heading in the wrong direction.

Visitors to Cook's office would sometimes be pointed towards a particular book on his bulging shelves. It was called *Scotland: The Real Divide*, published in Edinburgh in 1983, and the authors were Gordon Brown and Robin Cook. It was said at the time that Cook felt Brown had taken too much credit for the book, and that the resentment was one of the reasons for his irritation with him, but by the end of the 1980s Cook's complaint was different. He was a critic of the economic policy that was emerging under Smith and Brown, who were trying to rid Labour of the image of a spendthrift party on tax. 'That's what he used to believe,' Cook would say as he took the familiar volume in his hand. 'This is what we were going to do with the economy,' he would snort.

Brown had become a prominent figure, in part because his battles with Major on public spending made good parliamentary theatre. They really didn't like each other. Brown would always mutter of him, 'Not as nice as he looks.' Major, as Prime Minister, would tell his ministers that he never trusted Brown. Even now, fifteen years after they first met on the opposite sides of a Commons committee on the 1986 Budget, Major says he has barely spoken to Brown. While the Smith–Brown team was improving Labour's economic attack, Blair was spokesman on Energy and then, after 1989, on Employment. Although his public profile was still fuzzy, he was becoming better known in the party because of his willingness to unsettle the trade unions. They detected some unease about their attitudes. They were right.

1988 saw another change which shaped the careers of Blair and Brown and brought a reminder that politics is a trade driven as much by human frailties and eccentricities as by strategy, never mind logic. Just after the Labour conference in Brighton John Smith had a heart attack at home in Edinburgh. He was lucky to survive, and took three months off from politics. Brown immediately took over. Bryan Gould, who was Trade and Industry spokesman, had expected to deputize as shadow Chancellor since he was the next most senior Economic spokesman, but Brown was faster on his feet. Mandelson said at the time: 'Gould had no idea what was happening. He turned round and Gordon was making the running. He didn't even feel the stiletto.' In those days, Mandelson was delighted to see Brown prospering. He had an eye for a headline and a telling phrase in the Commons and he was exhilarated at the chance to take on the Chancellor, Nigel Lawson.

The shape of Labour in the nineties was starting to emerge. At the top the main characters had established the relationships that would determine the party's future. One of those which is most intriguing, because it is often misunderstood, was that between Brown and Smith.

The two had developed a close friendship during the eighties and Smith had championed Brown's rise to the top of the shadow Cabinet. It was shortly after Smith's heart attack that Brown overtook him, pushing Smith into second place in the poll. It is also true that Brown has written movingly about Smith's commitment to social justice, which he sees as the great purpose of politics. He cherished Smith's principles. They had become close friends and relied on each other's judgement. Yet there were complications.

Before Brown arrived at Westminster he and Smith were not at all close. Despite Brown's enthusiasm for devolution and his support for Smith when he was the minister in charge in the Callaghan government, they were from different political moulds. It is impossible to imagine Smith curling up in bed with a copy of *The Red Paper on Scotland*. He was quite out of sympathy with the left-wing critique of those later Wilson–Callaghan years and was an unashamed member of the pro-European Labour right – in favour of a mixed economy that didn't embrace more nationalized industries and against pretty well anything that became a rallying cry for the left in the late seventies. On these questions he was an ally of many of those who went on to form the SDP, though he felt betrayed by them and embarrassed by having it pointed out that on many of the insistent political issues of the time he was closer to the departed Jenkinsites than to Michael Foot.

Smith's loyalty to Labour had little to do with the approach crystallized in the 1983 manifesto. He described a number of its promises as 'bonkers' and never expected that Labour could come close to winning. Brown would, of course, abandon many of the commitments in that document as time went on, but he had come from a section of the party where Smith's views were regarded as reactionary and lodged in the past. Smith, in his pungent way, didn't bother to disguise his attitude to the left. About such prominent figures on the established left as Robin Cook, with whom he had fought over devolution, he had a lively scepticism. 'Wee Cookie's an odd one right enough,' he often said. So it would have been surprising had he been an early fan of Gordon Brown's. He wasn't.

All the factions and alliances were, however, shaped more by personality than creed. Brown and Cook were from the left, but they had fallen out for good. Smith was of the right – his ideological stablemates were Hattersley, Denis Healey, Jack Cunningham and Gerald Kaufman – but he respected Brown's intellect. Temperament and chemistry were more important than ideological positioning. His eventual bonding with Brown came about principally because of a shared attitude to politics, and it was in this that they demonstrated something which was quite distinct from the Blair approach which would develop in the nineties.

Smith is often misleadingly described as an Edinburgh lawyer. He was a lawyer and he did live in Edinburgh, but the description conceals more than it reveals. Though his demeanour and his style seemed to outsiders to define his character and his natural habitat, Smith was emphatically a West of Scotland man who kept with him a certain feeling for the radicalism that he had absorbed from his father in the schoolhouse in Ardrishaig in Argyll where he grew up and where the *New Statesman* would arrive by boat. He inherited the same kind of egalitarianism that was summed up in the title of a famous book about Scotland by George Davie called *The Democratic Intellect*. He believed in a society founded on equality of opportunity in education and a notion of individual worth that wasn't ordained by wealth or social position. Though Smith had never practised politics as a matter of class struggle, and was always uncomfortable with the language that went with that view, his instinct for the political trade was similar to the one Brown had absorbed in the manse.

This meant that on the scarred landscape that Kinnock inherited from Foot, Smith and Brown felt that they were engaged on similar business. Disputes about the 1983 manifesto were in the past: that document was somewhere in a dustbin that they hoped would never be opened again. Each was a party loyalist, willing to play it rough in Labour infighting if it was necessary, and were temperamentally committed to night-and-day opposition in the Commons, Smith the old student debater who loved cross-examination from the dispatch box and Brown the ferreter-out of government leaks who had a knack of embarrassing ministers with his revelations.

The ties were strong in the late eighties, but like so many political friendships they began to fray in the aftermath of the 1992 election defeat. Kinnock had started the campaign believing in victory, though he subsequently admitted that by the last weekend of the campaign he had sensed a decisive shift back to the Conservatives. Smith, oddly enough, hadn't felt it coming and was genuinely startled when his old friends Donald Dewar and Helen Liddell took him to one side at his own constituency count to tell him that he should accept that the plane waiting at Edinburgh airport to take the new Chancellor of the Exchequer to London in the small hours of the morning would not be required after all.

That election was a turning point because, once more, power began to shift. When Smith succeeded Kinnock in the summer – an assumption of leadership that seemed natural to most in the party – he began to pursue a policy that some of those who had become quite close to him believed was both cautious and defensive. Brown and Blair found themselves at odds with their old friend. He had acted as an opener of doors for Blair, as a benign boss to Brown, and he had schooled them in parliamentary tactics, first in the long all-night sessions on the 1983 employment bill when he led the attack for Labour with Brown and Blair in support. But those days were past.

In the few weeks before Smith succeeded Kinnock, Brown was tempted to stand for the leadership himself. But as well as supporters he had enemies. One union leader phoned a party official when he heard that Brown was wondering about a candidacy and said: 'If what I hear is true, it has to be stopped. When the mice start running around they have to be stamped on.' The recipient of the call believes it was prompted from Smith's office. Brown read the signs and decided to bide his time. Blair's reaction, however, was not altogether understanding. He told a close friend: 'Gordon's bottled out.' Instead, he himself considered running for the deputy's post under Smith. Brown couldn't, because two Scots in the top jobs would be unacceptable. But Blair was stopped too. He met Mandelson and agreed to listen to party soundings. However, another union leader, Bill Morris of the TGWU, emerged the next day to declare his support for Margaret Beckett, and within twenty-four hours Smith was giving interviews supporting her candidacy for the deputy's job. Blair was scuppered. Afterwards he was convinced that the intervention of Morris had been arranged by friends of Smith. These episodes confirmed that the subcutaneous rivalry of the previous couple of years could, under the pressures and fears of high office, be brought gasping to the surface. They showed that each, instinctively, wanted to get ahead of the other.

In mutual frustration Brown and Blair settled down to life under Smith, and found that they were thwarted. Blair was the angrier of the two. His affection for Smith went back to their first boozy meeting at the Commons in 1982 and he had learned the ways of Parliament at Smith's feet, but after the 1992 election he had become convinced that Labour was now the cautious party and that the tempo was all wrong. His own instincts were already leading him in a direction which ran counter to the party's received wisdom – on the role of the unions and on crime, most notably – and the target of much of his private criticism was Smith. Mandelson, now MP for Hartlepool, having left his party post just before the election, was another of the critics. Smith had never been a fan.

Mandelson now found himself in an outer circle of influence. There were other sceptics from the Kinnock circle of reformers. On the *Mirror*, Alastair Campbell's view was that progress was slowing down. Mandelson put it differently: 'It's not slowing down. It's gone into reverse.'

Blair was demonstrably unhappy. He would tell friends the same thing again and again: 'John is just so cautious. It's a disaster.' At times he appeared almost to be despairing, despite the Major government's own troubles after the ignominious and messy exit from the European Exchange Rate Mechanism (ERM) on Black Wednesday in September 1992. Smith was abroad on the day itself so his new shadow Chancellor, Brown, was in charge in London. Brown concluded immediately that this was the event that would in the end destroy John Major's government. Smith agreed, but his subsequent tactics dismayed Blair. He believed that the next election would now inevitably be lost by the Conservatives as long as Labour didn't foul up in opposition: his cautious instincts therefore led him to sit tight. Blair did not agree with him. Indeed, there are some (they claim to be tuned into the Blair antennae) who go so far as to say that he even wondered about getting out of politics at this stage. Blair now denies it, and there is no solid evidence to support the claim. There is no argument, however, about the distance that started to open up between Blair and Smith.

Blair found that he had an ally in the leader whom Smith had succeeded. He and Neil Kinnock had developed an affinity for each other in the late eighties, when Blair began to relish the kind of policy sallies that would later become one of the main characteristics of his leadership. He was on the move, and to his relief he found Kinnock – and, even more to his surprise, John Prescott – more supportive than he could have expected. There had been predictable and sometimes quite feisty union opposition, particularly to his formulations on secondary picketing which were designed to ditch a great deal of Labour lore on the subject, but he found that Kinnock's commitment to change was solid enough to see him through.

In the approach to the 1992 election, Kinnock had become a still more impatient leader. He wanted further change. So even when

Blair irritated parts of the trade union establishment and the parliamentary party by challenging some of the assumptions that had survived earlier Kinnock reforms, he found his leader more sympathetic than he might have expected. Blair remained scarred by the despair that had cocooned his party after the 1983 defeat and, like Kinnock, was determined to avoid its grip again. Both were given to dark moods and although Blair still cut a breezy figure he was ready with shadow Cabinet colleagues to talk about the chasm that might still await Labour round the next bend.

They shared that caution about the future, even when the bizarre upheavals of Margaret Thatcher's resignation in November 1990 appeared to give Labour some cause for glee. Offstage, however, Kinnock feared with some justification that the judgement of Michael Heseltine and the senior Tories who supported him was right: a Conservative Party with a new leader was going to be stronger in the coming election, whoever that leader might be. Blair thought the same. The run-up to the 1992 campaign had been bad enough, with Blair among those near the top of the party who sensed that a Conservative victory was imminent. That feeling of frustration was to become much worse.

With defeat and Kinnock's departure immediately afterwards, Blair and his friends wondered if they had given their lives to politics only to see them played out entirely in tedium on the opposition benches. And despite the problems the Conservatives were facing, in Europe and elsewhere, Labour was prey to a period of self-doubt.

There was little excitement in Smith's election in the summer of 1992. Denied the fireworks of a Brown or Blair challenge the contest was routine with hardly a moment of drama. Blair found that, in common with others on the front bench who thought of themselves as modernizers, his attitude to Smith had changed. Aware of Kinnock's raw feelings about his successor, who he believed had come close to conspiring against his own leadership when it was at its weakest, Blair's affection was now tempered with a sense that Smith's instinct for steadiness and safety was risking the whole enterprise into which Blair and others had been drawn in the eighties: the effort to reinvent the Labour Party. In those days it had been a rather ramshackle project. There was a good deal of back-of-an-envelope policy-making and only a patchy intellectual coherence in what was afoot, but faced with the reality of a fourth Conservative term the pace for Blair and his friends was quickening.

In Smith's camp, there was a quite different view. On party organization, they thought he alone could deliver change, only he could cajole the unions into a one-member-one-vote reform for the party. Only because he was trusted by the custodians of the block vote could he get them to open it up. He was respected by those whom he would have to persuade. That was true as far as it went. Smith had never lost his affection for the unions. When asked in the early eighties why a traditional Labour right-winger like himself – passionately pro-Europe and contemptuous of Bennite thinking – had never contemplated joining with the Social Democrats he would say: 'I am comfortable with the unions. They aren't. That's the big difference.' But by 1993 Blair was wondering openly if that cultural commitment could still be regarded as a strength.

Even while Smith was deep in messy negotiations to change party voting systems, which had been the knot that Kinnock had been unable to unravel in his time, his very accomplishment was starting to seem to Blair and a few like him as too much of a series of compromises.

It certainly allowed Smith his sweetest moment in arguments with the party, at the 1993 conference. He squeezed through his compromise on one-member-one-vote in Brighton, though it nearly slipped away. Opening up constituency selections to members' votes was an assault on union power; and though there would still be an electoral college for leadership elections (one third of the votes each for the parliamentary party, the unions and the constituency parties) the parties would let all the members vote and the unions would ballot. At lunchtime on the day of the vote Smith thought he had lost it, because the MSF (Manufacturing, Science and Finance) union wasn't on side. He called for Prescott who, in a famous barnstorming speech, swung the vote. Smith told Prescott he was going to resign if he lost, and though the idea was to appeal for re-election on the issue of reform, in confidence that the vote would be won in the end, defeat would have holed his leadership some-where near the waterline.

In the moments after the vote, won by a hairsbreadth after a traditional Labour conference day of vote switching, threatened skul-duggery and a good deal of confusion, he had the high spirits of a man who has just been spared the gallows. To his team, the closeness of that vote was evidence of how his caution in negotiation had been justified: it could be won only by stealth. To Blair, it was evidence that the future held only the prospect of more deals and more fixing. He had been privately very critical of Smith's speech to the TUC a couple of weeks before in which the leader had gone far too far in reassuring traditionalists, Blair thought, on full employment and workers' rights. Smith knew he needed the votes at the coming party conference in Brighton in a fortnight: Blair found Labour's positioning with the unions increasingly dispiriting.

And Brown was frustrated too. Having become shadow Chan-cellor in Smith's team, his instincts were to maintain the pattern that had been set in the last part of Kinnock's leadership. He was much more reluctant than Blair to be open about his feelings but those around him were clear that he was more unsettled than at any time since he had been elected to the front bench. There was one important contributory reason for this which caused him to lose his foothold in the shadow Cabinet elections and gave Blair an opportu-nity to make ground.

Brown had inherited from Smith's own years as shadow Chan-cellor a strong commitment to British membership of the European ERM and, as a result, his attack on the government after Black Wednesday was undermined. Some of his shadow Cabinet col-leagues who had doubts about Smith's European policy – notably Jack Straw, Robin Cook and David Blunkett – started to question the way Labour had prepared the whole argument. To Smith and Brown the priority was to exploit the government's manifest dis-comfort, by arguing that the party traditionally associated with sober economic management had lost its grip. But those who had never been keen on joining the ERM thought that there might be an easier case to make if Labour hadn't been pressing so hard for so long for membership. As so often in politics, Brown found that the tenor of the times told against him. Where a couple of years before he had been the most sure-footed member of the shadow Cabinet he was now finding life more difficult.

After 1992 he had the job of expunging from the public mind the memory of the 'tax and spend' label which the Conservatives had successfully hung round Labour's neck in the election campaign, helped by John Smith's 'shadow Budget'. By common consent in the shadow Cabinet afterwards, it had been a disaster. The sight of the Labour Treasury team posing on the steps of the Treasury – a most un-Smith-like piece of PR – had seemed hubristic, and so it proved. The spending plans duly unravelled. Now Brown was to tell the party that its attitude to economic management had to change if it was ever to win.

He was prominent, but his popularity in the party was weakening. In interviews he began to develop a relentless style, one that would become familiar in later years, which intensified the public feeling of a Labour Party that was strangely defensive, despite the government's trouble. In May 1993 Alan Watkins wrote in the *Observer* that Brown had been 'for some months now on a kind of automatic pilot which enables him to repeat meaningless phrases in monotone'.

By the autumn of that year he had slid to seventh, and bottom, in the vote for the constituency section of the national executive committee (NEC). Blair was sixth. It was the kind of result that was hardly likely to create a flicker of interest outside the fevered world in which they lived, but for Brown it was the first time that he had seen Blair edge ahead of him. He didn't like the feeling.

This was the background to a subtle but decisive change in their partnership. For as long as anyone in the Labour Party after 1992 could remember (the habit of recalling the days before the mid-eighties having been abandoned because it encouraged nightmares), the coming men had been Brown and Blair, in that order. In his beaming schoolmasterish way, Smith had blooded them and coached them through their parliamentary tests, and by the time the party was preparing for the 1992 election it was accepted well outside their circle – and emphatically believed by those around Brown – that they would never fight each other for the leadership.

At the time, that meant that Brown would be the candidate. From those first days in the windowless room he had been the senior figure, the wilier operator, the one who knew the most recondite byways of his party. He had worked the union circuit year after year and in the parliamentary party he was the star around which a group of MPs was starting to cluster, in the way that they do. By 1988, he had beaten Smith himself to come top of the shadow Cabinet poll and if, at any time up to 1992, the party had been asked whether it was Brown or Blair who would fight for the leadership under a modernizing banner the choice would have been clear. Blair knew it. Each considered one opportunity and decided against it – Brown to run against Smith for the leadership, aged forty-one, after Kinnock's resignation in 1992, and Blair to go for the deputy leadership. And it was at this stage that they discussed straightforwardly how they should proceed together. They agreed – and neither has ever denied what their friends acknowledge – that it would be foolish for them to fight each other. They pledged not to do so. At that stage, immediately after the third successive election defeat, Brown was clearly the more powerful figure. Therefore the deal was simple: Blair would defer to Brown.

This understanding has been the source of gossip and acrimony because it is held by some of those around Brown to constitute a promise broken. To any outsider, this will seem a rather literal interpretation of the kind of unwritten agreement that is made in politics all the time and is bound to be eroded by the ebb and flow of events. There was never a chance that such a commonsense discussion at a moment of transition for Labour after an election defeat could be expected to last indefinitely. But the way these conversations became elements in a subsequent struggle for supremacy, as if they were protocols to some great international peace treaty, reveals what was happening to their relationship. Inevitably it was changing as they began to feel that personally and individually they might be close to power.

The rivalry was conscious and was transmitted to the posses of camp followers who were beginning to gather around them. If Brown had his old network of allies and the advantage of his Scottish base, Blair had a much less secure place to stand. His time as Employment spokesman had made him more enemies than friends in some of the big unions, where he was already seen as someone ready to move too far too fast. In the party at large he was still a figure without the substance of Gordon Brown: his first conference speech, after all, had been only in 1990 and although his parliamentary performances had given him a certain Westminster profile it had none of the sharpness of Brown's. Now, though, the clearing of the undergrowth that always follows an election defeat offered space that they were both determined to fill.

Even then, those who watched these two trying to plan the way ahead – every journalist at Westminster, for example – were aware of how the natural laws of politics were almost bound to pit them against each other, as is the way of things. And among those who already appeared to have come to a cold-blooded assessment of what was most likely to happen were John Smith and Neil Kinnock.

Both had tilted towards Blair, Kinnock because his own experiences in the two general elections he fought as leader had moved him in that direction. One reason for this is obvious, though it is often overlooked. He had found that there was a great deal of English territory which was deeply inhospitable to a Labour leader from Scotland or Wales. All the pollsters told him that without recapturing what later became known as 'middle England' Labour could not win; he knew it to be true. After Smith was elected Kinnock suspected that his Scottishness would prove his greatest weakness, and in looking ahead to the next generation it was one of the reasons for favouring Blair. He came to believe – perhaps as early as 1990 – that Blair would beat Brown to it.

Smith's view was moving in the same direction, but his reasons were more complicated and, in the end, more telling in their effect on others in the party in the weeks ahead.

At this stage no one was preparing for a leadership election. Although Smith's health was a regular subject of mordant conversation, it was unthinkable to contemplate an election campaign under anyone else. He was enjoying the job, enjoying the government's difficulties, enjoying the first real prospect of power that he had known since the Callaghan government fell in 1979. Smith was usually beaming as he went about his business. He could claim (just) that Labour was now a one-member-one-vote party, and as 1994 began he seemed a confident figure.

It was against this background that Brown and Blair's prospects were changing: the names were starting to be mentioned in reverse order. Brown was having difficulties with some of his Treasury team and making demands on shadow Cabinet colleagues for assurances on spending which they were reluctant to give. Blair was shadow Home Secretary and enjoying a freewheeling argument with Michael Howard, a good Labour bogeyman, which gave him the perfect pitch on which to talk about a new kind of Labour Party and to start to employ a moral rhetoric which came naturally to him. Some of his colleagues didn't like that, even at this early stage, but they acknowledged its usefulness.

Smith knew that one or the other would probably succeed him. In early 1994 he was talking to two colleagues in the leader's rooms about the future. One who was present remembers: 'Smith stood at the window and looked over the river. He said, "People say that when I stand down Gordon's my successor. They say he's the son I've never had. That's not it at all. Tony is probably the one."' Smith had been saying something similar in private conversations with journalists for some time. Many of us heard him say: 'Blair's the man.' Roy Hattersley has a slightly different version. When he went to see Smith in April 1994 to tell him that he was going to stand down from the Commons, they had a brief conversation about leadership. Smith said that Blair was ahead for the moment, but there was no vacancy. Brown, he thought, was likely to prevail in the end. Smith was probably being mischievously ambiguous but his long-term prediction has not yet been put to the test.

This was the atmosphere that prevailed at the top of the party at the beginning of 1994. The leader, on jolly form, convinced that the government's economic problems and ugly disputes on Europe would give Labour the opening that had been so elusive for so long, thought he would be the next Prime Minister. Around him, however, there was simmering unhappiness. The shadow Cabinet was burdened by the personal antagonisms that had grown up in the long years of opposition and in the weary slog of reform. It was not a relentlessly happy band of brothers.

But Smith felt in charge. There was no direct threat to his leadership. He was enjoying his outings at the dispatch box. He was relishing the splinters flying in all directions from the Tory backbenches. He thought that at last Labour was beginning to find itself in tune with a public mood for change. He appeared to be in fine fettle when, on 11 May 1994, he went to the Park Lane Hotel in London to speak about Europe at a Labour fund-raising dinner. Next morning came his second heart attack. It was over.

3

One Leader

A melancholy frenzy followed Smith's death. Those around him were tearful and deflated, and the press decided to let the emotion flow. Politics appeared to come to a halt for a few days. But away from the sound of the torrential eulogies, there was quiet business to be done, and quickly. That was why the Labour chief whip, Derek Foster, made his way a day or two later on a private errand along the corridor behind the Speaker's chair to the empty rooms of the leader of the opposition under Big Ben. He retrieved a document for his own safe-keeping and left. No one knew he had been there.

It was a private paper commissioned by Smith himself a few months earlier. He had asked the chief whip for an honest assessment of the performance of the shadow Cabinet. Who was up and who was down; who was causing the government the most difficulty. Foster did not want his judgements coming to light in the course of the leadership election which was about to begin because he knew how fraught the atmosphere would become.

He had written in straightforward terms and his conclusion mirrored Smith's own. Brown was thought to be 'wading through treacle' as shadow Chancellor against Kenneth Clarke, troubled by his arguments with front bench colleagues about spending pledges which they wanted to make and he wanted to stop.

Blair, on the other hand, had found the job that suited him. As shadow Home Secretary he was able to start to develop a moral tone to his politics which, as events would prove, suited him much more than it suited many in his party. The Conservatives could be made to feel uncomfortable about crime, an issue traditionally their own, by a shadow Home Secretary who managed to coin a phrase that gave him, at last, a public identity. 'Tough on crime, and tough on the causes of crime' would, like most such phrases, come back to torment him. But it did its work.

And where did it come from? As Smith had known when he teased Blair about it round the shadow Cabinet table, it was not his own. Indeed, it had come from Brown, who had heard it in the United States. He and Colin Currie – the medical thriller writer, Colin Douglas – had developed a fine line in rhetorical inversions since the days spent in the mid-eighties contriving Labour slogans with Mandelson, and the origin of this one was pure Brown. But Blair had now made it his own and, as Foster noted in his memo to Smith, it had turned him into a national figure as well as a more substantial front bencher.

By contrast, Brown's troubles with colleagues were sapping his energy. Mo Mowlam, in particular, had a spiky relationship with him. She was an over-the-top, rumbustious, tactile woman; he was a man whose personal disciplines meant that hard work and frivolity were supposed to exist in separate compartments. He said nothing without having thought about it first. Mowlam was quite different. They found that they were colleagues who really didn't want to work together. But she was distraught nonetheless to be shuffled out of an economics job. She had enjoyed speaking about City affairs and had become popular in the party and in the Commons. She might have expected promotion. 'The bastards have given me Women,' she complained when she emerged from Smith's office with a new portfolio. Brown could expect no future favours from her. Mowlam was bitter and has never forgiven him.

It was a common enough view to be damaging to the shadow Chancellor. One of Brown's strong supporters at that time, later to join the Cabinet with him, says of that period: 'We all knew Gordon had the equipment to be the best leader. But could you imagine working under him? It was never on.' This came from someone whose ideological wellsprings might be thought to be the same as Brown's, and it was a judgement that was filtering through the front bench team. A shake of the head, the eyes turning upwards – 'Gordon's difficult,' they would say.

So Labour prepared for a leadership election with the rising generation in the shadow Cabinet elbowing each other around. After Smith's death, events moved fast. The trauma of those days transformed the relationship between Blair and Brown with the speed and force of a summer storm. Politics was transformed and the two men were left with a residue of hurt and misunderstanding which has never left them.

Twenty days passed between Smith's death and the public announcement that Brown would not challenge Blair for the leadership. It was a passionate time. Much of the personal drama was given decent cover first by a period of mourning and public reticence about potential candidates discussing the leadership and then by the demands of a European election campaign which had to be fought, however half-heartedly. But a political struggle was joined, and the relationship between Blair and Brown was now on fire. Rival camps were embroiled in battles that would be carried into government – the talk of betrayal and double-dealing had become especially bitter.

This was the whirlpool of events which turned Peter Mandelson in the course of a few days into the object of Brown's lasting disdain and at the same time the figure whom Blair believed indispensable to the team which he would install in Downing Street. In the end, instead of being the government's stabilizer, that triangular relationship threatened to unhinge it.

The previous ten years became a piece of history. The young brothers-in-arms had now outgrown all that. Politicians in every generation, in every party, find that the moment comes when friendships have to be put at risk or abandoned because the time is right to strike out alone, and Blair and Brown realized on the instant of Smith's death that, although those heady early days might sometimes help to rescue their relationship for the future, each was on his own now. In the previous months they had talked to colleagues about each other more openly than before. They were making their own ways in the shadow Cabinet, and Blair, for example, was discussing with Mandelson for the first time the possibility that he might over-take Brown and get to the leadership. He did not yet put it explicitly, but he wondered aloud with friends about whether Brown could recover the commanding position he once had.

Now, with Smith gone, Brown had to confront that political truth, which was exceptionally painful for him. Many of his friends and allies refused to recognize or simply did not believe the fact that in the later stages of Smith's leadership he had ceased to be the man most likely to succeed. The story of the six days between the leader's death and his funeral is the story of Brown's realization that he could not win.

The narrative has become muddied over the years, and some around Brown still insist that he did not reach his conclusion until the day before he met Blair to settle the leadership on the last day of May, the twentieth day after Smith's death. The occasion was the fabled Islington dinner – in fact an awkward and quite meagre meal – at which Brown formally told his old friend that he would not stand and would support him to make sure that the leadership would pass to him. In truth, Brown had known for more than a week that victory for him was probably not possible. He could fight, but the party would split and if he did win he would inherit a mess. If he lost to Blair, he would have to serve under a leader who would certainly believe him guilty of betrayal. The deal in 1992 that they would not challenge each other was hardly a legal document, signed in blood, but both of them felt it weighing on them.

Brown continued to listen to friends and family who produced elaborate explanations about how he might prevail in the party's electoral college, and he gave every impression to supporters in a wider circle that he was still game for the fight, but there were a few close to him who believe that even before Smith's funeral he had faced the truth.

This was the climax to the chapter that began with Smith's col-lapse in his Barbican flat at breakfast time on 12 May. Within a few minutes Murray Elder, the leader's chief of staff and Brown's friend from infancy, had told the shadow Chancellor. Brown immediately rang Blair on his mobile phone and found him in a car leaving

Aberdeen airport on his way to a European campaign meeting. He had already been alerted. Derry Irvine rang Blair a few minutes later to say that Smith had been pronounced dead at 9.15 a.m. On the intimate network which connected these characters at the centre of Labour's affairs, and the wider party that would choose a successor, there was an immediate mingling of grief and hard-headed calculation.

They were all in a state of shock. Elder had been close to Smith for fifteen years, when he left the Bank of England to work for the shadow Cabinet after the 1979 defeat. He had undergone the trauma of a heart transplant to save his own life in the late eighties and had a special feeling for Smith after his first heart attack in 1988. They climbed together, Elder the experienced mountaineer leading the rather more sedentary Smith to a series of highish Scottish peaks. Irvine was one of Smith's closest friends, a veteran of the uproarious Glasgow student days, and someone whose mind was turning to the possibility of a political career in government instead of a lawyer's swansong on the bench. And Blair and Brown, for all their irritation with aspects of the Smith regime, had lost their mentor. They didn't need to be told what that meant. In their shock, they had to start to plan.

It was not a choice between one and the other, mourning and scheming. Brown had been with Smith the night before at the Park Lane Hotel and it was a profound shock to be wakened seven or eight hours later to the news that he was dying. But no politician in his position is equipped to grieve in a vacuum. For someone who had even pondered a fight for the leadership after Neil Kinnock's resignation in 1992, and who had been at the top, or thereabouts, of the annual shadow Cabinet election since 1988, it was perfectly natural to think about what happened next while he was writing the tributes to Smith throughout the morning of 12 May. For Blair, it was the same.

All their expressions about Smith's leadership were subsumed in natural mourning. Now Brown was to be found writing obituaries. In the *Mirror* he wrote 'he put service to others first . . . his fearless sense of duty drove him on . . . like so many Scottish socialists before him his politics were shaped more by Kirk and community than by ideological theories'. There was an acknowledgement there of Brown's own long political journey, and it's hard to read what he wrote around this time without recognizing that he was instinctively writing elements of his own manifesto.

Although efforts were made to suggest that thoughts of the leadership election did not intrude, only a few hours passed before the first manoeuvres began. Politicians' instincts lead them to do this: the issue of leadership is never entirely submerged. It always disturbs the surface. Supporters of Blair and Brown found that they had been preparing subconsciously for this moment. The frustrations of the previous year ran deep.

Their irritation with the leadership had been obvious to all their colleagues, and so was the way in which they had become natural rivals. Others in the shadow Cabinet had nurtured leadership ambitions – Robin Cook was prey to them regularly, and John Prescott saw himself quite instinctively as a leader of a large group of MPs, many of them from the north of England, who considered themselves traditionalists rather than modernizers. But the centre of gravity seemed to be somewhere between Blair and Brown. To the hard-headed schemers of politics around party headquarters and the shadow Cabinet corridor that meant one thing. As the two had tentatively agreed two years before, they wouldn't split the forces of modernization. Only one would stand.

On the very day that Smith died, this was understood. The two most widely held assumptions around Westminster were that Blair and Brown could not afford to fight each other if one of them was to win, and that Blair had strengthened his position so much in recent months that he would not stand aside. At Brown's side at the time, Charlie Whelan's recollections are succinct: 'The idea that Tony and Gordon would ever fight it out to the end was always complete bollocks. As simple as that.' So what would Brown do?

He was in a black mood. But already the phones were ringing. A succession had to be organized. Around the principals, everyone could feel the first stirrings of a campaign. Once Blair was back from Aberdeen, and before the day was out, both camps had assembled. There was no sense of embarrassment in this. For politicians not to talk about succession at a wake would be very odd indeed, as Smith himself knew. He'd often enjoyed the old political adage 'where there's death there's hope', slapping his thigh with glee at the thought of some coming by-election. So across Westminster the first plans were laid. Mandelson called at Brown's flat briefly in the late morning and left more aware than ever of what he had long known: that the weight of Brown's personal history, his determination to lead and his single-mindedness about politics were still pushing him on.

Mandelson then did what came naturally: he began to talk to the press. The accounts of his private conversations with serious political correspondents late that morning agree that he was still trying out Brown's case. Told straightforwardly by one sage, Peter Riddell of *The Times*, that the augurs pointed to Blair, he said he wasn't yet sure and wanted to know why that was so. Like some others, Riddell read it as genuine uncertainty in Mandelson, a man who revels in his reputation as a Rasputin and enjoys slipping on a mantle of ruthlessness, but whose politics are emotional. A good deal of angst is often involved. The bond with Brown had been close. They spoke endlessly. The break didn't come in an instant.

But by early evening some of Brown's friends were gathering in a conclave and they were already disturbed by what they thought was happening among the Blairites. Smith had been dead only nine hours, but Douglas Henderson, MP for Newcastle North and an old friend of Brown's from Scotland, arrived from his own Millbank office with news. His room happened to be near Mandelson's, and he claimed to have heard conversations with Fleet Street from which he concluded that the Blair campaign had started to roll. 'We're half a lap behind,' he told them.

Over the next week, Mandelson gave quite contrary indications to some other members of the shadow Cabinet about his own preference, implying that he was not sure of what would happen. Bumping into Irvine, who expressed confidence that Blair would indeed become leader, Mandelson replied: 'I am not persuaded of that.'

The trouble was that Brown and the people around him no longer believed his old friend. If Mandelson was trying to preserve the tripartite relationship, the effort was doomed. Brown had gathered a team which had come to regard him with great suspicion. Although Mandelson had encouraged Brown to take on Whelan as his spokesman, the two were already operating in separate orbits as competitors. Whelan's interpretation of Mandelson's every move, relayed to Fleet Street in regular bulletins from his mobile phone, was that it was duplicitous. Mandelson had once been Brown's man, but no more.

On the afternoon of 12 May the Commons adjourned in mid-afternoon after formal tributes had been paid. Mandelson had arranged to meet an economist friend from New York who was in London and they repaired to the Pugin Room, a bar looking out from the Palace of Westminster over the Thames. While he was there, he received a pager message from Blair. Could they meet? The area around the Commons chamber was quiet. Everyone had gone home. So they sat down in one of the empty division lobbies that run alongside and talked alone for about ten minutes. Blair's message to Mandelson can be summed up in four words: 'Don't write me off.' Mandelson has since claimed that he was surprised at Blair's determination. If so, the surprise did not last long.

The *New Statesman* journalist Sarah Baxter, close to Blair, wrote in the London *Evening Standard* that afternoon predicting a Blair win. Alastair Campbell, who had been close to both men for years, appeared on BBC's *Newsnight* at the end of this first day and gave his view as a weather-beaten political editor: it would be Blair. The following morning, Mandelson's aide, Derek Draper, reported that his boss had decided on Blair. From the beginning, the Brown camp had decided that enemies had encircled them before they could organize themselves. A chorus was beginning, gathering strength in the papers the next morning. By the weekend Nick Brown, who was organizing MPs for the Brown team, could see the strength of the opposition. Three polls in the Sunday papers made Blair the public favourite to succeed, and Mandelson had popped up on Channel Four on Saturday night in anticipation – well-informed as to the polls' conclusions – to say that it was important for Labour to choose the leader 'who will play best at the box office'.

Smith's funeral was still five days away, but Brown is said by some of those closest to him to have absorbed the truth: it wouldn't be him. On Sunday the 15th he asked Philip Gould, the modernizers' pollster and focus group manipulator, to tell him who had the better chance of winning, and, by Gould's own account, got this reply: 'I said Tony, without hesitation. Gordon asked me why and I replied that Tony not only met the mood of the nation, he exemplified it. He would create for Labour and for Britain a sense of change, of a new beginning, which Gordon could not do.'

Gould was a weathervane for what Blair would call New Labour, his polling and voter research pointing in one direction: towards change. Gould's relentless pursuit of the Blairite 'project', a word of which he is very fond, has given him a reputation among non-Blairites for a mechanical pursuit of politics. His message to Brown that he could not change Britain was not welcome. Their friendship dissolved. Years later, when some of Gould's embarrassingly frank memos to Blair about the weaknesses of his government were leaked to *The Times* and the *Sun*, a Treasury colleague of Brown's said the Chancellor was greatly amused. They had restored relations by then but Brown retained some scepticism about the Gould number-crunching exercises with voters and focus groups.

It was now clear that Blair had the momentum in the race to be the candidate of change. Taken with the polls on that Sunday morning, and with the public declarations of Mandelson and Campbell for Blair (as they were interpreted by those around Brown), the sky was darkening. If Brown were to win, it could only be by pitting the party against what was claimed to be a public mood for Blair. In doing so Brown would have to challenge the very appetite for modernization that he had been trying to apply to economic policy in the previous two years. Even someone with less of a tendency to bouts of melancholy than Brown might have felt something of a victim at that moment. He was caught.

It was probably made worse for him by the insistence of many of those closest to him, friends and family, that he *must* fight and *could* win. Nick Brown and Andrew Smith were twisting arms in the parliamentary party; he had broad union support. One MP on the team reported that when he had suggested to John Edmonds, leader of the GMB (General and Municipal Boilermakers Union), that Blair might win, Edmonds had replied 'Over my dead body.' From his circle, Brown was under intense personal pressure to stand.

Smith's funeral was planned for Friday 20 May, and at the start of that week Brown was aware that Blair had secured a position in the public's and the party's mind from which he could not now be expected to retreat. It meant, Brown knew, that he would have to make the first move. Just at that delicate moment, when friends believe he was accepting that inevitability, the letter arrived from Mandelson that more than any other document in the whole saga settled the pattern of relations that would persist for years.

In it, Mandelson said that Brown was seen outside as 'the biggest intellectual force and strategic thinker that the party has' but that he already appeared to be running behind Blair, which made it difficult for Blair to withdraw. Brown already knew this. Mandelson went on to say that if Brown threw himself into an intensive campaign to recover his position it would weaken Blair, and added, 'Even then, I could not guarantee success.'

Mandelson wrote the letter on his laptop and before sending it round to Brown he showed it to Donald Dewar, a supporter of the shadow Chancellor. Dewar did not object to the wording of the letter, though he was distressed by the circumstances. Smith had been one of his oldest friends, and now he found himself involved in a leadership election that was bound to divide two of his close colleagues, Blair and Brown. Dewar's lugubrious commentary is remembered by many because it was often repeated: 'It's all most unfortunate. Most unfortunate.' Off the letter went.

By way of personal reassurance (at least in Mandelson's interpretation) it contained the phrase: 'Nobody is saying you are not capable/appropriate as leader.' The analysis continued: there were critics who would attack Brown's 'presentational difficulties' and he certainly had enemies, but the main objection was that the party would be damaged by a Blair–Brown contest. 'Because you would be appearing to come in as the second runner, you would be blamed for creating the split,' said Mandelson.

The wording is intriguing because in its use of the first person the letter reads as if it comes from Brown's personal adviser, a position from which those around the shadow Chancellor believed Mandelson had already removed himself. Mandelson has since insisted that he was still writing as the candid friend who had not yet abandoned Brown. He returned in the last poignant sentence to that voice: 'Will you let me know your wishes?'

This letter fizzed like an unruly firework in Brown's office. A member of his family could still describe it nearly seven years later as 'the most clever and devious letter I have ever seen'. It was viewed in the Brown camp as an effort to use his feelings of loyalty to Blair to force a guilty withdrawal from the contest, and moreover as an effort to portray Mandelson as a loyal colleague when they believed he had already become something quite different.

Mandelson has always expressed astonishment at that reading and (backed by Campbell) has insisted on the depth of his feeling for Brown and loyalty towards him. He told his biographer Donald Macintyre: '[If] Gordon had emerged there and then, and Tony had signalled his support, I would not have thought twice. My loyalty to Gordon was intense. He had always seemed to be the leader of the pack, the man whose brainpower, political judgement and personality were dominant.' But feelings were soured, and later in the week in the course of the funeral preparations, when reports carried back to Brown base camp that Mandelson was still talking around Westminster of his loyalty to Brown, they got worse. The common phrase was: 'Mandy's at it.' Henceforth he would always be 'at it'. Anything Mandelson did would be interpreted by those around Brown as part of a wider and inevitably hostile plan.

No other episode can catch quite as vividly the emotional fragility of the relationships that now linked these three. The very intensity of their dependence on each other over the years seemed to carry its own explosive charge. The draining days after Smith's death passed in an atmosphere that was inevitably heavy with personal recollection, so nerve ends were rubbed raw. With Blair and Brown thrown without warning into the contest that would decide their future, and the finely tuned emotions of Mandelson having to contend with accusations of treachery as well as the guilt that was evidently there, every contact was volatile.

Brown and Blair had spoken several times, the first in an arranged meeting at the home of Blair's brother, Bill, on the night of Smith's death. It was brief and they skated around the subject. Neither showed his hand. Each was being urged by groups of supporters to press on. Mo Mowlam was running Blair's campaign and her team calculated by that first Saturday, 14 May, that he already had a third of the parliamentary party in the bag; Brown's counters gave him much the same story. As with the soundings from the party outside, the message was unmistakable. In taking on Prescott, the nearest thing to a traditionalist candidate who was likely to emerge, one of them ought to give way or the cause of modernization would be put at risk. Most of the public comment suggested it should be Brown who should retreat. Tony Wright, from the vanguard of the modernizers, said on television that it now required from Brown an act of 'heroism and self-sacrifice'. By the start of the week of the funeral that was the dominant theme.

In private, however, Brown was being told something else, especially in Scotland, where his supporters were insisting that Blair seemed a weak candidate and was beatable. From the other side of the border the case that Mandelson had deployed for listening more carefully to public opinion and the box office – the 'middle England' argument – seemed much less important. Scottish Labour had escaped much of the trauma that had taken so much of England so far out of its reach. And Brown's supporters among MPs and in the wider party had, of course, none of the nervousness that was evident among English MPs about yet another Scot (after Smith) taking over. Despite the southern metropolitan current running strongly against Brown, some of those around him persisted long after he had realized that the fight was over.

Crucially, on the day before the funeral on 20 May, Brown knew that the political world was waiting for him and not Blair to decide. By this stage he had no realistic choice. He was still being urged to fight by his brothers, John and Andrew, and the inner circle that included Colin Currie, Murray Elder, Whelan and Nick Brown was still pressing him. In the shadow Cabinet Donald Dewar, now preparing one of the tributes for Smith's funeral, was already sensing that the cause was lost. Being a pessimist by nature, he read the runes clearly.

At Smith's funeral in Cluny Church, on a grey day in Morningside, Brown and Blair sat apart. There is a telling picture of them, separated by a couple of rows, both looking gaunt and pale and gazing straight ahead. Unlike most of their colleagues they knew the words of the hymns and seemed throughout to be a pair apart, which indeed they were. The service was a taxing one for everyone, deliberately plain and unadorned, with the 23rd Psalm sung in Gaelic unaccompanied. Dewar and Derry Irvine both spoke. The atmosphere was heavy. A few hours later, Brown and Blair met near the airport for a brief conversation. Each knew by now that Blair's momentum was increasing, with Fleet Street giving it a hefty push. Blair left for London and Brown went back home to his house in North Queensferry in Fife, overlooking the Firth of Forth. There he listened to his friends telling him, yet again, that he should fight on, but in the speech that they worked on through the night to be delivered the next day to the Welsh Labour conference in Swansea there is less evidence of that appetite for the struggle than there is of Brown's acceptance of the inevitable.

He chose to adapt one passage of Ecclesiastes – 'To everything there is a season, and a time to every purpose under Heaven . . .' This was a time to unite. 'Because we have travelled too far, too many miles together, for us now to lose sight of our destination. Together we have climbed too high for us not to achieve the summit. And it is near.' To some, these words were an indication that he would fight on. Blair feared as much. But they can be interpreted quite differently, as a laying down of the sword, an acceptance of the course of events and the need to do what was demanded of him. The words are intended to suggest that heroism, to use Tony Wright's word, is not always about a fight to the death. It is worth remembering that this was going on a mere nine days after Smith had collapsed, that no public campaign had yet occurred, and that Labour was about to try to maintain the fiction that only after the European elections at the beginning of June would minds be allowed to turn properly to the leadership issue. Brown's Swansea speech was misunderstood by some around Blair as a piece of grandstanding (it was delivered in the absence of Blair, who had originally been booked to speak and who didn't want Brown to go instead) but its tone, to those who knew Brown, was that of the man who was preparing for the sacrifice that many MPs were now asking him to make.

Brown is an enthusiastic student of American politics, and he is fascinated by the rhetoric of campaigns. One of his close friends in Washington is Bob Shrum, who was one of Al Gore's principal advisers in his struggle with George W. Bush during the 2000 Presidential campaign. But in a previous life, Shrum was famous for something else. As a speech writer for Edward Kennedy in his effort to take the Democratic nomination away from President Jimmy Carter in 1980 he wrote most of the address that Kennedy gave to the party convention in New York. It was a celebrated speech in its day – remembered for one phrase in particular, 'the dream will never die'. As a concession it is remembered by everyone who heard it as a classic piece of political theatre. It was exactly that tone that Brown tried to capture in Swansea. His stage, of course, was a much more modest one, his audience relatively small, and the occasion was still overshadowed by the funeral of the day before, but reading the words now it is hard not to conclude that the speech was made by a man looking forward to a distant crusade in the future rather than to an imminent victory.

Whether or not Brown was preparing to give way, the speech struck the edgy Blair camp as an appeal to Old Labour, and made them nervous. After discussing it with Blair, Mandelson spoke to *The Times* which carried a story on Monday 23 May to the effect that Blair was not going to abandon the cause of modernization. Set against the Swansea speech, the implication was that Brown was doing just that. But although he was irritated, Blair was also anxious to preserve the relationship with Brown when – as he now expected

– he became leader. Friends who spent most time with him in this period say he agonized aloud about Brown's feelings. He would say: 'We have to take care of Gordon.' This was rather more generous than some of his remarks a year or two before, when the strains had first appeared, but it reflected the reality of his new superiority. The truth is that they both realized quickly after Smith's death that the outcome was likely to be a Blair leadership, and it was in that period of just over a week, encompassing their own awkward meetings, the to-ings and fro-ings of Mandelson between the camps and the funeral itself, that all was settled.

A final act remained to be staged, but before that there was a period of frenzied campaigning of the sort that had been avoided (just) before the funeral. Brown's team lobbied hard, still believing they could convince their man that he might win. Two pieces of evidence, one much stronger than the other, convinced them otherwise. A survey for *On the Record* on BBC television on 29 May gave Blair a solid lead in all three sections of the electoral college which would decide the leadership and two days before, in the *Scotsman*, a survey of a number of Scottish Labour MPs showed Brown with only fifteen solid votes (to Blair's six) but said that six others who were natural Brown supporters wanted him to stand aside for Blair. This was interpreted in Westminster as evidence that even in Scotland Brown was not impregnable.

In the march of history, the *Scotsman* survey changed nothing, but it became another cudgel with which to batter Mandelson. Years later, one of Brown's closest advisers in that period said: 'We knew what Mandy did with that poll. He misinterpreted it to everyone. He probably fixed it himself.' Mandelson says he didn't twist it, though he showed it to MPs as a piece of interesting research; and it is certainly not true that the respected *Scotsman* correspondents of the time had been put up to it. The truth is that by this stage it was all becoming deeply painful in the Brown camp, and any bad news had to have Mandelson at its origin. By Monday night, 30 May, Gordon Brown was ready to tell his team that it was over.

The *Scotsman* episode illustrates how the passions released by the leadership contest had now entwined around the main characters, and how difficult it would be to escape those feelings. By the time Blair and Brown broke bread at Granita, a restaurant in north London, on 31 May, they were looking ahead to life under a Blair leadership but also aware that the events of the previous three weeks had changed their relationship permanently.

The idea of the dinner came from Blair's office. The Swansea speech had alarmed them. Brown was a powerful orator, and was capable of causing immense difficulty for Blair with the party if he felt that he had been pushed aside. Blair had only come to realize in the previous year that he might overtake Brown and he was still hesitant. Mandelson, well aware of Brown's sensitivity and the crushing sense of disappointment that he must be feeling, told Blair straightforwardly that he would have to promise that in any Labour government he would be a Chancellor with more power than any of those who had served Major or Thatcher. No one used the phrase 'dual premiership', but they accepted that Brown would be offered something which might seem like it.

This calculation was based on fear. Blair would be a leader with no experience of politics at the top level, and alongside him he would have a master strategist. If he offended Brown at this juncture, he could expect endless trouble. Mandelson had spent days and weekends with Brown over the years planning speeches, campaigns and strategies and he knew how potent a force he was. They decided they needed to go even further. Remembering the pact of 1992, when Blair and Brown had agreed not to challenge each other, they now agreed that Blair should tell Brown that he wanted to see him succeed him as Prime Minister in due course if the chance came. Pitched so far into the future, the promise seemed a safe one.

This piece of planning has an other-worldly air. A General Election was some way off. Labour had no notion what power would be like, if it came at all. Blair had never set foot in 10 Downing Street and had never even sat on the government side of the Commons. Yet here they were, about to discuss what might happen at the end of a second term of a Labour government. Their readiness to look so far ahead is an indication, first, of the momentum which had built up in the party in the cause of modernization and, second, of the sheer brazen confidence which Blair and Brown had developed. When Mandelson spoke to Blair about what he might do as Prime Minister in the course of a second term, he was listened to seriously.

Mandelson has since admitted another factor to friends: 'I was scared of Gordon.' It rang true with those who had watched them over the years. Brown was in charge and dominant. Mandelson encouraged and advised, but he never led. Where with some other members of the shadow Cabinet he could be openly manipulative, with Brown he was always careful. As Blair and Mandelson prepared in Blair's home in Islington for the climactic meeting of the leadership contest, Mandelson was aware of the consequences if the two had a row. As a wounded antagonist, Brown could destroy Blair's leadership.

The shadow Chancellor never gave any sign that he would relish that outcome. He seemed to want a settlement. But on what terms? On Tuesday 31 May Blair set off alone for Granita, on home territory, not far from his house in Richmond Crescent, Islington.

Brown had begun the evening with drinks at Westminster with his inner circle. He had dined with them the previous night and told them that he knew he must give way. They were not surprised. Even his most enthusiastic head-counter (Nick Brown) couldn't find evidence for optimism. Ed Balls, Brown's adviser, a former *Financial Times* leader writer, went with him by taxi and they arrived a little late at the restaurant.

A few minutes earlier the waiting Blair had been approached by the journalist Allison Pearson who was dining there with her husband. She had never met Blair, but introduced herself. She says he seemed happy – even anxious – to talk. Bubbling. 'What should we do?' he asked her, meaning the Labour Party. She remembers an exchange about the power of enlightened self-interest for good in society and about the need to do away with old Labour attitudes, the theme that was going to be Blair's message to his party. He was ready to talk politics. Then she heard him say: 'You know Gordon, of course?' Turning round, she realized that she had stumbled into something important. Brown was polite and they shared small-talk before she sped back to her table. Ed Balls stayed for a few minutes then left.

Blair and Brown sat in the back of the restaurant, facing each other with an exposed brick wall as a backdrop. As a place for a private conversation, Granita in those days had one of the worst rooms in London, its design fashionably spartan. It echoed. By chance, however, there was a diversion that night. The actress Susan Tully – who played Michelle in the BBC soap *EastEnders* – was sitting near the window at the front and was the evening's object of interest. The fact that Blair and Brown were carving up the next government at the back passed everyone by. They huddled privately, unnoticed.

There was practical business to transact. Brown wanted a decent deal for some of his supporters in the parliamentary party and for those close to him. Murray Elder, for example, stayed for a period in the leader's office. Then came the main subject, command over economic policy and quite significant chunks of social policy. There would be no difficulty about that, said Blair. A paper was subsequently negotiated, with Mandelson in the almost inevitable role of intermediary, and was published as a statement, an important indication of the place Brown would occupy in any future Labour government. But the most important words at that table did not concern such practical matters. They touched on a more distant future. What awaited Brown after a Blair premiership?

There has been a pretence on the part of some that Blair went to that encounter wholly unaware of what Brown would say. That is not true. The concession was coming, as Blair had known for two weeks that it almost certainly must. His problem was a different one. What could he say to preserve the loyalty that had developed between them but had been threatened in the course of the leadership contest? He had spoken around the time of Smith's funeral about his awareness of the agony Brown must be feeling, given his thundering ambition and his determination, and despite the moments of irritation in the previous few weeks, his friends believed he now wanted to soothe it.

One of Blair's most prominent characteristics now came into play.

As it is put by one colleague who was sacked by him, and has no particular political affection for him now: 'One of Tony's weaknesses is that whatever has just happened he always wants you to leave the room feeling happy.' He does not like awkwardnesses, or unspoken grudges. A discussion must end with both parties feeling as good as is possible. It is true of Blair that, unlike many other politicians, when he is behaving ruthlessly he likes it to be disguised. That is the view of a number of his closest supporters. So, on this occasion, faced with an old friend who'd been denied a long-held ambition and someone whose support he needed carefully to secure for the future, what did he do to allow him to leave feeling happier than he expected? Blair was guided by Mandelson's entreaties echoing in his head. Brown must be offered something more than a powerful Chancellorship. He needed to be given hope.

The combination, friends of both men believe, led them to discuss quite openly what might happen if Blair became Prime Minister and won a second term. As advised by Mandelson, Blair certainly made it clear that he hoped Brown would succeed him. Their assumption had always been that they would stick together and Blair saw no reason why that should change. But beyond that fraternal expression the accounts begin to diverge.

Blair was asked subsequently by one of his Downing Street intimates to answer a straightforward question. Did he say to Brown that he would stand down before the end of a second term in favour of Brown? Blair answered without a pause: 'Absolutely not.'

From the other side Brown has never claimed, even in semi-private circumstances, that such a promise was made but his colleagues were convinced at the time, and have been given no reason to change their minds since, that Blair expressed his hopes for an eventual Brown leadership in such strong terms that he gave the impression it would be a deliberate act on his part that would bring it about, not simply the passage of time.

Brown left the restaurant believing that Blair had committed himself to supporting his own succession to the premiership, if he was able to pass on the torch. No one in Brown's most intimate circle believes anything else. He has not spoken of it to anyone who would repeat it, and no one expects him to. But it is a hope – though it has been doused by *realpolitik* – that has been built into his Chancellorship.

Is it true? Blair wanted to soothe Brown and to keep his loyalty. His friends believe that he spoke directly about a succession. Who knew what might happen? There might come a moment when it would be possible to hand government on. But a promise? They doubt it. There is no such gift that a putative Prime Minister can offer.

As a historian, Brown knows that pledges of that sort are undeliverable. The attractions of office tend to grip you quickly and firmly. How often has power been handed over in a seamless transition amid conditions of stability and success. In British politics, there is no precedent. Circumstances change, the landscape alters, fate intervenes. But the next day, when they staged a comradely walk across New Palace Yard under Big Ben to announce that Brown would support Blair for leader, Brown believed that he had been given an assurance that Blair would try to time any departure from office to allow Brown to succeed.

None of this was written down. There is no firm evidence of what was said. Brown believed he had a near-promise of succession; Blair insists that nothing so clear could have been offered, and wasn't. The understanding was more like a misunderstanding. Like the princess and the pea it was there, even if no one could see it.

They had to pretend it wasn't there. Brown prepared his words in support of Blair's candidacy and Blair made sure that Robin Cook, in particular, was warned about what Brown was going to say and would leap on board. And then came the campaign proper, at last, in which Blair, Prescott and Margaret Beckett fought it out to what was a near-inevitable conclusion (Blair 57, Prescott 24, Beckett 19 per cent). Only then could Blair relax about Brown. When he appeared with the other candidates at the first public event of the campaign in Blackpool at the GMB conference for a question and answer session, broadcast live on *Panorama*, he was much more concerned about Prescott who seemed likely to be his deputy. But the words exchanged with Brown over dinner weren't a settlement that would last indefinitely.

Roy Jenkins, often described as Blair's history tutor, has compared the encounter between Blair and Brown in conversations with friends as reminding him of a talk he had with Harold Wilson as Prime Minister towards the end of his second administration, just before the 1970 General Election which he lost to Edward Heath. 'Roy,' said Wilson, 'you know I believe you to be my natural successor.' For all the byzantine plots which Wilson imagined Jenkins having organized against him, and for all their tension on Europe which was even then a difficult party problem, Jenkins believes that Wilson more than half-believed it when he said it. Might not the same have been true of Blair in Granita?

There is one piece of hard evidence which can be brought to bear on the conversation they had that night in relation to Brown succeeding Blair as party leader either during or at the end of a second term. Later, well into his leadership but before the election that brought him to power, Blair confided in a friend outside politics that he had learned the lesson of Margaret Thatcher, the Prime Minister who stayed too long. He'd seen from the opposition benches how her government split and sundered around her and how she couldn't see it; moreover, how her intimates huddled in a Downing Street bunker unaware of the coming catastrophe. Blair has often spoken of it. But on this occasion he said more. He would make sure to avoid it. He could not imagine wanting to serve a third term and he would find a way of making a timely exit.

Did Blair rehearse that thought with Brown as they dined together? It is the kind of political promise that is less a promise than a musing on what might be. Labour, after all, had not even won a first term, let alone a second. But it is the kind of talk to which politicians return again and again. It deals with the delicious uncertainties of their fate, one of the lures that draws them to their trade. Blair couldn't know whether he would ever be in a position to deliver on such a deal, before or after an election, or before or after a referendum. The fact that he has talked of it privately with others suggests it would be odd if he hadn't discussed it with Brown on that night. The political truth of that conversation is that Brown left the restaurant to return to his closest friends, defeated but not humiliated. He would remain publicly loyal to Blair but privately loyal to the ultimate ambition which had always driven his political progress. The lingering effect of the Granita conversation is obvious. Blair had made no binding promise of the succession, and Brown's character set him against wishful thinking. But even if there was no expectation, there could be hope.

From close to Blair comes this intriguing description of one of the great difficulties that continually faces him. 'We all know the truth about the second term. With every day that passes Gordon will make another cross on the calendar. Day after day after day.' And they don't need to ask why.

PART TWO

'Look Gordon, you'll have to accept the fact that the
Glass slipper fitted my foot and not yours'

4

The Alchemy of Power

Behind the bow window to the right of the black door of Number 10 sits the Prime Minister's press secretary. Early one evening, not long after Labour had moved excitedly but uneasily into Whitehall, Alastair Campbell sat with his feet up on his desk and turned his head to look through the net curtains. A happy stream of people was passing up Downing Street towards Number 11. Gordon Brown was having a party. Campbell watched them go and said to a visitor from Fleet Street: 'I wonder what he's up to now.'

Ministers and their courtiers seemed to be afflicted by the kind of suspicion immortalized in the reaction of the French statesman Clemenceau to the death of a rival at the negotiating table: 'I wonder what he could have meant by that?' Nothing could be as it seemed. If the Chancellor was having a party – *another* party! – he'd be working the crowd and spreading his word. Something was up. Something was always up. The air was heavy with intrigue.

That intensity of feeling was something that arrived with the cars that took the new ministers to their departments on 5 May 1997. A rising civil servant at the time, later to become a permanent secretary, says it was all something of a surprise to official Whitehall, especially those parts of it which saw the Cabinet at work close up. 'Of course we knew quite a bit about them. We had all done the usual homework and we had watched them operating in opposition. But we thought they were going to be rather *nicer*. We found that some of them really weren't very nice to each other at all.' The civil servants were surprised by the maturity of these disputes, which had clearly bubbled away for years. The government which they were about to

79

discover was defined by arguments and clashes of ambition in the years of opposition. It was these that Blair and Brown had to transform into the driving force of a government, like alchemists turning base metal into gold. But the last years in opposition were fraught with such volatility and uncertainty that there seemed no guarantee that the magic would work.

Insiders knew that power had come to Labour without the problems of opposition having been solved first. On the surface, the leadership contest of 1994 seemed to have been absorbed by everyone, and there was no direct challenge to Blair. Old grumblers did patrol the Commons corridors in search of a Labour Party they thought they had lost, and they would spit the word 'Blair!' at you in the way that the hard left had once said 'Kinnock!' or an earlier generation had learnt to say 'Wilson!' Long before the election, the leader knew that there were those who had already placed his name high in the pantheon of treachery, which was the certain fate of the modernizer. That was no surprise, and hardly a problem, since political victories at the polls have a way of encouraging subservience and good behaviour. The more serious dispute still pulsed just below the surface. In the eyes of Brown's circle, Blair's leadership was tainted with a touch of illegitimacy, as if he sat on a stolen throne.

'He wouldn't be there without Gordon and everybody knows it,' was the sentiment that drifted round the Commons. Blair certainly did know it. He knew that it was Brown's network that had first given him a route map in Labour politics and he acknowledged to friends that the hundreds of beneficial hours they had spent together had been his political education. The same did not apply to Brown. He was meticulously loyal in public, and even some who know him quite well have not heard him utter personal criticism of the leader, except with the occasional backhand stroke. But there is none of Blair's willingness to praise, as when he says 'Gordon is my Lloyd George'.

He kept his silence. Brown has never compared Blair to Attlee or Disraeli, because any such analogy would reflect their relative positions. He was not going to give Blair the satisfaction of a comparison that would emphasize his own position as the Prime Minister's junior partner.

The roots of the problem, that negotiated balance on which the Blair government would rest, are buried in the unresolved personal disputes which persisted long after the settlement of the leadership in 1994 and they also sprout from the nature of that deal, the sharing of power between Blair and Brown.

The divisions which were agreed in opposition gave Brown command over social, industrial and economic policy, and the advantage for Chancellor and Prime Minister was that power shared was not power halved. Indeed, they were able to appear as if by their division of the spoils each had become stronger, Blair as a quasi-presidential figure directing government strategy, making treaties and fighting wars and painting the big picture, with Brown as the all-powerful economic overlord. The disadvantage, however, was that the increased power generated by their arrangement seemed to be made more volatile by the division, depending on daily negotiations between the two. The deal made them stronger, but more vulnerable too.

The partnership had, of course, been nurtured by Mandelson and when the election was won it was he who stood at their shoulders. To Brown he was a reminder of the personal disaster of the leadership struggle, but to Blair he was the essential companion, the grand vizier whose presence at court was indispensable. Perhaps surprisingly, Blair was more convinced that his eagle eye was needed at his side than even Mandelson himself. On 1 May 1997 itself, the day Blair learned from his pollsters that he would win a majority which might be bigger even than Labour's in the fabled year of 1945, Mandelson was hoping for a ministerial post inside a Whitehall department – 'a proper job' – and told Blair so. He wanted to be a real minister running an administrative machine. Instead, Blair followed his instincts and made him Minister Without Portfolio in the Cabinet Office, through the corridor from Number 10 with fishing rights across Whitehall, a post which would play to Mandelson's strengths and encourage his weaknesses. He saw all but the most sensitive papers that landed on Blair's desk and stood at the confluence of all the streams of ministerial entreaty and administrative negotiation that flowed to the prime ministerial study. Blair told friends he needed him there. But from the Treasury across the street Mandelson's presence looked menacing and unwelcome. Mandelson was the necessary catalyst in the preparations for power. He was an essential part of the chemistry that sustained the partnership. His presence, however, had often been combustible.

The big breach between Brown and Mandelson had not come during the leadership battle itself, although Brown was furious and sore and many of his supporters had condemned Mandelson by the end of it. A second episode made the hurt worse. In the autumn of 1994, Blair decided (not for the last time) to try to apply his own balm to the wounds. At his suggestion the trio took the opportunity of a party meeting in southern England to repair in advance to the Chewton Glen Hotel in Hampshire for a long talk. They convened under the aegis of Colin Fisher, an advertising man who worked for the Shadow Communications Agency invented in the eighties by Mandelson as Labour's link with the world outside party headquarters. The idea was to dine and stay up talking, recapturing the bonhomie of late nights past and soothing the recent bruises of the leadership contest. The next morning all would be well. It wasn't.

At dinner in a private room Brown did what he always does: he demonstrated that he had been thinking and planning. He produced a blueprint for a party reorganization, worked out in detail. The substance of the plan is much less important than the reactions it provoked, and their consequences. Blair was embarrassed. He had prepared nothing similar and, according to those closest to him at the time, hadn't expected such a document to be produced. He noted that one of its main features was an important job at party headquarters for Michael Wills, a close Brown ally who would later become a minister.

It was Mandelson, not Blair, who seems to have intervened first, saying something like 'I don't think we can do this now . . .' He later told friends that Brown was livid and added: 'Gordon flashed me a look of such menace. It was terrible.' The evening limped on with Brown's plan put to one side. Blair went to bed, and Brown and Mandelson talked on their own. This conversation ushered in a period of nearly two years, leading almost to the election itself, through which their relations were so cool as to be in hibernation. Mandelson has referred to it since as one of the saddest passages of his life.

To an outsider this may seem excessively emotional. It reveals the passions that bound these three personalities together and their instability. What passed between Brown and Mandelson cannot be known for certain – the two were alone in Brown's room – but enough has been discussed with friends and recollected at regular intervals for it to be clear that Mandelson believed he was being challenged about his loyalty. One version has it that Brown challenged Mandelson about his reluctance to have Brown's reorganization plan discussed and said: 'If you and I agree, Tony will never resist. You've got to decide.' Brown's friends dispute the implied invitation to Mandelson to take sides against Blair, though they don't deny Brown's anger. Whatever the words, the outcome is not in doubt. Brown and Mandelson, warriors together in the eighties, parted and were never close again.

This was not a breach that could have occurred without intense emotion. The point at issue – Brown's reform plan – was hardly the Marshall Plan or the Treaty of Versailles. Yet it was a moment of high drama, infused with feelings which bubbled up from great depths. To Brown and Mandelson it was clear that the triple relationship was irrevocably over. In the years when there was none of the pressure of leadership, or the prospect of power, their feelings could be managed. Then it had been all for one and one for all. Now that Blair was clearly and solely the 'one', Brown found himself unable to be part of the brotherhood. Blair's primacy fatally disturbed the balance. All three had driven to Chewton Glen together the previous day. When Brown and Mandelson left, they went separately and in the knowledge that the breach between them might never be healed. Brown's sense of betrayal was much sharper than it had been four months earlier when the leadership was decided. Mandelson, he realized that night, would never be willing to side with him in a dispute with Blair. In that judgement, he was correct. 'He is the leader. We've got to help him,' Mandelson said during their argument in the hotel. Blair had Mandelson's loyalty, but there were miserable consequences. Meetings of the leader's team and senior members of the shadow Cabinet in Blair's room were often strange and prickly, leaving those who were not on the innermost loop puzzled and often embarrassed. Mandelson couldn't resist displaying his soreness at the rift with Brown. Brown showed no interest in restoring the old relationship. Blair, trying to find his own style as leader from a standing start, was wearied by the atmosphere.

'What can you do with Gordon?' Mandelson would say, about some Brown refusal to agree with a suggestion from the leader. And from Brown's cohorts the response came in a steady drift of stories about Mandelson's perfidy. Brown himself did not contribute to these. But shadow Cabinet colleagues began to recognize the closeness of the Brown group and the consequences of the loyalty which he demanded and received. MPs like Nick Brown, Nigel Griffiths, Andrew Smith and Douglas Henderson formed a phalanx of foot soldiers who were always on the move through the Commons corridors with news from Brown's office: some shadow minister's effort to push through a new spending commitment had been squashed; a new stratagem for the election was being drawn up with Gordon in charge; a Mandy criticism of Brown at some meeting had been slapped down by Blair.

Curiously, Charlie Whelan had arrived at Brown's side as the result of a request from Mandelson himself, when he was still helping the shadow Chancellor to build up his team towards the end of John Smith's leadership. Brown had got to know Whelan the previous year during the fight to get union support for the one-member-one-vote reform. He was working for the engineering union and demonstrating a streetwise grip of spin-doctoring (a term still unfamiliar at the time). His recruitment revealed much about Brown, his tactics and the nature of his gang. A cheery, rumpled character invariably wreathed in smoke and gossip, Whelan was an unlikely combination of public school communist (lapsed), City currency trader and Fleet Street intriguer. He loved the game, whatever it was, and played the part of the ragged-trousered boulevardier. News from Brown's office, or the latest whisper about Mandelson, was grist to a mill which ground away happily, with Whelan gleefully cranking the handle.

Whelan would have been an unimaginable component of the Blair circle that was being built. Where Brown's office thrummed with party gossip and kept some lines open to even the more exotic corners of the Labour left, Blair's was engaged (partly as a deliberate strategy and partly by instinct) in a different game. In the pursuit of power they were cultivating non-Labourites who might be brought on board, pursuing a determined Bowdlerization of political language to expunge the old words and setting out on a determined expedition towards the places in Fleet Street which no Labour leader had reached before. This was partly because Blair had no choice. If he couldn't find at least one feature writer on the *Daily Mail* who might be seduced into writing something pleasant about a Labour leader (and his spectacular conquest of Paul Johnson, though the infatuation wouldn't last, convinced him the effort was worthwhile), or make some progress towards an understanding with Rupert Murdoch, he might sacrifice some of those rightish votes which were beginning to detach themselves in great slabs from the Conservatives and pile up for Labour. But the tilt was more than a piece of strategy. Blair's restlessness, caught most dramatically in his assault on Clause IV in the first conference speech as leader, was obvious to everyone around him. He was patently fed up with the nuances of Labour lore that he saw as antiquated. Blair's enthusiasms lay outside his own party.

Brown, by contrast, has never felt that pull. Even when, as Chancellor, he was making a virtue of policing the spending plans inherited from the Conservative government he would happily socialize with parts of the union left, especially in Scotland. If there is a contradiction, it is one he has always tried to ride. Blair is different. When he made his last constituency speech on the eve of polling in 2001, at the Trimdon Labour Club in his Sedgefield constituency, he gestured to his agent, chairman and friend, John Burton, on the small stage beside him and said again what he had been telling his local party for eighteen years: that they had made government possible because they had been willing to change and to challenge the inherited ways. That, perhaps above all, was what he admired in them. It was a striking assertion of how he sees Labour's history in the eighties and nineties. Brown sees it differently, as just another turning in Labour's winding road. The fundamental direction, in Brown's view, remains the same.

In his constituency, Blair's union support came first from the right of the movement, through the GMB, and he has never spent much time cultivating the left. As Employment spokesman he was irritated by what he regarded as the reactionary instincts of the big unions on party reform and on legislation like the Shops Bill. They believed that he often paid lip service to the importance of the unions to the party; they were right. Brown's closeness to the union leaders, especially Bill Morris and Rodney Bickerstaffe, even as the party was changing its economic policy under his direction in ways that the public sector unions, in particular, did not enjoy, was as intimate as it had ever been. Those on the left who didn't like what they were learning about Blair, and had regarded John Smith as a helpful fixer rather than an ideological companion, now looked to Brown who had a particular nostalgic affection for some of the hard men of the left. In them he could feel some of the inherited passion of the Scottish socialists about whom he had written in his biography of James Maxton, the 'sea-green incorruptible leader of the Clydesiders'. He also admired their all-or-nothing attitude to politics. For Brown, the enemy's enemy is indeed your friend and once loyalty has been promised solidarity is everything.

With Whelan and Ed Balls, the Brown machine began to operate. There was one rule more important than all the others. Loyalty. Since his student days Brown was known as a leader of the pack. His natural authority wasn't expected to be challenged. In the three years between the leadership settlement and the General Election this was the most obvious feature of Brown's operation. Front bench colleagues became used to bruising interrogations and in the party at large it became obvious that Brown was fashioning a sphere of influence which would be controlled by him and which would be as powerful and self-contained in government as it was becoming in opposition.

In the preparations for power, Brown considered himself as important as Blair. Tax had been the undoing of Labour in 1992, and his job at its simplest was to make sure that the campaign would not unravel in the same way. The result was a period of what some members of the shadow Cabinet described at the time as brutality. The leader and the shadow Chancellor saw each other every day (speaking much more often than Blair and Prescott, his deputy) and they laid down policy. The idea that collective shadow Cabinet discussions could change Brown's mind was regarded by his colleagues as absurd, because they had reason to know better. They complained about it, mainly among themselves, but the urgency of the coming campaign suppressed revolts. For shadow ministers in their forties who had come into politics to serve in government the prospect of another defeat, stretching Labour's eighteen years of tormented opposition beyond two decades, was terrifying.

Those who got in Brown's way were cased aside. As health spokesman, Chris Smith irritated the Treasury team with speeches that seemed uncomfortably close to spending pledges. Asked privately at the time what he thought of one of Smith's hints about Labour's plans Brown's reply was emphatic (and accurate): 'Whoever is Health Secretary it will not be Chris Smith.' He was duly shuffled sideways by Blair soon afterwards. Brown's approach brought him some admirers, but lost him friends. One prominent front bencher at the time, a natural supporter of Brown's on the left, confessed after a couple of years in government: 'We were all right when we thought that Gordon was the one with the most brains and the best strategic mind. But we were also right about the way he behaved towards us. I hate saying it, but the thought of him as Prime Minister is unimaginable. Think of how he'd behave.'

Rough judgements of that sort were common in the couple of years leading up to the election. The party was being corralled and disciplined in ruthless fashion by Blair and Brown. The memory of the wavering and often feckless leadership of Foot; the knowledge of how it took Kinnock nearly ten years to create even the image of an alternative government; and their memory of the 1992 defeat – all this gave them their political justification for the way they ran the party. Brown was also a natural disciplinarian. He is a man always under control, and apart from the famous shambles he leaves in every office he inhabits, he believes in order. Decisions are made and then implemented; commitments are given and kept. His personality kept Labour in order.

If Labour was to find a creative space in which to reinvent itself ideologically it needed Brown's discipline and authority. But it also needed the iconoclastic impetus of Blair. Blair had developed a certain affection for the Labour tradition, but it always played second fiddle to his impatience for reform. Brown enjoyed addressing party meetings; Blair didn't. Brown was still wrestling with the intellectual problem of reconciling his embrace of many elements of the market economy with his affection for old ideals which he had always expressed in the language of socialism. Blair had very few items of such baggage on the voyage. His ideas had developed in the late seventies without any of Brown's painful rethinking and even recantation. One policy seemed to him to follow from the other – union reform, a resistance to high personal taxation, an admiration for the entrepreneurial spirit, a suspicion of collectivist solutions. When Stephen Byers, a junior spokesman on Employment, was fingered as the Blairite who had mused to journalists in a Blackpool fish restaurant at the 1996 party conference about the possibility of a break in the party's link with the unions, Blair was perfectly content. There was no reprimand. There was a good segment of the shadow Cabinet that thought their own definitions of 'socialist' were being cast aside, but Blair was carrying even the grumpy along with him. Blair was starting to invent a new Labour language; while Brown was laying the foundations for a new economic policy which would depend, he said, on rigour and prudence. Most of the malcontented and the frustrated did not have the energy to resist. If they were going to get to power, this was probably the only way.

From time to time frustration would break out in the open, usually followed by a claim by a shadow minister that remarks had been taken out of context. This was the case with a Robin Cook interview in the *Sunday Times* around conference time in 1996 in which he said this: 'There is a very real danger that we're ignoring the needs of a minority in society who find themselves in a very difficult position, usually through no fault of their own, so much so that when someone like me comes along and tries to redress the balance we're accused of having an odd political agenda.' Cook's reference to a balance that needed to be redressed was, of course, a straightforward criticism of Brown as well as Blair. In private, Cook and those with similar doubts were sniping at the shadow Chancellor often enough for Blair to become alarmed. He had the running feud between Brown and Mandelson, then at one of its peaks of antagonism, and he knew that there was a reluctant section of the shadow Cabinet which was making it obvious that it was being dragged along unenthusiastically by the shadow Chancellor. Frank Dobson, Chris Smith, Clare Short and John Prescott all wanted to make spending commitments that Brown denied them.

Strikingly, Prescott did little to use that uneasy mood to unsettle Blair further. There were a few minor explosions, but they changed nothing. Indeed, Prescott's acceptance of the drift of Blair's leadership was much more telling than any of his criticism. After all, the year before John Smith died he had told the party conference as Transport spokesman that if the railways were privatized they would be brought back into public ownership, and he had vented his prodigious rage after 1992 on 'the spin doctors . . . and people in smart suits who've never won an election in their lives', spreading his ire to encompass Bill Clinton's first winning campaign of that year – the one Blair admired so much – attacking 'Clintonism' as the kind of thinking that would destroy the Labour Party. That language melted away. He had sharp words with Blair in private about his attitude to rail privatization, which the leader was not minded to reverse, but their row was never taken to the airwaves by Prescott. He fumed with his friends, but carried on.

There was one early scare for Blair, when Prescott wasn't invited to a meeting with the party's new advertising agency in 1995. The deputy leader erupted, with good reason. It was a sizeable meeting, including several apparatchiks as well as Blair and Brown and Mandelson, of course, and it looked as if Prescott was deliberately being kept away. He was. It certainly wasn't his kind of gathering

– there were plenty of smart suits, and one of the main participants, Philip Gould, was well-established as the blackest of Prescott's *bêtes noires* – but his omission was a foolish mistake. Blair apologized personally, and subsequently took great care to avoid such gratuitous offence to Prescott who, if he had been tempted to resign at that time, could have caused awful trouble for his leader.

That meeting has another significance. It was held at the home of Chris Powell, chief executive of the advertising agency Boase, Masimi, Pollitt (BMP), which had been hired to make ads for the party. Chris is one of three brothers who have spun a thread that links the Thatcher and Blair governments. One, Charles (given a life peerage by Major), was Thatcher's private secretary for foreign affairs in Downing Street through all the turbulent years, seeing it through to the last days of stumbling resistance in 1990 when, with Bernard Ingham alongside him in the last ditch, he watched the members of the Cabinet peel away from her one by one. The second, Jonathan, was a Foreign Office man like Charles, enticed by Blair out of the British Embassy in Washington where he was a principal observer of the start of Clinton's Presidency. He took over the leader of the opposition's office and, in due time, took his place as chief of staff (a new role) in the Prime Minister's office.

Anyone sitting round Chris Powell's fireplace on that Saturday in 1995 would have seen how different this Labour administration would be from its predecessors. The Powell brothers exude exactly the kind of suave confidence that has Prescott's antennae twitching furiously. In the world of Them and Us, the Powells are Them – exactly the kind of confident, successful, public school-educated characters that part of the Labour Party still found sinister.

The only trade union figure in the room was Tom Sawyer, who had left the public service union, NUPE, to become Labour's general secretary and who was a veteran of the Kinnock reforms. He retained some scepticism about Blair, but he had jumped on board. There were two groups of participants in this meeting – Blair-Brown and the advisers. That was how the party was now being run. The roles taken by Mandelson, Gould and Alastair Campbell illustrated how the campaign would emanate from their thinking more than from any collective discussions the shadow Cabinet might have. Ten years before, in the mid-eighties, this collection of people would have been unimaginable.

A pattern was set. Although Blair's imperious leadership was developing from the memory of party nightmares past, and Brown's more from his conviction that only the rigorously steadfast survive in politics, they were agreed. There would be no nonsense. If they needed evidence to bolster their view they could watch the Conservative government benches, where Eurosceptics were gnawing away at John Major's premiership. He'd been at war with them since he signed the Maastricht Treaty barely a year after he succeeded Thatcher and Tory discipline was breaking down. Major's accidentally recorded remark after a television interview with Michael Brunson of ITN in 1993 in which he referred to some (unnamed) members of his Cabinet as 'bastards' allowed the public to savour for once the reality of life in government. From then on the public saw a Prime Minister wrestling with his party, even having to resort to the device of a surprise leadership election in 1995 to try to give himself new authority. For the opposition there seemed to be a lesson in all this.

Blair and Brown had spent almost all their shadow Cabinet careers in a Parliament gripped by one crisis or another. Nigel Lawson's resignation from the Treasury in 1989 and Geoffrey Howe's a year later broke the back of the Thatcher government, and the early part of Major's premiership from 1990 was defined not by his feisty defeat of Kinnock in the 1992 General Election but by Black Wednesday later that year and the fissure on Europe that opened up under his feet. Young reporters arriving to watch the comparatively arid Parliament of Blair's first term would hear tales from old hands of how the Commons had once been a place of melodrama and tears when votes mattered, rebellions shook the government, and the members' lobby outside the chamber in mid-evening was a bubbling pot of intrigue. Ministers couldn't afford to lose their fingertip feeling for the mood of the Commons or they'd be lost. From the late eighties until the Blair government was elected, Parliament was an unpredictable place with a will of its own. As in the seventies, when

Callaghan's Labour government was limping towards an election it knew it could not win, Major's government was finding it difficult to keep breathing.

By December 1995 it had lost, technically, its overall majority when the wilfully unpredictable right-winger John Gorst said he'd no longer cooperate with Tory whips because of a hospital crisis in his Hendon constituency. This came on top of a classic episode of slapstick politics, when the Chancellor, Kenneth Clarke, had to issue a statement through Conservative Central Office denying that he had threatened to resign over Europe. Denials of that sort from Chancellors are rare, with good reason. They speak of panic. Clarke's came in response to a BBC report by Jon Sopel revealing Clarke's frustration with Major, quoting a devastating phrase the Chancellor used to describe a Eurosceptical remark the Prime Minister had made to the *Daily Telegraph* – he called it 'a boomerang laden with high explosives'. Sopel's source was blown by fellow-lunchers in a Park Lane restaurant and Downing Street panicked.

This was life in the late Major years – crises and rumours of crises, trouble among ministers, trouble at party headquarters, Commons votes that always promised trouble and an atmosphere in which every phrase in every interview was assumed to carry a hidden meaning. By the turn of the year, a Gallup poll put Labour thirty-five points ahead of the Conservatives.

The scent of panic emanating from the government had a profound effect on the opposition. Blair became as obsessed by the sight of a crumbling administration as he was about his own party's past. Just as Kinnock had said 'never again' to Labour after the 1983 cataclysm, so Blair said to his shadow Cabinet: 'We can't ever let this happen to us.' It meant that Brown's natural taste for discipline and what some of his colleagues thought was an instinct for authoritarianism was allowed to flourish. He had one principal purpose: the construction of armour-plating around Labour's spending plans. Where Smith had made much of a commitment to 'full employment', that notoriously elusive concept, Brown spoke of fiscal caution and inflation-busting as the pillars of his policy. Colleagues who were looking forward to fighting an election in which they wanted to promise to outspend Major on public services did not enjoy the regime. Blair and Brown decided the priorities: even Prescott was kept at arm's length. He was often consulted only after announcements had been leaked to the papers and was unable to put his stamp on any significant piece of economic policy.

Blair had put Brown in charge of election strategy a few months after becoming leader. The manifesto would not be subject this time to the painful arguments on the national executive that had set previous election campaigns off to a miserable start. The NEC had been tamed so effectively that it was no longer a lion growling at the party leadership but a pussycat with manicured claws – and the bedrock of the campaign was to be the promise of economic competence. Labour knew – the whole country knew – that its reputation for economic recklessness was a folk memory that was embedded in politics. It had to be expunged. Brown's tactic was to announce at the beginning of the election year that a Labour government would preserve the Conservatives' lower and higher rates of income tax for the lifetime of a Parliament. When he revealed it, on the *Today* programme on 20 January 1997, his colleagues realized that it was the decision that would dictate their lives in government. Not that they had known it was coming. The strategy had been drawn up with Blair and Brown's advisers, with Prescott informed late on. The shadow Cabinet were not surprised by Brown's decision, though many of them grumbled about it in semi-private around the Commons, because they had been feeling the Brown lash for more than a year. And as for the secrecy? By now, it was all too familiar.

Brown knew the announcement was the most important, by far, that he would make before the election. He took very few colleagues into his confidence after it was agreed with Blair, until Sunday 19 January, the day before his speech was to be made. He had agreed to an interview on *Today* immediately after the 8 o'clock news on Monday morning. He then did two unusual things. He tried to speak to the rest of the shadow Cabinet, one by one. And Whelan started to put the message out that he'd be making a big announcement. *Today* presenters mingle in political circles and are used to pressure, unwelcome but unsurprising. But being rung at home on the night before an interview with a specific heavy-handed hint about what might prove a valuable line of questioning is unusual. 'You will ask about tax, won't you?' said Whelan. Was this an attempt to use the programme? Hardly. It suited their purposes; but it suited *Today*'s too. It was inconceivable that such an interview could have taken place without a question about tax. But it was handy to know how excited the Brown team was. They had something up their sleeves.

Meanwhile, Brown was ringing his colleagues. He had an amusing difficulty with Prescott, who was in Hong Kong. He was staying as the guest of the Governor at Government House and the plan was to send him a fax. But the Governor was Chris Patten, former Tory Party chairman. There was an election coming: what if Patten told his friend John Major? So a message was left for Prescott to ring Brown urgently.

Monday dawned. In those days *Today* was broadcast from the grubby but cosy Studio 4A in Broadcasting House and Brown arrived with not only Whelan in attendance but Balls too. This was unusual. They stood behind the glass with the editor and the studio managers as Brown, jacketless, made his announcement. Whelan was agitated when, after five minutes or so, the tax question hadn't been asked: had all his promptings been in vain? No. After dealing with public spending, we turned to the most important subject. But the statement by Brown, unambiguous as it was, was still a surprise. This is how the exchange went.

James Naughtie: Let's put this in context, because the other half of this equation is tax. Is all this really about personal taxation? Are you doing this so that you can say to people, 'I'm not going to put your taxes up'? Because you think that's a necessary condition for winning the election?

Gordon Brown: No, a taxation system has got to be based on principle. It's got to be based on the values of a society . . . It is because of the importance we attach to work and because people have been dealt such a harsh blow over these last few years that we will leave the basic rate of tax unchanged and we will leave the top rate of tax unchanged.

Naughtie: Ah, so this . . .

Brown: And what I want to do over time, when resources become available, is introduce what is absolutely vital for the low-paid in this country in particular, but to the benefit of everyone, a 10p starting rate of tax. But I will not make promises I cannot deliver and that will only be possible when we have the resources to do it.

Naughtie: Right, let's get this absolutely clear. This, at last, is the Brown statement on tax. In your first Budget, you will leave the basic rate and the top rate unchanged.

Brown: I will be making commitments for our manifesto which are commitments for a Parliament. And the basic rate and the top rate will remain unchanged.

Naughtie: Throughout the Parliament?

Brown: Yes.

There it was. Balls and Whelan were like a couple of football coaches who felt they'd scored a goal. They were gleeful. *Today* presenters, producers and reporters realized that a new front in the battle over tax had been opened. Fleet Street descended on Brown, which is what they had planned.

The most important phrase in Brown's revelation, delivered *in extenso* in a City speech that night, was 'the lifetime of a Parliament'. It was a commitment of the sort that no putative Chancellor had given before, and his party knew what it meant: Conservative spending plans would shape the early phase of Labour's first government for eighteen years. On the surface everything was about election preparation; underneath, the assumption was that they were heading for office and that discipline was all.

This meant that although power did thrust Labour's new ministers into the unknown, and they had to deal with the mystification and embarrassments of being Whitehall innocents, almost to a man and woman, they were expecting it. There was none of the slightly vague, rather naive, hopefulness that had kept the Kinnock team going in

1992, when one of them took a photograph of the leader of the opposition in his garden reading a briefing from the Cabinet Office and couldn't quite believe that the red box would have prime ministerial papers in it the following week. Five years later, Labour's leadership was serious. Peter Hennessy, Whitehall's most distinguished academic eavesdropper, chaired some training sessions for shadow ministers organized by the Fabian Society to explain what they should expect in their departments, and at one of them he was told by someone who he says remained close to Blair in government: 'You may see a change from a feudal system of barons to a more Napoleonic system.'

Striking though the phrase is, it tells only half the story. Napoleon wanted lucky generals, but none was lucky enough to share the imperial throne. From the outset, Brown had a place that none of his predecessors had occupied. At the start, it seemed to some startled officials as if the working day was one long conversation between the two, on the phone and in person, with interruptions for a few necessary meetings with others. John Major has spoken of his close relationship with Kenneth Clarke as Chancellor and records in his memoirs that they would always meet once a week. That does not tell the whole story, of course, because there would be other contacts day by day, but it describes the kind of relationship the Prime Minister thought it natural to have with his Chancellor. Blair's and Brown's was quite different, and it sent tremors through Whitehall from the moment they arrived in Downing Street.

Within a few days, officials were wondering what to do. Blair was working from a tiny room off the Cabinet Room itself on the ground floor at the back of Downing Street and there he would meet with Brown with the door closed. This broke a cardinal rule. Except in exceptional circumstances, or when there is a deliberate piece of late night political gossip to exchange over a glass, Prime Ministers and their senior ministers don't usually meet alone. Notes are always taken; as with Cabinet ministers generally, office phone calls are monitored by a private secretary listening on a line next door and notes kept unless there is a particular request that it shouldn't be done. Such a request is, of course, noted. Even the informalities of power are not allowed to pass unseen.

Instead, Brown's calls went straight through to the Prime Minister's study. He would drift in and out with no need to be cleared through by an official. Jonathan Powell guarded the approaches but Brown was not impeded. When he was not in the Treasury he took to working in a small room at the back of Number 11, just a short walk, via the connecting passage and straight down the Cabinet corridor behind the front door of Number 10, to Blair's office.

Civil servants eddying around that office realized that they had never seen a relationship of this kind before. Even the Cabinet Secretary, Robin Butler, who acted as a bridge from the Major to the Blair administration before he was succeeded on his retirement by Richard Wilson, and who had seen many strange things around Number 10 in his time, was taken aback. But when he was approached by some officials, early on, who were concerned that they were not able to monitor all the meetings between Prime Minister and Chancellor and were therefore in danger of losing the grip that it was their task to maintain, he used a remarkable phrase in giving them advice: 'Let them be,' he said. 'Blood is thicker than water.'

That Butler found himself referring to the relationship in family terms is revealing. He had seen close partnerships at the top of government before, but here was intimacy of a wholly different flavour. Thatcher and Lawson, for example, had been notably close from 1983 to 1987, when he was the intellectual engine of her second term and their mutual admiration was intense. But it soon soured after her third election victory, when Lawson believed she was jealous of the credit he received for it. Lawson tried and failed to stop the political disaster of the poll tax (to her fury) and found that she was ultimately more willing to see the resignation of her 'unassailable' Chancellor than to agree to remove from Number 10 her personal economic adviser and freemarket soothsayer, Alan Walters, with whom Lawson was battling over exchange rates and Europe and whose public interventions drove the Chancellor to despair. Even at its passionate height, Thatcher–Lawson hadn't seemed like a mingling of blood.

Blair–Brown always did. The relationship was not being forged in government. It was already established. In a government with almost no experience of the byways of Whitehall – Jack Cunningham, Gavin Strang, Margaret Beckett and John Morris were the veteran exceptions who had seen some minor action in the Callaghan years – there were no ministerial big cats prowling the corridors, familiar with the terrain. There were some, like David Blunkett, who had come from local government and had handled big budgets in their day, but many of them had spent their political lives running little more than a fax machine and a couple of secretaries. It was all a shock. In 1997 Blair was, of course, the first Prime Minister since Ramsay MacDonald, Labour's first Prime Minister in 1924, who had never set foot in a ministerial office occupied by a member of his own party until he became their master. A majority of his Cabinet had never even seen the Commons from the government side. In this atmosphere of enforced ignorance, Blair's team tried to establish control and it was not a surprise to the civil servants waiting for them (though it was still unsettling and often irritating) that they did it with a certain wild-eyed enthusiasm.

They had spent three years of preparation in opposition by exerting the sort of discipline that had not been seen within the Labour Party since the post-war government. Attlee had his own style, dismissing ministers from his office (and, on occasion from the government) with a single laconic sentence before turning back to the cricket scores rattling off the teleprinter he kept in his office for the purpose. Blair's regime was different, but it was meant to be similarly brisk. The result was an obsession with control. It was almost as if they were surprised it didn't come automatically with government and felt they had to try harder. Whatever nervousnesss lay underneath, they started to behave like enforcers.

The seeds of future trouble were sown. At the time, they thought it was the only way. A frantic pace was set. There is no clearer example of how the early exercise of power in government had its roots in opposition. Brown's announcement of independence for the Bank of England came after only three days, a shock to the system which disoriented officials in the Treasury who had read his speeches of the previous eighteen months without picking up the clues. He had argued the case for a different relationship between ministers and the Bank quite clearly earlier in the year, but in the preparations they made for how to deal with the new ministers the Treasury officials hadn't foreseen it. This was more important than the other matters of personal chemistry which made his relationship with his permanent secretary, Terry Burns, so tetchy and which led to his early departure. It also produced a rocky start to the Chancellor's relationship with the Governor of the Bank of England, Eddie George, who was surprised to have been brought late into the Chancellor's thinking. In the course of administering the shock, the Chancellor demonstrated one of his characteristics – the way that breezy good humour can spring out of taciturnity quite unexpectedly. At the same time that he was having such a difficult beginning with some Treasury officials, Brown made sure that weekend to ring a few ex-Chancellors to tell them what he was about to do, in a spirit that was somewhere between cheekiness and politeness. Norman Lamont, for example, had suffered a fairly humiliating defeat in Harrogate where he had fled from his redrawn Kingston constituency in the hope of staying in the Commons, and was rather touched to get a cheery call from Brown who told him: 'You'll be pleased to hear that I'm introducing your policy.' Brown was oozing confidence. Apart from the Prime Minister, only two or three ministers knew in advance and a handful of advisers in the Treasury and Number 10 were in on the preparations. Prescott and Cook were informed, but not consulted in a way that would allow them to object. The government as a whole did not know that interest rate policy was being handed over and that, as critics on the left would have it, the Bank of England was being privatized. It promised to introduce the oligarchic rule of the bankers that had been a bogey of the left for a generation. Brown, however, had convinced himself that it was the best way of conducting the anti-inflation strategy which he told himself was needed, so he did it without blinking.

When MPs unhappy with interest rates later complained to Brown that he had surrendered his power over the economy he told them that he could not have had stability without first putting the Bank in charge. He believes that it was the most important decision of the first term. He and Blair spoke about it just before the election. He said he was going to do it. Blair said: 'Fine.' That was the extent of the discussion. Brown's control of economic policy was absolute. Those around him knew that Blair wouldn't argue. The Prime Minister, at least for the first year or two, would not contest the central strategy of the Treasury. It was the Bank decision that caught the flavour of those first days, both Blair and Brown being anxious to appear virtuously decisive.

But the anxiety produced other kinds of decisiveness that were to cause trouble. Not many members of the public have read, or would want to read, Questions of Procedure for Ministers, though it is a document which is to each member of the government what Queen's Regulations are to a soldier. Blair's introduction to the 1997 edition (it is updated by every incoming Prime Minister) ends with the words: 'I commend the Code to all my ministerial colleagues.' This is misleading. The Ministerial Code, as it was to be called after 1997, consists of the instructions by which ministers live their lives – how they deal with each other across departments; what the chain of command is to the Cabinet Office; when the Prime Minister should be told of administrative changes and by whom; and how negotiations must be conducted with Downing Street. The point of publication, following John Major's decision to declassify the document in pursuit of 'openness', was to demonstrate the government's commitment to personal standards of behaviour. As it turned out, the rules were to cause Blair considerable trouble when the tide of sleaze began to lap around the government. But in the document there was one especially telling paragraph. It reads: 'In order to ensure the effective presentation of government policy, all major interviews and media appearances, both print and broadcast, should be agreed with the Number 10 Press Office before any commitments are entered into. The policy content of all major speeches, press releases and new policy initiatives should be cleared in good time with the Number 10 Private Office; the timing and form of announcements should be cleared with the Number 10 Press Office. Each department should keep a record of media contacts by both ministers and officials.'

This had several consequences. Leaving aside the brief spasm which passed through the proprietors of certain restaurants within a mile or two of Westminster, whose tables were playgrounds of ministerial gossip and mischief paid for by Fleet Street, some members of the government began to behave as if the last shreds of privacy and dignity had gone. Alastair Campbell, they realized, was now entitled by prime ministerial diktat to know everything about them – even their informal conversations with journalists – and they felt the formidable grip of the Number 10 Private Office tightening round them. The timing of Whitehall announcements has always been an obsession in Downing Street – any government needs to look as if its many arms and legs are roughly coordinated – but the new code went further. It established a new tone in government. Labour's pre-election effort to appear relaxed, unstuffy and loose-limbed and Blair's to present his team as a streetwise gang of individuals was now officially declared over. The era of control had begun.

The government's personality was defined as much by this pre-occupation with a culture of command as by Blair and Brown's early efforts to appear decisive and quick, and it revealed a lurking fear under the confidence that had seemed to characterize the first days. Blair had spent much of his time since becoming leader in cultivating Fleet Street, and he had been well schooled by Campbell in the ways of the tabloids. The capture of the *Sun* as a Labour-supporting paper in the run-up to the election was the greatest prize, to be treasured over the years and guarded with near-obsessive care, but Blair, with particular help from Anji Hunter, had also calmed the troubled breast of the *Daily Mail*. He suspected it wouldn't last, but at least he was promised a period in which it would not try to destroy his government simply because it carried the label 'Labour'. All this manoeuvring changed Blair. Now he could barely think of a strategy without automatically considering how it would play in the papers. Talking with Paddy Ashdown about the future of Labour–Liberal Democrat cooperation he was often open about the importance of avoiding offence to the papers which had been so painstakingly neutralized or brought into Labour's camp. More than any predecessor as Prime Minister – including Major, who was the despair of his staff for his habit of chewing over newspaper headlines and plunging into late-night rages as a result – Blair worried about how his government was portrayed.

With Philip Gould, the perpetual pollster, ready with daily readings of the public mood and Campbell in a closer position at his shoulder than any Downing Street press secretary had been before, Blair was often being presented with dark tidings about the reaction to some speech or policy announcement. Prime Ministers tend to have few people around them who can talk frankly, without choosing their words carefully. Campbell is one of them. 'Bollocks' and 'crap' often pepper his conversations with Blair, even when they are not alone and someone from one of the outer circles of power is in the room. Ministers from past governments affect shock at this. One Thatcher veteran said he could not begin to have imagined what would have happened to him if he had walked into Her study and announced: 'This speech is complete crap.' Campbell can do it happily, and he does. He has none of the polished deference of the natural civil servant, which holds cheekiness to be the greatest sin, and he speaks to the Prime Minister in private as he would speak to one of his journalistic clients. Blair takes it, every day.

The significance of Campbell's influence is that it reveals Blair's acknowledgement that his government would do nothing without first taking trouble and time to find out how it would be presented to the public gaze. To members of the government this was portrayed as a strength, the mechanism by which the muddles and dithering of the Major years would be prevented. In truth, the conception of how power would be exercised was as much an expression of nervousness.

Blair's 1997 government had none of the confidence of experience. It was building defences against what Blair thought were its great enemies – indiscipline among ministers, a slackening of reforming zeal, and a turning of the Fleet Street worm. That reflected the obsessions of opposition and fear of what failure would mean for a party that had grown used to the wilderness. The call for discipline covered a basic lack of trust: Cabinet colleagues were not to be empowered because that would endow them with the potential to wreck the new government's scheme. And so the levers of power were held by just two people. It was safer that way, as long as the two individuals thought alike and trusted each other. What no one could know for sure in 1997 was how that relationship would change in government and whether the fault lines opened up by the leadership contest would widen. And so this was how the Blair government came into being, pulsing with what Robin Butler had identified as the ties of blood between Prime Minister and Chancellor, which gave it its air of wild intensity. The volatile spirit infected its whole life.

5

A Cabinet Made for Two

No Prime Minister since the nineteenth century has spent more time avoiding formal meetings with Cabinet colleagues than Tony Blair. When they happen, they are brief. The real deals are done elsewhere, usually in the Prime Minister's study with only three or four people sitting around: and, as often as not, with only two. 'We are not a very collegiate government,' said one Cabinet minister, just before he was sacked. 'I'm afraid we don't really see very much of each other. It's a strange outfit.' From the start, it was to be a government of individuals, moving in their various orbits round the pair at the centre like planets whose orbits wobble under the influence of competing suns.

The patiently crafted relationship with Brown, handled with the delicacy that you might expend on an unstable bomb, had to be watched and tended in government ever more carefully. So in power, privacy became Blair's stamp. Civil servants soon dispensed with the old Whitehall habit of clearing Cabinet ministers' diaries for all of Thursday morning, and putting putative lunch guests on standby for cancellation. Weekly Cabinet meetings ended in under an hour, as if the clock on the mantelpiece behind the Prime Minister's head would sound an alarm if they let the discussion drag and the Lord Chancellor might turn into a pumpkin. At least once, the Cabinet were out on the street in under thirty-five minutes. For officials who remembered the Thatcher Cabinets, or the rambling hours of Callaghan and Wilson days when ministers still indulged themselves with long interventions and arguments and semi-confessional out-pourings, this was brevity that was almost indecent. Blair runs his

Cabinet as if it is a formal ritual, like some piece of parliamentary procedure that has to be observed, or a weekly church service from which everyone must be allowed to escape on time. The decisions are taken elsewhere.

Blair is quite open about how he would view a Cabinet that insisted on staging grand debates. With horror. He told Michael Cockerell on BBC television in 2000: 'The old days of Labour government where, I think, the meetings occasionally went on for two days and you had a show of hands at the end. Well – I mean – I shudder to think what would happen if we were running it like that.' He is unashamed, as usual, to use a Labour government as the example of how not to do things in Whitehall – his instinct to expunge his party's record in power is very strong – but he exaggerates. Harold Wilson certainly organized an occasional orgy of Cabinet meetings. Before deciding on his tour of European capitals in 1967 to discuss British entry to the Common Market, Wilson had seven full Cabinets between 18 April and 2 May, with two on the final day. Blair is wrong, however, about a show of hands being common. It wasn't. His horror is generalized and fuzzy, but it is real. He simply cannot imagine how a government can function with a Cabinet having to be consulted regularly. Think of what these warring ministers might do, he seems to suggest, and how long they would take to do it.

Blair sees ministers one by one on the secure territory of his own little office, with his own staff gathered around. He negotiates alone whenever he can. The Cabinet committee system, which Thatcher and Major still used as the engine of government, is much less important to Blair. It is even less important to Brown. This is despite his being given the prize by the Prime Minister of the chairmanship of the committee on economic affairs (EA in Cabinet Office jargon), which includes all the ministers with the big Whitehall budgets and is, alongside the overseas and defence policy committee, the most important sub-Cabinet group. Brown was the first Chancellor to chair this committee since Wilson retrieved it from his Chancellor in 1966 after the economic storms of his first two years in office. As part of his understanding with Blair in opposition, the committee chairmanship came with Brown's rations. But strangely he never seems to have relished it. Blair clearly doesn't regret not chairing it ('Tony doesn't like maths anyway,' says one sniffy spending minister) and Brown also does his main business elsewhere. A picture of Brown in the chair has been provided by a colleague sitting near him: 'He can't wait to get it over. Maybe that's why he's so rude to us. I don't know. But it's Gordon at his grumpiest. He's sometimes much more interested in what Balls says than he is in what we say. He scribbles away all the time on his pile of papers and sometimes doesn't seem to hear what we say. I'd say that they aren't anything like the meetings that outsiders maybe think we have.'

Like Blair, Brown operates on his own ground, in his own way. A nervous crocodile of ministers troops one by one to the Chancellor's Treasury sanctum for individual meetings round the huge table where he often does his negotiating. From the moment he arrived in the Treasury, committed to the inherited Conservative spending plans and a stern regime for ministers who wanted to spend, this has been his mechanism for control.

In the early years of government, the surprising outcome of this tendency for Blair and Brown each to want to work alone, doing their deals in bilateral negotiations with individual ministers, was that it allowed them to preserve their own relationship as the real centre of government. Blair's ceding of economic authority to Brown and the Chancellor's contentment that the Cabinet was not to be allowed to become a powerful and potentially rampant force, meant that they could operate in their own spheres and settle the big decisions between themselves alone, with no interference.

Intimacies were reserved for their separate circles of advisers and, most of all, for each other. One Cabinet minister puts it like this: 'What's the thing I hear the Prime Minister say most often? "I've got to clear this with Gordon." Or: "I'll square this with Gordon and it'll be fine." Or: "I'll take care of Gordon." It's the same all day, every day. That's how we work.'

At the start, the Treasury hated it. They had a more private Chancellor than they had ever known. His door would close and nothing could happen until it opened again. His secrecy was famous.

When Terry Burns was still his permanent secretary, before the instabilities of their rocky relationship persuaded him to get out, he asked one of the secretaries in Brown's private office one day in July when the Chancellor was proposing to go on holiday. One of them looked at the closed door, behind which the Chancellor was thundering away on his desktop computer, battering out some memo to a Cabinet colleague: 'We don't know. He won't tell us.' The character of any department changes with the personality of the Secretary of State, and Brown brought to the Treasury exactly the air of closeness and near-obsessive single-mindedness that had caused difficulty with so many shadow Cabinet colleagues in opposition. Government didn't change him: his officials realized that the Brown they had watched from afar was going to be the Chancellor they had to work with. He didn't care that it offended some quite grand Whitehall figures, like the (anonymous) official who told Peter Hennessy: 'The Chancellor is an anorak. He has the social skills of a whelk.' The Brown bonhomie is reserved for out-of-office activities.

In the office, he got an early reputation for gruffness. Some Treasury officials resented his importing of his own team – Balls, Sue Nye and his adviser Ed Miliband were around him, and Whelan was exactly the kind of rough diamond which that department is never going to value. He did not have the Treasury style, which is one of the reasons for Brown's loyalty to him. The Chancellor liked to work alone, didn't like being patronized by some of the officials who tried to, and wanted to make it obvious from the start that he would make his own decisions, many of them in private. By comparison, the Kenneth Clarke regime under Major had been louche. This seemed the age of the hair shirt. Brown, in fact, is a convivial man when he chooses and he is a genial host. But the Treasury found that at work he behaved more like a headmaster than an eager prefect. Some didn't like it.

Blair had the same effect on the officials who had expected to run his life. He brought his intimate circle into Downing Street with him, and it was to them that he always wanted to turn first – to Jonathan Powell; to Anji Hunter, who acted as part-confessor and part-coach; and above all to Alastair Campbell. In the early stages, one of his important civil service private secretaries, Moira Wallace, used to find it difficult to get into Blair's study at important moments (particularly when the Chancellor was there) and expressed her frustration to colleagues. It was an awkward handicap because she was the official in Number 10 who was meant to monitor the comprehensive spending review, the most important negotiation in the government's first year. Those who knew Blair well told her that it was no reflection on her professionalism or discretion. That was the way he worked. The Downing Street joke afterwards, a good-natured one, was that her next job was a most appropriate one, based on her experience with them: she was to run the Cabinet Office's social exclusion unit.

The Cabinet is encouraged to get on with its life as best it can, individuals dealing one by one with the Prime Minister or the Chancellor – to get money, to clear a speech, to shape a new policy, to recover from some public blunder or to conceal one from the public gaze – and the consequence is that many of the inherited problems in their relationships were allowed to fester through the first term. If Cabinets are families, this is one with a fractious history and a love of combat that seems to come naturally.

Sitting round the family dining table, the Cabinet preserves some old feuds, whose roots are deep in the past, and it crackles with the jealousies of ambition and political disappointment. This is hardly unique to the Blair government, of course. Major's 'bastards' were a source of carpet-chewing angst to him, and ministers who witnessed Thatcher's persistent humiliations of Geoffrey Howe in front of colleagues, especially after she removed him from the Foreign Office, speak of them still as exercises in public cruelty, shaking their heads at the memory. Sometimes outsiders do get over-excited about the personal disputes in politics, and forget that in the fevered world of a Cabinet there are bound to be strong ties of loyalty and strong enmities too. It is true of all parties. Even as the Labour Cabinet was bedding down, and surprising Whitehall with the maturity of its family disputes, there was a spectacular example of this in the shadow Cabinet across the floor of the Commons. One serious national newspaper editor was astonished in the course of a conversation with a leading Conservative just after the leadership election of 1997 to be told of a piece of gossip which even he found startling. The story he was told was that the shadow minister to whom he was speaking had concluded that a fellow member of the shadow Cabinet was – literally – 'possessed by the Devil'. So serious was this belief that an exorcist was consulted, who was apparently taken aback by the suggestion but who nonetheless agreed to make a visit to the House of Commons to sit anonymously in the public gallery and gaze down – presumably thinking cleansing thoughts – on the object of the accusation during question time. The editor, a sober and respectable figure, reeled away from the conversation convinced that politics was even stranger than he had always known. It's a useful reminder that it is indeed a rough old trade, and it attracts all sorts.

Every Cabinet accommodates rivalry and some hatred. Throughout the Wilson years, Jim Callaghan and Barbara Castle had a relationship that throbbed with distaste and envy and after their struggle over trade union reform at the fag end of the second Labour government of the sixties it became mutual loathing. Callaghan's first significant act on becoming Prime Minister in 1976 was to sack her. No one in the political front line was surprised. Edward Heath, once asked about the role of women in politics, said of his successor, Thatcher: 'I had one woman in my Cabinet. One too many.' So it goes.

Blair's Cabinet, however, has a family character of its own. The central tableau throughout the first term was a picture that told much of the story. The table tapers slightly at the ends, like a coffin, to give more junior members out on the wings a proper sight of the main activity at the centre, and every eye is drawn to the axis of power which runs from the Prime Minister's chair in front of the fireplace to the Chancellor directly across from him, about four feet away. The floor-to-ceiling windows let in quite a bit of light and it is a room which inevitably carries a certain grandeur from its history. Ministers' chairs are the ones used by Gladstone's last Cabinet; everyone knows that this is the room in which politics has been distilled for the last two centuries and more. Brown habitually sits with a pile of papers in front of him and always with a pen in hand. He is flanked by Cook on his right and Derry Irvine on his left. They were the three big beasts in the first term, with Prescott on one side of Blair across the table and the Cabinet Secretary (Sir Robin Butler and, after 1998, Sir Richard Wilson) on the other. The most recent arrivals at the table sit, as tradition dictates, at the ends of the table, from where it is sometimes difficult to hear and where irreverent commentaries on proceedings on centre stage can be whispered quite safely.

In the group of three ministers facing Blair across the width of the table the body language was absorbing from the start. Brown's physical behaviour in Cabinet fascinates his colleagues. While the Prime Minister is talking, unless he is directing a question to the Chancellor or giving him the floor, Brown is usually writing. His apparent absorption in his own thoughts borders on the rude. He acknowledges his colleagues only rarely, in breaks from the stream of note making. He has a distinctive hand, with big, sprawling letters. Sometimes, if he is organizing his thoughts on paper, he will write very fast in capitals. It is an unmistakable style, and because he writes at speed it becomes an athletic business. His whole posture seems to be directed at making his pen work hard and the paper scrunches up as he goes. When Brown is writing in Cabinet you can't miss it, even if you are a minister well below the salt. He writes instead of looking around. With Cook the conversation would be limited; with Irvine, their unspoken rivalry for the Prime Minister's ear makes dialogue awkward. Some restless members of the Cabinet describe them as the two bullies, who always behave warily towards each other. Brown is such a dominating figure with such physical presence that in the course of routine and frankly tedious meetings he is watched by everyone. 'I have no idea what he writes,' says one colleague who sits well outside the central group, 'but there's a lot of it.'

Another, no longer in Cabinet, is less charitable. 'It's obvious that he doesn't want to look at anyone except Tony. That's how power is shared out in the government. Gordon acknowledges the Prime Minister – as an equal as much as the boss – but no one else.' Most members of the Cabinet agree that Blair is careful to defer to his Chancellor in formal meetings. Every minister knows that they have divided the world into two parts – Brown's control of social and industrial policy as well as the economy means he treats the ministers involved as Treasury satraps while Blair adds to the obvious prime ministerial concerns of foreign policy, defence and Northern Ireland the need to fulfil campaign promises on health, the subject that by the beginning of the second term had become the nearest thing to a Blair policy obsession. In Cabinet, as in the daily round of Whitehall meetings, they operate as a duopoly. They don't argue across the Cabinet table – that's left for their daily private encounters – and Blair defers to Brown in the policy areas in which he's been given command. At Cabinet meetings everyone else – Irvine, Prescott, Cook and Straw included – is an onlooker.

But around this central group the Cabinet's lesser power games are played out. Blair has gone to considerable trouble to involve Prescott, having learnt early in their relationship how easy it would be to leave him feeling slighted. A deputy prime minister who strayed off the reservation into parts of the Labour Party where Blair's name is spoken like a curse would be a dangerous beast indeed. Some of Prescott's friends, never reconciled to Blairite thinking and practices, accuse the Prime Minister of patronizing him and, frankly, of exploiting Prescott's vain streak. Richard Caborn and Rosie Winterton, both ministers, would not use those words, but would sympathize with that view. The defence from Prescott is that he was able to make use of the authority he was given – for example, in leading negotiations at the Kyoto climate change conference where he was probably at the zenith of his parabola in power before it dipped back into the mire of transport policy. The settled Whitehall view after four years was that his vast department of Environment, Transport and the Regions had proved an empire that stretched too far, whose distant reaches had slipped out of control. The lines of command were very tangled by the end. And just as he prepared for his arranged move to the Cabinet Office, settled privately with Blair months before, he had his election fist fight in Rhyl with Craig Evans, the most celebrated egg-throwing protester of all, who could not have expected the straight left to the jaw that he got from the light heavyweight deputy prime minister.

Blair, who was in his constituency on 16 May when titbits of news began to arrive in the early evening of a streetfight involving his deputy, displayed signs of panic. He'd had an awkward encounter himself on camera earlier in the day with Sharron Storer, the partner of a cancer patient in Birmingham, who accused him of neglecting the NHS. Blair had appeared stuck for words, and stumbled. He looked shaken by the verbal assault, to which it was hard to summon up a quick diplomatic reply, and for some of those back at his campaign headquarters it revived ugly memories of the wobbly Blair of the WI speech in June 2000 and the fuel protests of the autumn. This was the image of the Prime Minister that they least wanted to re-create, and they were preparing for the worst headlines of the campaign. Then came Prescott. For an hour or so it looked as if Blair might have to think of sacking him. He spoke twice to his embarrassed deputy on the phone, and soon the truth dawned on those around Blair: Prescott's escapade would get a good deal of comic treatment which would be rather easier to handle than persistently awkward questions about NHS waiting lists and, as a bonus, it was an episode that would clip the deputy prime minister's wings. After this he'd not be in a strong position to deliver grandiloquent speeches about the government's 'vision', nor to appear as a deputy with a hold on Blair. His punch cost him political weight.

In any case, that weight has seldom been used to try to destabilize Blair. The Prime Minister found one of the most surprising features of the Cabinet, as he has confessed to his associates, not the bad blood that still flows around the table between the likes of Brown and Cook but the fact that Prescott has not drifted into a position of opposition. He has had plenty of disagreements – he thought Blair's interest in the Liberal Democrats was absurd, he still finds the language of entrepreneurship unsettling and shares late night regrets with his friends that Blair's Labour Party, as it seems to him, is irredeemably hostile to the trade unions. Yet he has never organized a Cabinet revolt of significance nor fomented organized discontent. There have been manoeuvres on regional policy and transport and efforts to promote the careers of his loyal friends, Caborn being the most obvious, running regional policy at the DETR then becoming trade minister at the DTI and finally Minister for Sport. But these have been matters of everyday politics, not major engagements. In his big arguments with Brown, on transport and especially the London Underground, he has often found himself more in sympathy with Number 10 than with the Chancellor. Compared with the activities of some senior ministers in the Major and Thatcher years Prescott's challenges have been expressions of dissent so polite that they have often passed unnoticed.

Prescott in government has been quite different from Blair's expectation of him in opposition. At the time of the leadership contest in 1994, Blair was worried. Although Prescott's formulation of 'traditional values in a modern setting' was an acknowledgement of the inevitability of change, Blair was conscious that he did not really understand him. 'I really am not sure if I can handle Prescott,' he said to colleagues during that campaign. 'I am never sure what he is going to do next.' But in government Blair has found Prescott easier to handle than any other minister. It brings him regular bulletins of thanks from Blair. Any visitor to Downing Street won't have to wait long for a prime ministerial tribute to his deputy. On the night the egg landed, Prescott benefited from that gratitude.

This is the (surprisingly) stable part of the family, enlivened by occasional talk of a Prescott late night explosion or a need for some tenderness, but in which there never seems to be the threat of fracture. There has never been a serious threat of resignation from him. Prescott has not played that game with any gusto. Even in his darker moods, roaring with frustration at the 'fancy boys' in Number 10 or another Gould memo based on voter focus groups ('all that glitters is not Gould' he once announced on the *Today* programme with a giggle), he prefers to boast of his loyalty, not his trouble-making.

But near the dormant volcano of the deputy prime minister at the Cabinet table rumbles the family feud that will not die. The old contest between Brown and Cook has swung back and forth between them for at least two decades. Most of the government believes that it was his knowledge of the depth of the feud and his fears about what it portended for the second term that caused Blair to take Cook from the Foreign Office on the day after his re-election and make him Leader of the Commons.

But strangely, it was not only a surprise to Cook, who spent a considerable part of the day inside Number 10 telephoning friends for advice about whether or not he should leave the government in anger. Brown didn't expect it either, and nor did the new Foreign Secretary, Jack Straw. As Home Secretary, he was preparing for an agreed move to the Department of Transport and the Regions, slimmed down as a result of the obvious difficulties which had caught up with Prescott. Straw had a meeting arranged with the permanent secretary of that department on election day itself. That move was anticipated by his own private office and Prescott's, which had organized the necessary briefings for an incoming minister and was utterly sure that it would be Straw. With David Blunkett given leave from Number 10 to drop broad public hints that he was to become Home Secretary, and Straw's move well-trailed with the usual string of prepared smoke signals from Blair's office, all seemed ready for a prepared piece of choreography at the top of the government. Blair had been talking for months about how he regarded Cook as a great success in Europe, and how his diplomacy in the Kosovo war had so impressed the Americans, and those around him took it as a signal that after all his early difficulties – in Kashmir with a silly hat and an ill-judged phrase, in Israel with a piece of bungled diplomacy, and with a public crisis in his private life in the government's first year – he had secured his place for the second term. So even Brown did not know what was about to happen when he flew from his own count in Fife back to London to join Blair at the outdoor celebration of victory at Millbank just after dawn on 8 June. Yet such was the history of the Brown–Cook relationship that it was assumed by their gossiping colleagues that it was Brown's pressure that made the change.

Even if the decision was Blair's own, without any direct suggestion from Brown, the belief that it was done to try to prevent a continuing public exchange of barbed speeches between Chancellor and Foreign

Secretary hardly reflects well on Downing Street. For most of the first term Cook and his circle had been complaining about Brown's coolness on the euro, often with only the thinnest diplomatic disguise. And soon after his demotion to Leader of the House (hailed by both Cook and Downing Street, in the threadbare language of such moments, as an exciting new challenge perfectly suited to his great talents) his former special adviser David Clark, who had long been battling on Cook's behalf with his counterparts in the Treasury, broke cover. On the very day that the new Parliament met for the first time, two weeks after the election, the Chancellor delivered his Mansion House speech and doused the euro enthusiasts with a cold shower. The watchword was delay. Clark gave an interpretation which chimed with Cook's own. He described the shuffling of the Foreign Secretary in words which members of the government could easily hear coming from the lips of the new Leader of the House: 'Mr Blair took the decision, we are told, to prevent the early months of his second term being dominated by headlines detailing Cook–Brown splits on the euro. There is, of course, a more orthodox way for the Prime Minister to prevent Cabinet splits: to reach a clear decision of his own and impose it on his colleagues. That he chose not to do so is a stark admission of personal weakness.'

The weakness claimed is not, of course, a failure to impose his view on 'colleagues' in the plural but on his Chancellor alone. Cabinet government in the Blair years has been seen by those at the centre of it as a simple struggle at the top of the government. The ministers who cluster round the throne can sometimes infect the atmosphere for good or ill, and they can succeed or fail in their own departmental endeavours with important consequences for the government, but only one among them matters alongside Blair. The result is that the Cabinet is seen by Labour MPs, and sometimes appears to see itself, as principally a reflection, even a victim, of that relationship.

In this case, Blair's moves had as much to do with freshening the top of his government as with a response to the difficulties between Brown and Cook. He confided afterwards to other members of the Cabinet that he wanted to keep Straw in the top three and not to be seen to be demoting him to Transport. The relationship between Blair and Straw had deepened considerably in the first term. That was part of the balance and the other changes were designed to keep Brown happy – the departure of Byers from the DTI to Transport and the arrival of Patricia Hewitt at the DTI, from the Treasury. None of Brown's supporters was eased out obviously and in economic and industrial policy, all the key positions were taken by ministers who looked first to the Treasury.

Cook hardly had time to feel aggrieved before he had an opportunity for glee. He was already meeting backbenchers with whom he had lost contact since he was sent to fly abroad for his country as Foreign Secretary in 1997, and had mischief in his eyes. He was careful not to be around when Downing Street and the chief whip's office made their blundering decisions about Select Committee lists which in July 2001 produced the biggest rebellion of the whole Blair era, and was able to say later that he advised against it, thus putting himself on the side of the backbench shop stewards who saw this as a test of parliamentary virility. Moreover, he could use the opportunity – and did – to promise procedural reforms which meant nothing to the public outside but were of immense importance to Labour MPs. For a deposed Foreign Secretary, it felt good to be seen as their champion in the Cabinet.

Blair, however, was cursed with the inevitability that, as with every reshuffle, the first of the second term would be seen again as a kind of tug-of-war between Brownites and Blairites.

The one that caused most anger in the Brown circle was the removal of Nick Brown as chief whip in July 1998, a tearful episode for him which also condemned him to Whitehall's notorious house of nightmares, the Ministry of Agriculture, Fisheries and Food (MAFF). Brown had been his namesake's most assiduous supporter, a head-counter and arm-twister on the backbenches for more than a decade and one of his closest advisers at the time of the leadership struggle. The Chancellor believed that he could protect him; but Blair was advised that it was dangerous to have a chief whip whose first loyalty lay with Number 11. He agreed.

At each following reshuffle the counting went on: how many

Blairites in, how many Brownites out? In the nature of such games, much of it was absurd. It did the Chancellor more harm than good to fight for the positions of some of his friends. Why, his colleagues wondered, was it worth it for Brown to argue for a return to a junior government job in 2001 for Nigel Griffiths, the Edinburgh South MP who is one of his long-time supporters, and had been sacked as competition minister in the DTI the year before? The appointment was interpreted by some in Downing Street as pointing up Brown's refusal to let go, which they regard as his biggest failing. Brown doesn't see why he should apologize for what he sees as proper loyalty to friends. Each change of personnel had become a Downing Street–Treasury test, a weakness which Blair tells colleagues he has recognized but can't fully expunge. There was some panic among Brown's friends, for example, on the morning of the 2001 reshuffle when it was thought for an hour or two that Charles Clarke was being promoted not to the Cabinet Office and the party chairmanship, where he ended up, but to a job in the Treasury. He is regarded as an enemy of Brown's and his arrival in Great George Street (where his father, Sir Otto, was a famous senior mandarin) would have been explosive. It seems that Blair never intended any such thing: but the thought was enough to send a frisson through the Brown camp. When Blair has a reshuffle, that's life.

The zealots encourage this talk still, despite the fact that the gossip around rival team selections has become something of a joke over the years, and the subject of ridicule in the press. It seems to be in the government's blood. The language was invented by the rival camps themselves, after all, not by any Fleet Street conspiracy, although when it was up and running there wasn't a political journalist whose nose didn't twitch at another twist in the story of a struggle for supremacy between supporters who were happy to have the Cabinet seen as the field on which battle could be joined. Whose foot soldiers had the higher ground? Who had the heavy artillery? Almost any minister will take you through the line-up with glee, pointing to Brown's most enthusiastic supporters – the Treasury chief secretary Andrew Smith, the Social Security secretary Alistair Darling, with Margaret Beckett retaining enough distance from Blairism to be counted a friend. They're backed up by others outside the full Cabinet – Nick Brown (who still attends Cabinet meetings as employment minister) and a clutch of second-ranking ministers circling in an outer orbit.

Blunkett? Blair's new best friend. Straw? Blair's joint leadership campaign manager all those years ago and the man with most interest in stopping a Brown succession. Alan Milburn at Health? Strongly for Blair, with a bag full of Treasury secrets from his time as chief secretary. Stephen Byers? A Blairite who was given the black spot by Brown when he was at the DTI and has scores to settle.

But the difficulty in a Cabinet with such self-conscious dividing lines is that the whole business of government becomes a struggle of personalities and its energies are directed inwards. The balance of power is measured every day, as with the tap on a barometer in the front hall of Downing Street. And the demotion of Robin Cook has set the pressure gauge spinning. His antipathy to Brown is overlaid by a new fury at being forced to leave the Foreign Office. He was distraught. He owes Blair no favours now and there are many Labour MPs who believe that in the course of the second term he will be the natural conduit for the unhappiness that is bound to arise on the backbenches, the focal point of the inevitable sporadic troubles that will arise from that source. He will be well placed to sharpen their focus. Cook's story, the dilemma of a minister caught between the Scylla and Charybdis of Brown and Blair (it is the kind of grand reference that Cook might well make), is the story of how one of the great questions of the second term – whether or not to give Britain a European currency – couldn't be disentangled from the Cabinet struggles that, like so many Prime Ministers before him, Blair had seen take a grip of his government.

It became the most dramatic example of how personal conflicts came to seem more important in the public eye than the substantive issues themselves. They did so because Blair's Cabinets have had one striking and maybe perplexing characteristic from the beginning. They have not been Blairite.

This does not seem a contradiction to anyone who is inside the government. From the start, Blair saw himself in a position of some solitude. He enjoyed it. Thatcher-like, he revelled in the image of the party leader and then the Prime Minister who was willing to swim against the current. He took care to fix his lines of control into the party, and to have his allies organize a more supportive NEC, but he also craved a reputation for a kind of political loneliness. He enjoyed moments when he could seem *different*. When one of his close supporters, Harriet Harman, stirred up a traditional Labour kerfuffle in opposition with her choice of a selective school for her son, Blair refused to take the party's side (despite Alastair Campbell's fury both at Harman's decision and Blair's support for it, which he made no effort to conceal from the press). In his own decision to choose a selective school for his oldest child, Euan, Blair was happy to let it be seen as the kind of decision that defined the break he had made with Labour's past. Each time he could hear the roar of disapproval from many members of the party, and the grunts of discontent from some of his own ministers, but as with Clause IV he wanted such episodes to make a point. From time to time, he wanted to stand alone.

Almost no one around the Cabinet table, with the possible exception of Derry Irvine, would be with the Prime Minister on all these questions. He nurtured rising ministers like Byers and Milburn in the language and practice of Blairism, but in the first term they were still learners. Geoff Hoon at Defence was loyal, but it is a department that has a way of separating its ministers from the rest of the government: they become figures apart, spending their days trying to reassure a nervous military and fighting an endless war with the Treasury about funding. Brown did not have close collaborators in the Cabinet's most powerful posts, but neither did Blair have colleagues who were willing to express themselves in his language. He always seemed to be a few strides ahead. Blunkett, still with a rich dash of authoritarianism from his days on the left in Sheffield, would be a Blairite radical in Education but stayed well clear of wider arguments about Europe, for example. Jack Straw signed up at the Home Office to a regime of reform which many party critics savaged as illiberal, but he resisted Blair on much of his constitutional reform programme. And so on. Apart from Mandelson, whose Cabinet career was dominated by his two enforced resignations in three years, there was only one all-round Blairite at the table and he was the boss.

Towards the end of the first term a complaint was made regularly by the Prime Minister – his Cabinet had too many weak links. This Prime Minister, elected in 1997 with a bigger majority than any one-party government since the Battle of Waterloo, and re-elected four years later with one that was nearly as great, was tormented by the thought that he had so far failed to construct a Cabinet in his own image. Blair was racked at the turn of the century by the thought that he might not have done enough to bed his ideas down. It was partly for this reason that he continued to talk to Mandelson.

After his resignation as Northern Ireland Secretary, he was still in regular touch with Downing Street. He and Blair decided that he should not be seen to visit Number 10 – if he was spotted there would follow a new season of Mandelson stories and speculations which neither of them wanted – but they talked a great deal. Casual callers to Powell's office would hear talk of 'Peter's' latest call or piece of advice or commentary on events. And there was only one Peter. Blair, all his friends concluded, was lonely without him.

This was not simply because of their intimacy, going back over so many years and involving so many joint operations and clandestine manoeuvres, but because Blair did not even now have a Cabinet with whom he felt he wanted to confide completely. Every Prime Minister has a Cabinet composed partly of favourites and partly of rivals, but in Blair's case he came to believe that his Labour Party had not yet produced a crop of first rank ministers. 'Can you explain to me,' he asked a new friend towards the end of the first term. 'Where are the people? Why don't I have more of them? I need some better people at the top. I know it. Where are they?' As he approached the re-election campaign, a number of his closest friends saw this self-questioning becoming something close to an obsession.

His critics complained that he was much too cautious in fertilizing the lower ranks of government with new talent and was reaping the reward, and he has expressed some guilt-tinged sympathy with that view. He has spent a good deal of time cultivating backbenchers, who are brought in groups to sit with him at the Cabinet table by the chairman of the parliamentary party, and therefore he has been made aware of their grumbles, but he is privately convinced that he has not yet shaped a party that will produce future Cabinets which will be better than the one he started with.

The consensus among the mandarins who have watched the Blair government since it arrived is that the Cabinet has been weak for two reasons – partly because of the Blair–Brown division of power and the necessary private negotiations that make it work, and partly because man for man and woman for woman it was not a group that was able to give departments a real sense of purpose. It was this weakness that Blair tried to correct in June 2001 with the arrival of Charles Clarke, Patricia Hewitt, Estelle Morris, Tessa Jowell and the new chief whip Hilary Armstrong. But it was still a reshuffle that demonstrated his limited scope for the kind of revolution part of him favoured.

The Scottish and Welsh Secretaries, Helen Liddell and Paul Murphy, stayed in place, for example. These have been awkward jobs since devolution, and each Secretary of State has had some difficult moments with the Parliament in Edinburgh or the Assembly in Cardiff, but Blair did not believe he could follow his instincts and abolish the posts. It would have been politically difficult, with menacing elections looming for Labour in both Scotland and Wales in the next couple of years, and the person who was most anxious to point this out to him was Brown. There is not a nuance in Scottish politics that he misses and he has kept up a stream of warnings to Blair about the dangers of the Nationalists: warnings which the Prime Minister was finding somewhat wearing even before the Parliament was opened in Edinburgh. He has a history of difficulty with the Scottish party and the Scottish press ('a bunch of wankers' in Campbell-speak) and displays in private the same kind of impatience that brought him trouble and embarrassment in Wales on the issue of 'London interference'.

So despite the government's rhetoric of change, it sometimes comes slowly. Blair believes he has no option but to run the Cabinet in the way that he has, because he would find a truly collegiate government a cumbersome animal, and because he has engineered with Brown a mechanism which delivers decisions quickly and irreversibly. They may have arguments and rows and each may stomp off from time to time. Each may complain to his intimates about the other. The early bloom of their relationship may have faded. But they still believe that the partnership works and that they need each other. Without Brown, Blair would find the conduct of economic, industrial and social policy a much more hazardous business because he believes that no alternative Chancellor could exert such formidable discipline, even if he were easier to placate at moments of anxiety. Brown also knows that Blair has conceded to him ground that all his predecessors in Number 10 have kept for themselves, and that, though he may feel a rising private frustration about his prospects for the succession, there is no value for him in creating an open Cabinet rift of the sort that occurred between the last five Prime Ministers and their Chancellors. Better to share power between two individuals who enjoyed working alone, than to invite a powerful Cabinet to line up behind one or the other on each important question. Nothing but danger could come from that.

In that sense the duopoly has remained stable, surviving despite the regular onsets in Downing Street of what feels like a political hurricane season, but the stability has come at a high cost. Blair has a Cabinet that at times has resented its impotence in policy-making, as well as some of the Prime Minister's own initiatives. When Derek Foster, the former opposition chief whip who was denied a Cabinet job by Blair, said this government 'wasn't fit to lick the boots' of the post-war Attlee government he irritated a good number of ministers but caused some others to mope privately about their powerlessness to influence the direction of policy.

But the signs at the start of the second term were not that there would be more attention paid to the Cabinet or to Parliament, but less. Blair's changes to the Downing Street machine, based on observations by a number of outside business figures who had looked at how decisions were taken and implemented, were building blocks to a Prime Minister's department based on the Cabinet Office.

It is not so named, but this central office of government which has always been the fear of the mandarinate is now in place. With

Powell, Campbell and Baroness (Sally) Morgan (replacing Hunter) in charge of three new sections the mating dance with the established civil service will have to continue until a final settlement is reached. No one doubts that the old Whitehall spectre of a Prime Minister's office more like the White House than the office of a parliamentary leader has now arrived. Whitehall now expects it to be the pattern for all governments in the future, and the centre to strengthen. Blair's command premiership has almost decreed that such a structure should be built. He will not dismantle it.

His relationship with Parliament is distant, compared to that of his recent predecessors. It is not surprising that a Prime Minister with a majority of 165 finds that he isn't fretting over the outcome of parliamentary votes, and he has been spared the horrors which John Major had to endure week after week when a Commons rebellion seemed to be scheduled on the weekly order paper. But Blair's attitude springs from something deeper than the comfort of a big majority. He has always been impatient with the Whitehall machine – a feeling sharpened with the approach of the 2001 election when 'delivery' of public services became the government's most pressing problem – and that restlessness about how government's work is done encompasses Parliament.

Blair prospered there in opposition, but he has never had the enjoyment for Parliament's habits or a lust for its charms in the way of John Smith and most of his predecessors in the Labour Party. When the Commons embroiled itself in a messy and sometimes ludicrous election of a new Speaker in the year before the General Election, he made it clear to his staff that his irritation went far beyond the fact that the process took seven hours. It seemed to him pointless that a Prime Minister should be wasting his time sitting in an office at Westminster waiting to complete a string of procedural votes. Why couldn't he get on with running the country?

He was unaware that the change of Prime Minister's Questions to a once-a-week outing would annoy some of his own backbenchers, though it did, and has tended to dismiss the possibility of genuine trouble among Labour MPs as fanciful. But at the start of the new Parliament, with a determined cross-party group of backbenchers, a sort of All-Star Awkward Squad, forming themselves into a campaign for changes to the select committee system, there were stirrings of trouble. They wanted a system that took power away from the whips and gave the Commons more freedom in calling the executive to account. With the wounded Cook, in place as Leader of the House, whose interest in reform converted him to support for proportional representation years ago, they believed they might be in a position to make serious mischief.

There were warning signs for Blair in the first term. As Speaker, Betty Boothroyd regularly scolded ministers who showed what she thought was contempt for parliamentary convention (the most common being the making of policy announcements to a morning press conference, or to the audience of the *Today* programme, before coming to make a statement at the dispatch box). Her surprise retirement was interpreted by those closest to her as a clear signal to the government that she disapproved strongly of its way of working. Blair's attitude to Parliament is not unlike his view of Cabinet government. Formal respect, but little commitment. He lusts after streamlined executive government, and is irritated by anything that gets in the way.

By the start of the second term the Blair style was set in stone: a Cabinet of ministers whose most important negotiations were directly with the Prime Minister or the Chancellor and who would seldom be invited to have a general discussion round the table. Government rested on the axis that ran from Number 10 to the Treasury and Blair gave the impression that he had no interest in running affairs in any other way. Ministerial meetings were as small, as short and as infrequent as they could decently be. And Downing Street itself was expanding, placing new departments in the chief whip's former residence in Number 12, with the happy symbolism that it squeezed Number 11 in its embrace.

Above all the government remained a kingdom divided between two rulers and their courts, commanding their own domains and responsible between themselves for solving those territorial disputes that arose. Around Blair and Brown the architecture of government reflected their own relationship, built on privacy and intimacy and with carefully erected defences which they hoped could resist the wildest storm.

The relationship and therefore the business of government was frustrating – sometimes infuriating both of them – and it caused their officials and political bag-carriers to lead lives of anxious rivalry and intrigue. But it was one from which there was no escape. They believed it still worked for them. And while it did, its imprint was on everything the government did.

PART THREE

EURO STAKES, ASCOT (V. HARD GOING)

6

Definitely Maybe

Sometimes the Chancellor rushes into the Prime Minister's office at such a speed that a path has to be cleared for him. Officials stand aside; doors fly open. It happened like this one Wednesday afternoon a few weeks before the date had been chosen for the General Election. So agitated was the Chancellor that one official was knocked aside as Brown raced for Blair's office. The door closed behind him and soon there was the sound of angry voices. They were arguing about Europe again.

Such moments are familiar to the civil servants who are jammed around the desks in the office just outside Blair's office next to the Cabinet Room. This particular argument, however, was a special one. Europe had been a source of disagreement since their earliest months in government and four years on was threatening to disturb the careful election plans. Ministers were pulled one way and then another by the debate. On this Wednesday Brown felt the balance tilting away from him, so he demanded a face-to-face meeting with the Prime Minister alone. They were arguing, as so often, about a few words.

In the confines of the Prime Minister's small ground floor office looking on to the Downing Street garden, the significance of a phrase was being dissected. Blair had used it in the Commons an hour or two earlier. Brown was upset by it. Each knew that it was like the shift of a tiny weight on a pair of finely-balanced scales, a tilt more powerful than it seemed. Their discussion was intensely important to them both, yet it was just as important that the world outside should know nothing of their disagreement. The surface of the waters had to remain undisturbed, though underneath their feet were churning furiously.

The tumult had come about without warning. At Prime Minister's Questions that day, 7 February, William Hague had asked Blair to clarify his definition of five words – 'early in the next Parliament'. This is the weary phrase that every minister had been trained to utter as the formula for the timing of the Treasury decision on whether to recommend British membership of the single currency, the trigger for a referendum. Hague asked a simple question: did 'early in the next Parliament' mean within a couple of years?

Blair was able to appear almost puzzled by the nature of the question: wasn't the answer obvious? He replied: 'Early in the next Parliament means exactly what it says. Early in the next Parliament would, of course, be within two years.' In one sense, this revealed nothing at all. What could be more straightforward? Yet those words produced a fusillade of phone calls from the Treasury to Downing Street, the angry meeting between the Prime Minister and his Chancellor, and a memorable aside from Blair to a member of his staff, delivered with a revealing grin: 'Let's say it was a slip of the tongue.' That would not only be the explanation to the public, but to the Chancellor of the Exchequer too.

This is the kind of episode that would seem baffling to an outsider allowed a peek behind the curtain of politics in Blair's government. To those at the centre the pattern was familiar and the exchanges seemed to carry an electric charge. Throughout the first term, Europe was the great national question that could not be allowed to become the great national question. The dangers were simply too great, because Blair and Brown found themselves drifting apart on the question of the euro, and it became an emblem of their differences. The Prime Minister came to believe that his commitment to British membership had to be clear if a referendum was to be won; the Chancellor began to try at every turn to keep that commitment vague and to insist that the Treasury alone was the 'guardian' – he invented the word for the role – of the economic decision that would precede any referendum. So it was a struggle for supremacy. In Brown's view, the Treasury was not to be pushed around by Blair.

When he heard the Prime Minister's description of the timescale, unsurprising and almost banal as it was, he fumed.

Lurking behind these arguments and this sensitivity was an even more dangerous problem for them both. The European debate gripped the government, as it had gripped all its predecessors for more than a generation, and acted as a cipher, a kind of second language which revealed a government divided and uncertain on this question despite its majority. From the first months in power, when they decided that a decision to join the euro should be put off, Blair and Brown inevitably came to be seen as the leaders of two distinct groups of ministers – one in favour of getting Britain into the euro and joining the central core of the EU as quickly as possible, another which was innately cautious and even hostile. The problem for Blair was that Brown's group was bigger and seemed likely to remain so.

The argument churned through the government in the eighteen months up to the 2001 General Election. No other issue of strategy had the same resonance. Although in principle the Prime Minister and Chancellor were both publicly committed, it was complicated by huge difficulties in timing, and by the determination of Brown and the Treasury to be the arbiters of the five tests that would trigger the referendum. The European question was not a division of principle between Number 10 and Number 11, but it was an argument about tactics that swung to and fro with such rapidity that it had as much effect inside the government as if it had been a fundamental dispute about the policy itself. Fortunately for the government, the Conservatives' decision to play the 'keep the pound' theme in William Hague's campaign allowed Labour to play a dead bat. The Prime Minister and Chancellor could both say that they promised a referendum and the Conservatives didn't. That was the divide, not the difference between them in Downing Street about the economic tests. For an election campaign, that would do. But the argument went on.

Blair and Brown tried to take some of the sting out of the issue only a week after polling. Brown went to the City to deliver his speech at Mansion House and gave a signal to the City that a judgement on the tests might be some way off. The idea was to give everyone a cold shower: the Chancellor was telling the City to calm down. Immediately the assumption was that he was pushing Blair. Intriguingly, the truth is different.

Blair himself had been involved in the drafting of the Mansion House speech. He approved of the downbeat signal. Despite his anxiety not to appear wobbly on his commitment to deeper integration in Europe, he had learnt in the previous year how dangerous for the government the timing of the argument could be. He, at least as much as Brown, wanted to turn down the heat.

Almost since the government was elected, the European argument has been monitored as a strategy for which the enthusiasm of one or other seems to wax and wane. The media's fascination is increased by the obvious way in which they have tried to keep their tactics on Europe to themselves.

A consequence of this is a remarkable one for the Cabinet, or at least remarkable for those outside who believed that their meetings might sometimes permit real debate. From the day it first convened on 8 May 1997, Labour's first Cabinet meeting for eighteen years, until the government was dissolved for the 2001 election there was not a single round-table discussion of policy on the single European currency. It was the unmentionable policy, the one that could only be handled by the Prime Minister and the Chancellor in their own way, between themselves and with selected groups of colleagues from time to time, as they saw fit. Just as set-piece arguments on the economy of the sort that marked important stages of the early Thatcher years were never encouraged, so the Euro discussion did not happen. Reflecting on this at the end of the first term, one minister said: 'I suppose you find it odd that we never had a proper debate about the euro round the Cabinet table. I'm afraid it isn't odd at all. This isn't a very collegiate government. We just don't debate things like that.' He shrugged.

Ministers had never been led to expect anything else. Prescott enlivened TV and radio interviews regularly by insisting that the euro decision would be a collective government decision when it came, but in practice that collective voice was a chorus which sprang to life when the Prime Minister and Chancellor had made their decision. There was no prospect that they would be overruled by their own Cabinet – the idea would strike Whitehall as absurd – and it was just as unlikely that the Cabinet would insist on arguing the subject through and forcing the pace if Blair and Brown decided that the moment had not come. So the balance was held between the enthusiasm in Downing Street for an early referendum if the conditions were right and a natural Treasury caution. Brown was no Eurosceptic, but he was determined to keep his own counsel. Above the door of that old Scottish changing house, Drummonds branch of the Royal Bank of Scotland at the top of Whitehall, there is a motto intended to be a cautionary word to any reckless customer. It says 'gang warily': proceed with caution. Brown was determined to gang warily towards the euro zone.

By the end of the first term, the reason John Prescott was saying publicly (and much more forcefully in private) that the decision whether or not to recommend British entry had to be taken by the Cabinet as a whole was not to emphasize that decisions of that sort were made collectively: it was to try to make sure that, for once, it did happen. On Europe, most ministers felt cut out and remote. They were distant observers. Outside Downing Street and the Foreign Office, ministers would hear of it on the Whitehall grapevine, in trembling messages that spoke of a tilt one way or the other between Number 10 and Number 11 or a new intervention by Robin Cook, as Foreign Secretary, another Mandelsonian ploy, or another snort from the Treasury in Mandelson's direction. As often as not it would be a message flashing up on the computer screens on ministerial desks around Whitehall, written by the Chancellor himself, reminding them that the position he had just repeated in the course of some remarks to the Cabinet remained the position of the entire government, and that his choice of wording was the only one that any minister could use.

No policy reveals more clearly the government's fault lines and the character of its principals. It ensnared them in personal feuds and struggles which were controlled and kept largely from the public gaze only by the lucky accident for Blair that he faced an opposition party that was continuing its own traditional internal struggle on Europe. But by the end of the first term, this was the issue that Blair knew he had to resolve. His Cabinet Secretary, Sir Richard Wilson, told his civil service colleagues that it was without question the policy that the government must settle early in the second term. Delay could bring untold political trouble. Yet in the week after their re-election, the Mansion House speech suggested that delay rather than decisiveness was the choice.

Every government since the fifties had found that Europe was a constitutional question that gnawed at their parties' vitals. The Conservatives were split on the Common Market from the moment it came into being, with the nationalist right at war with the emerging majority which thought of itself as internationalist and outward-looking. That division was given cover by the Thatcher victory in 1979. The Prime Minister was able to send semaphore signals with her handbag to those Tories who were instinctively hostile to European institutions, playing the part of the one-woman opposition to Brussels. But simultaneously, while the rhetoric was often antagonistic and sometimes even contemptuous of Europe, the Thatcher government followed broad Treasury and Foreign Office advice and dug in deeper. Thatcher's enthusiasm for the single market led her to agree in 1987 to the Single European Act, the piece of legislation which Eurosceptic Tories later came to regard as a pivotal moment in the history of integration.

The double game couldn't be played for ever: ultimately, Margaret Thatcher lost a Chancellor, Nigel Lawson, over exchange rate policy and a Foreign Secretary, Geoffrey Howe, over her hostility to Europe a year later. With Howe's departure in 1990, and his memorably savage resignation speech which thrilled half his party and horrified the rest, she turned within a month into a Prime Minister who could not command the support of her Cabinet and was gone. She paid for mistakes like the poll tax, but it was Europe that finished her. Labour's experience was less melodramatic but just as painful.

As Prime Minister, Harold Wilson weaved and dithered on Europe throughout his first two terms, but found when he returned to power in 1974 that this would no longer do. His own deputy,

Roy Jenkins, had led sixty-nine Labour MPs to the 'Aye' lobby to support Edward Heath's government on the principle of British membership and settle the matter in October 1971, and the only device Wilson could find to help him handle his party was the referendum, which he had dismissed with contempt when Tony Benn had first suggested it. The Cabinet were allowed to take different sides, thereby lifting the threadbare veil that was supposed to protect the government's divisions. But the party at large was not turned by the big Yes majority into a pro-European party. Michael Foot led Labour into the 1983 election waving a policy of renegotiation which was effectively a promise of European withdrawal, since the demands to be made of the other member states were known by everyone to be impossible to meet. Labour's gradual emergence as a pro-Europe party was greatly complicated by the presence of the Social Democrats. Jenkins, David Owen, Shirley Williams and Bill Rodgers had founded the SDP in March 1981 in large part as a challenge to Labour's anti-Europeanism and it was meant as a bolt hole for many on the Labour right who could not stomach it. The effect was to make it more difficult for some of Labour's most enthusiastic Europeans to argue their case inside the party: they were open to the charge of neo-Jenkinsite treachery.

So, as with the Tories, Labour's European scars were ugly. Blair is no political historian by instinct, but as he came to know Jenkins he absorbed the lesson of those battles.

Blair was only nine when the Macmillan government ran up against the 'Non' of General de Gaulle in 1963 with Edward Heath leading the British negotiations. As a student Blair hadn't attended the televised debate at the Oxford Union which was one of the few sparkling events in the 1975 referendum campaign. He had adopted the ritual hostility to the European Community as a putative Labour candidate in 1983 (it was hard to find a seat if you didn't in those days) and as part of the Kinnock generation shed it like a snakeskin sometime in the mid-eighties. But when he became Prime Minister he was still wary of economic and monetary union. The sight of the eviscerated remains of the Conservative Party after the 1997 election was testimony to the consuming power of the European argument,

John Major's government having devoured itself in the years since Black Wednesday on that very question. There were also plenty of ministers and Labour MPs who retained suspicions of the EU, and especially its plans for a single currency operating with interest rates set by one central bank. This central bank was the 'bosses' Europe' which had been demonized by much of the Labour Party in the seventies, the Europe that they believed wouldn't permit a British government to pursue its own economic and social policies.

So Blair had no stars in his eyes. Yet Roy Jenkins was on hand to try to instil some excitement. To many Labour MPs, Jenkins was a claret-stained ghost of battles long past but Blair enjoyed his company and valued his political wisdom. They dined together several times when Blair was opposition leader, Derry Irvine some-times acting in his familiar role as host and sommelier. They talked about the Liberal Democrats and proportional representation, of course, but also about Europe. Jenkins, after all, had been trying to encourage a pro-Europe Labour government since the 1959 General Election, and for the first time he had one. He was also determined to impart to Blair the lessons of prime ministerial uncertainty on Europe: in his view it meant disaster. This was the Chancellor of the Exchequer who, in his own words, had warned Wilson in 1970 about his European attitudes: 'What is most damaging to your repu-tation and position in the country is that you are believed, perhaps wrongly, to be devious, tricky, opportunistic.' There was an echo of those words in his warning to Blair. In Jenkins's view, Europe was one of those great questions which had the power to destroy any Prime Minister who handled it in a slippery fashion. So he was determined that Blair's eyes should be directed across the Channel, and that he shouldn't blink.

But Europe wasn't an issue that Blair could address as an intellec-tual puzzle to be solved. It touched on the most sensitive relation-ships among those around him. Most of all, it fell squarely between the spheres of influence of the Treasury and the Foreign Office – between Brown and Cook.

There is an old political adage, coined by Lloyd George, and a special favourite in the Labour Party, which laid down that there could be no friendships at the top in politics. Sometimes debts of loyalty and trust can survive power, but in the sense that completely open relationships become almost impossible to sustain in the struggles and negotiations of government, the rule is true. And turned on its head, another truth jumps out. Old enmities seldom pass away in politics. The difficulties between Brown and Cook are a spectacular example. For years they have maintained a spiky relationship, which has often slipped into open hostility. Government has mechanisms for concealing such feelings – Cabinet ministers can stand on stately platforms and appear to be partners in power, pursuing joint objectives – but in the human exchanges that determine the character of an administration old grudges seldom disappear.

Putting a date on the start of what is considered by their colleagues to be a genuine feud between Brown and Cook is difficult. By the time Brown began his political career at university, Cook was up and away, already on the threshold of Parliament which he reached, as MP for Edinburgh Central in 1974, nearly ten years before Brown. For someone with Cook's ambitions and talents as a left-wing orator in those days it was galling, as it was for many others higher up in the Labour establishment, to find the young student radical making such waves. Despite his contribution to *The Red Paper on Scotland*, for the rest of the seventies Cook found himself on the opposite side in the devolution debate that gripped Scotland.

Cook, convinced that devolution was a mistake, pressed for a 'No' vote in the referendum on 1 March 1979. With Tam Dalyell, and fellow figures on the left like Brian Wilson, he pitched himself against his party. Since Brown was running the Scottish party's devolution campaign in Edinburgh, by arguing against it at Westminster, Cook became a natural foe. Later, it got worse. At the end of the eighties, when Brown began to get his teeth into Labour's spending commitments as shadow Chief Secretary, Cook was the spokesman on Health and Social Services. He wanted to promise to spend more. Brown wouldn't let him. Cook accused Brown of making speeches away from Westminster which played to the party's desire for higher spending, but of arguing behind closed doors with his shadow Cabinet colleagues for a much more restrictive policy. Cook accused him of double-speak, and from then on their coolness dropped a few more degrees.

It was obvious to Cook's shadow Cabinet colleagues throughout the Kinnock years that he had a gimlet eye trained on the shadow chancellorship. He never got it, Smith being the natural successor to Hattersley. Brown in turn became Smith's natural choice when he became leader: Smith would not have chosen Cook, because the two men weren't close at that stage. When they had been rival campaign managers for Kinnock and Hattersley in 1983 there was some bad blood. Smith had bonded with Brown, but not with Cook.

Despite his notable prosecution of ministers over arms to Iraq at the height of the Major government's difficulties, it was Brown who had the more senior job under Smith. And even when Cook managed in one year to come top of the constituency section vote in the NEC elections and to head the shadow Cabinet poll – he would ask his colleagues if they, like him, suspected it might be a record – he was not offered the job he wanted. Blair had made his promise to Brown, and it was Foreign Affairs for Cook.

Their personal history became an important part of the European debate. Brown devised his five economic tests in autumn 1997, the moment at which the government decided against using its majority to have a honeymoon referendum on the euro, and from then on found that the Foreign Office was forcing the pace, trying to ease Downing Street into a more enthusiastic posture. Cook had been no Euro-enthusiast at first – as a seventies left-winger he had campaigned for a 'No' vote in the 1975 referendum on whether or not to stay in the Common Market – but sitting in the Foreign Secretary's grand square room looking out to St James's Park, where so many of his predecessors had cast their moist eyes towards the empire beyond the seas, he began to relish the politics of the European Union.

This was greatly encouraged by his permanent secretary, his fellow-Scot Sir John Kerr, who was a former ambassador to the EU in Brussels. They did not have a good relationship – when Kerr retired in February 2002, Foreign Office gossip had it that he had enjoyed his short time with Jack Straw more than his previous four years with Cook – but on European matters they had a shared interest in massaging Downing Street, and giving the Prime Minister an occasional slap. Europe was their bread and butter, the diplomatic marketplace where momentous constitutional negotiations were moving ahead, new relationships were being built with Russia and Eastern Europe and where, in the considerable space left by the end of the Mitterrand–Kohl era, a new generation of leaders had taken over. Cook was enjoying himself at last.

In the Treasury, it was quite different. Brown had a number of officials around him who still bore the ugly scars of the Major government's painful ejection from the ERM in 1992 on Black Wednesday, which Brown believed was the event that had made the long-term disintegration of that government inevitable. His closest adviser, Ed Balls, had always been unimpressed by some of the claims made for a common currency. In his previous life at the *Financial Times* he had shown what the Foreign Office thought were signs of scepticism. So the two great departments entered a traditional stand-off, with Blair holding the ring.

In all his economic arguments with Brown – whether over the minimum wage, pensions or public investment – Blair was conscious that he had given his Chancellor guarantees which created a kind of dual premiership on these questions. It was the same with Europe but Blair, with a Prime Minister's sense of his international role, wanted to shine on his own.

He relished his European ventures. He was quite different from Brown in that respect. The Chancellor enjoyed taking his summer breaks in Cape Cod, Massachusetts, where he'd work his way through the latest American economic tomes and historical biographies between games of tennis, and drink the political gossip from the Harvard diaspora that headed for the Atlantic shore in the summer. For Blair it was Tuscany or Provence, sun and chilled wine on the terrace. He might break off to have lunch with Lionel Jospin or to greet the Italian Prime Minister for an afternoon, but they were brief interludes. His were the wanderings of a happy

European, perching on a balcony for the Palio in Siena, lounging on the terrace of a shady *palazzo*. He became the only British Prime Minister of the modern era to muster a French accent respectable enough to use to address the National Assembly, an accent honed in a Paris bar where he'd spent a student summer. (Margaret Thatcher had learnt her speech for the opening of the Channel link in Lille by rote from a phonetic script, though she did it with such panache that François Mitterrand was fooled for a moment into thinking she must be fluent.) From the start Blair wanted more of Europe.

There was an obvious political incentive. When he came to office, the European left was in a beaten and bedraggled state. He was fresh and he had a mandate that everyone envied. At first, this caused him to be carried away. He went to a meeting of socialist leaders in Sweden and spoke about the lessons to be learned from his election as if he were lecturing a class of delinquents yet to be persuaded of the error of their ways. They didn't like it. Jospin, in particular, was offended because he thought (quite correctly) that Blair was expressing disdain for his style of socialism. Considerable repair work had to be done on the relationship, which has never been a particularly trusting one. The French socialists continued to believe that Blair had been too dazzled by aspects of Thatcherism: for them, Blair's 'third way' was a treacherous path. But after his fumbling start, Blair began to tread the European stage with more confidence.

The twice-yearly summits are generally more enjoyable for heads of government than for finance ministers, who are not allowed to steal their superiors' thunder and sometimes don't even attend. Blair has always been in his element at these meetings, though they can turn into festivals of tedium. Brown, by contrast, has never enjoyed the wearying sessions of finance ministers and has a reputation in the corridors of the Commission in Brussels for brusqueness and for seldom taking any trouble to acknowledge one of the commissioners' most precious possessions, their own *amour propre*. Towards the end of the first term, one of his favourite themes was the tendency of the commissioners to interfere in his handling of the economy. Just before the election he said in a BBC interview: 'I am not prepared for the European Commission to give us lectures about what the level of spending should be in this country.' The commissioners were guilty of 'unwarranted interference in British affairs'. Even in a pre-election atmosphere sharpened by Eurosceptic rhetoric, this was revealing about Brown's attitude to the EU, expressed in language which Blair would never use, even after a pep talk from Rupert Murdoch.

Brown's determined pursuit of stability and prudence have not needed the help of the EU, he argues. The British government has done it alone. In all his repetitions of the formula agreed in 1997, the measures which the government will apply to the economy when it believes the time is right to join the euro, Brown uses phrases almost identical to Blair's, but he stresses the primacy of the Treasury in making the judgement. And even the Prime Minister has seemed to acknowledge that the process is being driven from there. Asked at the beginning of 2001 whether it was he or Mr Brown who would be deciding whether the test had been met he sounded hesitant: 'I very much hope it will be both of us together. That would be the normal way of doing it.' An extraordinarily tentative prime ministerial thought.

In that hint of doubt about how the decision will be made in the course of the second term lies the awareness of how their efforts to march in step have often seemed to falter. In the middle of the first term, Blair began to address the political nature of the euro decision; Brown always prefers to rest on the economic realities. He echoes the Prime Minister's commitment to a European future – telling the CBI in 1999 that the Labour Party of the eighties was wrong and irresponsibly anti-European – but for the second half of the first term he devoted considerable energy inside government to trying to rein in the European debate. When Mandelson and Byers strayed off the reservation fenced in by the Treasury and talked about the benefits of the single currency, they were told by Brown to stick to the line: nothing must disturb the policy of 'wait and see'. While Blair was being attacked by the most aggressively pro-euro figures in business and among Conservatives and Liberal Democrats for failing to give an early lead, Brown stuck remorselessly to his text: 'the decisive test as to whether and when we will enter will be based on the five economic tests', he said in New York in autumn 1999.

The timing would be a Treasury decision, and no one else's. The tests were sufficiently subjective to permit it to be made at a politically convenient moment. The judgements about the effect on jobs and on the City, the criteria for investment and flexibility, weren't matters of mathematical precision, and even the most difficult, the achievement of convergence of 'business cycles and structures', was loose enough to keep a roomful of economists arguing for a month. The tests didn't tie Brown down, they freed him up. And that was their point.

Brown's caution has never been fully-fledged scepticism. He gave a clear glimpse of his thinking in a private speech to a meeting of the Anglo-French Colloque, a political-economic discussion group, in Versailles in January 2001. Knowing that his words would find their way to the appropriate quarters quite quickly – they were in the hands of the French and German governments, not to mention Robin Cook in the Foreign Office, within a few hours – he delivered a notably enthusiastic pro-Europe speech, refusing to give any clear hints on euro membership but taking the opportunity to try to change his image as a grudging European. He also took the opportunity in Versailles to have a private meeting with the head of Nissan's European operations to discuss a big investment in north-east England. Nissan was worried about Britain staying outside the euro. After half an hour in private with Brown, the Nissan executive left happily and the investment was announced soon afterwards. The message was clear. Brown might be cautious, but he hoped one day, like Blair, to take Britain into the euro, as long as it was done on his terms and in his own good time.

From the moment he put the government's policy to the Commons in October 1997 he was determined to keep the decision to himself. The policy, according to one Downing Street adviser, became 'as much a matter of Gordon's psychology as economics'. No one could deviate from the formula; no one could rush the Treasury along.

One day the Chancellor would announce that the tests had been met, when it suited him. Until then, everyone could wait – including the Prime Minister. This caused immense frustration in the minority of the Cabinet that felt, with Blair, that it should be one of the purposes of their government to change the national mood on Europe and prepare for entry into the single currency. But Blair was unwilling during the early stages of his premiership to try to recapture ground he had already ceded to Brown. It was part of their compact.

Brown was allowed to set the rules and it meant that his long-standing dispute with Mandelson took a new turn, that his old rivalry with Cook became the talk of the government, and that the strains with Number 10 intensified in the last year of the first term. His reluctance to let the euro debate open up posed an awkward question which Blair would soon be forced to answer: how great was this government's real enthusiasm for Europe?

Its European difficulties are inseparable from its difficulties with its own personality. Blair's attitude has been markedly different from that of his Chancellor, and Brown's difficult relations with Mandelson and Cook have greatly complicated the stealthy progress on membership of the euro which has always been Blair's aim. In his pre-election assignations with the Liberal Democrats before 1997 he was perfectly clear that he was an enthusiast. Despite his efforts to reassure the Eurosceptic press that he was not what they would call a Brussels softie, he was evidently looking to the prospect of political operations on a wider stage; and when it opened up for him, he duly revelled in it. In Downing Street he made sure that the tone was aggressively euro friendly.

Blair's European policy adviser was Roger Liddle, Mandelson's old friend from the Vauxhall Labour Party, who left to join the Social Democrats in 1981 and spent more than ten years working closely with Roy Jenkins and Bill Rodgers in cementing the merger with the Liberals. After he rejoined Labour he was appointed by Blair to the policy unit and there were no ideological hurdles for him to surmount: it was a perfect fit. Like Derek Scott, a former SDP candidate who became an economic adviser in the policy unit (and whose relations with Brown had the quality of permafrost), he was evidence of Blair's contentment in shrugging off a sense of party loyalty. With Mandelson as minister in the Cabinet Office next door with a roving brief and a corridor taking him straight into Number 10 there was a pro-European whiff in the air.

Liddle is a bustling, rotund figure with a jovial obsession for politics. In the Labour Party, then in the SDP, then in the Liberal Democrats and once again back in the Labour Party he was a campaigner and fixer who did not seem to change. He is a man whose distinctive giggle can be heard in the next room and whose eyebrows shoot to the top of his head with excitement several times in the course of the briefest conversation. He had a brush with disaster in summer 1998 when he was alleged to have helped Derek Draper, a former Mandelson aide working as a lobbyist, with contacts in government. It was a classic minor political embarrassment for the government – and a significant illustration of Blair's style. Though Liddle, who was distrusted by some ministers simply on account of his SDP–Lib Dem past, could easily have been thrown overboard, Blair refused to do it. Liddle stayed in the policy unit working on European policy from the position of an ardent enthusiast for closer integration and the single currency.

Mandelson's appointment to the Department of Trade and Industry in July 1998 was intended as part of the preparation for the coming argument over the euro. The deal agreed in 1997, with Brown managing the famous five economic tests which were to settle the timing, committed the government to the principle. Every minister knew, however, that a rocky slope lay ahead of them. Brown's natural interest was in securing the economic stability at home on which his credibility rested. He knew that his decision before the 1997 election to stick to Conservative spending plans in the first phase of government, and to promise not to raise basic tax rates for the lifetime of a Parliament, would make him a deeply unpopular Chancellor in his own party unless he could prove within four years or so that it had delivered sustainable growth. He was uninterested in European adventures. He and Blair might repeat the same phrases about Labour's Europeanism and its friendliness in principle to the euro, but in his mind a referendum campaign was an unwanted distraction.

Pro-Europeans around Blair saw it as an issue that was putting more distance between him and Brown. They would gossip about Brown's dinners with sceptics like the American financier and journalist Irwin Steltzer (a courtier and fixer of Rupert Murdoch's) as evidence that he was playing the other side of the street. Not that Downing Street was ignoring the sceptic press. A great deal of energy was devoted to the reassurance of Murdoch and his editors – Alastair Campbell has a nervous system that is tuned carefully to the *Sun*, and a pen that is always ready to dash off a signed article by the Prime Minister saying that the national interest will never be sold off. Such articles, or friendly briefings to journalists on Eurosceptic newspapers, are carefully timed. Whenever the argument heats up a signed article will appear, almost always written by Campbell.

The 2001 General Election campaign provided a delicious example. Two weeks before polling day Blair captured the lead story in the *Financial Times* with an interview for the paper in which he sounded enthusiastic about the prospect of euro membership when the circumstances were right. A stream of soothing balm was directed at the City. On the same day the *Sun* carried an article under Blair's name which was carefully crafted to sit happily with the government's formula but to invite the interpretation that this was a Prime Minister who would never bounce his country into some foreign currency, an assurance which duly appeared on the front page in a form that made it sound like a sigh of relief from Wapping. In Downing Street, the judgement was that the crossover readership would be small.

Such moments were revealing because they displayed Blair's own uncertainty at the end of the first term. The most enthusiastic Europeans in his circle had no doubt about his cast of mind: 'He is intellectually committed to British involvement in Europe. That means inside the euro. He wants the influence that brings. He'll do it,' one said, even as the traditional mixed smoke signals were pouring out of the Number 10 chimney in the run-up to the General Election. The trouble for the enthusiasts was that it seemed Blair's careful gavotte with Brown had been going on for so long that neither of them knew how to stop dancing.

Blair also knew that however much he might want to express more enthusiasm before the election there were two good excuses for caution. One was public opinion, still weighted heavily against the euro; the other was placating Brown. He didn't need a crystal ball to know what might happen if Brown felt manipulated. He had seen the results up close.

In the summer of 2000 there was a serious explosion on European policy. It was a bad time for Blair on other fronts and in May he was lucky to be able to ride out what could have been a destructive storm.

The trouble began, once again, with a phrase that seemed innocent enough. Just like Blair's later answer to Hague, the words themselves were innocent, but they were uttered by Mandelson, and that was enough to provoke a protest. On 17 May he observed: 'The fact is that as long as we are outside the euro, there is little we can do to protect industry against destabilizing swings in the value of sterling.' Nothing in that sentence would have disturbed Blair in the slightest. Indeed, Alastair Campbell's briefing to lobby journalists that afternoon was going to deal with it as an unsurprising statement of fact. That was the plan before Brown's arrival in Blair's office. The door was closed and those nearby heard what one later described as 'a hell of a noise'.

After the door was opened, Blair spoke to Campbell and the Downing Street line changed. Ministers were all to be bound by the 'prepare and decide' policy on the euro, which wouldn't be compromised by any pro- or anti- statements while the judgement on the five economic tests was awaited. All speeches on these matters would be cleared with the Chancellor before they were made. Mandelson's remark, of course, was considered by Brown to be a cheeky piece of propagandizing. The previous month Mandelson had told a GMB union conference in Belfast that Britain should 'take [our] place at its heart and shape it to our ends'. On the day of his second intervention, the Trade and Industry Secretary Stephen Byers told the Commons that the government mustn't slip back into its previously cautious posture of 'wait and see'. In the Treasury this amounted to something like insubordination. The relationship between Brown and Byers was already bad. The Chancellor had recognized in Mandelson as Secretary of State at the DTI someone who could prosecute the European case vigorously in industry and business: with Byers he wasn't so alarmed, but he was irritated for different reasons. Mandelson was a combatant on Europe worthy of a fight. Byers wasn't. Around Brown's office, Byers was a name to be bracketed with the weaker brethren in the Cabinet. With the bigger beasts – Mandelson and Cook – he was one of the three troublesome ministers who took every opportunity to speak positively about the euro. The Chancellor wasn't having it.

The euro affair coincided with the onset of a fever that weakened the government for nearly six months. Indeed, even as Mandelson was stirring passions with his remarks, Philip Gould was beginning a two-day session with one of his focus groups, which would be condensed in a memo which reeked of gloom, the most alarming report Blair had received from him since taking office. Gould's message to Blair in May 2000 was not only that Labour support was beginning to sag and sink – voters apparently thought he was 'soft on crime' and didn't like it – but that for the first time since he became Conservative leader William Hague was looking like a credible figure 'speaking for the mainstream majority'.

Far from allaying public disenchantment the government embarked instead on a wild summer of misjudgements and mistakes. Blair missed the early part of it so as to be able to spend time with his family after the birth of his son Leo on 20 May and he was fortunate in the interpretation of some of the pictures of a greying and seemingly weary Prime Minister which appeared on his trips to and from Chequers. The charitable assumption was that he was having interrupted nights and was helping out at home. This was only partly true. He was also going through his most difficult time as Prime Minister.

First there was Brown's speech on 26 May 2000 about elitism at Oxford – the Laura Spence business – which sent Downing Street into a spin and caused warnings to be given to Cook and Prescott not to be tempted into follow-up speeches that might be lumped together in the public mind as a resumption of some class war. Then, even more embarrassingly, there came Blair's own debacle at the Women's Institute conference on 7 June, which enlivened the country's television screens with the unexpected image of a Prime Minister being heckled and slow-handclapped by an audience which he might have expected to coo happily at tales of his new-born son. On the lonely-looking stage at Wembley Arena he seemed an uncertain and shaken figure, unable to conceal his bewilderment. Here was a flustered Prime Minister who was starting to get it wrong.

Political luck sometimes turns like the run of a malign pack of cards, and on it went. Far from the summer recess bringing some calm to politics, everything seemed to heat up. Soon Blair was embroiled with the fuel protesters, who had managed to turn a popular grievance about the price of petrol into a kind of guerrilla campaign which block-aded roads and closed petrol stations, isolating refineries and turning a prime ministerial visit to John Prescott's Hull constituency for a celebration dinner into an embarrassing cross-country scuttle.

Blair had to get a grip. But the Treasury was horrified when he said in a press conference that the government would resolve the crisis in twenty-four hours – 'crazy' was the word that floated around Brown's office – and it was the Chancellor who argued successfully for a measured concession to the protesters, price cuts which were put in the context of an environmental strategy and which could be made to seem part of a long-term strategy. The policy worked, and it was seen in Whitehall as an illustration of Brown as a steadying influence. There had been distinct signs of panic in Number 10. It was an episode after which Blair had to reassert his authority. Europe was the obvious area in which he could demonstrate that after a shaky summer he was a Prime Minister back in charge. The ambassador to the EU, Sir Stephen Wall, was recalled to take charge of an EU unit inside the Cabinet Office which was to be the political power-house on matters European. Never mind that the Chancellor would keep the five tests in the Treasury; the Downing Street machine would set the political pace. From this point on, Blair began to acknowledge the political dimension of the debate in a way that he had resisted in the past. He agreed with Roy Jenkins's tart remark at the time: 'You cannot convert the British public in a fortnight after previously taking the view that the euro is a subject you must not discuss, rather like the Victorian attitude to piano legs.' The curtains around the piano legs would have to be swept aside.

Blair had felt it necessary to seize the initiative from his ministers because in the period of about six weeks that encompassed the latest Mandelson affair and the birth of his son, he was said by colleagues to be in despair about the state of relationships around him. Brown was fizzing about Mandelson's friskiness: Cook was newly resentful towards Brown – while he sat on the Commons front bench he'd had the humiliation of having to censor a European speech on Downing Street instructions to pacify the Treasury, the full text having already been made available to the Press Gallery upstairs. Foreign secretaries do not enjoy looking foolish. Everywhere Blair turned there was trouble. Philip Gould continued to warn that Hague was on the rise. And Campbell, the Cerberus at the gate, was having a hard time keeping the sceptical press at bay. Even he couldn't stop the *Sun* running a front page editorial on 24 June calling Blair 'the most dangerous man in Britain' because of his 'weakness' for the euro. The skies were darkening.

There appeared now to be two governments. Blair, his advisers and a trio of ministers were trying to keep the euro argument on the move, believing that the first groundwork had to be laid for the distant referendum. The Prime Minister was being told by pro-euro business leaders and union enthusiasts like Sir Ken Jackson of the AEEU that he had to show leadership, and he confessed to his staff that he was stung by the accusations of weakness that were flying around his head. But the Treasury was an immovable object. Brown knew that his caution reflected the views of a majority of the Cabinet. The Deputy Prime Minister John Prescott, the Home Secretary Jack Straw and the Education Secretary David Blunkett were all with him. So Blair not only appeared weak to the public – the satirists were beginning to get to grips with the grin and the glottal stops – but he knew that inside government his authority was also being undermined.

At the height of the trouble, on 15 July, Brown made his annual Mansion House speech. He laid out the policy – a successful single currency would be good for Britain, but the five economic tests were sacrosanct and couldn't be prejudged. There was a telling sentence about the origin of the policy. It was the Chancellor himself, of course, who had made the first statement to the Commons and he chose to underline that fact once more: '. . . the policy set out in October 1997, repeated by the Prime Minister in February 1999, has not changed and will not change'. Blair was carefully depicted in a supporting role.

There was to be no backsliding from dissident enthusiasts within the Treasury either. Three days before the speech, when the *Financial Times* published a story saying that Brown's officials believed that the tests might be met 'within two years', there was an unusual public denial from the Treasury. This was a subject on which no doubt could be allowed.

Everyone at 10 Downing Street knew that the problem was festering. As time went by Cook, Mandelson and Byers were bound to try to force the pace on Europe once more, such was their irritation with Brown. It was just as obvious that the Chancellor had set his course and would not be diverted. He was in charge of the timetable and he was convinced that politically it would be foolish for Labour to open up the European debate before the election. He wanted a prolonged silence.

Blair had to respond. He did so in two ways. First, he began to plan a European venture of his own. He'd try to transform the atmosphere with what George Bush Sr. had called 'the vision thing'. Work began on a speech to be made in Warsaw in October. Second, he'd adopt his characteristic approach to personal disputes. There would be a gathering of friends, after which everyone would feel much better.

He called a meeting in his office with Brown and Mandelson to thrash it all out. He meant this to be an opportunity to restore old bonds, and he dramatized the gesture by deciding that Brown and Mandelson would run the 2001 election campaign together. It might have been a statement of faith that the improbable could be made to happen and peace would break out. Those around him doubted it. One member of the Cabinet said: 'When I heard about it I thought for the first time that Tony had flipped his lid.' The scepticism was justified.

There were the traditional difficulties in arranging the get-together. The Chancellor was busy. Diaries were full. Mandelson suspected Brown of avoiding him; Brown suspected Mandelson of organizing the whole thing to reassert his influence. Blair finally got them to sit down together in his little room, between the Cabinet Room at the back of Number 10 and the officials' room on the other side. This is a plain but a sunny room, its windows giving out on to the garden, and it is notably uncluttered. There are Blair family photographs on the desk, and little else. Blair likes it that way. He and the Chancellor sat in the armchairs, Mandelson on the sofa. By the accounts of the participants that circulated immediately after-wards in their closest circles, the meeting was a grisly encounter and an utter failure. Blair was uncertain; Brown was irritable and aggressive; Mandelson was nervy and hesitant. He seemed to want to leave. If Blair needed a demonstration of how the old feelings still held them in thrall he had it.

Through the winter into 2001, the message was spread to the world outside that 'Gordon and Peter' were having a ball and cooking up a spectacular election campaign. It wasn't true. The preparations were certainly being made; both were turning their formidable tactical brains to the campaign; each was happy to answer questions in public about the other with a cheery assurance that they were friends, as ever. Underneath, however, there were familiar strains.

Brown wanted to suppress the euro debate entirely before the election. He and Blair had their scripts neatly dovetailed. Each insisted that there were no political objections in principle to membership and that when the moment came they would campaign with vigour for a 'Yes' in the promised referendum. But the moment had not yet come. In Seoul Blair said in October that if he were asked then to vote he would say 'No'; Brown said that he wouldn't rush in and put at risk 'economic stability or the discipline that has created sustained growth'. They marched in step. But the government was now carrying another burden: its reputation for news management, which spawned a phrase that clung to Downing Street – control freakery. Thanks in large part to the summer's weird cycle of events and the desperate efforts to fight back, the government was seen as an outfit that was as interested in appearance as the substance of policy. It was touched by the curse of spin.

One consequence was that the more carefully the statements on the euro were choreographed, the more they were interpreted as clever public relations. There was a problem of belief. Blair saw his Warsaw speech as something of an answer. He worked hard. Drafts were solicited from a gallery of euro thinkers. The historian Timothy Garton-Ash (a distinctly non-Labour figure) was asked for his thoughts; Charles Grant of the Centre for European Reform, a fervent Labour supporter of closer European ties, was an important influence. The phrase that lodged in the public mind after the speech, however, was inserted by Campbell. He suggested that Blair should say of the new Europe that it was 'a superpower, but not a superstate'.

Blair was bolder on Europe in this speech than he had ever been before, speaking of the importance of enlargement to the east – set in train by the Nice Treaty – and of reform in Brussels. And in one paragraph he summed up his own frustrations of the previous years: 'British policy towards the rest of Europe over half a century has been marked by gross misjudgements, mistaking what we wanted to be the case with what *was* the case; hesitation, alienation, incomprehension, with the occasional burst of enlightened brilliance'. He deliberately followed that sentence up with a restatement of the government's policy on the euro, saying that the five tests had to be met if Britain's economic strength wasn't to be put at risk.

But the signal from Warsaw wasn't a cautious one. Blair wanted to escape from the arguments in his Cabinet about Europe and, though he knew that public opinion and most of the press were vigorously hostile to euro membership, he appeared to have embarked on a new course.

The Warsaw speech was intended by Blair as evidence that he wanted to break free from the domestic argument about the euro and play on a wider stage. Like every Prime Minister since the fifties he felt the lure of the European challenge, just as even the instinctively suspicious Margaret Thatcher had been unable to resist the opportunity to plunge into the argument about national destiny and the European future. Yet Blair was still the cautious observer of the polls, the papers and the national mood. The message from Gould wasn't changing; the editorials were still bashing Brussels. He had to balance his enthusiasm with a public sense of wariness.

Just before the election, he spoke to Rupert Murdoch, which he does regularly. He valued the support of the *Sun*, which Campbell believed had been one of the foundations of the shift in opinion before 1997, and he was fearful that Europe could undermine Murdoch's decision to let that paper, and *The Times*, continue to support Labour. He asked Blair directly whether there would be an early referendum if Labour won. Blair assured him that there would not be.

This was not a difficult pledge to give, since the exchange rate would make a decision in the early part of the Parliament impossible and Blair had already committed himself to a sober assessment of the five tests on a Brown timetable. But nonetheless he felt it wise to be clear with Murdoch: he could guarantee that the editors of *The Times* and the *Sun* would not be embarrassed by his European policy if they urged their readers to vote Labour.

The plan was to dampen down the debate. Blair did not follow the advice of his party's more avid Europeans – the Mandelson–Liddle axis – and he decided not to make an early move to prepare public opinion for a referendum. Instead, he agreed with Brown to deliver the sober Mansion House speech and play for time. The Conservative leadership election helped, with Downing Street happy to make mischief at the possibility of the election of the pro-euro Kenneth Clarke, planting a story in the *Sun* to the effect that if he were elected Blair might consider having the referendum on the same day as the next General Election, forcing the Tory leader to argue for 'Yes' on one ballot paper in support of the government, but 'No' on the other against Labour. It would not need a Machiavelli to suspect that the intention was to encourage some Tory members to vote for Iain Duncan Smith instead, the preferred choice of Downing Street for opposition leader.

The government prepared for a long delay, happy to allow the impression to gain ground that there would be no referendum in this Parliament. The Treasury view was put nicely by Ed Balls in a contribution to a private Labour Party seminar in early July, which was tape-recorded and subsequently leaked (with a suspicious lack of embarrassment on the Treasury's part). He said: 'We have to be careful in the second term that we maintain our position as pro-European realists. We know there are big debates to be had on Europe, on taxation, on the euro, on economic reform, on political reform. The most important thing for us as a party is to keep focused on the need to stay united, stick to a long-term agenda and not to do anything in the short term which would divide us.' Stability and investment in public services might otherwise be threatened, he said.

That 'Euro realist' position contrasts with the enthusiasm which Blair has often embraced. But it was the authentic Treasury voice. For the moment, Downing Street seemed happy to let it set the tone for the government.

The desire shown by Blair in his Warsaw speech to break free had not yet reached its moment of fulfilment. Inside Downing Street Campbell was determined that public opinion was still far too hostile for the government to challenge it with a burst of euro enthusiasm. Jack Straw at the Foreign Office could be trusted not to go gooey-eyed at Brussels, given his distinctly sceptical political pedigree leading back to his days as Barbara Castle's bag-carrier in the early seventies. Both Blair and Brown hoped one day to operate in the euro zone, but Brown's characteristic caution at the consequences of a decision made at the wrong moment was the prevailing tone.

Officials in Downing Street who criticized the Treasury's nervous-ness at any speech or interview or casual remark that smacked of enthusiasm had to accept that, although Blair himself might express occasional frustration with Brown, the guardian of the five tests, it was the Chancellor who controlled the timetable.

The Cabinet waited and watched. Ministers gossiped, and some of them, like Byers and Cook, looked for progress. But the chances of a round table discussion in which the government could set a collective strategy on the euro and the referendum were nil. Such things, they now knew, didn't happen. The debate was driven by Number 10 and Number 11 and the decision had been made to let it idle in neutral. Until that changed, no one would move. They were definite. Maybe.

7

Rival Obsessions

Paddy Ashdown is not a politician who sprays his audiences with cultural references. Nor does he have the irritating weakness of the political opera-goer who can't hear a ministerial speech without being tempted into a Wagnerian reference. Yet after the climax of his political affair with Blair had passed he did offer a telling description of the Prime Minister. 'I think he was a bit like Don Giovanni. He meant it at the time.'

The description is warm rather than bitter, and Ashdown had no reason to see himself as the victim of a serial seducer. There were more dangers for Blair in his pursuit of the Liberal Democrats than there were for Ashdown, who became the first third-party leader to sit in formal circumstances in the Cabinet Room since his long-forgotten Liberal predecessors had their last taste of coalition in the Second World War before subsiding into parliamentary obscurity for a generation. The recklessness was all on the Prime Minister's side. He was operating without the support of most of his Cabinet, and with no visible supporting tide of encouragement from the Labour Party at large.

For a Prime Minister whose leadership throughout his first term was overwhelmingly cautious, this was by far his boldest personal manoeuvre. He had intended it to be even bolder, musing about a formal coalition even when he had been told by his private pollsters in May 1997 that he was heading for a comfortable victory, one that might expand into a rout of the opposition. He drew back only at the last moment. But more than a year after the election, sitting on his huge majority and untroubled by any jitters in his Cabinet or his party, he was able to say to a close friend outside the Labour Party words which would have given most of his Cabinet the vapours: 'I still wish I had put Ashdown in the Cabinet.'

It was a remarkable revelation, and an insight into Blair's purpose in courting the Liberal Democrats even after he was convinced that he could govern comfortably on his own. This strategy was no lifeboat, painted yellow: it was a search for congenial travelling companions. And in these efforts he was more alone than in almost anything else he did in the first term.

In the early days of the government only Robin Cook among senior ministers was willing to behave benignly in the direction of the third party, and Mandelson, outside the Cabinet in the first year as Blair's ministerial fixer, was the oiler of wheels. For many Labour MPs Mandelson's enthusiasm was the proof that they should turn away. He had his supporters in the intake of young MPs in 1997 (there were a number who knew that their political careers had been largely invented by his successful remarketing of Labour) but more of them were hostile. They would smile at him as he flitted through the crowd at a Downing Street reception for new MPs, or in the Commons tea room, then turn and tell the latest story of some new piece of Mandelsonian gossip about his influence in the Prime Minister's office or about a new collision with Brown.

Blair appeared to care little about this. Mandelson was his most loyal operator, a one-man kitchen Cabinet with sensitive ears and flashing eyes: he heard all the secrets and missed nothing. His unpopularity among many MPs appeared to be of no consequence to the Prime Minister. Indeed, Blair seemed to value him as an opportunity to open up some distance between 'independent' Downing Street and the Labour Party. Like Thatcher before him he enjoyed from his earliest times in office the sensation of being a leader who could sometimes appear deliberately at odds with his party. Just as she had on arrival offended one-nation grandees and aristocrats, so Blair was prepared to use Mandelson to stir up the traditionalist Labour tribe. And if there was one issue guaranteed to make Labour MPs feel that they were being not merely stirred up but thrown bodily into a blender it was cooperation with the

Liberal Democrats. It was a deliciously volatile combination. In his support for cooperation with the Liberal Democrats in government Blair was challenging Labour to make a break with its recent past. He knew it was desperately unpopular among party activists, and that MPs were coming back from their constituencies reporting bewilderment among their members about why Ashdown was deemed to matter, but the Prime Minister wanted them all to know that he didn't care. One of his staff says: 'He enjoyed that feeling almost more than anything else.'

One of their intimates recalls Brown telling the Prime Minister straightforwardly, 'You're on your own. I'm having nothing to do with it.' That was an attitude shared by John Prescott (who fumed and giggled all at once when anyone mentioned the Liberal Democrats), by Jack Straw, by the then chief whip Nick Brown, and by a majority of other members of the Cabinet. Brown and Prescott told Blair from the first that they weren't interested and exuded a good deal of contempt for the exercise. They had never been part of Blair's cosy encounters with Liberal Democrats in opposition and found it even more extraordinary in government that a Prime Minister with a majority of 179 wanted to bring a third party into the outer chambers of government and continued to talk, vaguely but insistently, about coalition, proportional representation and a reshaping of the political system. But he did none the less.

And the truth about the constitutional arguments in the government just after it was elected is that Brown's suspicions about the dealings with the Liberal Democrats had a counterpart in Blair. From the start he was nervous about devolution, and expressed private doubts to many colleagues. But he found himself pulled along, for one inescapable reason: 'It's Gordon's passion. So we're doing it.' As things turned out, however, it was Brown's passion which turned into legislation and a Scottish parliament. Blair's came to nothing tangible – no moves towards coalition, a nervous drawing back from electoral reform and, after the 2001 election, a new distance from the Liberal Democrats.

Devolution did bring Blair some success, but great bursts of embarrassment and political trouble too. He claimed credit, naturally, for the referendums that established an Assembly in Cardiff and a Parliament in Edinburgh, coming back to the city of his birth on the afternoon of the 'Yes' vote to drive down the Royal Mile and hail the completion of the task which had first been handed to John Smith as a junior minister in the late seventies, who even then had thought it a poisoned cup. It sweetened over the years. Smith became a genuine reformer and by the time of his leadership the Scottish party had put aside the doubts and divisions of the seventies. So Blair could drink happily in celebration with the Scottish party. But in private he worried and fretted about devolution. It didn't stir him as it did Brown. The north-east of England MPs whom he'd known for fifteen years were still unreconciled to a local powerhouse Parliament to the north of them in Edinburgh, and Blair was being poked by Prescott to encourage regional government in England. Blair was, and is, deeply sceptical and the Whitehall advice has been that it promises to be an administrative nightmare. So although he was willing to be innovative in the composition of his government, thinking unthinkable things with the Liberal Democrats, he was conservative on devolution.

For the two principals, this was another awkwardness that had to be managed. Brown would have the Scottish Parliament that he's campaigned for through nearly three decades; Blair would have his way with the Liberal Democrats: or at least he would sit in the Cabinet Room with them, even if neither party could agree that coalition made sense. The two stories reveal how their partnership depended on an agreement that they could stay apart on these matters, following parallel paths that would never really involve any awkward political reconciliation. Pragmatic considerations would determine how long each journey lasted. Unsurprisingly, Brown's was better mapped and he had fewer policy issues to divert him.

The first meeting of the so-called Joint Consultative Committee with the Liberal Democrats took place in the Cabinet Room on 17 September 1997 and it was one of the more revealing tableaux of the early days of the Blair government. For the Prime Minister and the leader of the Liberal Democrats this was a picture that had shimmered in their minds for years. But there was no Chancellor or deputy prime minister present, no feeling of a Cabinet that had decided to make this happen.

This JCC brought four Liberal Democrats into the antechamber of government, letting them sign the Official Secrets Act and enjoy a first modest acquaintance with the machinery of government. Alongside the full Cabinet committees it was a minnow, but its very presence was important enough for the Chancellor to be careful to make a point of ignoring it. Various ministers were brought in by Blair as its remit was tentatively extended from constitutional reform, but Brown did not once sit at the table in the whole first term. It was his choice and Blair hardly tried to dissuade him.

Brown's absence had one happy consequence for Ashdown. He sat in the Chancellor's chair, directly across the table from the Prime Minister. The two sides were arranged as if for a negotiation, with Blair, Cook, Donald Dewar and Mandelson on one side and Ashdown, Alan Beith, Menzies Campbell and Lord Holme on the other. Brown's presence would have produced an amusing awkwardness. He'd have joined Blair on the government side and would have had to look at Ashdown sitting in his chair. It was never likely to happen. Another absentee whose significance was underestimated in 1997 was Charles Kennedy. He was never part of Ashdown's closest entourage.

Brown's distance revealed a powerful and insistent undercurrent that flowed just under the surface of the new government, attracting Blair and repelling Brown. It was a force that the Prime Minister encouraged, indeed had conjured up from the depths, and one that his Chancellor resisted. For both of them it became one of the ways in which they developed different political characters in power, showing how differently they regarded their party. No political question revealed more clearly in the early days how these two men who had made their pact on the economy and public services still saw Labour through different eyes. But it allowed each of them the minor luxury of a personal talisman to venerate in contrast to the other's. In a way, they both needed the Liberal Democrats.

For Blair they were the manifestation of his unease with his own party. He wanted to send a clear signal about the inclusiveness of his new party that distinguished it from the narrow tribalism of Labour in the 1970s and 1980s. From the moment he assumed the leadership he had begun to weave schemes with Paddy Ashdown which for both Labour and Liberal Democrat leader soon seemed to lead to one end – coalition. It was the logic in their minds and though Blair faltered at the last, and had moments of doubt throughout, he never lost the sense of a job uncompleted. For him it would remain 'the project'. Even after the 2001 election, when the Liberal Democrats' fifty-two seats and the Conservative disaster gave them every reason to distance themselves a little from Labour, Blair retained a belief that a centre-left alliance might some day make sense. In his mind, it was sleeping and not dead. He was prepared to breathe new life into it, to woo the Liberal Democrats again, if he needed to.

Brown never believed in it. He had been outside the Blair–Ashdown conversations in opposition and was brought in late in the day for one set-piece talk with Ashdown which he carried off without complaint but which was never followed up. For him it was a moment of politeness undertaken at Blair's request, and no more. To those unhappy at the general drift of policy under Blair and its consequences for economic policy, Brown could point contentedly to his own party loyalty when it came to contacts with the enemy. He was surprised that Blair attached so much importance to his session with Ashdown – there had been several requests for it before Brown agreed – and would joke about it to his staff.

But the striking difference in their attitude to the third party never became a *casus belli* between them. The truth about the politics of cooperation and putative coalition is that for each of them it was a useful way of backing away from the other, of staking out two separate territories among their MPs. Brown's apparent intransigence reassured the old Labour hardcore; Blair's intellectual engagement with another party's philosophy attracted the smart young things – Stephen Twigg, Tony Wright – and extended the natural boundary of his government.

For Brown, it made political sense to let Blair carry on and to keep his own distance. 'Gordon knows the movement hates them,' says one of his associates about the Liberal Democrats. In speeches and in conversation Brown deliberately calls them 'the Liberals' still, a quite conscious effort to irritate them. When Blair spoke of a 'new politics' that might be built on inter-party consultations, Brown muttered about what Labour might do on its own; while Blair was being pursued by amorous Liberal Democrats and calculating how best to respond to their advances, Brown was conspicuously elsewhere.

No episode in their preparations for power reveals more clearly how their different backgrounds in the party had produced quite distinct political strategies for government. For Blair it was a hope that he could persuade his party – or maybe bundle it – into cooperation with others, and eventually into some form of broad coalition. By the time he became leader he had almost reached that conclusion: within months it had become an objective of his leadership. An intriguing thought was becoming flesh. But for most of his ministers there was nothing in the least bit intriguing about it. For that reason it had to be kept secret, not only from the mass of the party – which would have convulsed itself had it known – but even from modernizing companions who were already disturbed by the suspicion that Blair was getting too cosy with Ashdown and who might have become dangerously agitated had they known anything like the truth.

When, three years after the event, one of Brown's closest colleagues was shown Ashdown's diary entries for the six months leading up to the 1997 election he was startled at the depth of the relationship. The Chancellor's men had thought they knew it all: they didn't.

For Blair, the idea had germinated early. At Smith's funeral itself he had revealed his thinking. After the service, and the departure of the funeral party for Iona, the company had repaired to the Signet Library in the Old Parliament House where in traditional fashion the funereal mood was leavened with drink and serious political gossip. A leading Scottish Liberal Democrat figure was speaking to Blair and decided to talk frankly: 'When you win, don't forget the

Liberals.' Blair's response was decisive: 'Don't worry. I can assure you that I won't.' This was before the leadership campaign proper, at a moment when any such talk in public by one of the candidates would have been damaging, perhaps even fatal. It was therefore a startling statement, almost sacrilegious to some, and it hinted at what was to come.

The previous summer Paddy Ashdown had been given a first glimpse of Blair's interest in what Liberal Democrats always call 'realignment', the moment when they imagine the trumpet sounding and the walls around the old parties tumbling down. The two men and their wives dined together for the first time, and when they met again at Ashdown's house in Kennington, south London, about six months later it was obvious that they shared an impatience with the way party politics worked. There was no talk of pacts or coalitions, but plenty about what Ashdown called in his notes a new pluralism.

Standing behind it was the figure who had done a great deal to manoeuvre Blair in this direction and who was still bent on a strategy for Labour that he had first conceived nearly forty years before, Lord Jenkins of Hillhead. Roy Jenkins was of course an ogre to most of the MPs and unions who had elected Blair. This was the Labour deputy leader who led the rebellion in 1971 that gave Ted Heath's government the Commons votes to take Britain into Europe; the Home Secretary who left the Labour government in 1976 for the fabled purlieus of Brussels as the first (and only) British President of the European Commission; the majestic soothsayer who had spoken of the coming disintegration of Labour in the depths of its trauma after the 1979 defeat; above all, the relentless old schemer who had put together the Gang of Four, founded the Social Democratic Party in 1981 and tormented Labour through the eighties. In short, the Traitor Jenkins.

Blair felt none of this. Having discovered his politics late, he was curiously immune to the folk tales of betrayal which were passed around among others. Instead, he discovered Jenkins the Political Sage. It was in the course of their conversations that Blair began to develop a theory of what had happened to Labour and how it could be changed. He became fascinated by the way that what he saw as the triumph of Victorian Liberalism had been dissipated in the century that followed. A nineteenth century that spoke of progress was followed by one that was marked above all by conservatism. So Blair concluded. It's a theme that he still brings up in conversations with colleagues, and evidently cherishes. Labour, the argument goes, failed to fulfil the promise of its founders and handed much of the century to the Tories. Rather than revelling in the stories of the 1945 Labour government, the staple diet of Labour MPs when the sky turns black, Blair developed an almost permanent sense of frustration with the past.

Brown looked back in a quite different spirit. He had become fascinated by 1920s politics as a student and it was to the Red Clydesiders that he turned for his Ph.D. They were rebellious socialists whom he admired and found inspiring and his biography of James Maxton, the most charismatic of them and the founder of the Independent Labour Party, showed that fire hadn't dimmed. Its opening sentence recalls a protest meeting in Glasgow in the early twenties which was said by those present to have demonstrated more enthusiasm than anything that had been seen since the campaign for the Reform Act nearly a hundred years before. Brown quotes a veteran of the march as saying that for many of them there it was the most inspiring hour of their lives.

Though it is a book that acknowledges the failure of the Clydesiders to change politics in the way that they wanted, and dwells on the reasons for it, it crackles with the kind of nostalgia for earlier Labour struggles which is quite absent in Blair's credo. They have different heroes.

So the ease with which Blair began to talk to Ashdown about realignment and another transformation in Labour sprang from an attitude to his party which was quite different from Brown's and the one cherished by most of his colleagues. Within four months of his election as leader he was insisting privately to Ashdown that his was no tactical manoeuvre but something more profound. 'You can trust me on this,' he said when Ashdown came to his home at the end of the summer in 1994.

For any Liberal Democrat leader this would be dizzying. However, Ashdown had enough sangfroid to be aware that it was likely that Blair would swing back and forth when questions of close cooperation and coalition arose, as they were bound to. And sure enough, he did. In the two and half years up to the election there were moments when Blair was preoccupied with the dangers of their association, not least from its possible discovery by the Conservative-leaning newspapers who were now the subject of Labour's most earnest wooing. Above all he continued to baulk at electoral reform for Westminster which for Ashdown was the key to everything but which Blair knew to be something even recruits to the newest of New Labour were not nearly ready to digest. To Ashdown, it was as if Blair wanted the world that proportional representation would bring without all the trouble of having to bring it about. And indeed in government Blair showed no more inclination to embrace PR, not only because he knew most of his party and a majority of his Cabinet were set against it, but because he seemed genuinely unpersuaded in his own mind. He had a radical view about the make-up of his government, but not about the voting system for Westminster. He was prepared to embark on the intellectual reform of Labour but not simultaneously to hand over the mechanisms of control that the first-past-the-post system bestows on clear electoral winners. To Liberal Democrats, this was not taking the plunge, but paddling with your socks on.

In May 1995, Blair was ready to talk to Ashdown in front of some of his colleagues at Derry Irvine's table, fuelled by his fine wine. Brown was not among them. Robin Cook, who had long been an enthusiast for PR, was chosen by Blair to work on a strategy with Robert Maclennan for the Liberal Democrats and there began a series of meetings which would tie both parties into some kind of arrangement in the event of a Labour victory or a hung parliament. There could be no going back now without causing severe embarrassment.

But even then Blair's difficulties were obvious. A mere month after the Irvine dinner Ashdown received a phone call of such nervousness from Blair that he concluded 'he's been got at', probably by Brown. The Cook–Maclennan meetings were to be kept secret until after the Labour conference in October 1996 and Blair was saying that he couldn't see the electorate, let alone the Labour Party, supporting PR. They were a pair of nervous suitors at this stage, neither of them sure of how far their parties would let them go. Ashdown knew that asking Liberal Democrats to stand aside in some seats to help Labour would be anathema to them; Blair knew that Labour blood boiled at the thought of deals with other parties, raising spectres of Ramsay MacDonald and alleged coalition traitors from Labour's past. When Blair gave an interview in *The Times* in September 1995, floating the idea of more inter-party cooperation, it gave Ashdown a fright. Elements in his own party did indeed want nothing to do with Labour and it gave him a few awkward moments at his conference. It was all very sticky.

But the truth, known to only a few, was that the groundwork for possible coalition was already being laid. Blair's talk was bold. Squashed together in John Major's plane coming back from Yitzhak Rabin's funeral in Israel in November 1995, Blair raised with Ashdown the possibility of seat-by-seat pacts in south-west England, and this time it was Ashdown who knew that his party would have a seizure. So it went, back and forth. Sometimes Ashdown prodded and pushed, sometimes Blair. Jenkins hovered overhead, feeding Blair with the historical imperatives that inspired him. Day by day Blair became more used to the idea that he might one day lead a government which had another party in it. It was in sustaining this relationship, maybe more than any other in opposition, that Blair had come to depend on Peter Mandelson. He was one of the few around the leader who had a relish for the cross-party conversations. Alastair Campbell, who had become Blair's spokesman in September 1994, had a robust suspicion of all Liberals. The vast majority of the shadow Cabinet, had they known of the sweet nothings being whispered between the leaders, would have paled at the thought. But Mandelson was different.

He was Blair's agent throughout, and Ashdown had presented him with a perfect partner in Lord Holme of Cheltenham, whose enjoyment of some of the darker arts of politics is a legend in his

party. He had been an operator from the days of the Lib–Lab pact
in the seventies, when David Steel did a deal with Callaghan's
tottering government with the express intention of giving the Liberals
a taste of the compromises of government so that they might lose
virginity as painlessly as possible. It had no effect on government
policy that anyone could discern clearly, but it served its purposes.
Throughout the negotiations with the Labour defectors, the forma-
tion of the SDP and the eventual merger, Holme was the key figure,
a suave and polished negotiator with a love of the good life and a
tactician's political brain. His ploys against David Owen when he
started to distance himself from the Liberals as SDP leader were
famous, positively Mandelsonian in their exploitation of the press.
He was Ashdown's closest collaborator and the natural link to
Mandelson. They began to talk a great deal, and their instinctive
love of the secret side of politics egged them on. With every contact
and each proposal they sensed the leaders edging closer together,
and were happy to nudge them on. Holme would say as the election
approached: 'Mark my words. This will end with the spelling out
of one word, and that word is coalition.' Even old colleagues, aware
of Holme's closeness to some Labour figures, were wary. But he
meant it, because Mandelson had told him.

Indeed, so confident had Mandelson become that he almost fell
into an elephant trap of his own making. His old friend Roger Liddle
was by 1994 a Liberal Democrat who was developing a convenient
affection for Blair: it was the lack of leaders like Blair, he thought,
that had persuaded him to join Roy Jenkins in the SDP in 1981.
He and Mandelson decided to write an account of what a new
Labour government would be like. In effect it would be a trailer for
Blair's manifesto. As a result it was exceedingly carefully worded,
to the extent that parts of it sank into banality, and chunks of it had
to be approved by members of the shadow Cabinet, notably Brown,
who vetted the economic chapters with a lack of enthusiasm which
he did not conceal from Mandelson. At the Irvine dinner Cook was
highly amused to find a copy of the book and a novel by Albert
Camus side by side and asked Irvine what he could possibly find
in common between them. Entitled *The Blair Revolution: Can New*

Labour Deliver?, it is a volume which has suffered much mockery over the years. Mandelson almost made it worse with an overenthusiastic chapter on inter-party relations.

What appeared to be a synopsis of the book's passages on cross-party cooperation and possible coalition found its way to the *Observer* and was published. There was a hurricane. Mandelson had to deny that he would contemplate any such thing: there was much talk of misquotation and misleading interpretation. And, sure enough, when the book did appear in 1996 it dealt with the difficult question of PR and 'realignment' in strictly neutral terms. The original version had been nearer the truth, of course. The enthusiasm which even then was being stoked up between Blair and Ashdown was still judged a little hot for the parties, or the electorate.

In this period, Blair can be seen in a position which would become familiar to him in office. Mandelson was by his side, ready with the encouraging word, the tactical ploy or the quick defensive play, but he was largely on his own. Cook would do the negotiating with Maclennan but he was never a genuine Blair intimate; Irvine would be supportive but could hardly be deployed in the party where he was still a somewhat shadowy figure; and most of the shadow Cabinet could not be trusted with the secret. If not alone, Blair was certainly not surrounded by supporters determined to see him through.

The thought of coalition politics was anathema to almost everyone who was preparing to serve in a Blair Cabinet. Cook was the only figure in the front rank who would speak enthusiastically about PR, and the idea of bringing the Liberal Democrats into a majority Labour government was not one that even he would be willing to argue for in public. Yet the messages from Downing Street convinced Holme and Ashdown that eventual coalition was in Blair's mind. He mused with intimates about Ashdown (probably as Home Secretary) and Menzies Campbell (as Defence Secretary) coming in. Blair enjoyed thinking these radical thoughts. His problem was the explosion in his own party that would follow and, much as he was willing to juggle the gelignite, with Blair there was a bedrock of caution. His leader's speech in 1995 in Blackpool dispensing with Clause IV, once the holy of holies in Labour's catechism, had been phrased carefully enough to prevent possible trouble in the audience in the Winter Gardens. He wanted most of them to realize the implications of what he had said well after he had finished and was safely off the platform. He wanted to shock and startle, but to protect himself too. With the coalition talk, it was much the same.

The curious twist in his relations with the Liberal Democrats was that he was still not convinced of the case for electoral reform for the Commons. He told Ashdown regularly that he wasn't persuaded of its benefits. Ashdown found it hard to understand how a Labour leader could think happily of coalition but not of the change to the system that would make it more likely, and from time to time inevitable. Usually the argument was put the other way round – the case for PR led to an acceptance of coalition as a consequence. Blair revealed in his conversations with Ashdown that he was less interested in a radical reshaping of the Commons than simply in jerking Labour out of old thinking, the urge that had driven him since his first rather bewildered days in the battered parliamentary party after its 1983 collapse. The evidence suggests that Blair had not thought the entire process of coalition politics through. He simply wanted to start. Ashdown, being leader of a party where talk of party realignment was the stuff of life, knew what it might mean. Two years into the Labour government, with the Joint Consultative Committee meeting regularly in the Cabinet Room, he was prepared to contemplate privately the winding up of his party in ten years' time. If Labour was changing in the way Liberal Democrats wanted, Ashdown would wonder aloud, then would there in time be any reason for the Liberal Democrats to exist? Like Blair he was taking a position that many in his party would regard as treasonable. With more than 3,000 local councillors by this time, his party was thinking of its own future.

Blair and Ashdown met like lovers in a clandestine affair, sometimes at Blair's home in Islington, sometimes at Ashdown's home near the Oval in south London where they would sit round the small kitchen table talking of revolutions that most Labour MPs had never contemplated. Their wives were sometimes present, and the relationship soon became much less of a negotiation and more of a political friendship of the sort that neither could have with some of their closest colleagues. The two wives embraced publicly when they went to the Strangers' Gallery in the House of Lords to hear Blair's first Queen's Speech being read in 1997. Blair simply didn't talk to Brown about cooperation between the parties in the way that he did with Ashdown, and Ashdown was aware that there was deep suspicion at the top of his own party about what he might brew up with Blair. When Brown went to see Ashdown in December 1996, after Blair's repeated entreaties, he expressed disbelief to his friends that in the course of their conversation about economic and social policy Ashdown had said he was concerned that there were some aspects of Labour thinking that might not go down well with Alan Beith, his deputy. Brown's staff say that there was hilarity in his office at the idea that Beith mattered at all.

But the affair went on. By the time the election came along on 1 May 1997, Blair and Ashdown knew each other's minds well. Blair was resisting a gold-plated promise on PR but he wanted Liberal Democrats in his government. Ashdown saw his opportunity to get a toehold in government for the first time in the modern history of British liberalism, but he had his own doubts. His party would be by far the weaker partner, unless there was an unexpectedly close result and a hung Parliament, and a number of his MPs feared that they would be swallowed up by the Labour Party in a messy merger which would bring them little but ridicule in their constituencies. So Ashdown asked Blair, when they spoke on polling day, to be careful. This was an extraordinary conversation. A Labour Prime Minister-in-waiting who knew that he was heading for a commanding majority, probably in three figures, was willing to bring a third party into his government and was being told by the leader of that party that he must watch his language, in case it upset some Liberal Democrat MPs. The word 'merger', Ashdown said, must never be used. They agreed that some participation in a Cabinet committee might be the best way to 'heal the schism', a phrase that Blair liked to use to describe his purpose.

To Blair, Ashdown seemed to be the one who was now showing the greater nervousness. Hence, a year later Blair was able to say

The student Rector of Edinburgh University displays a physical
echo of James Maxton, the spirit of Red Clydeside, fifty years on.

Labour Old and New. On the threshold of a parliamentary career,
before his trial run in the 1982 by-election, Blair meets Michael Foot.

A leadership secured with a smile. The poignant moment of
victory for Blair in 1994, and a squeeze of congratulations from the
friend who stood aside, when friendship still seemed simple.

The other friend, Bill Clinton, in 10 Downing Street.

How Prime Ministers get it wrong. The women don't want to
know that he and Brown don't disagree on the Euro.

The man behind the smile … Alastair Campbell looks for trouble.

The Iron Chancellor as the Cabinet sees him, listening behind his defences.

One shirt-sleeved and one jacketed, but eyes dead ahead, the two campaigners move as one but stay apart, catching the cool flavour of the 2001 campaign at Millbank.

Even in war, all the world's a stage. The Blairs in India, 2002.

ruefully to some intimates (though certainly not to Brown) that he wished he had gone further himself. Would Ashdown the Cabinet minister have been disowned by a significant section of his party for collaborating in the implementation of the Labour policies which had won the election? It seemed to Blair that it was just such an outcome that Ashdown feared. The picture of a Liberal Democrat leader being more nervous about coalition and merger than a Labour Prime Minister with a newly won majority of 179 still causes amusement, and a good deal of astonishment, in the Brown camp. They simply cannot understand Blair's attitude.

There were to be no Cabinet jobs, only the Joint Consultative Committee. Blair intended it to be seen as something more important than it was. It would meet in the Cabinet Room itself – many Cabinet committees labour away in much less grand surroundings – and the Cabinet Secretary himself would be on hand to give it the appropriate Whitehall imprimatur. Senior civil servants in attendance, however, saw it rather differently. 'They loved the Cabinet Room and all the officials fussing around,' one of them says. 'But frankly we thought it was all a bit of joke. I'm afraid we giggled quite a bit after some of the meetings. In terms of government business it was meaningless. Rather laughable, I'm afraid.'

If Blair's intention was to heal the schism that he believed had separated the anti-Conservative parties in an artificial way, this was a thin and temporary repair. It was not much strengthened by the government's reaction to the Jenkins Commission on electoral reform, which Liberal Democrats saw as the proper price of their involvement in government. When Roy Jenkins emerged in 1998 with his plan for a modified version of the alternative vote system it was set adrift and allowed to sail away towards the horizon. There was not a whimper of support from a single minister. Blair had other obsessions by then, and saw no need to pretend that he was more attracted by PR than he had been when he first started to see Ashdown. The Labour manifesto of 2001 touched on the subject only in the most cursory fashion, and as if to acknowledge the truth the Liberal Democrats' own manifesto reduced it to a lower priority than in any such document for more than thirty years. In his leader's speeches in the campaign, Charles Kennedy gave little more than a brief ritual genuflection to electoral reform.

When Ashdown was gone, Kennedy deliberately pushed part of his legacy to one side. He said on BBC television during the election campaign: 'We have a joint Cabinet committee which discusses constitutional reform issues. In the best part of my two years as leader, it's only met twice. Why? Because I'm not blinded by the lights of the Cabinet Room at Number 10 Downing Street and I'm not in favour of meetings for the sake of it.' Even allowing for the party loyalty which has to be on show during a campaign, this was a brusque dismissal of the strategy which had dominated the last years of Ashdown's leadership. Kennedy sees little for his party in the level of cooperation offered by Blair, and the tentative affair between the parties has turned into something close to estrangement. Charles Kennedy says:

Since the 2001 election there seems to be a lessening in the appetite in and around Number 10 for further constitutional reform initiatives, something I regret, but perhaps in part a product of other internal Labour party and trades union tensions.

But my hunch remains that the day will come when it becomes in Labour's longer-term interests to revisit certain of these issues – and when they do the Liberal Democrats should be ready and up for that moment.

Kennedy was from a different generation. He was the happy recipient of a surge in support for the Liberal Democrats and found that a campaign based on extra investment in public services was popular, seeming to outflank Labour. There was little point in talking about closer ties, even if he thought that Blair was still interested. He was seen by both Blair and Brown as a leader without the gravitas which they thought Ashdown had developed (to their surprise) and although his relations with Brown were perfectly cordial – they both swam in the Scottish pond – everything had shifted down a gear.

Ashdown is right to say that, like Don Giovanni, Blair 'meant it at the time', because he did have bursts of passion about his desire to change Labour's thinking about cooperation across party lines. But the ardour cooled quickly after each burst, helped by his knowledge that the Cabinet was not Blairite, in the sense that it did not subscribe to 'the project' as it had been hatched in the Prime Minister's mind. Ministers might be quite happy to contemplate some previously unthinkable things in economic and social policy but this was still a Cabinet representing a party that had spent long years out of power and wanted to enjoy victory. Labour MPs who had beaten Liberal Democrats in the General Election were telling the party whips of their fury at any suggestion of too close a relationship with the enemy. Fortunately for Blair, they did not know the whole truth. Nor did Nick Brown, the chief whip, who had little knowledge of the intimate nature of Blair's conversations with Ashdown. 'Healing the schism' with the Liberal Democrats would have produced an instant Labour schism of its own if he had.

In power, Blair understood that as well as his party not sharing his thinking, the Liberal Democrat members had not yet been won over by Ashdown. It was much easier to be cosy to Labour notionally in opposition than when it was a massively powerful party of government. So he kept his enthusiasm for the private encounters with Ashdown, which still took place, away from the prying eyes of his ministers. The JCC met regularly, and for most members of the government its proceedings mattered not at all. Different Cabinet ministers were taken along from time to time and the discussions were duly minuted, but in the life of the government it had little significance. One senior minister puts it like this: 'There are some Cabinet committees you want to sit on. It's important that you are there. You have input in some of the big decisions at least. With the Liberal thing there doesn't seem much point. It obviously means something to Tony but nobody else takes it very seriously at all.' That is a common view among ministers in the senior ranks; there are other views which are more hostile. It is one of the few subjects on which Prescott has often felt it safe to disagree with Blair in public. In many interviews he has said that everyone knows what he thinks about Liberals. He never has to add: 'Not much.'

Prescott would not serve in a coalition Cabinet and everyone knows it. But Blair has never abandoned his urge. From time to time it breaks the surface for a moment. He told Robert Harris in May 2000 in an interview: 'I've never given up on that goal, and I still believe it can be achieved.' Most of the time, however, this is a passion that dare not speak its name.

Blair's most radical thought about the kind of government he wanted to lead was, therefore, one that he couldn't easily share with his colleagues. He often had to conceal it. By contrast, the trouble with his most innovative change – devolution to Scotland and Wales – was not in concealing his enthusiasm but in keeping his misgivings private.

Blair did confess his doubts to a small group of Labour MPs who went to see him before the 1997 election. They were anti-devolutionists, still convinced that the policy was an appeasement of nationalism and would fail. They thought, as a large section of the Labour Party had thought in the seventies, that the SNP in Scotland would be energized, the Conservatives in England would be given a banner to raise and that the government would find itself paddling once more in the mire which had sucked down the Callaghan government in 1979. The MPs, among them the veteran anti-devolutionist Tam Dalyell, put their case to Blair. They were on a hopeless mission. They wouldn't be able to persuade him to abandon the party commitment to devolution, as they knew before they arrived. But Blair was surprisingly open with them. He revealed that he was troubled by the politics of devolution, and fearful that the constitutional complications would hobble his government. And he said something else: that his relationship with Brown was essential to the success of a future Labour government, and that it could not survive what Brown would consider betrayal on devolution.

Blair's interest in 'healing the schism' between the non-Conservative parties in British politics was a feeble thing compared to Brown's adamantine commitment to devolution. For a quarter of a century he had argued for a Parliament in Edinburgh, and his feelings about devolution had been a still point in the turning world of his economic views. The editor of *The Red Paper* in 1975 was writing about a Scotland with a Parliament, just as the Iron Chancellor, with his fiscal rules and his love of prudence, was determined that the Labour government would legislate for devolution in its first Queen's Speech. Blair's nagging worries about the consequences and his suspicion that it was a distraction from the government's main business were not going to be allowed to delay things.

But even Brown had to accept referendum procedures which infuriated some of the most dedicated devolutionists. Despite Labour's absolute commitment to a Parliament, on the model devised by the cross-party Scottish Constitutional Convention, Blair announced a year before the General Election that there would be a referendum with two questions, the second giving voters the chance to decide whether or not the Parliament should have tax-raising powers. For the true believers this was in itself a betrayal. What if the Parliament were approved but not allowed a measure of control on taxation? Its legitimacy would be sabotaged and all the old arguments about irresponsible talking shops would return. The Liberal Democrats, in particular, were furious. Blair wouldn't give ground to them. He told Ashdown that there were many English nationalists in his party who wanted devolution to die, and if it was to survive he had to have his hand strengthened by a two-question referendum. There was no other way. Blair needed the two-question referendum to give devolution legitimacy. If the Liberal Democrats didn't like it, too bad. He could hardly undermine a policy which had come to be seen as something of a memorial to John Smith but he had developed a nagging fear about what became known as 'the English backlash'. Without a referendum he believed he would find it hard to defend. His own Scottish party was deeply unhappy – any referendum had been ruled out repeatedly as unnecessary – and the Liberal Democrats spoke of betrayal, but Blair insisted.

It was held on 11 September 1997, before the late summer glow of the election honeymoon had faded, and the government duly won a clear 'Yes' answer to both questions. The legislation which had to follow was likely to provide more of a difficulty than the Scottish electorate which, after all, had voted overwhelmingly for devolutionist or nationalist parties in the five General Elections past. The legislation was based on a plan drawn up in the first fretful six weeks of the government's life and the Cabinet negotiations were further complicated by the oldest rule of politics, the one that says everyone knows everyone else's past.

The Scottish Secretary and First Minister designate Donald Dewar had to argue his case in a ministerial committee (DSWR – Devolution to Scotland, Wales and the Regions) chaired by Derry Irvine. They had been students in Glasgow together, but their friendship was broken. Long after their buoyant days as young debaters in a notable gang of livewires and wits that included John Smith and Menzies Campbell, Dewar's wife, Alison, left him for Irvine with their son and daughter. Not surprisingly, Irvine and Dewar were not regular companions thereafter. There was some nervousness in government about how they would work together. But Dewar got into the habit of coming off the sleeper from Glasgow to London every week and having private breakfasts with Irvine in his apartment at the Lords. They made it work, though it was not easy for either of them.

It wasn't surprising that other members of the Cabinet looked in on these devolution arguments with a certain awe and mystification. Everyone seemed tied up with everyone else in Scotland: different generations like Brown's and Dewar's seemed to be connected by shared experiences that were passed on down the years. Added to the wariness of ministers like Jack Straw about the devolution exercise itself – what would independent-minded northern constituencies like his in Blackburn do when the English complaints became too loud for comfort? – was a degree of irritation at the assertiveness of the Scottish mafia in Cabinet. But Irvine, in fact, was disturbed by the drift of Dewar's first paper to the committee: like Straw he did not want to see the centre of power in Whitehall weakened too much. Blair sympathized with that view. Brown did not.

Blair told Irvine that he did not want a plan that seemed in any way to impinge on Westminster's ultimate sovereignty. The subjects devolved to Scotland must be clearly delineated and Westminster's powers in other matters must be clear and unaffected. He also sought a promise to cut the number of Scots MPs at Westminster and said that when that could be agreed he wanted the Edinburgh Parliament reduced in size by the same proportion. This infuriated his Scottish ministers who disagreed profoundly with the view that the new Parliament should have to wax and wane with Westminster. But the issue of Scottish MPs was to be kicked off into the future, so that row was postponed.

During the Cabinet's arguments on devolution Irvine had the advantage not so much of prime ministerial patronage but of his own patronage of the Prime Minister. He found it difficult to avoid using the old description 'young Blair' when he was off duty, and in the early days of government every minister with well-tuned political antennae knew that he and Blair spoke to each other a great deal, a call coming on many mornings from Number 10 to the Irvine apartment in the Victoria Tower high above the House of Lords. They gossiped about everything. This gave Irvine the clout that comes with such intimacies. In the early days of the government, no one could afford to offend him. It was too risky.

Ministers found this galling. Privately, they complained about his style. One minister who had been treated at a Cabinet committee like a trembling witness who'd come to court with a threadbare story said after her first experience of the Irvine treatment: 'I don't think I have ever met a ruder man.' This was a high accolade. It made Irvine a few enemies, and he became the Flashman of the Cabinet, routinely described by his colleagues as a bully. Stories would circulate of humiliating interrogations of ministers who hadn't mastered a brief. As in a courtroom, he would pause to glance with a raised eyebrow at a colleague who was encouraged to share his scepticism about the case being made, and there would be the sort of derisory grunts that come only from the unpersuaded. 'You've got to remember that we can't stand him – but he probably doesn't know it,' one quite senior member of the Cabinet said in the early days. In fact, Irvine understood quite well that he wasn't especially popular. His position in the government had not come as the result of a conventional political career and his power flowed from one source alone: his old pupil. The advantage was that it gave him independence. He had no network of supporters that had to be nurtured and massaged. He dealt directly with the Prime Minister, and no one else was in a position to intervene.

Irvine mastered his devolution brief and got on with it. Having launched himself as a constitutional reformer, Blair wanted the legislation to pass quickly and with as little collateral damage to the party as possible. But no one believed that when Blair had gone anyone would find the word 'devolution' engraved on his heart. In conversation he would raise his eyes heavenwards and hope it would soon be over. He was encouraged in this by Straw, who spoke of the importance of maintaining 'executive democracy', by which he meant the power of the central bureaucracy in London, parliamentary sovereignty for Westminster in as many areas of policy as possible, and no change to the first-past-the-post system for election to the Commons. The ministers who agreed with Straw were reconciled to PR in Scotland – long since agreed by the Labour Party, largely as a defence against the chances of an outright Nationalist majority in Edinburgh in years to come – but the devolution argument was drenched in suspicion.

Blair's worries were compounded after the Scottish Parliament and the Welsh Assembly were elected. The campaign in Scotland was awkward, and in its later stages Brown was sent up to give it some weight. This caused some resentment on Dewar's part, but Blair was in a state of mild panic about what was happening beyond England's borders. 'He looked up there and saw nothing but trouble,' one of his officials says. Some of the trouble was of his own making. In Wales, the choice of Alun Michael as leader in the Assembly was unpopular and politically humiliating for Michael himself, who eventually had to give way to Rhodri Morgan, the party's popular choice, whom Blair had decided to oppose for his 'old Labour' sympathies (Morgan prefers the neat description 'classic Labour'). In Scotland, the new administration, a Labour partnership with the Liberal Democrats, stumbled into a series of embarrassing bungles, found itself in a street fight with the Scottish press and had a troubled infancy.

These constitutional innovations were radical steps by any measure, but they left Blair uneasy. His instincts for reform were just that: instincts rather than plans. Where Brown had beavered away on devolution for twenty years, and in common with every Scots politician of his generation knew every turning in the maze, Blair had inherited a commitment whose complications he had never had to bother to master in the way that he would have had to had he been a Scottish MP. When he began to ponder the likely unpopularity in England of a Parliament that appeared to give Scotland special powers, and therefore advantages, he got the jitters. Along with Irvine, oozing with the instinctive caution of the lawyer playing a canny hand, he watched the pace being set by Dewar, with Brown's support, with alarm.

The paradox of Blair's first term is that he led a government which produced more radical changes to the constitution than any since before World War I but couldn't shake off a nervousness about the whole exercise. Three years after he came to power, nearly two dozen bills had gone through the Commons reshaping the insti tutions of the United Kingdom, and yet he chose never to devote a major speech entirely to constitutional matters. It was almost as if he didn't like the very thing he had committed so much of his legislative time to. Brown was different.

Though he has in general been notably reluctant to involve himself in public debate about questions that aren't Treasury preoccupations he has pushed and harried on devolution. One of his colleagues, who watched the progress of devolution with Straw-like alarm, offers a picture.

'Gordon is obsessed by Scotland. Obsessed. He reads the Scottish papers. Talks about it all the time. Of course he's terrified that there will be separation. Devolution has always been his thing. He pushed the pace on. Tony went along with it. Not very enthusiastically, but he went along.'

But in politics such observations seldom come without an explanation that tries to identify the motive. 'Now Gordon talks all the time about regionalism and the need to solve "the English question". He knows, of course, that if England isn't reconciled to Scottish devolution and the regions are sorted out there will never be a Scottish leader of the party. The penny has dropped. It happened about two years ago. He talks about it all the time.'

That interpretation of Brown's motives may not be entirely unfair, but it ignores that pulse of devolution that those around Blair have sometimes been unable to feel. For Scots politicians of all parties the years of the constitutional debates of the seventies were invigorating, bloody, memorable ones. There was a comic demonstration of it at Dewar's funeral in October 2000 in Glasgow Cathedral.

Blair read a lesson from Isaiah about the obligation to help the humble and the needy and Brown delivered the principal tribute from the pulpit. It was a congregation which represented a Scotland whose byways Dewar knew intimately, representing every party and faction as if they were a small community gathered for a town meeting. Everyone seemed to know everyone else. Indeed the funeral arrangements were attended by arguments of the sort that Dewar the politician would have found hilarious – an emissary from London declaring that Glasgow City Council's finest china wasn't good enough for the reception after the service; officials of the Scottish Executive trying to reroute the cortège on its way to the crematorium to avoid the City Hall in George Square because of a dispute with the council leaders; a jockeying among clerics for position and the sight of one of the most distinguished among them being seated by chance behind a large stone pillar, to his evident discomfort. It was a melancholy day for Dewar's friends but not without the traditional piquancy of the political funeral.

Brown's address was delivered as if it was a political speech, almost a rallying cry. He turned from his recollections of an old friend (with whom he'd been having some painful arguments in the year or so up to his death) to his theme of social justice. In the day or two before, while Brown was thumping away at his keyboard in the Chancellor's office in the Treasury, writing a tribute that would match the occasion, there were discussions in Number 10 about how 'political' the address could afford to be. 'We decided that Gordon could push out the boat a little quite safely. It was quite right that he should talk about the importance of social justice and the rest of it,' an official said after the funeral. A friend of Brown's found it laughable. 'Can you imagine some prat from Number 10 telling Gordon what to say at Donald's funeral?' he said, sipping strong tea from one of Glasgow City Council's finest china cups, safely approved for the wake.

It was a tribal occasion. Blair, sitting in the front row with Brown, Irvine and the Prince of Wales, felt again the self-awareness of the Scotland that was being shaped by his own devolution of power. His colleagues believe that it's an awareness tinged with foreboding. A Parliament that begins to think for itself, an electorate that looks to Edinburgh and not London, Nationalists who are ready to exploit any dispute with London and win easy votes as a result – they are Downing Street nightmares. Devolution changed the shape of the British state within a year of the election of the Blair government. For the Prime Minister, however, it was a change that tingled with apprehension.

Blair's caution and his willingness to think the unthinkable always march hand in hand. For years before the election he was happy to contemplate coalition, whatever his party thought about it. About devolution, his inherited revolution, he was apprehensive. Alongside him, in Brown he had a Chancellor who saw radicalism in a quite different light. His was a party belief, a Labour loyalist's line. The Liberal Democrats wouldn't be welcome in the Cabinet Room if he were Prime Minister, all his friends knew, but on the constitution itself he'd draw on the beliefs of early twentieth-century Scottish socialists, who still cast a spell on him, and battle for a kind of Home Rule.

On the day of the referendum result, in September 1997, Blair flew to Edinburgh and then Cardiff to mark the moment. It was something of a triumph for him, and he grinned at the crowds. A friend of Brown's who was watching, said: 'What does it mean to him?' The unspoken answer was: 'Not much.' But Blair revelled in the success of the referendums like a professional. Eighteen years before it had been the Scottish referendum that marked the beginning of the end of the Callaghan government. This Labour government had succeeded where its predecessor had failed, and Blair could justifiably feel that he had completed the work that John Smith had begun.

His worries about devolution increased after Dewar's sudden

death; in Downing Street the leadership of Henry McLeish in Scotland was thought to be of a distinctly less commanding sort, and Blair's nervousness returned. A Prime Minister who worried as much as Blair about the efficiency of the Downing Street machine and wanted to streamline Whitehall was never likely to be a natural devolver, and Blair is not.

This was not as contradictory as it seemed. Brown, as is his habit, had built a strategy on one of his political principles, in this case devolution. That commitment was sacrosanct. If it meant a joint administration with the Liberal Democrats in Edinburgh, so be it. That was a consequence which would have to be managed. But for Westminster, Brown saw no principle involved. He did not believe in electoral reform for its own sake, nor in encouraging coalition. Scotland was important; the Liberal Democrats weren't.

Once again Blair and Brown came to a settlement from different starting points. Neither undermined the other's strategy, though neither felt it necessary to show great enthusiasm for it. They balanced their rival obsessions and let them flourish.

8

Money

Labour has often had trouble with money. It has always caused envy and guilt, and it brought squalls of uncertainty to the government. Blair may have exploited the sleazy episodes in the Major years to help swell his 1997 majority but when his own ministers began to slip and slide into the same muddy pools he found it even more difficult to deal with in public than his predecessors. He could boast of a Parliamentary Commissioner for Standards, a new Commons committee and new rules of disclosure for election donations but money made the government uncomfortable.

Clean government and financial propriety were not the only difficulties. Deep inside Labour there still lay a feeling of awkwardness about the rich, even about the half-rich. With Blair's regime came a new language as well as new policies. They intended to change the image of Labour as the party whose former Chancellor, Denis Healey, had promised to 'tax the rich until the pips squeak' in the seventies, turning it into a party that was at ease with wealth and its benefits. For Blair, the mantra of 'traditional Labour values in a modern setting' did not mean holding on to the value that equated wealth with greed and exploitation. Social justice and financial success were to be allowed to co-exist.

The sensitivity of the issue could be gauged by the awkwardness with which Blair spoke about it. At the start of the 2001 campaign he was asked by Jeremy Paxman on *Newsnight* whether he thought it was acceptable for the gap between rich and poor to widen under his premiership. His reply was evasive because Blair knew that he would offend his party with a more blunt one. Nonetheless he stubbornly refused to condemn the pursuit of wealth: 'It is acceptable for those people on lower incomes to have their incomes raised. It is unacceptable that they're not given the chances. To me the key thing is not whether the gap between those who – the person who earns the most in the country and the person who earns the least – is distant or not.' Blair's answer was revealing. His government was committed to a sustained attack on child poverty at home – a preoccupation of Brown's – and attempts at debt reduction across the developing world as part of a global effort to slow down and even reverse the spread of poverty around the world, another policy to which Brown has devoted a great deal of personal attention, and Blair has no difficulty with those objectives. Some of his warmest words for his Chancellor have been about them. But he has never believed that a concern about poverty should be matched by a nervousness about wealth.

On this question, perhaps more than on any other, his instincts have drawn him away from much of his party. Roy Hattersley, who for all his life in the Commons was associated with the loyalist Labour right, assumed the role of doom-laden pamphleteer from the Lords in his retirement from front-line politics, taking to the pages of newspapers right and left to denounce Blairism as a betrayal of Labour values because it was, above all, an elitist creed that had lost any interest in equality. Just after Blair's re-election, Hattersley said that he had even considered resigning from the party, which for a former deputy leader would have been an act with a guaranteed public effect. He had long since severed links with Downing Street, and is regarded there with some bitterness for obvious reasons, but his themes have unsettled Blair.

To the Blair of 1983, Labour seemed to have nothing to offer the professional middle classes. He went along with the party's election manifesto in public, despite his private doubts, but in the gloomy years that followed one of his preoccupations, much more than it was Kinnock's, was finding a political language that dispensed with the class envy which he still found uncomfortable. He was perfectly at one with the instincts of his constituency party, which, like most of the others in County Durham, leaned generally towards the right of the party, where he was not expected to indulge in bloodcurdling assaults on the rich and privileged. So early on, with friends like his agent John Burton, he experimented with a new language. A different attitude to wealth was part of it. Even during the height of Thatcherism, he wanted to associate Labour with a commitment to successful people as well as the downtrodden. His legal friends in London were comfortably off, even if most of them would not end up as Irvine-like millionaires at the Bar, and Blair was determined that Labour should not be a party that decried them. He had little idea where precisely such determination might lead, but in his early period in the Commons his private contempt was directed firmly at those on the left whom he believed to be imbued with a hatred of success.

This was hardly an incongruous posture for Blair. Before 1983 he had been a reasonably successful barrister who would probably have been making several hundred thousand pounds a year in the nineties had he stayed at the Bar and developed in the way that was predicted by Irvine, his head of chambers. Moreover, as a barrister he was self-employed. That status does not seem a particular hardship to those outside the law, given the rewards that are available for success, but it did mean that before entering Parliament Blair had become used to the fact that he was responsible for the size of his own income. If he was a success, he would probably become quite rich; if his cases dried up he would be scraping a living at the scruffy end of the profession. By the time he became an MP he was used to controlling his own financial destiny and was quite sensitive about money, a sensitivity no doubt sharpened by the fact that his income dropped by more than half when he was elected.

Blair came from a comfortable, though not spectacularly well-heeled middle-class background. His father, Leo, was a law lecturer in Adelaide, Edinburgh and Durham and practised as a barrister on the Newcastle circuit while Blair was at The Chorister School at Durham Cathedral. There was enough money to send Blair, and his older brother Bill, to Fettes. Theirs was not a household where money was a regular worry. When he began to show an interest in political ideas (as distinct from political activity) at Oxford, it was natural that he would match his creed to his own experiences. Blair never showed any sign of rejecting his family's status or outlook and was never one of those political figures who either buries the past or turns publicly against it. His father had been a youthful communist in Glasgow before the war, and Blair well knew the story of his disillusionment with the revolutionary left.

He has never shown an interest in class politics, unlike some members of his Cabinet who were formidable leftists in their day. Charles Clarke, his choice for Cabinet Office fixer and party chairman after the government's re-election, was left-wing president of the National Union of Students when Blair was in his last, politics-free year at Oxford. Alan Milburn and Stephen Byers both went on package tours to the far left in the seventies, all-in excursions to the self-contained world of Trotskyite certainty, when the clenched fist and the 'Internationale' were on show for the last time at party conferences. Blair was nowhere near such gatherings. His early years in the Labour Party, partly at the time when he shared a flat in London with his fellow-barrister Charlie Falconer, did not involve the kind of infighting that scarred the likes of Mandelson, and when he had his first electoral outing, in the Beaconsfield by-election in 1982, he described himself, safely, as a Labour centrist.

So when in power Blair spoke of his interest in allowing success to flourish, he was not adopting a new line. He was simply letting the old frustration show. He never accompanied his arguments for social justice, and equality of opportunity, with a balancing assault on the well-off and when Brown and he discussed the possibility of a 50 per cent upper tax rate in the run-up to the 1997 election Blair was strongly against an increase. He was certainly concerned not to lose the sympathy of some Conservative newspapers which were being won round to him, or at least tiptoeing towards disinterest, but he had no ideological appetite for higher taxes themselves.

Brown approaches the problem of wealth from the other end. While Blair has spent much of his political life finding a way of reconciling his belief in community obligations to his instinct for success and prosperity, Brown had undergone a transition from the editor of *The Red Paper* who spoke about defeating the logic of capitalism and establishing street committees for an assault on the forces of privilege and power. By the time Brown fought Edinburgh South in 1979, he was a fixture of the conventional left and a pillar of the Scottish party. His attitude to taxation in those days was that the well-off should pay heavily for their success. The Brown of 1979 would not have supported the Brown of 1997 in holding the 40 per cent top rate: he would have been a rigorous pip-squeezer of the rich. At that time, the right was deeply suspicious of him, thinking him too young, too ambitious and far too sure of himself.

The confidence had a good deal to do with a certain kind of rage that he managed to preserve from his more radical days. His book on James Maxton was published in 1986, three years after he became an MP, and his visceral sympathy for the controlled anger that fuelled the Independent Labour Party of the 1920s and 1930s is still obvious. His account of Maxton's life acknowledges the failure of his political ambitions, but his conclusion on the last page is worth quoting. First he cites Maxton's defence of the individual, that 'people must never be allowed to become ants in an ant-hill,' then Brown adds:

Cold, bureaucratic state socialism held no attractions for him. For Maxton the only test of socialist progress was in the improvement of the individual and thus the community. Greater educational opportunities would not only free exceptional people to realize their exceptional talents but allow common people to make the most of their common humanity, and ordinary people to realize their extraordinary potentials. The social equality he supported was not for the sake of equality but for the sake of liberty.

This is as good a summary of Brown's political outlook (or, at least, how he would like to have it interpreted) as there is. In his maiden speech in 1983 he spoke largely about poverty in his own constituency, in which he said that 15,000 people were dependent on means-tested benefits, and that in Scotland by his calculation more than a fifth of the population was living under the poverty line as defined by Whitehall. He went on: 'This is all because the government's philosophy is that the rich must get rich by way of tax cuts and that the poor must become poorer to ensure true prosperity.'

Brown's attitude was anchored in his background. His father was a minister who was more interested in social balm than fire and brimstone. He had often recalled that his family did not seem to want for anything, and though a Church of Scotland manse in the fifties was not usually a luxurious place, it was not uncomfortable either. The message he says he absorbed from his father's way of life and his sermons was that an individual's worth should be treasured and celebrated, and that social divisions should be ignored. This was the egalitarian strain that ran through church and school in Scotland (when they were at their best, though in some places they were often at their worst) and it explains much about Brown's own political wanderings thereafter. Kirkcaldy, where his family moved when he was three, was a typical Scottish town of its size, neither noticeably deprived nor obviously prosperous. There were substantial sandstone houses marching along the seafront, but little ostentatious wealth. The town's reputation elsewhere in Scotland came from a piece of doggerel from a poem of the day describing a train journey through Fife, which every schoolchild knew:

> And ye ken right well, by the queer-like smell,
> That the next stop is Kirkcaldy.

This was a reference to the town's linoleum factory, long gone now, which produced a distinctive pong, almost rivalling the heavy fumes from the Edinburgh breweries on the other side of the Firth of Forth but not as pleasant. More Scots of that generation would know Kirkcaldy for linoleum than for the fact that it produced Adam Smith, author of *Wealth of Nations*, who was the rediscovered hero of the Conservative Party at the time of Brown's arrival at Westminster, his formulation of the practical and moral force of markets having become the platform on which Margaret Thatcher wanted to build a new economy in the eighties. Brown had read Smith, of course, at Edinburgh and returned to him years later when he discovered the late-night delights of the Treasury library where, after clearing his desk, he would repair and reread texts from eighteenth-century Scotland (especially David Hume) which – to the amazement of some less bookish parliamentary colleagues – he said he found relaxing and stimulating.

In his student days and afterwards Brown lived modestly. He was famous for muddle and never even flirted with an elegant phase. When he moved into his own flat in Marchmont Road in Edinburgh in the seventies it retained the flavour of a student nest almost until he left for the house he bought in his constituency in North Queensferry at the end of the eighties. He lived in a cocoon of books and papers in a flat that sometimes felt like a railway junction, because it was a stopping-off place for friends and acquaintances, a trading exchange for political gossip and intrigue and a place where people felt that if they stayed long enough they would eventually meet half of Edinburgh and many of its most interesting visitors. When Brown taught politics at Glasgow College of Technology in the late seventies, and worked in current affairs at Scottish Television in the early eighties, he still lived in Edinburgh and showed no sign at all of wanting to fit himself into a smooth professional mould. Even after he had been an MP for three years or so, when a visiting camera crew from the BBC arrived to film a long interview we found ourselves assisting in clearing a corner of his living room to create a suitable background – a temporary, tidy stage set – so that the subject wouldn't be surrounded by too much clutter. Brown's attitude to his own environment was not that of an aspirant social show-off. He needed enough money only to keep his political ambitions moving. It was never an end in itself.

The only show to interest Brown was on the political stage. He would devote a great deal of energy to political calculation – and, as some rivals in the Scottish Labour Party would have it, ruthlessness. He enjoyed hell-raising on a platform, but he was only Flash Gordon at these public moments. He dressed conservatively and never seemed to want to discard the ties which he had continued to wear even when he was a student railing against the Edinburgh University establishment, standing out from his fellow-troublemakers who were devotees of the stained T-shirt and the Che Guevara beard. By contrast, during his left-wing phase at Aberdeen University and later in Edinburgh politics, Brown's Cabinet colleague Alistair Darling was fashionably decked out in a combat jacket which in those days was a badge of earnestness. Thinking of Brown in a combat jacket is like thinking of Derry Irvine in a kaftan.

The outline of the radical young politician with a traditional side lies somewhere under the current figure of the conservatively dressed Chancellor doing his Whitehall rounds, like the first sketch for a painting lurking behind the final layers of colour. It is the authentic Gordon Brown. When Sarah Macaulay encouraged him to go shopping for new suits, he was persuaded only to choose four at the Savile Row tailors Norton and Townsend that were the 'cheap' cut, at £500 each, indistinguishable from the style of those that he had long favoured, usually dark blue or black with no fancy accoutrements. The four new ones were absolutely identical. They were to be his uniform for work. His wife-to-be was also allowed to choose him a tie for his first Budget, designed by Paul Smith. It was, like many of his other ones, red but with the merest hint of a distinguishing pattern. Brown the impatient intellectual radical of old has always been Brown the conformist about himself. Not much has changed.

Both Blair and Brown are of the generation that grew up while former rigidities of class were loosening, and an old order was turning to dust. It was no longer easy to know someone's social geography precisely. The children of the fifties were the generation that broke free from the austerity visited on their parents yet they were years distant from Thatcher's Children, born in the City big bang and raised to feel no embarrassment about money and material things, ready to chatter happily about the size of their mortgage as if it was another kitchen gadget. Life for that generation was increasingly about doing deals, shopping for financial services, buying PEPs and Tessas and ISAs and learning the language of money. Blair and Brown, in their own ways, reveal personally how difficult this transition has been for Labour. Brown is an uncomfortable propagandist for the world of liquid money and a life of risks, because his character seems set against it. Blair has tried to cast off all embarrassment about money with a swashbuckling defence of enterprise and success, and even a kind of hedonism among the winners who've made it, but he too has found it difficult to find a language which encompasses the public service commitments that are still Labour's boast and the freewheeling life he also admires.

The character who was the emblem of this difficulty in the first term was Geoffrey Robinson. He is a man who always seems to be smiling, even when he is not. He is a cheery glad-hander by nature, in politics and business, and for most of his time in politics he had a great deal to be cheery about. His successful career in the car industry which brought him the chief executive's chair at Jaguar allowed him to build on a fortune which he had been able to amass from his family firm. But it was a career of snakes as well as ladders, and the crash of an up-and-down outfit called TransTec because of its failure to deliver on a Ford contract (a failure of which Robinson has always insisted he was unaware) was expensive, not only in the loss of millions but in providing an episode that, despite his denial of direct investment, has dogged him, giving him the reputation of someone who always enjoyed sailing close to the wind. Robinson is a natural swashbuckler and a man of mystery. He made a fortune in the motor industry, bought a Tuscan *palazzo*, and moved into a Grosvenor House apartment on Park Lane with striped-trousered attendants on call. What other Labour MP can say that a shadowy Belgian millionairess left him a huge legacy which was tucked safely in an offshore trust for a rainy day? Madame de Bourgeois provided one of the exotic pages in the Robinson story which made him a most unlikely intimate of Brown's. Yet he was.

In the opposition years it was Robinson's money which, in part, funded Brown's extensive research operation, costing many tens of thousands of pounds. He oiled the wheels, and became part of the Brown circle, entertaining them and running a kind of permanent economic soirée for the team. Without him Brown's outfit would not have been the well-rehearsed gang it was when he got to the Treasury. Robinson, jovially and generously, gave it its private style.

He subverted Brown's straightforward tastes, and was the playboy of his team. In government it took less than two years for the rollercoaster to come off the rails, and for Robinson to be forced out, causing Blair's first personal crisis and exposing the government's intimate relationships to an unforgiving glare.

Everyone's character was revealed, sometimes cruelly but accurately, in the events that followed Peter Mandelson's request for a loan from Robinson to help him buy a house in the terminally trendy Notting Hill. He needed £373,000 and Robinson was happy to oblige.

When Blair appointed Mandelson to the Department of Trade and Industry in 1998 the arrangement could no longer remain the secret that it had been because Mandelson's ministerial activities could in theory have directly affected Robinson's business concerns. The Prime Minister should have been told. He wasn't. Mandelson's colleagues were astonished when the first leak of the story appeared. In fact it was a leak of a leak, because the information from an early copy of Paul Routledge's unauthorized biography of Mandelson found its way to the *Guardian*. Blair was angry that he hadn't known, and naturally suspicious that the information had come from the Treasury in the knowledge that it would probably force Mandelson from the government. He did not accuse Brown directly, but it deepened his distaste for the Chancellor's circle – led by Charlie Whelan and Ed Balls with sympathetic journalists like Routledge alongside – which he associated, simply, with intrigue and, now, the biggest political embarrassment of his premiership.

The first Mandelson affair threw the government into a state of panic. There was some quiet amusement at his predicament among ministers who feared him, but also mystification. One member of the Cabinet said: 'Peter is somebody who'll give you advice about a problem in a flash. He hardly has to think. In a few seconds he would have told any of us how to neutralize something like this – how to write to the Cabinet Secretary, the permanent secretary and so on – and how to take the sting out. You'd be safe; you'd be covered. But when it's himself, he can't see it.' Mandelson, the master tactician, walked to his doom. The DTI was investigating a company with which Robinson was connected. It was possible to argue that the Department's Chinese walls were sufficiently robust to allow Mandelson to say that it would be absurd to suggest that as Secretary of State he could intervene in a sensitive business investigation of the quasi-judicial sort that is always running inside the department. But the affair had such built-in drama and intrigue that it would not submit to such easy answers. For four days, over the pre-Christmas weekend, Mandelson tried to find a way out of the pit, but on the day before Christmas Eve he tumbled into it.

He tried to rearrange the financing of his house with the help of his family. He insisted that his arrangement with Robinson was a private deal between friends which therefore presented no conflict of interest for either of them. He said he had not breached the Ministerial Code. No law had been broken, no formal government convention had been breached. But, from the beginning, Mandelson's history made his position hopeless.

A good number of Labour MPs were luxuriating in his misfortune, just as he had been photographed luxuriating in a reclining chair in the elegant minimalism of his Notting Hill drawing room. Mandelson, who, in the opposition years could change a career with a raised eyebrow or a whispered word in the leader's office, was faced by well-populated backbenches whose MPs believed that their lowly status could be blamed on him. In this respect, his power was greatly exaggerated, but that hardly mattered. So enthusiastically and stylishly had he played the part of the Prince of Darkness that manoeuvres and plots of which he knew almost nothing were bundled up and laid at his door. Prescott and the others in the Cabinet who resented his power were happy to give the stories a fair wind. So when he began to slip and slide on the stories leaking out about the loan, a section of the party put on its happy face. You could have looked around the Cabinet table and missed the look of grief on the faces of Prescott, Cook, Straw, Blunkett, Mo Mowlam and, of course, Gordon Brown. Mandelson spoke to Blair (when the Prime Minister was in any case preoccupied with the renewed bombing of Iraq) at least twice over the weekend and they tried to find a way of rearranging his finances to wipe the Robinson

slate clean. The effort lasted only two days before it collapsed in a
heap.

Twenty-four hours later they were talking about possible resignation, the moment in such crises when resignation almost always
becomes inevitable. The press was hostile, revelling in a story which
had one of its favourite characters struggling against the kind of
inexorable forces that had damned a series of Tory ministers and
given Labour its pre-election air of moral superiority. The sight of
the Prince sinking in the same muddy pond raised Fleet Street's
spirits in those traditionally quiet news days before Christmas. The
more he persisted in his explanations, in an increasingly desperate
series of interviews, the more it was seen as a fruitless effort to stop
a tide that was bound to overwhelm him. It duly did on Wednesday
morning, Blair having told him straightforwardly the previous night
that resignation was probably inevitable. He sweetened the conversation with the assurance that a clean break would allow the possibility of a quick return to the Cabinet, and an invitation to come to
Chequers for the night after the resignation was evidence that he
meant it. Mandelson knew he would serve a short sentence, and
there would be time off for good behaviour. He was back in the
government, in Belfast, in less than a year.

But Mandelson's conversations with Blair are only one side of
the story. He spoke privately to Brown through the days up to
resignation. Although the revelation about the loan was contained
in Routledge's biography, and was therefore assumed by Mandelson
to come from his contacts and cronies in the Brown circle, the
two old friends spoke in what appears to have been a frank and
emotional way. Despite the relationship's freeze before the election,
they were now thrown together again for a moment. Brown told
Mandelson he wanted to try to help. Mandelson's suspicions of
those around Brown were temporarily eclipsed by the Chancellor's
apparent distress at his predicament, and although he knew that
the Chancellor had almost certainly known of the loan since the
deal had been done in 1996, he did not appear to blame him
directly for the way the story emerged. It seemed as if Mandelson
wanted to believe in Brown's innocence. The closeness wasn't

maintained for long, but for a day or two the pull of the old days almost brought the strange pair together once more. Those closest to Brown insist that despite the hostility which had built up over the leadership question, and the coldness that was often obvious between them, Brown was not one of those who enjoyed watching Mandelson's departure. They corresponded at this time, engaging in the kind of personal contact that had stopped after the falling-out in opposition. In the government's first crisis, the older loyalties did peep through the gloom, but only for a moment. Brown's sympathy was limited, and it was clear from his conversations at the time that he was much more concerned about damage to the government from the affair than the plight of Mandelson. A more cynical view is that Brown, having witnessed the removal he so longed for, could afford to be generous to Mandelson once his departure was inevitable.

As for Blair, he tried to save Mandelson until it became obvious that he could do no more. He was getting advice from Campbell, who knew over the weekend that Fleet Street thought Mandelson was finished, and that ministers seldom survive such judgements. In any case, he had long been aware of Mandelson's penchant for danger, always riding his bike with his hands away from the handlebars. This was true of his private life, of his conversations with journalists which produced colourful descriptions of ministerial colleagues in newspapers without much doubt about the source, and of the kind of impulse that let him accept the loan of a car for the election campaign from James Palumbo, proprietor of the London club, The Ministry of Sound. To some colleagues, anxious to avoid the impression of any financial indebtedness, that seemed rash.

Everyone in Downing Street also knew that Campbell often displayed some semi-public irritation at what he considered Mandelson's egocentricity. 'If he didn't think about himself all the time, we'd all be much better off – including him,' one friend heard him say. Campbell helped him to think through some possible survival strategies over the weekend but it seems certain that he never shared Mandelson's early confidence that the storm would subside in the Christmas glow. He knew that Fleet Street was showing an alarming interest in Robinson's business affairs, and the thrilling confluence of a secret loan, the Robinson millions and Blair's best friend was going to be irresistible. After the weekend he did not try to persuade Mandelson to stay and they both wept when the moment came for Mandelson to admit that his struggle for survival was over. Since then their relationship has never returned to the closeness that bound them together in the run-up to the 1997 election.

The loan affair revealed how tangled this web of feelings and obligations had become. These weren't ministers and advisers making executive decisions round a political board-room table; it was a family in agony. Brown still seems to have been both upset and relieved. Blair was determined that even if the proper course was for Mandelson to go, he was not going to lose his confidant – they wouldn't stop talking for a single day. And Campbell, reading the runes of the government's first public ministerial bust-up, was reinforced in his view that Mandelson, for all his tactical brilliance, always had a phial of poison somewhere on his person. Three years later, that judgement would help to condemn Mandelson once again, this time in circumstances which left him convinced that he had been the victim of an injustice perpetrated in panic. With Robinson, though, there was no such agreement. They both had to go and they knew it.

Compared with the effect of any of the policy arguments of the first couple of years, the Mandelson affair was draining on Blair. He skated along in the polls, which still seemed reluctant to display any serious weakening of the government's support, but he was damaged by it. The public had had its first glimpse of life behind the front door, and sensed the passions and the competing loyalties flowing between those who were in command. For the first time, Blair was pictured as a lonely Prime Minister. He still had the rest of the gang, with Brown the dominant Chancellor at his side, but somehow the world outside Downing Street sensed correctly that Mandelson's departure reinforced in Blair the feeling that continued to disturb him for the rest of the first term – that he was short of Cabinet friends. Any true Blairites were to be found in the learners' pool at the end of the table and not clustered around him in the centre.

Brown, whatever human pangs for Mandelson's plight he might have felt, was certainly strengthened by his departure.

In all the commentaries about the issues of judgement in the affair, Blair noted (though his newspaper reading is thin and selective and usually filtered by Campbell) that it was he who was being fingered as a Prime Minister who did not seem to be in control. Yet Brown had known about the loan for two years, and had also been the champion and protector of Robinson, whom he regarded as something of a magician in devising schemes for bringing public and private money together in capital projects. This rosy view was not shared across Whitehall, and there were places where Robinson's touch was not considered so sure. He was Brown's man. Yet while Brown appeared to shrug off the affair with a wave of his arm and a grunt, Blair saw himself portrayed as the man who had languished in innocence, who hadn't been told about the loan and had been powerless to prevent the self-destruction of Mandelson. Some around Blair fumed at Brown's success in stepping cleanly and completely out of the Robinson affair. The Prime Minister was often referred to in print as 'Teflon Tony', with a surface on which nothing unpleasant would stick. Suddenly it started to be said in Downing Street that an even more remarkable alloy had been developed in Number 11 next door. Brown's reputation never suffered seriously at the hands of Robinson.

There was a flurry in the press about a flat that he bought in an unprepossessing corner of Great Smith Street, Westminster, for £130,000, which had been sold by the receivers dealing with the collapsed empire of Robert Maxwell, but Fleet Street's best efforts failed to come up with anything remotely dodgy about the deal. Brown denied emphatically any knowledge of the flat's connection to a Maxwell company. Everyone concluded that it was indeed a coincidence. The flat in question was a small, plain affair in a grim modern block across the road from Church House, Westminster, and was a telling example of Brown's attitude to his personal finances. It was a good buy, a clever investment and a functional place to live. There was nothing showy about it. The spotlight passed over the Chancellor once more.

This pattern began to irritate some in the Prime Minister's circle. One or two of them who tended to stay out of the playground fights between Blairites and Brownites began to make a point of discussing with journalists the skill of the Chancellor, as they saw it, in being absent in times of trouble. They even argued that when Blair was deep in the Kosovo conflict, playing with the inevitable political risks that military action involves, Brown should have been more supportive publicly, and should have attended more meetings of the Cabinet sub-committee established to monitor the campaign, to which he often sent the Treasury Chief Secretary, then Alan Milburn, to fill in for him. The Treasury argument that diplomatic and military matters were not for the Chancellor, and that his role was only as banker and accountant for the Kosovo policy, was technically correct but by mid-term a view was settling on some of those close to Blair's office: 'Gordon's gone missing again.' It usually meant, they claimed, that there was trouble. Like Macavity the Mystery Cat, he often wasn't there.

As Prime Minister it was Blair who had to clear up after Robinson and Mandelson. Once Mandelson and Robinson were off the scene, however, one enduring problem remained. The Prime Minister, unlike the Chancellor, was stuck with the image of running a party which loved big money.

In opposition, Labour had begun serious fund-raising beyond its traditional base in the eighties under Kinnock. A few business people began to be attracted by reform, and the party worked them hard. Grand dinners were held in fine hotels and the well-heeled began to be drawn into Labour's circle. £500 here, £1,000 there, the occasional cheque for much more – by the time Blair became leader a rather healthy pattern was developing. With his own skills of persuasion he was able to open the pockets of some unlikely donors, businessmen who had never supported Labour before. He did so with the help, above all, of Michael Levy, who had made his fortune in the music industry and became almost a personal fund-raiser for the leader and his party in the mid-nineties. No one is sure how much of Labour's £25 million for the 1997 election campaign he raised, but the estimates go from £7 million to £10 million. By any measure, he has laid a huge clutch of golden eggs. Blair rewarded him with a peerage, and a role as an informal, back-channel Middle East envoy, an arrangement which (naturally) some in the Foreign Office did not like at all. Levy is a hospitable man, entertaining in high style in north London, but he also possesses the instinct for secrecy that makes good business. He seemed to be able to conjure vast sums from dinner guests whom he gathered round to meet and hear the Prime Minister, soliciting the cheques after the departure of Blair, in whose presence the sordid matter of fund-raising was not discussed.

Levy's style is not to everyone's taste. One business figure in Scotland, who was considering a donation to Labour, was outraged to be approached by Levy and asked the blunt question: 'How much are you worth?' He declined to answer. Later he complained to the Labour Party directly, claiming that Levy had followed up his first question with the suggestion that he might consider giving a million pounds, which is what Levy thought he could afford. Labour received nothing as a result.

This was the consequence of Labour's realization in the nineties that it was going to have to replicate the Conservatives' well-tuned methods of corporate and individual fund-raising to finance ever more expensive election campaigns. Though Blair argues that legislation passed in 2000 will put a hold on the ambitions of the super-rich to buy into political parties by placing limits on individual donations, stopping contributions from overseas and opening up detailed accounts to public scrutiny, his first term was financed by methods which had traditionally been attacked and scorned by Labour. It left him open to the charge that the 'purer than pure' government was behaving in exactly the same way as Tory governments of the past which it sought to portray as prey to special interests.

It was Levy who was instrumental in guiding to the Prime Minister's office one of the most unwelcome guests of the whole first term, unwelcome in the sense that he turned out to be the bearer of embarrassment and near-scandal. In the view of some members of the Cabinet – perhaps most – Bernie Ecclestone, the boss of Formula 1, should never have been allowed there. His route to the

Prime Minister was assisted by having as one of his advisers David Ward, who acted as a lobbyist for Formula 1 (he is mad about fast cars) and was formerly on the staff of John Smith. He has a high personal reputation with many Labour Party insiders and his presence at Ecclestone's side certainly smoothed his path. With Ward's help, and Levy's knowledge on the grapevine that Ecclestone was considering a large donation, he was invited into Downing Street.

Men like Ecclestone enjoy the frisson of the chief executive's handshake, and nothing less will do. The fact that his offer of a million pounds came at a time when the government was engaged in a sensitive and complicated argument about the future of tobacco advertising, a staple of Formula 1's success, was a disaster for Blair. To the outside world it was either conspiratorial or naive. Neither is an attractive prime ministerial trait.

So Levy's influence was valuable to Blair but dangerous, too. He operated from within the 'high value donation unit' – as might be guessed from its title, located in the party's Millbank headquarters, where politics was translated routinely into the style and practice of management. It was from this office that strange signals would sporadically emerge. Levy's deputy, Amanda Delew, wrote in one party memo not long after the 1997 election: 'Major donors expect to be invited to Number 10. If this cannot take place then income levels may be affected.' This memo, which reads like something addressed to a supermarket sales team, was discussing how far the door of the Prime Minister's office should be opened to the rich and generous. Blair's Downing Street has never operated on the scale of Bill Clinton's White House, where nights in the Lincoln Bedroom were arranged for important donors, but the natural desire to make the 'new' party a rich and successful one as well as the natural party of government brought some new habits.

Just as the first Mandelson resignation cast a shaft of light into the heart of the government and allowed outsiders to see the forces which drove it, so his second departure was the most telling and alarming political event Blair had to face in approaching the re-election campaign. Even more than the horrors of a foot and mouth crisis apparently mismanaged by the Ministry of Agriculture, which had long since become an object of contempt in his office – 'useless' was Blair's own description of the officials in charge at MAFF – the dangers posed by another Mandelson affair, in which an uncomfortable link between money and influence in government was again suggested, seemed to sound an ominous knell. The argument about what Mandelson said in a phone call to a junior Home Office minister, Mike O'Brien, about a passport application for the Hinduja brothers became secondary. The Hindujas gave a donation of £1 million to fund the Faith Zone of the Dome – although the subsequent tax liability to the New Millennium Experience Company and tickets given to the family reduced the value of their donation to around £365,000. As well as 1,000 free tickets, their complimentary entrance passes were generous – allowing them, if they had wanted, to take a party of sixty people into the Dome free every day of the year. The controversy surrounding their name was persistent enough to ensure that any donation – even for a quasi-religious display in the Dome – was politically sensitive. The worry for Blair was the fear that there might be more awkward questions to come, and the knowledge that there were newspaper libraries with extensive collections of pictures of him as Prime Minister with the Hindujas unsettled him. Money, power, favours and friends became too potent a cocktail.

The report into the whole affair by Sir Anthony Hammond QC is not a document that explains Mandelson's resignation. It merely describes the confusion and uncertainty that surrounded a sensitive matter in which two brothers whose activities had long been the subject of warnings to the government from the security and intelligence agencies appeared to be able to get access to ministers which looked too easy. Unlike the Robinson affair of 1998, this one was not going to be allowed to run on. Although the first story of Mandelson's alleged role in supporting a passport application, which appeared in the *Observer*, did not signal the end of the Northern Ireland Secretary, within a few days Downing Street had decided that he must go. When Mandelson arrived in Blair's office it was to find the Prime Minister drafting a resignation statement for him. He emerged in a scene of memorable distress to say that he had decided to leave the government, and a few hours later he sat beside Blair shorn of his habitual jauntiness on the front bench in the Commons to listen to rampant Conservative mockery. Blair looked as if he had suffered a family bereavement: he and Mandelson had the look of a ruined couple. The closest of his friendships had been severed by the government's anxiety about its rich friends and its network of hangers-on, and the fear that the catch-all label of sleaze might yet stick to Labour in the way that Blair had managed to affix it to Major before the 1997 election.

The second Mandelson affair revealed how nervous Blair was about the danger that seemed to attach to his old friends – 'not again' was the Downing Street phrase of the moment – and something close to panic about the taint of bad money. There was nothing for it but a clean break. Mandelson would remain a friend, in more regular contact than almost any Labour MP knew, but his Cabinet career had to be terminated again. Blair's fear of another scandal was such that he had no doubt he must go.

Labour knew how sensitive these matters were. The party was awash with cash in the mid-nineties. The preparations for the 1997 election had identified a treasure trove of donations, and it seemed that everyone now wanted to be part of Blair's 'project'. They seemed likely to stay in power: why not jump on board? For those with the money to play a hunch, what was the sensible alternative?

Although the defence offered around Downing Street of the big donors was that none had landed the leader in as much trouble as William Hague found with Michael Ashcroft, Belize financier and Conservative Party treasurer, the gloss of New Labour was sometimes tacky to the touch. The early showbiz parties (discreetly toned down as the years went by) and the luring of such donors as the Tory philanthropist and businessman Christopher Ondaatje allowed the government to be portrayed as an outfit dazzled by the rich. The image was dangerous for Blair, because it meant, for example, that when the Millennium Dome became the butt of a national joke or the phrase 'Cool Britannia' became decidedly un-cool, he could be pictured as flighty rather than serious, a stylist and performer rather than a deliverer. This infuriated Downing Street, of course, when Blair was deep in the hands-on diplomacy and negotiations of Northern Ireland or Kosovo but it was an image that left its mark.

The government therefore developed a peculiar double personality. It was half-Prudence and half-Good-Time Girl. Brown's persona as Chancellor was uncompromisingly grim. From the start, he was the dark-suited bank manager gloomily wondering about the state of the overdraft. He wouldn't break his fiscal rules, invented by him and policed by him, and would never be anything but prudent. He would produce record levels of public investment, he said, but in his own good time. This attitude of unbending solemnity suited him, of course. There was a time, after a year or so at the Treasury, when it was suggested that he should try to smile more during television interviews. The party was concerned that he was appearing too dogged and downbeat. But give Brown a microphone and a camera and he is serious. It is his nature. His three-point plans, occasionally extending to ten-point plans, are famously grim litanies for interviewers to tangle with, and his style developed in government into a verbal reflection of his physical black-suited presence at the dispatch box or on the Treasury steps. He was immovable.

His policy was his personality. Having exerted a discipline on shadow Cabinet colleagues which would have been unimaginable a decade earlier (in the days when policy was made on the hoof in the Commons, and often didn't last until the end of the day) he was utterly convinced that success for the government depended on the tone being maintained in government. It did not make him popular. Though the City of London began to see a Chancellor who seemed to believe in the stability it held so dear, despite his refusal to put on a white tie for the Lord Mayor at his Mansion House dinner, the Labour Party felt uneasy. One minister recalls the early days: 'To be quite honest I dreaded going to my party meetings in the constituency. They were horrible. Here we were, the Labour government with the biggest majority in history and we were being told there were all sorts of things we couldn't do. Well, my people wanted them done. There's no doubt that when this government started, Gordon was not appreciated.' Yet everything had prepared him for this. No one could imagine a new Brown appearing at the dispatch box in a light grey suit, grinning from ear to ear and playing the economy like an accordion. Even when he produced his Budget surprises, at least one in each year's box, they were rabbits that seemed to be allowed out of the hat on sufferance. If they didn't behave, they were to go straight back in.

The first year was a difficult one for Brown. Although he was able to start to lay the foundations for the minimum wage, the welfare-to-work programme and to introduce some significant City reforms as well as give the Bank of England independence on interest rates, he found the euro tripping him up and in the spring he had the unhappy sight of a motion being debated at the Scottish Labour Party conference – and carried – which described reductions in benefits for lone-parent families as 'economically inept, morally repugnant and spiritually bereft'. The selection of words was guaranteed to send the Chancellor into a whirlwind rage, from which there was no chance of his backing down. He was the Iron Chancellor who would not bend, however hot the flames, and it was the image he cultivated just as naturally as he would conduct one of his broadcast interviews, refusing to give any ground. He had worked it out in his own mind, and that was that.

This was a political strength for Brown, despite the grumblings from his backbenches in the early days, with interest rates going up and a rigid spending regime in place. He was able to appear the solid figure alongside Blair whom it was impossible to imagine being dislodged. He spoke and answered questions on his own terms; he was resolutely a party man with no time for the rhetoric of the 'third way' or PR; he was assiduous in his conversations with backbenchers, trying to evangelize them in support of a fiscal attitude which those of them who had thought about it had never expected to see from a Labour government. He had one message: he would be the first Labour Chancellor who would finish a full term with a reputation which would rest principally on his management of the economy. That was the purpose of it all. In political terms, and crucially in terms of the media, Brown was massively successful. Four years of his dour uncompromising surface and barrage of statistics effectively machine-gunned any critics. When the electorate came to judge Labour's first term, the economy was hardly on the political agenda. He had made Labour safe, it seemed.

Brown's worst period coincided, of course, with Blair's. The troubled summer of 2000 reached its climax with the fuel disputes of the autumn. The danger for Blair was that he would look like a Prime Minister who was losing touch with the everyday concerns of the country; the danger for Brown, at least in his own mind, was that he might look like a Chancellor who could be pushed around. Where Blair instinctively tries to put himself in the position of those who are demanding a change of course – his technique is to try to demonstrate his sympathy with their complaint, and to mollify their feelings – Brown is more inclined to restate the policy and simply declare that if it is properly implemented it will work. This was illustrated neatly at a press conference in 2001 when the two sat side by side at Millbank, as they often did, to answer early morning questions. They were asked about the discontent felt by travellers on the railways. Brown laid out the policy – a thing of facts and figures – almost without taking breath. Coming in, Blair's message was, in effect: 'I feel your pain.' It was an encapsulation of their different instincts. In the fuel protests Blair was shaken by the image of chaos which was building up; Brown's concern was directed principally to making sure that no policy mistakes were made in conceding a quick victory to fuel protesters in a way that would prejudice his long-term economic game. Brown insisted that no immediate concession be made to the fuel protesters, reckoning correctly that the coherence of the protest would unravel as time passed. When, in his autumn statement, Brown finally acknowledged the issue, he was hailed. It was a command performance of economic authority.

Brown's handling of the fuel crisis was a microcosm of the two comprehensive spending reviews that dominated the first two years of the government. Brown had his disciplined strategy; he believed it would provide the revenues the government would want for public investment to build up into the first years of the century; he would give no ground. The first review was tough. Ministers who had expected to be able to argue politically for the exemptions and exceptions which are the stuff of spending negotiations with the Treasury found their paths blocked. Defence, in particular, found the Chancellor unsympathetic to their claims for increased spending. But they later found that Blair had been affected by the Kosovo crisis and the performance of senior military figures in it. He was on their side. So the then defence secretary, George Robertson, and Sir Charles Guthrie, the chief of staff, appealed directly to Number 10 over the Chancellor's head. They won. Brown was unconvinced by their arguments, and made it clear to Blair that he did not accept the settlement which the Prime Minister had approved. But of all the decisions in the two comprehensive spending reviews, this was the only significant one in which the Prime Minister most obviously took control. Otherwise, it was Brown's regime that ruled.

As the end of the first term approached, the same minister who confessed that he had found constituency party meetings difficult in the first years said: 'Nowadays, it's all forgotten. Gordon is God.' Apart from his stumble over pensions – the 75p increase was a piece of calculation that, unusually for Brown, misjudged the party mood rather badly – he was beginning to emerge as a consciously redistributive Chancellor. He spoke about poverty, and the minimum wage and the welfare-to-work scheme and more generous pensions – this was the message the party wanted to hear. While Blair began to try to lead his party on to yet another mine-strewn battlefield in the public services, opening up the debate about how best to inject private money without undermining the ethos of state provision, Brown was moving, rhetorically, in another direction. To listen to their speeches you might have imagined them in different governments, or at least in competing factions. They chose to emphasize different things – Blair talking about the need for radical solutions to pressing problems of public funding, Brown about the importance of creating a more equal society. They argued that the two were compatible, two sides of the same coin. If that was true, it was also true that their two faces were on different sides. In making the government's case they often seemed to take the same policy and interpret it in two entirely contrasting ways – Brown emphasizing his objective of pursuing a policy that was a development of what he was almost willing to say was socialist thinking, Blair arguing that if the urge to reform was allowed to slacken the old ways would return and decline would set in. In Labour Party terms they often sounded as if Brown was the traditionalist and Blair the iconoclast.

In the debate about the funding of private services, Brown appeared in his speeches to be the Chancellor who was trying to adapt the policies required in the new century to Labour's traditional instincts. While Blair was as impatient as ever, a weathervane searching for a new wind, Brown was playing the part of the reassurer. Compared with the Brown who alarmed his party after 1997 with his sternness, this was a Chancellor who wanted to reconnect to old networks.

Their public and private attitudes to money make up a prism through which it's possible to glimpse their characters. Brown retains an urge to redistribute wealth, though he has no interest in creating the kind of socialist society to which he was once committed, while Blair, although he argues the same case for 'fairness' and equality of opportunity as Brown, is relaxed about rich people remaining rich. It does not embarrass him.

Many of the Blair government's family problems were connected to money and its place in Labour's life. If it was to be 'New' Labour, surely the old nervousness about the rich must go. But if it was to be 'New' Labour it must also retain an ascetic probity, a sense of a government unbesmirched by the 'Loadsamoney' culture that had become such a part of the prosperous, devil-may-care nineties. In the personalities of its leading pair, it found an ideal solution: Blair the easy-going meritocrat, comfortable holidaying in Tuscan luxury; Brown the image of restraint down to the cut-price champagne at his own wedding.

Wearing their contrasting robes, they often find themselves together on a mission – or in arguing a case – and realize that although their political strength lies in staying together as a pair, they are pushing as hard as they can inside the relationship to nurture their own approaches and their own political personalities. Only by seeming to strain against each other can they claim for

Labour the broad, inclusive, political territory necessary to secure their place in power. In their approach to money, the big tent of politics is shown at its most inclusive. It was a technique, and an expression, that had a very specific origin that owed little to Dunfermline or Sedgefield, however, and rather more to Hope, Arkansas.

9
Brother-in-Arms

Bill Clinton was famous in the White House for losing his temper. He would rage. Especially when he was sinking into the mire of the Monica Lewinsky affair in the last two years of his presidency, he was capable of spectacular explosions which would erupt without warning and turn the President into a red-faced screamer. Blair was stoking up one of these Vesuvial displays during the preparations for the Kosovo war. Those who witnessed one telephone call made from the Oval Office to Blair in May 1999 knew that Clinton was displaying the telltale signs of an approaching storm and, since he and Blair spoke often enough to have dispensed with any need for diplomatic niceties, his staff expected the skies to break open.

The President was calling to remind the Prime Minister of the nature of their relationship. Friends they might be, but one was the leader of a modest European power and the other was President of the United States. Clinton saw no case for sending American ground troops to Kosovo to expel the Serb forces of Slobodan Milosevic until the bombing campaign which had begun in March had done its work – he'd told the American people in a televised speech on the first day of the bombing, 'I do not intend to put our troops in Kosovo to fight a war.' Blair disagreed. He was, according to a close adviser, 'possessed by that war' which he had spoken of as a moral crusade and had decided that, despite the reservations of other European countries and the United States, a ground force should be assembled. But Clinton was incensed. He spoke to Blair, in a conversation described by someone who heard it at the Washington end as 'testy', and the purpose was to remind him who was the senior partner in the operation. American troops would be committed by Clinton, not by Blair.

The conversation was remarkable not because it was tense and deliberately blunt on Clinton's side, but because it was the first time he and Blair had had an important strategic disagreement and, in the end, it occurred without the usual explosion. The President came close to letting loose one of his famous rages, which were kept private and seen only by West Wing staff or political intimates, a group in which Blair could be counted. But he was spared the blast. The call was evidence to those who heard of it in Whitehall and in Washington of how important the relationship had become to both of them. Blair was prepared to push Clinton to the limit; Clinton was prepared to control his temper, even with someone with whom he was accustomed to behave quite naturally and who he knew wouldn't mind hearing him in full ranting mode.

Afterwards, Blair did admit that they had had a frank conversation about his determination to prepare for a ground invasion. 'The bottom line for me was that we can't lose this,' he said in an interview on the American PBS network later that year. He insisted that Clinton had never ruled out using ground troops against Serb forces if they did not withdraw and allow the ethnically cleansed Albanian refugees to retrace the path of their trek through the hills and to return home. He knew, however, that Clinton was deeply reluctant to move, knowing that public opinion was unlikely to support a dangerous campaign and that few Americans had even the fuzziest idea of where or what Kosovo was. The Joint Chiefs of Staff were against a ground assault, and Clinton had no interest in trying to change their minds. Blair was as open about the fact that he believed a ground war might become necessary to back up the air campaign as Clinton was determined that it should never come to that.

The crisis was the moment when their relationship matured. It was also the most dangerous moment to date of Blair's premiership, as he acknowledged to his staff. There was no public appetite for a costly ground war, and in the Labour Party there was deep unease about NATO's airborne campaign against Serbia and Milosevic. After the seventy-eight days of bombing started in March, Blair spoke of the war as a moral duty. 'I was convinced that once we started it, we had to finish it. If we hadn't done so, it would have really given encouragement to dictators everywhere,' he said. He was on a course from which he was not prepared to deviate, and it was Clinton who felt that he had to try to calm the crusader spirit which was evident in Downing Street and the Foreign Office for what he suspected might be a step too far. But in the arguments between London and Washington Clinton had played something of the big brother to Blair.

For each of them the alliance was important. Clinton's staff believe that in the last two years of his presidency he spoke to Blair for longer than to all other world leaders put together. In Downing Street, Clinton is known to have had a huge personal influence on Blair. One of his aides involved in liaison with Washington even claiming that the political links between them ran as deep as any Blair had at home, apart from those with Brown. The connection with Clinton has been one of the most important strands of Blair's premiership, a personal channel that brought him political benefits, particularly in Northern Ireland, and also did a good deal to shape his style. They became so close that when he rang the White House in January 1998 to tell Clinton, 'I'm thinking of you', in the midst of the Lewinsky scandal that had seized Washington and was threatening his presidency, it was more than a polite gesture from a leader doing the right thing.

Apart from fighting a Balkans war, keeping a warlike presence to back up sanctions against Iraq and negotiating in Northern Ireland, they talked more and more as time went on about their own political obsession – the search for a language to describe the politics that they called, vaguely, 'the third way'. They developed an intimate friendship, though Blair had moments of incomprehension at Clinton's sexual escapades and confessed privately that he found some of Clinton's behaviour 'weird'.

Their first encounter was just after Clinton's election in 1992 in the campaign against George Bush Sr in which Clinton had styled himself a New Democrat. Labour had lost the General Election under Kinnock six months before Clinton's victory and Blair and

Brown decided together to go to the United States in January 1993 to try to identify the trick they had missed. The Democrats had successfully challenged a sitting right-of-centre President who was campaigning on a promise of 'no new taxes'. Clinton had somehow neutralized the tax question, appealing to traditional Democrat voters with an economic programme promising help for the lower-paid, while reassuring vast swathes of relatively prosperous suburban America where Republicans had been winning elections for a generation that his social thinking was no threat. It would be odd if there weren't lessons to be learnt from Clinton's experience. And anyway, Clinton was about to be President of the United States. So the New Labour embryos decided to go.

At home, their leader, John Smith, was not pleased. When reports began to come from Washington about Labour's 'coming men' riding into town, he rang Mandelson in a fury. What were Blair and Brown up to? Although Mandelson had just been elected for the first time in Hartlepool and was no longer a party official, Smith knew that he would be aware of exactly what was happening on the trip. He had always been suspicious of Mandelson, and immune to his charms, but this was an angrier Smith than Mandelson had ever experienced. The burden of the leader's complaint was that Blair and Brown were taking it upon themselves to import American ideas to the Labour Party. Why? He wanted to know the whole story, because he was suspicious that they were up to something. Of course, he was right. Smith bluntly rejected the need to study the Democratic example. The media baron and Labour supporter Clive Hollick had received a similar response six months earlier when, inspired by the Democrats, he wrote a memo called 'Campaign '96', in which he argued for 'a new Labour Party, new policies on tax and trade union links'. He presented these findings at a meeting with John Smith, Murray Elder and David Ward, Smith's policy adviser. Smith's reply reflected his confidence that Labour did not need to embrace the risk of radical change but could just wait for the Conservatives to implode: 'This is all very interesting, but I think you will find that it will be our turn next time.'

But Blair and Brown were plunging into bracing waters in Wash-

ington, refreshing themselves with the feeling of being among winners. From the moment they arrived there it seemed inevitable that
the place would influence their outlook. The Clinton phenomenon,
even then, seemed to Blair to be the kind of transformation in a
political atmosphere that Labour should one day try to achieve.
For Brown, his book-bags bulging with political biographies and
economic texts, it was his dream city: everyone talked about politics,
all the time. Obsessives were welcome. Brown would charge through
the bookshops like a hoover, scooping up every political commentary
he could find, while Blair was getting to know the diplomat at the
British Embassy on Massachusetts Avenue who had been assigned
to the Clinton campaign as the Foreign Office watcher, Jonathan
Powell. Blair and the gangly, bubble-haired Powell, who had helped
to plan the visit, have a natural physical symmetry. They gesticulate.
Their enthusiasm is wide-eyed and they are instinctive people-
watchers and gossips. So the two found themselves feeding each
other's enthusiasm. Politics in that freezing January seemed fun.
Washington was expectant. Back in London, Labour had nothing
to look forward to, except five or so years of opposition. A weary,
grey Kinnock was gone after nine embattled years as leader and
although the two shadow Cabinet ministers knew that they would
prosper under Smith's tutelage, and although they still counted
themselves his close friends, they also expected a period in the party
when their modernization plans were less prized in the leader's office
than they had been. So they focused on Clinton: how had he fought
a campaign in which he said there was one issue – the famous sign
on his wall said 'it's the economy, stupid' – while dealing with the
tax question that had bedevilled the two last Democratic presidential
candidates and had haunted Kinnock? They wanted cheerful news
for a change.

The trip was also a first, symbolic break with party thinking at
home. In retrospect, Blair has identified it as a moment when a new
vista opened up. Clinton was managing to harness some old Democrat principles of 'fairness' to a social agenda that reassured middle-
income voters that they wouldn't find his administration a drag on
their ambition – exactly the message that Blair and Brown would

decipher and imprint on the Labour Party. But the intellectual departure would not be welcomed universally at home.

Two days after Clinton's inauguration, Prescott appeared on *Weekend World* on ITV and dismissed the Democrats as an outfit with nothing to teach Labour. Criticizing the advertising techniques and outside advisers who had clustered round Kinnock's office up to the election, he laid into the Democrats for engaging in cosmetic politics. 'It's not about strengthening a party – all the ideas from Clinton are an elite few running a party on the basis of the information they get from the polls. That is not the way the Labour Party has been run, and while we've tried it in the last couple of elections, it does seem that we've lost, doesn't it?' Prescott particularly enjoyed making the attack on a programme on which Mandelson had worked as a producer in the early eighties. He warmed to his theme: 'I do not think it's been proven that Clinton won the election because he broke his contacts with the trade unions . . . We've gone chasing the extra two per cent from the Liberals on this basis: if we get rid of the vested interest . . . we could have proportional representation. This has dominated our thinking. That is Clintonism.' Whatever it was, Blair and Brown were keen on it.

Some groundwork had been done over the previous five years. After the 1987 campaign one of the Democrats' veteran pollsters, Joe Napolitan, had written a report for Labour which expressed surprise that it was not employing the relatively new techniques of focus group research which, he argued, would identify much more clearly the voters' reasons for refusing to turn to Labour. In the years that followed, Philip Gould developed those techniques and by the early nineties, to the sound of contemptuous snorts from some on the left who saw them as another piece of Mandelsonian wizardry, it was established as Labour's way.

After the '92 election, American advice poured in. Stan Greenberg was the Democrat pollster who turned up in 1993 to try to impart the lessons of the Clinton campaign, on which Gould had worked. Between them they persuaded Blair and Brown that Clinton's experience could explain how to approach the economic issue. Labour had to resist promising what people did not believe they could deliver, but at the same time convince them they could promise them opportunity. What could be simpler? With the evidence of what the Conservatives had successfully pinned on Labour in the campaign ('Labour's tax bombshell'), it was this advice that helped to persuade them that the promises of Labour in opposition had to be underpinned by a commitment to fiscal discipline that voters would believe.

The other message from the Clinton campaign was, of course, that in fighting against an incumbent who was struggling with the economy there was no point in devoting every speech and every statement to criticism that sounded negative. There had to be 'hope', a natural word for Clinton to use for the corny reason that he came from Hope, Arkansas. So when Blair and Brown went to Washington they encountered a campaign team that had somehow translated the language of attack – against the Bush economic record – into something that seemed uplifting. It was what Labour had never been able to do at any time since Blair and Brown were in their early teens.

Both were fascinated by American politics. Brown's first visit had been to the Democratic Convention in San Francisco in 1984, where Walter Mondale was the presidential nominee preparing a challenge to Ronald Reagan that led to disaster. He said taxes would have to go up. His defeat gave a rampant Reagan a landslide second term. Brown watched the convention from the floor, absorbed in the politics of the Democrats' effort to find a way of thwarting Reagan, the Great Conservative. It was a catastrophe comparable to Labour's 1983 failure against Thatcher, but there was much to learn.

The first thing Brown heard when he arrived in San Francisco from London and stood at the back of the convention hall was a speech from Jesse Jackson talking about the young who felt dispossessed and in despair. Jackson said he wanted them to have 'hope in their brains, not dope in their veins'. Brown was aware that this was a preacher's style more suited to Harlem than downtown Dunfermline, but he repeated the phrase for days, apparently fascinated by how such a glib formulation could be turned to political uses. The other memorable speech at that convention was the speech of the Governor of New York, Mario Cuomo, about poverty and opportunity which brought him national celebrity and gave some lustre to an event which would otherwise be remembered only as a defeat in the making.

Brown's visit, which ended in his first immersion in Washington, made a profound impression on him. He saw a Democratic Party going through many of the same contortions that Labour was suffering, though without the implacable institutional party difficulties, and it was in the United States that he began to try to find ways of resolving the conflicts between his instincts as a socialist and the economic world that was beginning to take shape in the eighties. When the century ended he was still using the United States as a sounding board. Apart from his inevitable involvement with the George W. Bush administration, and the obsession shared with every finance minister for each utterance by Alan Greenspan, the chairman of the Federal Reserve, it was to America that Brown turned for new ideas – on welfare, particularly.

The 1984 visit wasn't simply a quick dip in America for Brown. It was obvious to all of us there that he was starting an affair with the place which has gone on ever since. Though he found himself in San Francisco dressed more for Edinburgh than California, it didn't stop him heading for the mountains of Yosemite National Park, in a suit. By the time he got back to London a few weeks later he was hooked on the USA.

Between them Blair and Brown were a pair who found the Americans at the right moment. Brown had fought four elections for Labour, the first as a losing candidate, and Blair three. They were impatient for a Labour government.

The Democrat evidence encouraged them in their view that Labour could not afford to wait for Major's government to make mistakes and expect to reap the automatic benefit. Smith was utterly committed to some aspects of party reform, but Brown and Blair felt that the years ahead might be overcautious. Smith's gifts at the dispatch box were well known, but the lesson from the United States was that bashing Major would not be enough. The 1992 conference had been turned from the familiar Labour post-election wake into something different by Black Wednesday and the chaos of exit from the ERM. Politics was awash with stories of Major having come close to breakdown (much exaggerated), of the Chancellor, Norman Lamont, 'singing in the bath' despite the disaster, delighting in the break with fixed exchange rates. The Conservative government was sagging on the ropes. Labour enjoyed a false flush of optimism.

But neither Blair nor Brown believed that the next election could be won simply by claiming that Labour would be better than a bad bunch. Brown, appointed shadow Chancellor by Smith, had already decided that he should maintain a ruthless command of the party's spending plans. It was a decision which was reinforced by the 1993 visit to Washington.

They were hypnotized by Clinton's early days. And paradoxically, Blair absorbed one early lesson that had little to do with winning elections. After his first visit in 1993, during which Clinton's supporters had been talking of the whirlwind first months about to start in the White House, he watched in fascination as the new President stumbled into a series of political elephant traps and seemed about to throw away the advantages of goodwill he had won in the campaign. He became embroiled, most notably, in a row about gays in the military as a result of his desire to fulfil a campaign pledge to some of the interest groups which had supported his campaign. It turned into an ugly social battle which opened up old wounds and gave Clinton, the new Commander-in-Chief, unnecessary trouble with a military establishment that was already suspicious of him. Alongside that problem he found himself in a pickle over the MX missile programme. In the White House he had made the blunder of appointing a schoolboy friend, Mack McLarty, as chief of staff without establishing first whether he was up to the job. He wasn't. The place was running at half speed. From across the Atlantic, Blair was bemused. He had expected Slick Willie and he saw Blundering Bill. After he became leader he remembered this as clearly as he remembered Clinton's skill in the campaign. He told the shadow Cabinet before the 1997 election: 'Never forget that it's easy to throw it all away in six months.'

Clinton's slide to the Democrats' disaster in the mid-term elections of 1994 seemed to be an undoing of the campaign themes that he used to such effect in 1992. He'd been hammered by the populist Republican Newt Gingrich and his anti-government message, all tax cuts and lower federal spending. Clinton's response in the next two years was to absorb the evident rage of the electorate and, to the anger of some of his strongest supporters, to tailor his social and economic policies to assuage those feelings. Liberals were despondent, but fortunately for him the Gingrich revolution on Capitol Hill spiralled out of control. Clinton was able to force the Republicans into a Budget crisis which at one point briefly shut down the whole Federal Government (because there was no authority to pay day-to-day bills), after which he was able to present himself as the defender of government programmes like medicare and social security against the radicals of the right. It saw him through the 1996 re-election campaign.

Blair's first proper meeting with Clinton was in the spring of that election year in Washington. The agent of the rendezvous was Sidney Blumenthal, a writer on *The New Yorker* who had become convinced in the eighties that the Governor of Arkansas, though young and Washington-innocent, was a good bet for 1992. Blumenthal played his hunch in the magazine, got to know the Clintons and such was the chemistry that he found himself translated eventually to the White House as special assistant to the President after Clinton's 1996 victory. There he sat in the boiler room of the Clinton political operation, a natural adviser and campaigner, gripped by the melodramatic dips and dives of American politics. He comes from Chicago, where at the age of twelve he spent his first campaign as a precinct runner for the famed Democratic Party machine, and saw his first presidential candidate at a torchlit Kennedy rally in 1960. Leaving newspapers for magazines in the early nineties, Blumenthal was becoming more interested in Bill Clinton than journalism. Having met Blair on his 1993 visit he was a natural host in 1996 when the Labour leader came to Washington and he gave a dinner for Blair at his home to introduce him to Hillary Clinton. The next day, Blair spent an hour at the White House with her husband.

When Blumenthal joined Clinton's staff, part of his job was to develop the network with Labour which had been growing for years, in the expectation that Blair would be in Downing Street within a year. The relationship was carefully planned, and was certainly helped by Clinton's desire to make a contrast with the White House–Downing Street relationship in the Major years.

It had been undermined by Clinton's stubborn belief that during his 1992 campaign Major's government had helped his Republican opponents to scour Home Office records to find any information that might be held on Clinton from his time as a Rhodes Scholar in Oxford in the sixties. The story, broken by Blumenthal himself during the 1992 campaign, was that the Republicans hoped to turn up something embarrassing, perhaps a drugs revelation, that would damage Clinton. No matter that Major denied it, the Home Secretary denied it and the American ambassador in London at the time – Ray Seitz – denied it. Clinton believed that there had been a dirty deal, and he never forgot it. As a result his relationship with Major was civil, and at times verged on warmth, but was never close. When Blair came along in 1997, Clinton knew not only that they shared some political ideas about how to harness a market economy for public purposes but that whoever Blair was, he was not Major. The consequence for Blair was an even jauntier welcome than he might otherwise have received.

While Blair, as opposition leader, was matching Clinton and getting regular memos from Philip Gould on Clinton's re-election campaign, Brown was developing his own distinctive network across the Atlantic. He was especially fascinated by Robert Reich, Clinton's first Secretary of Labor, who left the administration in the first term fed up with Clinton's paling social objectives and apparent fiscal conservatism. His willingness to go as far as he did in compromising with the Republican majority on Capitol Hill over the federal budget distressed Reich, who became disillusioned with the drift. In the Labor Department, he was well known for his frustration and, for the e-mails which arrived regularly from his wife, a left-wing economist, which often circulated round the office. One of the regular refrains was: 'Your President is an asshole.' Reich went.

In office, while Blair developed his own relationship with Clinton (Chancellors not being involved in wars, peace negotiations and missiles) Brown renewed his own links. His key contact became Larry Summers, now president of Harvard, and Clinton's last Treasury Secretary. Summers is a large, jowly, jovial man who was known in the White House as a somewhat shambling figure, whose shirt tail often dangled behind him. He liked Brown when they became involved in the inevitable business of G8 summits and the IMF at which the administration and the Blair government were always doing deals. Summers had taught Ed Balls when he was a Kennedy Scholar at Harvard in the eighties and he had first met Brown in the course of the 1993 visit when he was deputy Treasury Secretary to Lloyd Bentsen.

Brown became fascinated by the American economists who were in Summers's circle. He began to take holidays on Cape Cod. Anyone who thought Brown was heading for Massachusetts for a spot of whale-watching or gentle surfing on the Atlantic swell was mistaken. He would head off to a small town called Wellfleet, on the curve of the tail of Cape Cod, south of Provincetown. This was the summer home to a group of American economists who cluster there, like painters at St Ives but with calculators instead of oils in their beach bags.

Labour MPs would not be surprised to find Brown there, as happy as a sandboy. Among those who go there for the summer are the economists Barry Bluestone and Bob Kuttner, who is sometimes described as the nearest American equivalent to Old Labour. Summers comes down from Harvard and is in some ways the centrepiece of this beachside salon. It is a congenial atmosphere for Brown: books, talk, social theories, with the odd tennis match to stretch a muscle or two. He couldn't imagine a happier way of spending a summer holiday.

In his effort to build a bridge between his intellectual background and the marketplace in which the Treasury has to operate he finds American ideas on welfare stimulating. How do you balance an assault on welfare dependency with proper care for social provision? How can a tax system be geared to encourage enterprise but lift the low-paid, especially against the background of an American tradition tilted against direct provision by the state? His Treasury officials say that Brown comes back from the United States, every time, as if he's found a new supply of adrenalin.

Blair has not been to Wellfleet. It would not be his scene. A beach barbecue with economists, with their Laffer curves and growth theories and graphs, comes near to his idea of hell. Instead, he had Clinton.

The President rang Blair on the night of his election in his car travelling from Stansted airport to the Royal Festival Hall for the victory party. Jonathan Powell had kept in close touch with Clinton's staff after he left the Diplomatic Service to become Blair's chief of staff in 1994 and from the first day in Downing Street the channel to the White House was open, with the telephone on Blair's desk marked with the single word 'Washington' in frequent use from the start. Between those who would work in Number 10 and those in power in Washington there was already a patchwork of contacts. Philip Gould had worked with the Democrats' pollsters for years. Now the President's and Prime Minister's staffs were intermingling.

The significance for Blair was not simply in having a President with whom he could have a good personal relationship and whom he could persuade, for example, to throw his energies into the Northern Ireland negotiations, but in feeling that he had a kindred political spirit. Clinton saw himself as the inheritor of a progressive tradition that embraced Franklin D. Roosevelt and Harry Truman and, before them at the start of the twentieth century, Teddy Roosevelt and Woodrow Wilson. The essence of it, in his view, was a determination to shape change rather than be shaped by it.

In a speech at Princeton University in October 2000 Clinton quoted FDR, saying that orthodox government had to be replaced with 'bold, persistent experimentation'. In the same speech he argued that progressive politics wasn't defined by a particular set of policy programmes but by the underlying belief that new economic and social conditions always demanded 'a new approach to government'. Clinton's approach to government changed several times in his eight years in the White House, veering from liberal to quite conservative on the old scale, but his argument was an appealing one to a British Prime Minister who was anxious to break away from what he thought was a stultifying tradition in his party. To Blair, anxious to develop in office some kind of intellectual momentum that could build on the party modernization that had begun a decade before, Clinton seemed heaven-sent.

But there was much less enthusiasm elsewhere on the Labour front bench. Prescott had clambered on board, but he was still suspicious of modernization. He equated closeness to Clinton with a desire, as he had put it in his *Weekend World* interview four years before, to break the party's links with the trade unions. This was a struggle, he thought, 'for the heart and soul of the Labour Party'.

He was right to believe that Blair wanted to move on from the removal of Clause IV from the party constitution to a reconstruction of the party. He felt no commitment to the place of the unions in its councils, which he thought anachronistic. He wanted to pitch a 'big tent' into which, as Clinton had done with the Democrats, he could persuade people who felt no visceral connection to the party. The enlightened self-interest of voters was to be the engine of reform. If the Labour Party spoke to them about their aspirations, they would support it without worrying about whether they were 'socialists' or not. These were the ideas that demanded Blair part company with the left of his party for good. A *Tribune* editorial said that his purpose was to make Labour 'even more bland in pursuit of elusive affluent working-class and centrist middle-class votes'. He might not want to accept the adjective bland, but Blair would not deny his search for those lost votes. If the Clinton experience helped, so be it.

The criticism of the 'third way' approach from the left was that it appeared to be insubstantial, maybe even vacuous. Blair, it was argued, had understood some important lessons about campaigning and public appeal from Clinton, but was there a genuine new approach to economic management and social change in the two countries, as was claimed?

The language Blair used to describe government that steered a course between abandoned ideas of state socialism and a society of unfettered free markets seemed nebulous. It was neither old left nor new right: but was it something which was best described in the negative, a prescription that got its character from what it *wasn't*? Even Clinton, speaking a few weeks before leaving office, described the concept in terms that seemed almost infinitely malleable and incapable of giving offence to anyone: 'a way back to enduring values; a way beyond a government profoundly indifferent to people's problems; a way forward to meet the challenges of today and tomorrow'. This was the kind of formulation that Brown found infuriatingly vague, all aspiration and no bite. He has never liked the 'third way' as a description of his own policy, preferring to leave the label to Blair.

Debate with Clinton about the future of left-of-centre politics went on through their negotiations over Northern Ireland and the Balkans and the worries over the state of Russia, the three subjects that occupied most of their time together. In Ireland, Blair was able to play to Clinton's obsessive interest in hands-on negotiations; Clinton happily plunged into the thicket of Belfast politics and spent three years engaged intimately with leading figures in all the parties, turning his St Patrick's Day parties in the White House into outings for almost anyone in Dublin or Belfast who had a connection with the peace talks. He took great care to include the Ulster Unionists, with David Trimble a regular visitor, and he smoothed paths for them on Capitol Hill which had previously been blocked. Having granted visas to Gerry Adams of Sinn Fein during Major's time (against the firm advice of his ambassador in London) he was in a position to exert some influence on the Republicans, which he did several times on Blair's behalf. By the time he left office it had not been enough to produce the progress of decommissioning which Blair needed, but in their valedictory messages to each other Blair acknowledged – accurately – that without Clinton's energetic absorption in the process the Good Friday Agreement of 1998 might well have been still-born.

The practical Clinton was a valuable friend. Blair, however, got more from him than assistance in tight spots. He was a Prime Minister who had never seen the inside of a ministerial office before he took office and indeed had only visited Downing Street once before May 1997 – when Major invited him to a reception for Clinton. So ready access to the White House was an extraordinary bonus. They behaved together as if they had been operating in the international arena for years, even when Blair was still learning how European summits worked (or didn't). Anyone observing Blair's first visit to the White House in February 1998 was granted a vivid picture of the enthusiasm of Clinton's embrace.

Clinton held the biggest dinner that the White House had seen since Richard Nixon left office. It was deliberately staged to surround Blair with glamour and glitz. The tables in the East Room were set with 'Eisenhower gold baseplates, Reagan china and Kennedy Morgantown crystal'. The vermeil and silver historical candelabra centrepieces were surrounded by hypericum berries with gold tapered candles.

The Blairs stayed until midnight, with the 240 guests. Clinton's Hollywood gang was out in force with a surprised Blair finding himself hugged by Barbra Streisand in the White House lobby. Stevie Wonder and Elton John did a cabaret in an auditorium erected above the White House swimming pool. The high command of the Senate and the House of Representatives was in attendance and Clinton's Cabinet hobnobbed with some slightly overawed Blair ministers who had come out with him for a seminar at the White House on the Third Way. One of them, Alan Milburn, announced that he discovered that in the official guest house across Lafayette Square from the White House (with the appropriate name of Blair House) he was sleeping in Eisenhower's bed. No one knew whether or not to believe him. After it was over, and Blair was heading to Camp David for the weekend, he remarked to an acquaintance: 'Not bad, eh?' and laughed. Clinton had put on a show.

Blair also witnessed the President's handling of pressure at the height of the Lewinsky scandal, which had reached a new peak just as he arrived for his official visit. Clinton's popularity was plunging, his critics were advancing on him in force, and he was facing the American press for the first time for weeks (since the obligatory East Room press conference for a visiting head of government couldn't be cancelled). As he waited with Clinton in an anteroom before entering the arena, Blair told his colleagues later, he was astonished by the President's seeming calm. Knowing that his presidency was in peril, and knowing that his dissemblings about Lewinsky were almost certain to emerge some day, he nonetheless managed to behave as if this were a normal press conference on another Friday morning. To Blair's surprise he betrayed no sign of nervousness, let alone panic. A few minutes later, at the twin podia in the East Room, Blair looked much the more nervous of the two, even when the CNN White House correspondent Wolf Blitzer put one of the celebrated questions of the whole affair to Clinton: 'Mr President, what is your message to the Lewinsky family today?'

Puzzled as he was by Clinton's handling of the scandal, just as he was bewildered at the stupidity of the affair with Lewinsky, Blair saw in Washington the opportunity to establish a powerful personal alliance that was invaluable to him. He was the least experienced leader in the bigger countries of the European Union, yet his relationship with Clinton was by far the strongest. His willingness to press Clinton on the ground troops issue was evidence of how he understood the advantages of his position.

At the height of the Balkan crisis, by chance, NATO leaders met in Washington to celebrate the 50th anniversary of the Alliance. Cook went with Blair and so did George Robertson, who would end up as Blair's candidate for the NATO secretary-generalship, with Clinton's strong support. In this conflict, to the despair of elements of the Labour left who were appalled by the decision to launch air strikes against Serbia, just as they were trying to persuade Blair (with no success at all) to change his support for sanctions in Iraq, Blair found himself lifted by the challenges of action in the field. He was well into his second year in power, and those around him noted a new phase in his style. He was less nervous about attacks from his critics in the party than ever before and was revelling in his foreign role which, in Kosovo, would be bound to stir up more criticism. Despite the horrors of the Bosnian war in the mid-nineties, there were many Labour MPs who would not support the bombing of Serbia. Sixteen of them signed a Commons motion condemning NATO's policy.

The first half of 1999 was an extraordinary period for Blair. In

January he went on an official visit to be received by Nelson Mandela in Pretoria, in May he received the Charlemagne Prize in Aachen and said he wanted to end 'uncertainty and Europhobia' in Britain, and in the intervening period he found himself in what was called 'a war of liberation' in Kosovo. After the Albanian refugees began to return to Kosovo under the protection of NATO troops in July, the reconstruction of a civil society would prove difficult, violent and long but Blair became so committed to the campaign against Milosevic that he emerged in those months as the most hawkish of the European leaders. He was pushing Europe, and he was pushing the Americans. One White House official told a senior British correspondent in Washington just before the NATO conference in April: 'The leader of this NATO coalition isn't Bill Clinton, it's Tony Blair.'

He became convinced, despite the nervousness of the Foreign Office, that ground troops would be needed in Kosovo if refugees were to come home in sufficient numbers to justify the action. The air campaign would not be enough. The displaced had fled through the mountains, to Albania and Macedonia, and the issue was whether the Serb forces in Kosovo could be stopped by an air campaign, with troops coming in afterwards, or whether there would be a ground war. The difficulties were huge, with terrain which was inhospitable to any quick action on the ground, and Clinton was clearly disturbed by the enthusiasm which Blair displayed for a ground war when he came to Washington in April for the NATO summit. The State Department and the Pentagon were alarmed, and Clinton was told that public opinion – the barometer that always hovered somewhere in sight – was not ready.

The American strategy in Kosovo had been implemented by General Wesley Clark, who was sacked six weeks after the campaign ended successfully. He reflected in his memoirs that this was the war that Washington did not want. The White House was intensely nervous, the State Department and the Pentagon were at loggerheads, and the President simply wanted to avoid being drawn in too deeply. In that context, Blair's urgings to Clinton about the prospects for a ground campaign were unwelcome.

The crisis passed with Milosevic's decision to draw back, under the pressure of the air campaign and diplomatic muscle from the Russians, and the crossing of the Macedonian border into Kosovo by the international force in the early summer was an almost bloodless exercise. In the effort to restore civil society in Kosovo there was much violence to come – the KFOR force of troops found none of their subsequent manoeuvres as easy as the entry into Kosovo itself – but for Blair the episode demonstrated the importance of clarity and determination. To his critics it was exactly as they expected when he invited Margaret Thatcher to Downing Street soon after his election and praised her because 'she knew the direction she was going in'. He had, in their view, succumbed to the temptations of semi-presidential power. On this occasion, however, the real President had been more cautious. Blair has never subsequently expressed regret for having tried to persuade Clinton to commit ground troops. Indeed, since he thinks that Clinton was persuadable (although there is no objective evidence for the belief) he wonders if he should have pressed harder.

The Kosovo episode as a piece of prime ministerial politics rather than military strategy is an intriguing part of the Blair story. To Cabinet colleagues around him it was the time when he found his confidence. Not all of them approved of his enthusiasm. 'I couldn't believe how fond he became of the generals,' one of them said at the time. 'It happens to all of them I suppose, but with Tony it was very quick. He loves the way they work.' By the time NATO troops assembled on the Macedonian border with Kosovo at the beginning of June, Blair was immersed in the politics of war. 'He was energized by it every morning. It was one of the periods – like the Northern Ireland negotiations – where he became completely absorbed and thought of very little else.' Critics found the leadership style a little messianic, and the left began to assemble its caricature of the Prime Minister as a trigger-happy sidekick of the United States who was content sometimes to criticize the White House for hesitation or lack of purpose. The picture is caught in the Kosovo cartoons of Steve Bell, Blair's most savage assailant, in the *Guardian* where the Prime Minister appears as a bulging-eyed Dr Strangelove driven by demons to launch another air raid or press another button.

When a fifty-mile-long military convoy moved into place in the darkness of a June night in the Macedonian hills ready to enter Kosovo, the British troops squeezed into the trucks did not feel they were part of an American-led NATO force. They spoke of it as Blair's campaign. At first light on Saturday 12 June the order was given to move at 4 a.m., on a balmy morning in the hills. The first sound was of a huge swarm of helicopters coming out of the gloom, Chinooks with trucks and armoured cars suspended under them filling the sky. The sight was extraordinary. At the front of the convoy, at the Blace crossing where the first entry into Kosovo would be made, a soldier who knew his cinema and knew his Prime Minister recalled the scene from *Apocalypse Now* where the helicopters fly in to the sound of the *Ride of the Valkyries*. 'The question this morning,' he said as he prepared to drive over the border with his men, 'is: "Who does it better? Francis Ford Coppola or Alastair Campbell?"'

Blair saw the campaign as a moral duty. He wasn't dragged into it. He leapt at it. Although the Kosovo campaign did not recast the political landscape at home, for him it was the first moment of danger in Downing Street. Even with a majority of 179 a war that went wrong would be fatal. If the war had become a catastrophe for NATO it would not have been a responsibility which Blair could have passed to anyone else. The decisions were his, and he was the leader in the Alliance who had become the most hawkish. And it had become especially obvious that Brown was not prepared to connect himself to the military crisis in the Balkans. Around Blair it was asked if the Chancellor's silence was the action of a minister concerned to preserve diplomatic propriety or a minister saying, once again, you're on your own. Without Kosovo, Blair's subsequent premiership might have had a different tone. It helped to persuade him that Downing Street should be the centre of a 'command and control' administration, not simply the enabler of collegiate government. In the first half of 1999 the hesitant, cautious Blair of the first two years, talking radically but proceeding gingerly in many policy areas, changed in the course of the military campaign. The Prime Minister with no experience was now a Washington intimate who had tangled with a President in war. In Germany and France he was seen as a restless (and perhaps reckless) leader with a greater relish for action than they had expected.

The surge of energy that clearly affected Blair during the Kosovo campaign was not entirely beneficial to him. He was different from the Blair who had taken Clinton's call of congratulations on 2 May 1997. With someone else in the White House, without the Balkan crisis, without the fascination for American campaign techniques which he was importing for the Labour Party, the Blair years would have taken a much more tentative course. Clinton was the Big Friend who made a difference. Only Thatcher's relationship with Reagan in the post-war era compared with the Blair–Clinton alliance.

John Prescott's worries about Clintonization were becoming flesh. Blair was talking to the White House night and day and Clinton was acting as a supplementary Northern Ireland Secretary in trying to keep the Good Friday Agreement alive. And in the Treasury Brown was nurturing his own American influences. They were as strong as Blair's, but they were inevitably absorbed elsewhere than in the Oval Office and its environs, where only Prime Ministers are allowed to do their deals. Each of them was revealing an absorption in Clinton's America, Blair as a student of the exercise of presidential power and Brown as the Chancellor who had a cultural fascination with the temple of capitalism and its high priests, especially Alan Greenspan. Their government was doomed to fret about Europe, like all its predecessors, but in adopting models for government they had become Atlanticists. The American experience revealed them as they are – Brown at the beach, but with economists talking markets and politics, and Blair in Washington, itching to play his role on the biggest stage, a map of the world.

PART FOUR

Rough guide to the Brownies

PART FOUR

10

Friends

One night in 1998, just before the World Cup began in France, Gordon Brown was entertaining the Scotland football manager, Craig Brown, and some of his players to wish them good luck. He had filled the first-floor reception room in Number 11 with friends and acquaintances. Half of Scotland seemed to be there, and the joint was jumping. Brown made a cheery speech (with the traditional misplaced optimism) and so did Donald Dewar, then Scottish Secretary. The Prime Minister was standing by the door, having just slipped in without fuss. Someone said to him: 'Great gathering.' He laughed and said: 'It certainly is. The alternative government?'

Brown pulled Blair into the throng and they worked the crowd together, the Prime Minister's throwaway line forgotten in the hubbub. It had certainly been a joke, but one that evidently leapt naturally to Blair's lips, without much effort. Brown was in his element, his court at play. And Blair, whose own court is just as important to him, had understood the scene the moment he walked in. They were swept up together a moment later, mingling as best friends, with Brown (who had been a resolute travelling fan at the fiascos and passing moments of excitement at Scotland World Cup matches since the seventies) indulging in what seemed like some good-natured patronizing of his neighbour and guest. They were with friends. But whose friends?

There is no parallel in the modern era in Britain for the rival gangs of supporters who follow Blair and Brown. Although most successful politicians can count on an assemblage of loyalists and camp-followers who are willing to fight their cause year after year – it is almost

233

impossible to survive for long at the top without one – the role of friends in the relationship between these two is remarkable. Each depends on a group of close supporters, connected to a wider army, and they have survived as distinct armies in government. Indeed, one of the characteristics of the relationship is that power has not brought the two courts together but has tended to exaggerate their individual characters. They exert such a powerful influence on their two leaders, and the atmosphere inside is so intense, that they have become as much the architects of the relationship as Blair and Brown themselves.

At moments of crisis each man turns inwards to his supporters. In Number 10 and its environs Blair had four or five intimates, led by Alastair Campbell and Anji Hunter, who circled him from morning to night. In the Treasury, Brown depends in the same way on Ed Balls, his personal secretary Sue Nye and Ed Miliband. Beyond these inner rings are the orbits of friends and political supporters with relatively little overlap between their respective constellations. After the 2001 election, for example, Campbell, Hunter and Blair's political secretary Sally Morgan (elevated to a peerage and a ministerial job for the second term before taking Hunter's job when she left Blair's side to join BP in 2002) all knew that Robin Cook was to be moved from the Foreign Office before Brown did.

The two personalities have created this universe, because they crave intimacy and privacy. When they are not together they enter their own worlds, which seem to have separate existences inside the government. Blair's aides work for a man, not a team of ministers; in Brown's office every speech is crafted to build up the Chancellor, not the government. The duopoly, bringing together two self-contained men with their own ambitions and pride, means that parallel teams were bound to spring up. The result was rivalry.

When the fuel protesters managed to summon up chaos from nowhere in September 2000, Blair and Brown had to decide quickly how to respond. From the Treasury came one interpretation: 'Blair's panicking. Gordon's going to have to sort it out.' From Number 10, a different line. 'Gordon's got to get this one right. Tony understands how serious this is.' Afterwards, the argument from the Blair camp was that he had managed the crisis, getting Brown to make the modest concessions that would get the tankers moving again. From Brown's side, it was said that the prime ministerial hand had to be held and his nerve steadied (the more convincing story). At every turn, the supporting chorus picks up its champion's theme and sends out the signal. In a government with two centres of power, there was no alternative. They were doomed to compete.

With two men who have a great capacity to inspire personal loyalty, any competition is bound to be passionate. But in the groups of friends one in particular has given the rivalry an ongoing emotional instability. Mandelson's dispute with Brown was one of the obstacles around which Blair had to construct his government, as awkward as if it had been a physical barrier built across Downing Street.

The first election campaign imposed its own discipline, and the early days in government were marked by a studied civility between Brown and Mandelson as if distant memories of the old days were being revived. But it was only a brief interlude. The pattern had been set in the opposition years and it was still the underlying template of government. Many ministers who've had enough proximity to the three of them to get a glimpse of the passions have chosen the word 'marriage' to describe the setting, because they're struck by the instinctive pull that Blair and Brown have for each other and the sense of obligation that lies between them, and also because they see Mandelson as the complicating agent in the *ménage*, a figure who fascinates each of them almost, but not quite, as much as they fascinate each other.

Blair has been tempted into using the word 'marriage' himself once or twice, but only in private. He dislikes it as a description, hardly surprisingly. He cannot, however, stop some of those around him looking at the bonds that tie him to Brown and Mandelson as links which they suspect that he feels (or fears) are as indissoluble in politics as is the anchor in his private life that binds him exceptionally strongly to his family.

The friends of Blair and Brown circulate around the separate points of this triangle, and over the years they have absorbed the passions that it contains. In turn, they have given back to the two men loyalties which are coloured by the tempestuous quality of the relationship and one consequence has been a heightened atmosphere and lots of trouble. Mandelson has never been the leader of a gang and has made his relationships one by one – close friends they may become, but they are not friends who run as a pack. It's possible, by contrast, to see Blair and Brown as the street fighters in *West Side Story*, leading the Jets and the Sharks through the alleyways on some new adventure, all flying fists and exuberant yells. There's always a scrap to be had, and always a new buzz to enjoy with the gang.

After one Budget a story spread around Whitehall that Blair had taken Brown to Chequers to work over his Budget speech because the Prime Minister thought it needed a new tone. From the Treasury came quite a different tale, of Downing Street ideas overruled by the Chancellor, who alone had the strategic vision. That kind of running commentary on their personal dealings became the daily conversation of Whitehall. Where the truth lay, or whether the story was accidental or malign, became increasingly difficult to know. Blair and Brown dealt with each other so much, on the phone and in person, and kept so much of their conversations to themselves, that they preserved the mystique of whatever passed between them. Even if there hadn't been a row, no one could prove that there hadn't been. In politics, a remorselessly speculative trade, that meant gossip and trouble.

Their friends were their sustenance and sometimes their weakness. The most striking characteristic of these groups, and the telling evidence of their importance, is that they have hardly changed in years.

When Blair reshaped Downing Street after his re-election, taking another step towards the creation of a Prime Minister's department in all but name, it was no break with the practices of the first term. The three pillars of his reconstruction were Jonathan Powell, Alastair Campbell and, at first, Hunter. Blair was building on the existing foundations. It would be the old gang who would make his office more powerful and it was clearly intended that it should direct policy from the centre in an even more rigorous fashion than in the first four years. He told one questioner on a train journey during the election campaign that he was still frustrated after four years with the sluggishness of Whitehall, using the slightly chilling phrase: 'The Prime Minister's writ must run.' The foot and mouth crisis, in particular, convinced Blair in spring 2001 that the government machine was antiquated and he solicited outside advice from business and academia about how best to rebore its cylinders. Business people like Don Cruickshank, chairman of the London Stock Exchange, were asked for prescriptions. Blair appointed Wendy Thomson, from the independent Audit Commission, to run the reform programme for the civil service. But inside Downing Street he turned to old friends.

He has known Anji Hunter since they were teenagers in Scotland. Apart from a short break in the early nineties, she worked for him for thirteen years. She is two years younger than Blair, attended boarding school in St Andrews and met him through a mutual friend when he was seventeen. He has lightheartedly suggested that he attempted a seduction and was sent packing: 'My first defeat.' The fact that he felt secure enough to make the joke illustrated the kind of relationship they had. It was settled.

At first Hunter was a secretary, but with Blair on the shadow Cabinet she had assumed a different role, the kind of half-fixer, half-adviser that politicians need as their conduit to the outside world. It involves a level of trust which must be absolute, because there is no one outside the family who will know as much about the frailties and foibles of the boss. In his public life, she was by Blair's side for most of his career and saw every turn in his transformation from gawping new boy to greying Prime Minister. Her husky voice and the plume of cigarette smoke that often trailed behind her were part of the Blair picture. Whether at the Women's Institute annual conference or in the White House, her mobile phone was close by, vibrating with the messages which flow to and fro in the Blair circle. She heard and saw almost everything.

As a result she was the object of jealousy and some hostility. To Labour MPs anxious to get access to the inner reaches of Downing Street she was the keeper of the key who had to be persuaded; to those who have criticized the side of Blair which is usually caricatured as 'presidentialism' she was the unelected courtier who was as likely to bite your head off as to let you through. Senior ministers may not have had to negotiate to pass her portals but almost everyone else did. And for Blair she operated not only as a filter, keeping out unwelcome visitors and problems, but as an emissary in the parliamentary party, Fleet Street and beyond where she carried messages to the world outside and returned with the answers, with news and with the latest gossip fresh for the Prime Minister's office.

She was part of a wider intelligence network. All governments need them, so that in Downing Street they can feel the trembling from the most distant corners of the web. Intelligence is the bloodstream of politics, bringing news of danger. For example, after the 2001 election it was believed that one junior minister was having an affair which, if it had been revealed, would have been particularly damaging to the government. The minister was not reappointed.

Hunter was an important cog in that machine and Blair also used her for personal tasks – soothing a bruised colleague, dealing with an MP whose marriage was in trouble or who had been bereaved, fixing a necessary social encounter with a newspaper figure who needed some timely massage, and all the other tasks that a political machine demands, day and night. Outside Blair's family there was no one closer. It was his constant refrain and the easiest way of pushing aside any problem: 'Speak to Anji.' With the family itself her relationship had a different quality and there was some strain with Cherie Booth, who was much closer to Baroness (Sally) Morgan. Hunter and Morgan had an up-and-down relationship in Number 10 before Morgan left for the Cabinet Office and the Lords at the start of the second term. The two women were competitors for the Prime Minister's ear. But it was Hunter whose throaty whisper was usually the one he heard first. Her intimacy was strictly at work, not at home. But for Blair-watchers it was not surprising that she prospered after the second election victory. This time, however, it did not last. Within six months, Hunter had decided to take up an offer made by BP before the election. The decision had nothing to do with a deteriorating relationship with Blair – they stayed tuned to the same wavelength – but seemed a signal of the way that the 'family' around him would have to change.

Sally Morgan became head of government relations at 12 Downing Street, from which the chief whip had now had to decamp, and one of the pillars of the Blair official household disappeared. But the story of the Blair years cannot be told without Hunter's presence permeating the first term and the start of the second. 'I need her. It's as simple as that,' Blair used to say. It was true. One of her tasks over the years was to cultivate parts of the press that were more difficult for other members of the Blair circle to reach. While Alastair Campbell tried to play most of the tabloids like an old violin, with only the occasional screech and broken string, it was Hunter who was one of the links in the all-important relationship – in Blair's mind – with the *Daily Mail*. It was she, for example, who played the part of Cupid in Blair's strange waltz with Paul Johnson, the irascible but gushing columnist once memorably described by Richard Ingrams as looking like 'an explosion in a pubic hair factory'. She spoke to him a great deal, and arranged the meetings which allowed the infatuation to develop. Johnson fell for Blair in the mid-nineties, writing in the *Mail* of their dinners and discussions as if he were announcing the discovery of a personal treasure trove of political talent and telling readers that they might be witnessing the coming to power of a great man. It went spectacularly sour, as such fevered dalliances in Fleet Street mostly do, but it served Blair's purpose well. The Labour leader who was happy to cultivate a 'middle England' appeal, and have it described as such, had found, albeit temporarily, a trumpet to make the appropriate noise. Subsequent blasts from Johnson announcing the turning of Blair from promising statesman to near-corrupt control freak weren't a surprise, and the Downing Street view was that his purpose had been served in opposition. Goodbye.

Hunter's speciality was the use of antennae which stretched well outside the Labour Party. Before power made it easier to find newspaper acolytes, the widening of Blair's circle in Conservative newspapers had a great deal to do with her skills. She didn't look or sound like a political hack and she appeared to epitomize a change of style in the Labour leadership. It was valuable for Blair to have an intelligence operative who could also wield a steely charm.

The charm of Alastair Campbell escapes some people. With Hunter, he was the backbone of Blair's operation since soon after he became leader. Campbell does, in fact, have a soft side to his personality, but it is usually concealed behind impenetrable layers of rigid muscle and some of those with whom he deals, in press and broadcasting as in politics, have hardly seen a hint of it.

One of the moments when his defences came down briefly was early in the first term on a Blair visit to New York where Campbell shared with reporters some of the family difficulties that came with his job. He'd argued with one of his children before leaving and as he departed his son said to him: 'You want a good soundbite? Here's one – you're a crap dad.' Blair told his first biographer Jon Sopel that just as he was sure his name would be mud in his house for spending so much time writing, the same was true in the Blair home because of his many enforced absences. The Downing Street gang have the feel of an extended family about them. It is not a controlled office environment of the sort that Blair's business heroes cherish.

Campbell and Hunter often played a 'tough-cop-soft-cop' routine, with Campbell almost always in the role of the baton-waving thug. Eyes blazing, mouth curling and finger jabbing he can reduce a young reporter, or a feeble backbencher, to jelly. Hunter's techniques were more subtle, entreaties for help that sometimes worked where directness had failed. Since Campbell's arrival at Blair's side in 1995 her job was not to deal directly with journalists day-to-day, though she knows a vast number, but to persuade the hostile or the fearful that Blair's office was not just an organized bullying shop. It was an equally ruthless tactic.

No press secretary in the history of Downing Street has been as famous as Campbell or as influential. He was bequeathed part of this fame unintentionally by his predecessor but three, Bernard Ingham. Ingham was the voice of the Iron Lady and created for the public mind the image which Margaret Thatcher wore like a perfectly tailored dress. He understood her appeal and her instincts because he sympathized with them, and gave them a language, all decisiveness and instinctive action. In turn, she conducted her premiership in character, the character which he had accurately sensed and described to Fleet Street and the broadcasters. He did so behind the flimsy veil of the unattributable lobby briefings which he fought successfully to preserve for a little longer. It was his skill and flair in the Thatcher era that was the foundation for the Campbell years.

Ingham's relationship to his Prime Minister, however, was quite different from Campbell's. He played by civil service rules – he couldn't imagine attending a Conservative Party conference, for example – and was never part of the kind of circle that Campbell helped to create around Blair. Ingham was the professional servant in the outer office, not the courtier at the bedroom door. His devotion to Thatcher was probably as great as Campbell's to Blair but even at the end, when he gave his last despairing advice to her as she headed for catastrophe in the leadership election of 1990, there was a little distance. No outsider has ever heard him call Thatcher 'Margaret'. By contrast, except in formal gatherings in the Westminster village, Campbell would hardly bother to refer to his boss as 'Prime Minister'.

As a lobby correspondent for part of the eighties Campbell understood Ingham's brilliance in sculpting the outline of Thatcher for those he was briefing. Before long they knew what she would think about almost anything, how she would respond to any political situation, what language she would use. Thatcher was herself, but 'Maggie' was Ingham's creation. Campbell learned his lesson, and when he began to advise Kinnock informally and to sense the rhythms of an opposition leader's office while he was at the *Mirror* as political editor he adapted Ingham's techniques. It was, he thought, what Labour needed.

Campbell was Ingham with a souped-up engine and twin exhausts, a pulsating propaganda machine that was meant to spin routine announcements into something interesting every day, with powers sanctioned by the Prime Minister giving it a terrifying energy. Campbell was everywhere. He was playing the Fleet Street field, picking off cowed backbenchers to help in some piece of mischief against the Conservatives, reminding ministers that their loyalty lay to one man (and his press secretary) and, most of all, sitting at Blair's side when he made most of his decisions. With Mandelson, before he was promoted from the Cabinet Office to the DTI, he was the omnipresent adviser.

His old acquaintance Ingham was horrified at what had happened to his former job: 'The things this lot do . . . I couldn't begin to have contemplated some of it. They're bullies. They break every rule. I'd have been thrown out on my ear in a minute if I'd tried any of it. They're an appalling bunch.' The eyebrows jump with Healeyesque ferocity and he snorts. The unattributable briefings of his day had gone and Campbell was speaking for direct quotation. This gave the Number 10 briefings a bogus flavour of excitement, which can be dispelled in a moment by a visit to the official Number 10 website, and it heightened the aura of Campbell himself. He was, said the opposition and many a Labour MP, more important than some Cabinet ministers.

Everyone knew it to be true. No significant announcement could be planned by any department without Campbell approving, in meticulous detail, the timing of the statement, the wording of the press release, the arrangements for interviews with the minister on radio and television and the decision as to whether it might be worthwhile flying a kite a day or two in advance in a friendly newspaper.

The criticism became familiar as Campbell bedded down. He demanded more Number 10 control of the individual press offices in Whitehall departments, almost always manned by senior civil servants who were meant to be able to work as easily for ministers of either party and who were professional information officers. Some of them moved jobs or took early retirement, and nearly all of them grumbled. Andy Wood at the Northern Ireland Office, whose Whitehall service stretched back through the Thatcher years to Callaghan's Number 10 press office, was dismissed by Mo Mowlam, the Secretary of State, because of problems of 'chemistry' and he made public his disgust at what he thought was happening to the Government Information Service, always conceived as a source of straight information and background free of party-political embellishment.

The Campbell style took shape, with the crafted slogan and the message carved in stone as its main elements. There was always a line, and it had to be followed. In Blair's mind there was still the spooky memory of life in the early eighties, when Labour had no style, no consistency and, as a result, no message. That was why he resisted the efforts of some of his colleagues who tried to persuade him, as delicately as they could, to rein Campbell in. 'Ali is the best. He is loyal. He stays,' was Blair's response. No other Prime Minister in the media age had created and sustained a professional friendship like it. There were odd rows about a headline that had gone wrong, a briefing too far or a piece of gossip. Blair was furious when stories appeared after a family holiday in the Seychelles implying that he had rescued a drowning man. He hadn't. He had encountered a Scandinavian tourist. But they subsided as surely as the sun rose the next morning. What Campbell wanted, he got.

The more the metropolitan cynics giggled and the broadsheets sniffed (especially the *Guardian*, which Campbell regarded as a puffed-up enemy and not a friend) the more he bent to his task. Through the first term he controlled his office like the operations room of a ship at war. The tiniest blip on the radar screen was monitored, and the guns would swing round. Campbell is a regular caller to the BBC in the early morning. If there's a headline on Radio 4 at six o'clock which he doesn't like, he'll complain. Why was a headline about Geoffrey Robinson's business affairs or the troubles of the Leicester East MP Keith Vaz more important than some 'good news' announcement coming later in the day about lower crime figures or good results in primary schools? Among his favourite words are 'garbage' and 'crap'. The theory is not that a rude phone call will change a headline (it won't, unless there is an obvious factual inaccuracy) but that a regular sense of being watched will induce a sense of defensiveness. BBC producers and correspondents try to make sure it doesn't.

During the 2001 campaign the style was exported to Millbank Tower. Radio and television editors would receive organized barrages of calls after news programmes giving lists of complaints about the choice of interviewees or the adjectives used by a presenter.

The opposition parties played the same game, of course, but without the same practised ease.

Campbell runs his regime as if it were a firm of nightclub bouncers. An editor needed bawling out. A correspondent may have had to be singled out for a humiliating aside at a lobby briefing (as one left the room early one day, Campbell called after him, 'Need a drink, do we?'). A backbencher may have been reminded that the Prime Minister might find room in his diary for a visit to the constituency if a loyal silence was preserved. He once outraged the *Mirror*, the government's most loyal cheerleader, by passing one of its scoops to the *Sun*. He commanded Blair's guest lists, even arranging for Richard Desmond, the porn millionaire who bought the *Express*, to visit Blair at Downing Street and Chequers, a favour which outraged dozens of sacked *Express* journalists and especially the former editor Rosie Boycott, a friend of Blair's whom Desmond had discarded.

Campbell's chamber was the political heart of the government, the place where all the lines crossed. In Cabinet, ministers found it difficult to plug into each other's lives. There were old friendships that could provide networks across departments, and of course ministers tried to help each other out in struggles with the Treasury or in swinging the balance in the Prime Minister's mind on the minimum wage, or the tube, or pensions, or the housing budget. But one Cabinet minister put it like this: 'We don't socialize very much. The Commons is quiet these days, because late night votes hardly matter. We just don't hang around much. It's quite strange. There's not much mingling at all.' More than in any government since the sixties ministerial lives were being lived inside departments. But they all had to have a lifeline to the centre and from the start Campbell, and Mandelson in his first year as Minister Without Portfolio in the Cabinet Office, saw a vast amount of prime ministerial paperwork.

They didn't see such documents as the weekly 'Red Book' from the Joint Intelligence Committee, with its update from the security and intelligence agencies, or more sensitive material from the Foreign Office or Defence, but almost everything else passed across their desks. Describing Campbell as a press secretary missed the point.

By the time they all arrived in Downing Street he was part of Blair's personality, a component in every strategy and a presence in every room where the Prime Minister had to operate. During the Kosovo war he sat in on meetings with the Defence Chiefs of Staff. He was not the still small voice in his head, but the big loud heckler at his shoulder.

The Campbell phenomenon is a clue to the nature of Blair's gang. He was a fabled Fleet Street figure in his day, a boozer and bagpipe player whose history was exotic. From Cambridge he went on a whim to train half-heartedly as a casino croupier but ended up as a kilted busker round Europe, and then wrote amateur porn for the magazine *Forum* before throwing himself on the tabloids. He played rough with the hard men of the newspaper trade who knock on a victim's door all day and all night before they give up, and loved the wild life of the Street in the last days of its heady self-indulgence, before the accountants and the computers took over. About that time, the bottle clobbered him and he broke down. He hasn't touched alcohol since, but in an odd way he is still the same over-the-top character. And that is what Blair enjoys.

For this Prime Minister has a weakness for the charismatics. It would be hard to find someone less like Campbell than Blair's student spiritual guru Peter Thomson, and yet there is something they share – a certain gift of the glittering eye. Blair seems always to have been attracted by that kind of intensity and directness. Sometimes their relationship seems to have a theatrical quality to it. It allows Campbell an openness in the Prime Minister's office which has astonished some visitors. Campbell has no inhibitions. Though Blair only draws on ripe language in moments of real anxiety – even Milosevic is a mere 'shit' – and never does so in front of outsiders, Campbell lets his vocabulary run free. He also has a characteristic grunt, often accompanied by a twist in the upper lip, which is a challenge to the person who has just spoken. Tell me why I should not be contemptuous of this, it says. Blair gets it regularly.

Blair's critics interpret it as weakness. He himself argues that there was never any doubt who was boss, and can cite instances where Campbell had to apologize to him for a foul-up in the press.

But Campbell was so powerful that he was assumed to be the source, rightly or wrongly, of almost every word that came out of Number 10. The most famous phrase in this category, which infuriated and wounded Brown in the middle of the first term, was the claim in the *Observer* on 18 January 1998, that someone close to Blair in Number 10 had described Brown as having 'psychological flaws'. Campbell was everyone's favourite culprit, because in such circumstances he always was. He has always denied, on and off the record, using the phrase. He insists it did not come from him and in evidence to the Commons Public Administration Committee denied briefing 'against any member of the Cabinet'. Around Brown these denials still ring with an uncertain note. The Chancellor himself doesn't talk of it: some of his staff do, and they still believe that the trail led back to Campbell's office.

The report on 18 January 1998 was one of many critical of the Chancellor around that time, and the reason was obvious. Paul Routledge, the *Mirror* commentator and dedicated sceptic of all things Blairite, had published his biography of Brown, a detailed and sometimes racy account of his life which was prepared, as the book announced on its cover, with the Chancellor's 'full cooperation'. Perhaps it was the 'full' that set Downing Street off. Although Brown was not quoted in the book as criticizing Blair directly, it fairly reflected his grudges and grumbles and gave them voice. In Downing Street, it was as if a hand grenade had landed in the front hall. Through the next few weeks newspaper front pages were pockmarked with the fallout, a shower of anti-Brown stories. The 'psychological flaws' accusation was the most biting, but there were others. Outsiders glimpsed for the first time how trust might reside inside the two circles of advisers but not often between them.

Campbell and Hunter formed the circle of intimates who were Blair's armour. Brown wears a similar protective suit. His most important adviser is Ed Balls, who was only twenty-seven when around the same time as Charlie Whelan he joined Brown in 1994. After Whelan departed, to gasps of relief in Blair's office and in Campbell's, in January 1999 Balls was left as the Chancellor's principal political lieutenant. He is a disarmingly cheery soul, given much more to laughing than to dark conspiracies, but he has created a fearsome reputation for himself. When he arrived at Brown's side from the *Financial Times*, he was thought of as a hired economic brain. He was; but he came to be much more. With Whelan he was a partner in an operation that had as much interest in preserving and enhancing Brown's political power in the government and the party as worrying about the next spending round or the preparations for entering the euro. They weren't Treasury men, they were 'Gordon's men'. Number 10 Downing Street was therefore an outfit which had to be treated like any other part of government. The centre of their world was Brown's office and it was from there that they sent their messages to the world, not from mission control in Blair's office or, worse, from Campbell's.

They knew from the start that Blair found Brown's affection for Whelan a puzzle and had tried to persuade Brown not to bring him into government. Campbell defended him when the first euro row blew up in the autumn after the election, though he told Blair directly that he thought Whelan had behaved dangerously and foolishly in his telephone briefings and in his loose talk. Fortunately, they thought in Number 10, the Chancellor had been embarrassed too. But it took Blair's office eighteen months to lever Whelan out and fill the Treasury press secretary's job with a career civil servant once more, just as in the old days. Brown kept his loyalty to his old bodyguard – he continued to see him regularly and to solicit his advice – and Whelan and Balls are still a pair seen together around the watering holes of SW1 on the Chancellor's business. As Campbell and Hunter rode shotgun for the Prime Minister, so do Whelan and Balls for their man, with his special adviser, Ian Austin, pulling the strings with the media.

Blair's relations with Balls are civil, because, after the difficult first days in which officials complained to the Cabinet Secretary about their exclusion from Blair–Brown meetings, an arrangement was reached by which many of their discussions would be attended by one official from each side. Jeremy Heywood, a Treasury civil servant seconded to Number 10 as Blair's principal private secretary, was one such official until he moved on in July 2001, and the other was Balls. Officialdom was relieved that a regular pattern had been re-established, and some precious aides-memoires recorded for the files, despite the habit of Blair and Brown of huddling together alone almost every day, and of talking on unmonitored telephones at all hours.

So Balls straddles the official and the personally political in Brown's office. He helps to write speeches, though Brown will still sit for hours at his desk working on his own words, and he deals with many financial journalists. 'It's not Brown, it's Balls,' Michael Heseltine crowed in an unusually 'risqué' analysis at a Tory Party conference of one speech from the Chancellor. This irritates Downing Street a great deal, because, especially in the arguments over the euro, the Prime Minister's office believes it can spot a Balls briefing when they see it fashioned into an elegant column in one of the broadsheets. It is a suspicious relationship, because the stakes are high. Even if Brown were a minister who had been promoted to Chancellor they would still keep a sharp watch on his people (whom they saw, where they lunched, where their networks stretched – all the human intelligence of politics) but with his installation as the twin pillar of the government Balls became a quite different creature, whose every move had special interest and significance.

The contacts are strained. If a particularly disturbing story has appeared touching on either the Prime Minister or the Chancellor there will be an atmosphere for a while. Whether because of Brown's fury about the 'psychological flaws', Blair's anger at Treasury briefings about the euro, irritation at rival interpretations being circulated about disputes over the tube or Post Office privatization or BBC funding, a story will take wing and fly. Campbell will be asked by Blair to explain to Brown what happened; or Balls will have to account for his movements. They are all used to it now, and one of the frustrations which Blair has confessed to his circle is that it has almost become the way of the world. There is no genuine prospect of a stop to it.

One channel did exist which was used to defuse some of the personal tension. Brown's secretary Sue Nye is Hunter's old friend. In opposition days they were matey in the shadow Cabinet corridor and could be found together in a wine bar from time to time consoling each other by sharing, in strict privacy, their latest worries about one of their bosses. From the start they managed to have a solid relationship even when Blair and Brown were paddling in choppy water. Nye is married to Gavyn Davies, a Brown adviser of long standing, former Goldman Sachs economist and, since January 2000, Chairman of the BBC. She is a Labour Party veteran, having toiled at party headquarters and in the parliamentary party before Brown had arrived at Westminster. She knows the party intimately, and although she shares the contempt of the Blairites for some past periods – her years in Kinnock's office when he was leader pitched her into battle with the hard left – she has the characteristic that Brown has tried to preserve in his office: a residual warmth for Labour history. Nye's importance for Number 10, however, was not simply in her party loyalty (which is almost as impregnable as her loyalty to Brown) but her resilient friendship with Anji Hunter. They sometimes talked more freely one to the other than their employers, and they were in the fortunate position of knowing (with Campbell and Balls, and sometimes Powell and Mandelson – the only others in that innermost loop) the detail of what had passed between Blair and Brown and, perhaps just as importantly, the state of mind of each of them when a particular encounter was over. Between them they formed a safety valve.

These were the individuals who were the closest to Blair and Brown in their offices and they set the tone for the wider groups of friends who operate in Parliament and beyond. They illustrated, too, one of the most striking features of the Blair–Brown relationship, the presence of strong women.

Each of them is married to one. Cherie Booth is a woman of strong opinions – still to the left of her husband. However, despite her decision to pursue her career at the Bar with as little interference from government duties as possible (indeed, sometimes challenging government decisions in her field of employment law without worrying about comment in the press) she has been careful to avoid the Hillary Clinton model. Her references in public to any issue of political significance can be counted on a few fingers: she has resisted almost all temptation. But anyone who has the faintest brush with the Blair family is aware of her importance to the Prime Minister, and her refusal to hide her opinions under some affected simpering exterior. This has caused some friction with the Chancellor. Those who see most of them together are convinced that theirs is now a very cool relationship indeed. Each is possessed of an eloquent body language. Even when the words are friendly, Booth and Brown don't demonstrate any physical warmth.

But they have had to learn to be close neighbours. On coming to power, the Blairs moved into the flat above the shop in Number 11, because it provided room for a family. Number 10's flat did not. Number 11 is hardly spacious, let alone palatial, but it accommodates the Blairs and their four children, three of them in their teens. Brown moved alone into the flat at the top of Number 10. Towards the end of the first term, of course, the personal focus and the long lenses shifted dramatically from Cherie Booth and the Blairs' baby, Leo, born in June 2000, to Brown. His marriage to Sarah Macaulay in August was a surprise, not because she had emerged out of the blue (she hadn't) but because Brown, in character, managed to keep the wedding a secret. He rang Whelan the night before and the late editions of the newspapers managed to break the news, but Brown succeeded in having the ceremony he wanted, not in his local church in Inverkeithing, but in his own front room with the local Church of Scotland minister performing the traditional ceremony before a group of only their closest friends. His brother John was best man. The bridesmaid and pageboy were the children of Sue Nye and Gavyn Davies and there was no place for the metropolitan glitterati: everyone there was either a family member of one of them, a close professional colleague or a lifelong friend. Whelan, for example, was not there. Nor were the Blairs, who were due to begin their summer holiday and had learnt of the wedding plans only twenty-four hours before they took place.

For Brown this was an extraordinary day. It was not only the culmination of a relationship stretching back over a few years and the start of a new era in his personal life, but it marked the end of a period in which his bachelor status had caused him trouble and misery. Long before he turned fifty in February 2001, his marriage plans – or, more accurately, the lack of them – were a source of good copy for the diary columnists. When he did allow a photograph to be published of a dinner date with Sarah Macaulay before the 1997 Budget it was widely described as some kind of put-up job, contrasted with his famous reluctance to be open about his private life. Brown was irritated and offended by this, but typically reluctant to do much about it. His unhappiness was compounded by his knowledge that for some years past his single status had given rise to rumours that he was gay. As with many such Westminster whispers, which attach themselves to the most unlikely characters from time to time, no one could produce a sliver of evidence for the assertion. This was not surprising, because Brown's friends insist that the story has no basis in fact. It did not stop it being peddled, often with the friend-of-a-friend attribution which many politicians know to their cost can quickly appear to become something more substantial in the retelling.

The closest Brown came to a public discussion of the matter came in a recording for *Desert Island Discs* on Radio 4 in the year before the 1997 General Election. At the time, at least one Conservative front bencher was stating 'as a fact' in various Westminster bars that Brown was gay. Some newspapers were said to have startling material which would find its way out. It was a cloud that hovered around him, and he knew of it. So when Sue Lawley interviewed him about his eight records, his book and his luxury, she decided to raise the question. He said that in some ways he was surprised that marriage hadn't happened and Lawley carried on. Surely it wasn't surprising that people were curious: 'It is something that middle-aged men and women have to put up with. People want to know whether you're gay or whether there's some flaw in your personality that you haven't made a relationship.'

Brown waffled in what was evidently some embarrassment and irritation, saying again that he had thought marriage might happen and it hadn't, but he left Broadcasting House furious. There was not much he could do, except to depend on Whelan to offer laddish hints about his love life and his interest in women – hardly a happy media strategy on which to have to embark. His best hope was that the questions would simply subside, but he was well aware that his natural tendency to keep his private life private would allow the old rumours to linger. Even in planning the wedding, however, he wasn't persuaded to ignore his natural instincts. The ceremony was private, the party was deliberately modest, and he left for his American honeymoon in his brother's car. The one concession to the media was a scrambled photocall in the back garden that included an exchanged kiss between Mr and Mrs Brown of some awkwardness. There are few more authentic pictures of the real Brown than those from his wedding, portraits of a man uncomfortable at the mingling of the public and private, ill-at-ease with the expected opening up of a life for public observation and comment. The bride was elegantly attired in an ivory two-piece silk suit. The bridegroom did not, however, use the excuse of his wedding to deviate from sartorial orthodoxy: a sober suit with the regulation red tie was his choice. He could have been delivering a Budget statement.

Brown has usually conducted himself like this. Although the student affair with Princess Marguerite of Romania had an inescapable air of improbability and panache about it, subsequent relationships have been conducted privately. For much of the eighties his close friend Marion Caldwell, then an Edinburgh solicitor, stayed well out of the public eye, and in the nineties a relationship with the broadcaster Sheena McDonald was kept very discreet. Brown has always been reluctant to open himself up as an object of public curiosity, and still shies away from personal interviews which might demand that too many innermost thoughts spill out. He has always been determined to keep the curtains drawn round his private life.

There was a touching illustration of his concern for privacy on the morning after his wedding. Whelan was touring the TV and radio studios as the obvious commentator on proceedings, indulging in some happy observations of the I-told-you-so sort. After saying on GMTV that, of course, the wedding wasn't really a surprise because the couple had been more or less living together for years, he received a phone call at the TV studios from someone close to Brown. It had not been prompted by Brown himself, but the message was that perhaps Whelan shouldn't have said what he had, because Brown's mother might have been watching. Even the shock-proof Whelan was surprised that a Chancellor of the Exchequer in his fiftieth year might have to worry on such grounds.

The point of the story is not that Brown comes from a grim or straitlaced family. He does not. It is that he has a natural feeling for the boundaries between the private and the public which, in his mind, are inviolable. To many others in public life, and Blair is among them, this caution seems excessive and sometimes off-putting but it has always been a part of his character. Public displays of emotion, unless in pursuit of the political cause, are not enjoyable.

Brown the university radical grew out of Brown the conventional schoolboy, and one has not entirely replaced the other. His politics were always personal and energetic, but the sixteen-year-old who arrived in Edinburgh in 1967 and was thrown immediately into the trauma of his eye operations, with the fear of blindness in the background, was a character who had to leap from spotty adolescence to self-reliance very quickly. Colleagues from that era recall someone who was never a carefree youth. Adulthood, like political seriousness, came on quickly.

His lifeline at that time was his family, his father especially. He and his brothers, the older John and the younger Andrew, have stayed close and supportive. It is inconceivable that he would take a major turning in his life without talking it through with them first. Brown is not someone who seems ever to have felt his family slipping into a more distant orbit with the years. It is as close as it was when he was growing up in Kirkcaldy, listening to his father preach on Sunday mornings. His view has always been that these solid foundations must never be allowed to erode in his mind.

The closeness extends to the circle outside his Treasury office. It is striking that three of his most intimate friends are veterans of his student days. The thriller writer Colin Currie was a contributor to *Student* when Brown was editor. Wilf Stevenson, who became director of the British Film Institute, was also part of the gang. Murray Elder – now Lord Elder of Kirkcaldy, sitting on the Labour benches in the Lords – goes back even further. He and Brown went to nursery school together, played rugby and went to Edinburgh as students, coming together in politics again in the eighties when Elder emerged from a period at the Bank of England to work for Denis Healey and then John Smith, whose chief of staff he became in 1992. These are Brown's closest friends; they have all known him for well over thirty years. It is still to them that he returns. With his wife and his brothers, they are the private circle to which he confides his deepest feelings. They seldom travel any wider.

Rigorous privacy has never been of such concern to Blair. From the beginning, the circles that influenced him have been looser. Some of this can be traced back to his youth. Unlike Brown's youthful and traumatic immersion in university life, Blair was nineteen when he left Fettes and had a carefree air which may have concealed some of his ambition and his working habits at Oxford, but was nonetheless in character. He enjoyed being the centre of attention, whether at the microphone for Ugly Rumours in the seventies gear that pinpoints the year almost exactly, or at a St John's College party eyeing up an elegant woman who used to walk around the college leading a kitten on a lead. His gang then was eclectic and so it has remained.

He is still in contact with some of his student friends, none of whom went into serious politics. Socially his contacts are as likely to be from the law, or from the Islington circles in which the Blairs used to live before Downing Street, as from the Labour Party. He is close to his agent and chairman in Sedgefield, John Burton, with whom he won the selection in 1983 and who supported him during the early days of modernization against some awkward opposition, but in London his private circles have never been politically obsessive. Campbell and Hunter were office figures who, despite their professional closeness to Blair, were not fixtures at home. Brown guards his private life with determination, but it is paradoxical that his private and public lives are intertwined more completely than Blair's. With Brown it is hard to say where politics stops and the other life begins. They are tributaries of the same stream.

Blair, though he is less concerned at the inevitable intrusions that come with high office than Brown has always been, has separated his lives more clearly. Some episodes have alarmed his family, usually involving schools. Public comments made by the headmaster of the London Oratory School, the Catholic school in Fulham where Euan was sent from Islington, are known by friends to have infuriated both of his parents. But Blair himself was able to make a joke at the time of the election of the incident in which Euan's friends left him drunk in Leicester Square and he was delivered home by the police. Although it was embarrassing and something of a family torment, it could eventually be spoken of lightly. In private, Blair has little of the obsessive concern with control that has come to be associated with his government. He finds it possible to relax.

Blair and Brown's political friends tell much the same story. Blair's political soulmates are a colourful, even eccentric bunch. The lead trio sets the tone – Mandelson, Irvine and Lord Falconer of Thoroton, never known in Downing Street as anything other but Charlie. They appear to provide Blair with much of what he needs.

Mandelson tells friends that, despite his two resignations, 'our relationship has never missed a beat'. Those who are in a position to know believe it to be true. Blair has despaired of Mandelson from time to time but it never seems to last for more than a few hours. He always comes back. During his first period out of Cabinet Mandelson was staying with friends one weekend while Blair was at a summit abroad. In the course of the Saturday the phone rang several times for Mandelson. It was the Prime Minister seeking advice. The disasters for Mandelson which led to his two resignations were seen in Downing Street as lapses of judgement on the part of someone who had always flirted with danger in public and in private, the moth that flew too close to the flame. But they did not destroy Blair's relationship with Mandelson. Although Campbell, even before the election, became greatly irritated by what he regarded as Mandelson's egocentricity – he told friends that he found his self-preening to be a pain – Blair has never wavered. On the day of the second resignation the stricken faces of the Prime Minister and the Northern Ireland Secretary suggested that they had been driven asunder, and the next day Andrew Grice, political editor of the *Independent* and an old friend and contact of Mandelson's, wrote words which were taken at Westminster to reflect Mandelson's own feelings – 'it's a parting of the ways'. It wasn't. To the irritation of Labour MPs who rather enjoyed seeing Mandelson cut down from on high, Blair retains him as a trusted confidant. They talked on the phone daily before and after the 2001 election.

It is the same with Irvine. Blair's debt goes back to his pupil-barrister days in 1976 and to the introduction he provided to John Smith and the top of the Labour Party. Irvine's 'young Blair' shivered through the public relations disaster of Irvine's choice of Pugin-design wallpaper for his official apartments in the House of Lords, and an absurd row about the modernization of the Lord Chancellor's formal garb which turned into a Trollopian debate among officials in the Lords about his wig. When Irvine made an ill-judged speech to the Society of Labour Lawyers soliciting funds from people whom he could promote to the bench if he so wished, some of Blair's colleagues hoped it might be the end. When Irvine's apology to the Lords turned out not to be an apology at all, but a simple assertion of his own integrity and honesty, the Downing Street view was that it was another perplexing blunder. Everyone knew that, in the Lords most of all, a grovelling apology from a minister in trouble worked wonders and cleared the air. Yet there was never a hint in the post-election reshuffle that there would be a new Lord Chancellor. Blair's gratitude and affection run too deep. The phone calls may not be as frequent as they once were but he still talks to Irvine more often than to any other member of the Cabinet save Brown.

Falconer, too, had to walk through fire. As the inheritor of the Millennium Dome from Mandelson he found himself in charge of one of the great political disasters of the Blair years. Despite the figures showing that it was Britain's most popular visitor attraction in 2000 and the opinion polls claiming that most visitors would come back a second time, Falconer struggled to give any substance to a project which by the turn of the century seemed metaphorically as well as literally empty. By the start of the second term it was a forlorn sight on the Thames at Greenwich, with its insides ripped out. The lights at the top of the metal arms supporting the roof still winked over London; but the Dome was dead. Nothing was heard of Blair's boast that it would be the first paragraph of Labour's election manifesto, because it symbolized so much about the new Britain that his government was bringing into being. Indeed, such was the nervousness about the Dome being used by the Conservatives as a symbol of emptiness and a costly triumph of flummery over substance that Labour was startled, as well as relieved, to find that the Tories decided to make little of it in the 2001 campaign.

Charlie Falconer is not a politician who looks as if he has had to soak up many punches. Indeed in some ways he is not a politician at all. A friend of Blair's from Scotland (Falconer also knew Amanda Mackenzie-Stuart), he carries the easy bonhomie of the confident and slightly louche lawyer, a few locks of hair splayed over his collar and a cheery smile usually completing the picture. He is well-fed and witty, a natural Blair companion who manages never to appear too serious, even when his brain is trying to work out the latest line of defence for the Dome, which kept it busy for many months. One senior civil servant, who is privately rather fond of him, says: 'Charlie is marvellous in a way. And he is obviously important to the Prime Minister. But the truth is that he is not really very political, in the sense of knowing things that most politicians expect to know. He's quite different. Derry is much the same – hopeless at some of the obvious political things. You could say they know nothing. But they're terribly important.' Falconer, however, did become a fixture at the Millbank election headquarters in the re-election campaign and displayed the energy for which his frame is often a disguise. On the night of the Prescott punch he turned instantly into the defence lawyer, scrutinizing television pictures again and again to come to a conclusion about the incident. One who was there said: 'He was transformed. It was as if he was at the police station having a first look at the evidence. He was making a legal judgement about what exactly had happened. When he slapped his hand and said "that's it – we're OK, I think", I thought the place was going to erupt in applause. His advice to Blair on the night was an important element in the Prime Minister's tactics with Prescott.'

Some of Blair's closest colleagues, excepting Mandelson who is steeped in Labour lore, were not cast in the political mould. And these are often the ones he would socialize with by choice, perhaps over a fine bottle of wine from Irvine's cellar. He would enjoy it more than an evening of heavy politics with some of his more earnest Cabinet colleagues.

Earnestness is more of a quality in the Brown camp. Although Balls and his friends exhibit a fair streak of hedonism – they are capable of spectacular drinking sprees – the Brownites have a high seriousness that is encouraged from the top. Geoffrey Robinson, Paymaster General before his fall over the Mandelson home loan, is an intriguing exception. Robinson is a high roller, whose business affairs have been subject frequently to critical scrutiny and investigation, and who seems at first glance to be a most unlikely Brown intimate. He lives during the week in a rented Park Lane apartment and has large houses in England and in Tuscany. He is gregarious and generous with his favours, feeding guests to their limits and acting as a rumbustious host. Brown and his entourage enjoyed Robinson's company and political gossip, Brown even taking to using the Grosvenor House health club for a period where he could be found on some mornings pedalling away on the cycling machine in a fair old sweat. Although party-loving Robinson was loyally on-side throughout, especially in pressing the case across government for public–private partnerships which had become a treasured Brown mechanism for pulling more money into the public sector while policing the golden rules of fiscal prudence. Robinson, whose business inventiveness has got him into trouble as well as bringing him a personal fortune, was a supporter who stayed signed up to the team.

From each of the groups of friends comes some of the character that makes Blair and Brown what they are. Blair's is a more relaxed circle, and not only because as Prime Minister he is not consumed by the usual political ambitions about how to take the last step to the summit. It is a reflection of his character in office as well as his personality. He has resisted complete absorption in politics, even in Number 10. Brown, on the other hand, has an attraction to the intricacies of the political world which never flags. He wakes up to political thoughts, and takes them to bed at night. Since his student days he has wrestled with the effort of pulling together a set of socialist instincts with the practical demands put on an early twenty-first century government in a global economy. That is where his energy goes.

The result is that with rare exceptions like the exotic Robinson, by Brown's standards a flamboyant dandy, his political friends tend to have seriousness in common. Alistair Darling, Secretary of State for Work and Pensions, is a little cheerier than he sometimes appears. Andrew Smith, chief secretary to the Treasury, is not. In the junior ranks of the government those who take their lead from the Treasury tend to adopt the style of Douglas Alexander, promoted spectacularly by Brown to an important role in the re-election campaign at Millbank although he was only elected in Paisley South in a by-election in November 1997 and appointed Minister for E-Commerce and Competitiveness after the 2001 election. As a clever economist who used to work for Brown (and whose sister, Wendy, is a minister in the Scottish Executive in Edinburgh), Alexander epitomizes some-thing of the spirit of those whom the parliamentary party identifies as Brownites. They are serious-minded but they are not political innocents. They know how to play the game and understand the thrill of the cut and thrust of the deft political manoeuvre. Although Blair's Cabinet at the start of the second term showed a tilt away from established Brownite figures – Charles Clarke's appointment to the Cabinet Office being the most obvious evidence of the shift – there is still a gang of supporters sprayed around the backbenches and throughout the government who regard Brown as the leader of a movement to which they belong. They don't plot directly against Blair, and will always protest their collective loyalty to the govern-ment, but they doff their caps first in the direction of the Chancellor's office.

Blair's inner circle is fiercely loyal and protective and will struggle for him in the last ditch; so will Brown's. The difference between their wider circles is that where Blair has wide support among those who have prospered under his leadership and who stand to gain most from his patronage, there is an anxiety among some ministers most loyal to him that Blair's political commitment may not be as strong as they would wish. A Blairite Cabinet minister bluntly articulated an anxiety shared among New Labour sympathizers: 'My fear is simple. It is that many of Tony's friends are there because the weather is still fine and that they could disappear very quickly in a storm. If he were to go suddenly, or if we were hitting really serious, serious trouble, I'm not sure what they would do. The difference with Gordon is that he has believers. Some of us don't want Gordon to be Prime Minister – but maybe his people want it more.'

That is where the story of the friends turns into a story about the future, and about the way Blair and Brown are appealing to their party. With their closest advisers and confidants helping them on they are engaged in a double game. Day by day they are continuing to make their established partnership work. Rows come and go but the decisions are made. There is no serious threat that Brown will resign, nor that Blair will walk away. They make it work because they must. It is how the government functions. But alongside the daily meetings and phone calls, entreaties and passages of angry silence, there was, at the start of the second term, a new game starting to take shape.

Blair, the Prime Minister who turned Labour into the most dominant electoral force Britain had seen for more than a century, was beginning to look to a second term as the period in which, like all long-serving Prime Ministers, he would try to find and secure his place in history. Where would he find it? And Brown, aware of a stirring deep in his party that spoke of coming discontent and trouble over the drift of policy, was wondering how to preserve the public loyalty which he has shown to Blair while building an alternative future for Labour under his direction, which his speeches, writings and political strategy all suggest that he sees glimmering somewhere ahead.

11

I Believe

The Arab League ambassadors who came as observers to Labour's conference in 2000 had a surprise when they met the Prime Minister on the penultimate day. At the party's reception for them he quoted from the Koran. Those guests who enquired as to whether a helpful handbag of quotes had been provided by the Foreign Office found that the source was not an assiduous diplomat's briefing but Blair himself. He was able to do it for a remarkably straightforward reason. He had the Koran by his bed, and was reading it.

Blair may be the only Prime Minister elected in the twentieth century to have opened the book with intent, apart from Anthony Eden, who studied Persian and Arabic at Oxford and may have had recourse to some of its exhortations when, in his wife's unforgettable phrase, the Suez Canal was flowing through his drawing room in 1956. Blair had no such background, and it was not Saddam Hussein or the debate about sanctions on Iraq that took him to the Koran. He was intrigued by its moral code. It is safe to say that there is not another member of his Cabinet who keeps a holy book by the bedside. Blair is alone among them in having a burning fascination for the spiritual, and no one can explain him without understanding that sometimes that feeling is more important to him than politics.

And despite saying in the year before he became Prime Minister that he was not fond of politicians who wore God on their sleeves, in the American way, Blair can easily be tempted. Indeed he revealed that his interest in the Koran was kindled by Chelsea Clinton, the President's daughter, who carries a copy everywhere, and he has picked up the habit. 'I carry a copy of the book with me whenever

I can, to give me inspiration and courage,' he told *Muslim News* in March 2000, saying that he found the Koran clear and reflective, revealing 'the concept of love and fellowship as the guiding spirits of humanity'. And all from a President's daughter.

Notwithstanding Margaret Thatcher's recitation of a prayer of St Francis of Assisi taken from her handbag on the steps of Number 10 in 1979, this is the kind of remark that no other modern British Prime Minister would have made. Not since Gladstone has a party leader spoken of religion like Blair. It's a practice that makes most of his Cabinet colleagues uncomfortable. A number of them are practising Christians, but most are not. None would be willing to slip so easily into spiritual mode.

Some of them find it scary. When he said in an interview in September 2000, after the miserable summer of fumbles and mistakes, 'I am a man with a mission', it rang true to ministers who have come to know him as someone driven by something inside. They have come to realize that it is not a conventional political philosophy that keeps him going. Many politicians live for the hours when they can tease out policy arguments, test them against political history, ruminate on the character of governments and ministers past. They think of themselves as pieces in a fascinating though sometimes infuriating political jigsaw that can never be complete. In their different ways, Brown, Cook, Blunkett and Straw are all like that. Blair is not. He has as much political energy, but it seems to come from a different source. He doesn't draw on the usual wellsprings of politics.

He doesn't feed on Labour's tradition, for the simple reason that even after he became leader he was unable to shake off the feeling that the story of Labour and the twentieth century is a story of failure. He contrasts the success of Gladstonian and Asquithian Liberals over a period of about fifty years from the last quarter of the nineteenth century onwards with the patchy story of Labour in the twentieth. He is as ready as the next Labour politician to eulogize the Attlee post-war government for the invention of the NHS or the strengthening of the welfare state – although at moments of high frustration with Labour he will point out that Beveridge and Keynes were Liberals – but underneath Blair has a more melancholy view of his party's history. His address at the Labour Party's 100th birthday at the Old Vic in February 2000 betrayed some of that unease. Any of his predecessors as leader would have been happier at the event. His rather gloomy view of Labour history was one of the reasons for his conference speech about the 'forces of conservatism' in 1999, which was not driven simply by a desire to appear more combative and perhaps partisan. Paradoxically, he found himself in trouble for making a speech which appeared to dismiss all Conservatives as hopeless reactionaries, when the convictions revealed in the speech derived more from a sense of failure on his own side.

Much of his politics flows from that negative feeling about his party. His own political convictions sprang from his interest in ethics at Oxford, rather than from an enjoyment of political activity, and he was aware when he was first attracted to Labour that it was a party which was burdened by a heavy sense of defeatism. In the seventies it was riven by ideological disputes and weary of government. Soon after he joined it, he concluded that it was facing schism and might splinter into fragments. His parliamentary career in the eighties consisted of dispensing with many of the attitudes and policies he had adopted as a young candidate. It was a bonfire of the promises. Unilateralism, opposition to the Common Market, support for nationalization, opposition to the sale of council houses – into the flames they went. Consequently, for Blair, there wasn't much in the ashes of old policies or in the litany of failed Labour governments from which he could draw inspiration. No Labour character figures in Blair's mind in the way that Maxton engrossed and spurred Brown. So he looked to other sources for his political energy and vision.

Such was his sense of distance from Labour's past that he developed a habit of sometimes referring to his party as 'they' instead of 'we' and to the embarrassment of his staff he has not managed to lose it in Downing Street. In arguing in the nineties for New Labour and then 'the third way', Blair was not simply trying to invent a new political language – as Thatcher had – but was consciously trying to put to rest the first hundred years of Labour's history. He might give the traditional conference speech boasts about the party's achievements, but twenty-two years of power in a hundred years didn't strike Blair as anything but failure.

Additionally, he had grown up with no sense of belonging to the Labour Party. His father had been an active Conservative and his own party membership came long after he had assembled a package of beliefs that weren't absorbed from formal politics. His religious interests at Oxford, which have remained with him almost unchanged ever since, led him to his interest in ideas of community from which he found his way to politics. Blair's political beliefs are unusual for a British leader in not coming from a framework of ideology. Even John Major was more steeped in his party's ideology than Blair.

The feeling of disaffection with his party's history, a history which has never gripped him in the way it mesmerized Brown as a teenage student, explains a good deal of Blair's impatience with colleagues and party traditionalists. When Roy Hattersley began his running commentary on the failures of the government after 1997, usually targeted directly at Blair, Downing Street affected to be amused. When the former deputy leader wrote savagely about Blair on the morning of a conference speech in Blackpool, however, there was genuine anger; and by the start of the second term the tone in Blair's office was contemptuous. 'How much did he get for that one?' they'd ask of the latest piece of savagery in the *Daily Mail*. 'When did he last say anything sensible in the Lords?' Publicly, the Prime Minister was said to be untroubled by anything Hattersley said; privately he seethed. Part of the reason is that he sees his own leadership as the natural and logical consequence of the Kinnock–Hattersley reforms and, according to his friends, he regards his old colleague as 'gutless' in refusing to accept it.

There's another reason. Blair knows that he has indeed been engaged on exactly the kind of rewriting of the Labour idea that Hattersley finds offensive. When he wrote just after re-election that Blair's devotion to meritocracy was a *coup d'état* against Labour's 'legitimate philosophy' because it betrayed the disadvantaged by its concentration on rewarding success, his ringing crescendo peaked with: 'I do not know what distresses me more, the apostasy or the naivety.' Blair would not plead guilty to naivety – his approach has been studied. Apostasy he might regard as a compliment. He would accept that he has indeed abandoned what he'd call 'old thinking' about equality of outcome, replacing it with a commitment to equality of opportunity. Hattersley's words wound only because Downing Street knows that the transformation – which he describes as a betrayal – is undeniable. It can't be disguised. It was Blair's specific intention.

Blair's beliefs involve a conscious rejection of the past, almost for its own sake. Throughout the Thatcher years he watched from the sparsely covered opposition benches as she wrote a new political language, with Nigel Lawson its supervising grammarian and Bernard Ingham and Norman Tebbit the trumpets who gave it voice. Blair used to listen in wonderment. Before he and Brown began to stir together just before the 1987 election, with Mandelson shaping the relationship, Blair would talk wide-eyed of Thatcher's success in reworking the geometry of politics. 'She's changed it all,' he would say. 'She speaks in a different way. She's made her own style.' It had a profound effect on him. Here was a Prime Minister who came to power determined to make amends for the failures of Edward Heath's last Conservative government, as she saw them, and to assuage her own guilt for her part in it. In doing so she turned her party to her way of thinking (or enough of it, at least, to allow her eleven years in office). This was achieved, Blair thought, more by stubborn attack than by negotiation. She simply demanded new thinking, persisted and got it. That was the lesson he absorbed. He admired her for that, and made no apologies to colleagues who were startled and privately appalled when he invited her to Downing Street after the 1997 election to talk about the early days of government. No other member of his Cabinet would have contemplated such an action. Blair, however, enjoyed the sense of being made in a different mould and was amused by the fuss. She hasn't been back – but he doesn't regret it. Just after he became leader in 1994 Thatcher said in a BBC interview: 'I see a lot of socialism behind their front bench, but not in Mr Blair. I think he genuinely has moved.' It didn't bother him.

Blair in pursuit of political ends is a Prime Minister who shows little concern about the means. If his party thinks it is being insulted, he doesn't care. If he's accused of being too close to the Liberal Democrats, he cuddles up closer. If he is said to be too ingratiating towards George W. Bush, he takes the chance once more to defend the Americans' thinking about the 'war on terrorism'. When he decided to bring Charles Clarke into the Cabinet as fixer and all-purpose government voice in the Cabinet Office ('Minister for the *Today* programme' and 'enforcer' are two of the titles that tradition-ally go with the job) he made him party chairman without dreaming of consulting Labour's national executive, which for generations has elected chairmen by the happy rules of Buggins's Turn, to preside over the monthly meetings and have a week of celebrity by the seaside chairing the party conference. Like Thatcher, Blair is often his own opposition, relishing the collisions with his party. They animate him and are one source of his political energy.

Belief for Blair is an attitude to life rather than a set of conventional political positions. He revels in his *difference*. In politics he is an outsider who has found his way in, and who seems determined not to be constrained within the usual boundaries. Brown, by contrast, has spent his life on the inside and is the politician who only steps out on his own terms. He does not see politics as a pond into which he's chosen to dive but as the natural habitat which nurtures him and lets him breathe. This is one of the differences between them that has enabled them to survive as a pair. They are not doubles who replicate each other's instincts and attitudes, but creatures from fundamentally different environments.

As much as Blair never wants to lose the feel of the outsider, Brown cherishes the opposite. From the moment he started to write in *Student* and fall for the charms of campus politics in Edinburgh, he has been on the inside looking out. The attitudes he strikes in government lead directly back to his early politics. Like Blair he went through the process of ditching early obsessions, in his case the heady assault on 'the logic of capitalism' in the *Red Paper* period, and although he was never as strident either on unilateralism or in the anti-Europe cause as many of his generation on the left, all that had been cleared away by the mid-eighties. Yet with Brown there were threads that always led back to early days. His rhetoric as Chancellor, even as the iron disciplinarian of the spending reviews, is still replete with references to equality and social justice. Although the word 'redistribution' was held to be too much of a reminder of Labour tax-and-spend attitudes long gone, and was therefore buried, Brown has always been happy to argue for his politics as natural products of an egalitarian instinct, which he interprets as a commitment to equality of opportunity.

As a schoolboy he'd written about poverty. His father insisted that his children understand what it meant to have to struggle in life; Brown always says that one of the debts he owes him is the importance of a feeling for equality. It explains a great deal about Chancellor Brown, but of course it also poses some questions. He was the minister who fought the backbenches on benefit changes – forced by the Treasury on the Social Security department – and who tangled with the sprightliest old warhorse of them all, Barbara Castle, on pensions and refused to budge in the face of her entreaties and campaigns to accept the restoration of the earnings link.

He was defeated on pensions at the 2000 party conference, and in his re-election campaign Blair said he regarded the 75p rise as the biggest mistake of the first term. It was a mistake he was quite content to lay at the Treasury's door, saying pointedly in his leader's speech at the conference: 'I tell you now – as Gordon made crystal clear yesterday – we get the message.' Brown appeared to believe that, with his big increases in the minimum income guarantee, he was making his commitment obvious, but within a month he had to backtrack and announce increases in the basic state pension of £5 for a single person and £8 for a couple so that 'all pensioners – the very poor, those on modest incomes and the relatively comfortable – share in the rising prosperity of the nation'. He was scrambling to recover lost ground.

Brown has presented a dual personality to his party and the public. One half of him is the austere accountant and stealth-taxer, the Silas Marner of Great George Street. In the first comprehensive spending review in 1997 he bullied the Cabinet into accepting

Conservative spending plans and even those who had got used to his methods in opposition were surprised at the ferocity with which he guarded his defences. There would be no backsliding. He told his colleagues that it was the election promise on which the government would stand or fall. Blair managed a joke about it in his 1999 conference speech, telling the party: 'You've never had it so prudent.' This was the Brown who gazed beetle-browed at the electorate after each of his early budgets promising that the pain would allow some later pleasure. But it couldn't happen without the pain. The message was unwelcome among some colleagues who began to talk about a Labour government seeming not to be a Labour government at all. Weren't they supposed to spend more than Major? Brown said no. He had his fiscal rules and they would not be broken, above all the Golden Rule laying down that, over the course of an economic cycle, borrowing would all be used for investment and not for current spending, the day-to-day running costs of government. In real terms spending rose by only 1.3 per cent a year over the Parliament, a lower average figure than the Major government managed, and in his first two years it actually fell by an average of 1 per cent a year in real terms. Fiscal rules, prudence and the bogey of boom and bust became the building blocks of every Brown speech and the patois of Whitehall. In the way that politicians always tune instinctively into a new dialect, just as schoolchildren will pick up the slang of the moment, Brown's disciplined repetitions ensured that the whole government began to speak in the language of the Treasury.

But Brown insists that he is not a mechanical Chancellor, concerned simply with the economic efficiency and progress which it is his job to produce. His obsession with stability is indeed an obsession: it is a belief that drives him. When he is asked to write or speak about his political beliefs he invariably chooses a theme of social justice. His own justification for everything he does in the Treasury is assessed in these terms. If the prudence of which he speaks cannot be shown by the end of his Chancellorship to have improved social justice he will, in his own terms, have failed. He convinced himself in opposition that rigour was necessary if the economic conditions he required were going to be produced. He therefore found no difficulty in arguing to sceptical colleagues that Conservative spending plans had to be respected for two years, and that the agreement to stick to existing tax rates for the whole Parliament be kept. The Bank of England decision, disliked by the left because it was deemed to put interest rate policy in the hands of the City, was similarly not awkward for him because his political thinking was dominated by the end rather than the means.

By the end of the first term, although the word 'redistribution' was still outside the approved lexicon and Brown talked about 'balance' instead, he was almost willing to put himself in the context of a socialist tradition. On the morning after the Budget in which he had decided to offer no direct tax cuts but a substantial new investment in health and education he was asked on the *Today* programme if he thought of himself sometimes as a socialist Chancellor. He replied: 'I think of myself as being fair – yes.' Explaining what he meant, he said: 'If it means equality of opportunity so that more people in our country have the chance of realizing their opportunities, then that's what I want to do.' He did not suggest that it was an outdated label, only that he wanted to interpret in his own way what it might mean.

Brown's language is interesting, because although it replicates Blair's themes about the economy so that there is no danger of gaps appearing between them, the Chancellor has always tried to retain for himself the mantle of the minister who thinks about the poor. It was the subject of his maiden speech, his 1983 book about Scotland with Robin Cook, and his efforts to promote the cause of debt reduction in the developing world. Nothing is more important to Brown than reminding his party that he hasn't lost that concern, an accusation heard often during the first couple of years of austerity from the left-wing Campaign Group and individual critics like Ken Livingstone.

One way Brown responded was to try to turn the question of debt in the developing world into a personal crusade. In opposition, he and Clare Short were not especially close, and when she spoke on transport they had the familiar battles about spending commitments. Brown thought she was a loose cannon whose opinions arrived loudly and long before her thoughts were in order. In government, as International Development Secretary, she and Brown shared one of the more surprising alliances in the Cabinet. Had Blair wanted to move her in 2001, Brown would have fought to keep her in post. He didn't have to, but the message to Number 10 was clear. Their bond was a strategy on debt devised between them which Brown claims offers the hope that child poverty can be greatly reduced and, in some countries, virtually eliminated. He has spent a great deal of time on the subject, with fellow finance ministers and leaders in the development movement, and his colleagues, Blair in particular, are happy to acknowledge it as a genuinely original effort. Brown insisted by mid-2001 that twenty-three countries had had their huge debts cancelled because of their efforts, although aid agencies are still arguing that on average only a third of debt repayments have been removed and many of the forty-one countries identified as being in need of help in 1999 were still crippled.

For Brown, however, it was a significant area of his chancellorship. It is a part of his job that confers no political benefits directly, either to Brown personally or to Labour. Elections are not won and lost over arguments about Third World debt. But Brown has made time for his debt reduction strategy to matter deeply to him. It is particularly his own. When he delivered the Gilbert Murray Memorial Lecture at Oxford at the beginning of 2000 to mark the founding of Oxfam in the early forties, a passionate Brown in full flow could be heard: 'John F. Kennedy once warned us that if a free society cannot help the many who are poor, it cannot save the few who are rich. But I believe that we start our considerations from something more fundamental – our dependence on each other.' This led to a perhaps unlikely friendship with the Archbishop of Canterbury, George Carey. Carey, who has entertained Brown and his wife privately at Lambeth Palace, found himself a welcome guest in the Treasury, his first experience of such intimacy with a Chancellor. 'I think he is a quite remarkable and deep man,' says Carey of Brown. The relationship is not one which Brown has publicized but it is strong.

Brown's main public boast is the New Deal programme but he

is just as proud of his work on debt relief. For Brown, sometimes assailed as the man who told the first Blair government it could not spend enough on the things it wanted, it is an important touchstone. Without it, he would feel greatly diminished.

He would also be seen as a dour and ruthless Chancellor, because he and Blair conducted the first comprehensive spending review, laying down plans for three years, with the vigour of an inquisition. It was a two-man job, with Brown the driving force. There were moments when Blair might feel it necessary to moderate Treasury enthusiasm for a particular figure, after being lobbied by some minister concerned that his department's great causes were going to be jeopardized, but it was an operation of notable joint ruthlessness. The two Cabinet committees – on economic affairs and public spending (both chaired by Brown anyway) – were effectively bypassed. No collective discussions were allowed to disturb the course of the spending discussions which were conducted with individual ministers who found they had no right of appeal. They were given the figures for the next three years of spending, and that was that. There was no star chamber of the sort that Willie Whitelaw had to convene in the early Thatcher years to hear appeals and adjudicate on tricky disputes with the Treasury. The Blair–Brown regime was less forgiving at the start than the Iron Lady's. What is more, the system of public service agreements introduced by Brown, which were the instruments by which the spending plans were controlled, meant that departments could only get the next tranche of their entitlement when they had demonstrated that the policy objectives set for them had been achieved. They had to defend their 'outcomes', the word that along with 'delivery' was to become almost an encapsulation of the purpose of power under Blair and Brown.

Nothing like this had been done before. In the post-war era, no Chancellor had been given so much raw power. The Whitehall wiring all seemed to run back to Brown's desk. With the Cabinet structure giving way to something close to a dual premiership – or at least a partnership in which the Prime Minister did not lay much store by his second title, First Lord of the Treasury – Brown was able to put an imprint on the government that was a statement of his own conviction, that without discipline there could be no progress.

Brown is a politician whose beliefs are obvious, never far from the surface of his performance in government. Though he tries to play down the redistributive effects of his policy, aware that it may open up some difficulties for the 'third way' talk of Blair, he has been a Chancellor who has manipulated the tax system with zeal in ways which he believes will shift money to the right places. He is criticized in the opposition parties for having done it in ways which have produced more damage than benefits – the 'stealth taxes' on pensions and business would have been a juicy target for a stronger Conservative Party in the 2001 election – but as ever with Brown his purposes are obvious. It is the same with his notion of 'fairness'. Where Blair is ever-anxious not to appear to decry success, Brown is much readier with rhetorical assaults on 'fat cats'. They are, of course, pursuing the same policy, in particular a top rate of tax which they have never seriously considered raising since 1997, but describe the objects of their policy in different ways. Brown still has a penchant for regular attacks on privilege. It sometimes unnerves Blair, who is vulnerable to the charge that his education was a gilded path. But Brown enjoys it. It led him, however, into one of his most embarrassing blunders.

It became the Laura Spence affair. Laura, an A-level student in north Tyneside, had a headmaster who decided to make public his disappointment that, despite having ten of her eleven GCSE results at the top A-starred level (the other being a mere A) she had failed to get a place at Magdalen College, Oxford, and was bound instead for Harvard. There was no argument about Laura's brilliance. Her school expected her to get A grades in all her A-level subjects. It was pointed out that she was also a Grade 8 violinist (the most advanced level) and was about to reach the same grade on her viola. The local press took up her cause, noting that Oxford took fewer than 2 per cent of its students from north-east England (the Cambridge figure was only 3 per cent), compared with 43 per cent from London and the south-east.

That week Brown was due to address a TUC lunch to mark

thirty years of the Equal Pay Act. In his office, his adviser Ed Miliband (whose brother David, now MP for South Shields, was head of the policy unit across the street in Number 10) briefed him about the case. Alastair Campbell had already discussed it in Number 10 after the Newcastle *Journal* headline had been spotted by Blair's 'media monitoring unit' and they realised Brown was due to be speaking about equality. Maybe there was a point to be made here? Miliband gave the Chancellor the bare bones of the story. Brown was sympathetic and angry. He told the lunch that he and the Education Secretary, David Blunkett, thought Laura's story was an 'absolute scandal'. He then spoke in a language which, for the obvious reason of his public school background and Oxbridge education, the Prime Minister would not have used: 'This is an interview system that is more reminiscent of the old-boy network and the old-school tie than genuine justice in our society. It is about time we had an end to that old Britain when what matters to some people is the privileges you were born with rather than the potential you actually have. I say it is time that these old universities open their doors to women and people from all backgrounds.'

Brown let it all pour out. His feelings about privilege were on display, and all the more obvious because as Chancellor he has tended to speak so cautiously, making his points with a machine-like monotony. In this speech, the brakes were off.

But unusually for Brown, who seldom utters a sentence without having considered carefully all the possible consequences, his facts were garbled. Laura had applied to read medicine at Magdalen, where there were twenty-three applicants for five places, and a dozen of the other candidates had GCSE scores as good as hers. (Brown had referred mistakenly to her A-level results: at this stage she hadn't sat the exams.) Of the five who were accepted for the course, two were from state schools and three from ethnic minorities. Laura didn't go to Harvard to read medicine: she decided to read biochemistry. Oxford colleges insisted that it would have been very unlikely that she could not have found a medical place elsewhere in Oxford. She was not sent packing with no alternative but to leave the country. And the Harvard 'scholarship' was not equivalent to a scholarship award in Britain, only the usual means-tested assistance offered by that university (a place, as Brown's critics pointed out, which could easily give Oxbridge some lessons in 'elitism'). But Laura had already become a symbol of 'old Britain', stuffy attitudes and the persistence of class-based education. She seemed less bothered about it than some of her supporters, telling the *Harvard Crimson* campus newspaper that she was 'kind of upset at the time' after an intense interview but adding: 'I wasn't thinking that I had been discriminated against.'

Brown found himself in trouble. In Number 10, Blair was furious although the two men did not have a face-to-face row about it. He was made vulnerable by Brown's sally, because everyone writing or commenting on the case would, naturally, contrast the Fettes–Oxford path that he followed with Brown's from Kirkcaldy High School to Edinburgh as if they were evidence of a great social divide. *The Economist* was typical: '. . . the whole government, in pressing home this attack, while being led by Mr Blair, a privately-educated, Oxford graduate who sends his son to an "elitist", selective school, is guilty of hypocrisy and opportunism'.

Advisers in Number 10 spoke of the Chancellor with real bitterness. Later in the summer, after Blair had slipped into his own stream of troubles they were blaming him for raising the Old Labour spectre. Brown's friends know that he was embarrassed by the revelations of his factual inaccuracy – nothing can make him lose his temper faster than the knowledge that he's been lured into an avoidable mistake – but, just as importantly, they say he has never expressed any regret for the question he raised. He appeared not at all disturbed that senior Oxford dons, a number of them Labour supporters, turned on him and accused him of ignorance, like the scientist Richard Dawkins, who said cheekily that if he did represent New Labour he should do something new and depart from political precedent by apologizing. The fact that joining in the chorus was the Chancellor of the University, Roy Jenkins, did not, of course, increase the chances of a Brown apology, although Jenkins managed a barb aimed with characteristic accuracy: 'If he had wanted to launch a great attack I would have thought his alma mater, Edinburgh, was a better target, since it has more Etonians than Oxford at the present time.'

Brown, although irritated at the revelation of the muddled facts, has never revised his general attitude to the Oxbridge system. He was happy for it to be known where he was positioned. He didn't like the system, and he wanted to say it.

The episode is telling. In the wider Labour Party, Brown found that there was sympathy for his approach. What if he had mangled the odd fact? He was talking, at last, about 'them and us'. And for Brown it was important that his party credentials were burnished. His 75p a week pension award had been announced in the Budget only a few weeks earlier, giving him by far his worst bout of personal publicity since coming to office. The Social Security department could be blamed by some of those in the Chancellor's circle, but that strategy was scuppered by the knowledge, enthusiastically peddled by the Treasury for three years, that nothing in that department could happen without passing through the Chancellor's all-powerful hands. There could not be a better moment for him to take an attitude of the sort that characterized the Laura Spence affair: here was a Chancellor who, though he might make mistakes on pensions, was willing to declare a passion for fairness.

Laura Spence was the unwitting agent of his effort to recover ground lost in the pensions argument: a political point was made. Brown thought he was seen to be on the side of those who wanted more access to excellence – among them women and pupils from state schools. It probably suited Brown that one of his assailants in the row that followed his speech was Blair's old housemaster from Fettes, Eric Anderson. He wrote in the magazine of Lincoln College, Oxford, of which he was the recently retired Rector, that Brown's remarks were deeply offensive: 'I have not seen Oxford so angry about anything.' But the fact that Anderson had left Oxford to become Provost of Eton was seen by those around Brown as useful. Forget the efforts of most Oxford dons to recruit more widely from state schools . . . this had become a political battle of attitudes. Brown was happy to send out his signal. The party would know where he stood.

For some of those on the Labour backbenches who were grumbling about Brown's 'fiscal terrorism' it was a welcome, even overdue, signal. Wasn't it the historic role of Labour ministers to challenge the establishment? In the parts of the party where Brown had his strongest traditional support, the parts that were deeply unsympathetic to Blair's approach to government, the incident was a blast of heat from the old days, fetid though it may have seemed in the senior common rooms of Oxford and the rarified corridors of Whitehall.

In the wide sweep of the first term, the Laura Spence affair did not have serious consequences for the government and was quickly overtaken by events that were much more alarming for Downing Street. Yet it demonstrated a fundamental aspect of Brown's political persona. He is not a minister who will ever be willing to change his fundamental attitudes. Despite the political journey he made from the seventies to the nineties he was displaying the political beliefs which he has kept with him. They are attitudes about wealth, power and social balance. Blair's beliefs are more philosophical than political, a series of instincts which are unconnected in his mind to party-political strategies or obligations.

Where Blair has been anxious to demonstrate that there are no sacred cows grazing on his patch, and has enjoyed the role of the iconoclast who sees a virtue in dismantling the history of his party, Brown has played the opposite role. Even as he espouses some of the language of the supply-side economists of the Thatcher–Reagan years, he is making an effort to remind his party that he retains some of the instincts of the traditional Labour man. Prime Minister and Chancellor often use the same words to describe their beliefs – a hatred of poverty, encouragement for the innovative, a commitment to educational opportunity, a modernized country – but in the accompaniment that runs underneath they reveal their different preoccupations. Blair is anxious to break free, and Brown wants to hold on.

One of Brown's strongest ministerial supporters puts it like this, without embarrassment: 'If you read Gordon's speeches you can see the shape of the party that he would run if he became leader. It's obvious that it's different from Tony's even though they've agreed on the direction the government has taken up to now. Gordon thinks of himself as a Labour man. Tony doesn't. It's the real difference between them.'

Clive Soley, former chairman of the parliamentary party, has had many conversations with Blair about his beliefs and attitudes, and speaks from the position of an agnostic who is interested in Labour's history and beliefs. He expresses the relative positions of Prime Minister and Chancellor thus: 'Tony is a Christian Radical and Gordon is a Christian Socialist. That's the distinction.' By that he means that Brown keeps with him a system of beliefs with which to apply prescriptions in the hope of achieving his ends, and Blair does not. He operates much more by instinct. Soley's acknowledgement of a shared link between their attitude to power and their policies, and their private beliefs is significant.

Blair, of course, is open about his religious life. He is a member of the Church of England but usually worships with his family at a Catholic church; his wife and children are baptized Catholics. Since his time with Peter Thomson at Oxford he has been, more or less, a practising High Anglican though without some of the ritualistic obsessions that sometimes come with that particular strand of Christianity. He is not afraid to draw on it, to the bafflement of some of his colleagues. Prescott, for example, who is resolute in his agnosticism, will not criticize Blair directly for his religious stand but finds it slightly mystifying. From inside the Catholic Church many have speculated that he will one day convert. He did take communion regularly from at least one Catholic priest but after a discussion with the late Cardinal Basil Hume, a close friend, that technically improper practice stopped. Blair could not resist a slightly waspish remark. After agreeing that he would refrain from receiving communion if the Catholic Church was troubled by it he added, 'I wonder what Jesus would have made of it.' Intriguingly, he used a formulation that has become something of a catchphrase among evangelical Christians. No apology there.

Blair's beliefs have caused him some difficulty, and not only from those in his party who find public expressions of religious faith unsettling and inappropriate in government. With the late Cardinal Winning in Glasgow, Blair had a very rocky relationship. In the West of Scotland, Labour is closely associated with the Catholic Church and the Cardinal was a figure of some importance, a Labour-supporting man on social questions but a churchman who was deeply conservative on theological matters, notably abortion. He objected to Blair's position on abortion – that he and his family wouldn't practise it but that he respected the right of others to take a different view. It was evidence, the Cardinal thought, of hypocrisy. Blair was offended. They managed to avoid running into each other on several prime ministerial visits to Scotland, and relations remained badly strained. Despite such problems arising from his willingness to discuss religion – no other post-war Prime Minister showed such an inclination, nor attended church so regularly – Blair has been happy not to retreat.

By chance, he found himself having to address a Faith in the Future conference, made up of a largely black evangelical audience, the very day after his son Euan's escapades in Leicester Square. Blair made a suitably chagrined reference to the incident and then departed from his text to quote a Longfellow poem: '. . . for thine own purpose, thou has sent the strife and the discouragement . . .' He said it was a poem he had turned to the previous night. He went on: 'Faith is important for another reason, too. Faith is and should be in the end the best expression of community, the best expression that there's something bigger than us as individuals.'

Speaking to Hunter Davies in the *Mail on Sunday* during the election campaign, he was frank about his feelings, and even the fact that he had to deal with the incident alone:

I was very worried at the time. But now, looking back, it was pretty hilarious . . . It had been such an awful day for me. I can't remember all the exact details of the day, but it was bad. I think it finished with me being pretty rubbishy at Prime Minister's Question Time. Then next day I had an important speech to make. So I had lots to think about. Plus Cherie was away with her mother and the baby on a short holiday. That left me in charge of the family. At first, I was so busy I didn't have much time to worry about Euan's absence. I wasn't in best shape anyway, with all the other things going on. It was quite late when I started getting worried. I rang some people to find out where he was. Then the police got in touch. It wasn't till 1.30 in the morning that he was located. When he did get home, he wasn't, er, all that well. I was desperate for a good night's sleep because I had a busy day coming up, but I didn't get much sleep that night at all. It was terrible at the time, with all those other things happening, but now in retrospect I can laugh about it. Next morning I was making a speech to some black church leaders. The news about Euan had come by then. They said they were going to say a prayer for me. That was sweet. I was touched by that.

It is impossible to imagine Brown speaking publicly in this way, not because he might not agree with some of the sentiments, but because he is not a politician who can mix the personal and political with Blair's insouciance. He keeps what religious feelings he has to himself. Though he does not go regularly to his local Church of Scotland in Fife, his wedding was conducted with the traditional ceremony and he has never appeared to lose his ties with that faith.

His public attitude to belief, however, is conditioned by a tradition that is quite alien to Blair. In Brown's childhood, religion was a private matter. Outpourings of enthusiasm were not encouraged, nor appreciated. Displays of fervour were generally regarded in Scotland as deeply improper. Religion was about private codes of behaviour. The Catholic way, with which Blair is familiar and very comfortable, has a style that is much less constrained. Reared in a cathedral choir school where Anglo-Catholic practice was the life-style, Blair gravitated naturally into the enthusiastic Christianity of the sort practised by Peter Thomson. It was not the over-the-top evangelism of the university 'God Squad' but it had an unselfcon-scious character which would not have seemed at home in fifties Kirkcaldy. Blair, though not a tub-thumping zealot, has built into his politics an overt spiritual tone which he finds comfortable, even necessary as a motivational reminder of why he's there. Brown keeps his religious beliefs private – even some quite close friends are not sure what they are. He much prefers the echoes of an old socialist language to the ethereal 'peaceful, very beautiful religious faith' which Blair finds in the Koran, though occasionally he is prepared to admit the truth of the adage that Labour owes a greater debt to Methodism than to Marx. A particular Scottish instance is described by Brown in his biography of Maxton, as the newly elected Red Clydesiders departed for London in 1922 from St Enoch's Square, Glasgow, on the night train to the sounds of vast crowds singing Psalm 124 ('Now Israel may say and truly, if that the Lord had not our cause maintained . . .'). Brown adds: 'Not sentiments widely heard in Bolshevik Russia, and the declaration issued earlier in the day owed more to the Bible than to Bolshevism, more to the traditions of the Scottish Covenanters than those of Soviet Communism.' The crowd also joined the William Morris Choir in singing 'Jerusalem', not an anthem often associated with Glasgow.

Cabinet colleagues who wonder why the rows – whether about the benefits policy or Mandelson or Campbell or Laura Spence – have never severed the link between Brown and Blair speculate privately about whether they have enough of a 'belief in belief' in common to retain a fundamental relationship. In the Cabinet there are very few who have been quite so marked by early religious and cultural influences (Blunkett, a serious Christian Socialist, being one notable exception) and some are repelled by Blair's overt attraction to religion. 'Tony's in his Jesus mood again,' one minister has said more than once, without much affection. Brown has none of that tone, but his politics are shaped as much by his background, in which a moral code was important, as Blair's.

Brown's private attitudes may be a deliberately protected mystery, but a description of the Chancellor without reference to the benign Calvinistic influences of his youth would be pointless. Blair, the Koran and the Bible packed carefully by Downing Street staff for every trip, can't be understood without his spiritual baggage. And their relationship, beset by gales and storms, gets some of its surprising resilience from that background. If Blair's public professions of religious faith seem soupy and off-putting to some of his colleagues, and Brown springs from a religious tradition which is often accused of implanting a repressed and guilt-ridden conscience, it nonetheless gives them something in common. At Donald Dewar's funeral, when Blair read from Isaiah and, a few minutes later, Brown delivered his own address, part sermon, part political rallying cry, each seemed at home and both knew it.

Blair lacks the armour of ideology; he has cast aside the shield of clannish party obligation. And what has allowed him to do this is a fundamental inner confidence – the confidence of a natural philosopher who has found a still point around which the intellectual and moral challenges of everyday politics can swirl and be dispatched. Blair's spiritual sense is, like his politics, inclusive rather than dogmatic. God lives, it seems, in a big tent as well.

The crucial distinguishing feature is not a doctrinal one, however, but in the distinct quality of the belief that each man has. Brown, a historian by training, a traditionalist by nostalgic instinct and a technician in practice, has a robust exoskeleton of conviction that roots him in his party. His certainties straddle the inner world and the political world outside. To him, they seem one.

12

Blair and Brown

The Cabinet table is like a psychological chessboard. The games are multidimensional and the lines of attack and defence cross each other in a pattern that is always changing. With each move, a new prospect opens up. But whatever the game plan, one axis never shifts.

The pulse that beats between Blair and Brown is their government's supply of nervous energy. Yet that same strength, which has allowed a Prime Minister and Chancellor to pool their powers and dominate a political era, has given their government a vulnerability, an inner contradiction that it is doomed to resolve in the end. Ministers argue about who is weak and who is strong, and who is the more manipulative of the two. They wonder how Blair and Brown can hold the balance between their personal commitment to each other and their rivalry. So they watch every move with eyes trained to spot the slightest shift of power and the moment when the endgame begins.

When Blair and Brown are together, they behave like brothers or young friends, leaning into each other, Blair touching and Brown grinning, making natural eye contact, understanding each other's reactions as only a close couple can. The notion of an estranged pair of battling ministers, each trying to outdo the other, is inconceivable. Their disputes and sulks don't undermine the closeness; they are the dark reflection of it.

Being part of the government involves studying this psychology. No one in the Cabinet can treat the duopoly of Prime Minister and Chancellor simply as the mechanism by which power is exercised in government. They are all drawn into the undercurrents of the relationship. Blair and Brown seem to their colleagues to need each other, aware that each provides something distinctive. Blair continues to speak of his admiration for Brown's intellect and force; Brown accepts Blair's skill in having colonized a vast tract of the political middle ground for the Labour Party. Each knows that without the other he would be much more feeble. So there is dependence, and that has bred a closeness which gives their government a distinct flavour. It's too strong for some tastes, imparting emotional tension to much of the business of government, but it is inescapable. More than most political partnerships, this one is psychologically compelling to those around.

At Chequers, alone except for perhaps one or two advisers and perhaps one minister involved in a specific subject to be thrashed out, they'll try to sort out some difficulty with a White Paper, or a Budget speech. Those who have been present at these almost private moments report that they are still capable of presenting the old picture of a pair of collaborators who speak an exclusive private language accompanied by an exchange of physical gestures – a grunt, a raised eyebrow, a dismissive wave – that comprise a personal code that they both understand without having to think. They're aware that it was their bonded, concentrated power at the centre of government that allowed an administration of more or less completely inexperienced ministers to manage the first term in a way that produced the second big majority. At those moments, the axis seems the most solid in politics.

But they complicate that simple contented image by the frustration they both display. Blair has wondered aloud to more than one colleague, on a number of occasions, whether he might have to sack Brown. Brown has grumbled about Blair and some of his social policy objectives, and allowed his friends to continue to put about the belief that there is a promise of the inheritance, given by Blair, that must be fulfilled. This parallel contest is as absorbing as the unified front that allows them to divide and rule, the means by which they control their government.

At least one colleague has grown weary of the difficult side of the relationship, especially as it seems as if it is the one that now dominates. He has known them for more than fifteen years and watched every move. 'It was a warm, bonded relationship. It really was. Now it is merely a professional relationship, not underpinned by warmth or much emotion any more. It's sustained simply by the need to exist.'

That bleak account of a union drained of the old passion portrays them as a close couple whose knowledge of each other is as intimate as ever, but whose relations have become routine. Through the re-election campaign it was obvious that some of the fire has cooled. Blair would throw his jacket off at a press conference and plunge into one of his head-shaking, confessional mini-speeches, apparently asking questions of himself. Brown would remain dark-suited beside him, eyes down and unflinching, scribbling away in his large scrawl on sheets of paper piled on top of newspaper cuttings and a copy of the Red Book. The physical relaxation just would not come, and the flow of jokes seemed strained.

By 2001, Brown, his colleagues thought, might have been sunnier. Mandelson was gone. The double act which Blair had planned for the campaign was destroyed before it could begin by Mandelson's unexpected departure from the Cabinet for the second time in January. Yet Brown did not relax. With his friend and loyalist, Douglas Alexander, they ran an efficient campaign with hardly a serious blip, but it was thought by the Blair camp to have a rather grim flavour. One member of the Cabinet put it like this at the end: 'We had a campaign run by two Presbyterians, two sons of the manse. The result was that it was serious and bloody boring. At the party afterwards you'd almost have thought that we'd lost.' This seems a harsh judgement on any campaign that produced an overall Commons majority of 167, but it reveals how the personal styles of Blair and Brown are becoming more distinct in the eyes of their colleagues. One resolute and dark, the Iron Chancellor, the other more relaxed than he was for most of the first term and apparently less concerned about the difficulties that lie ahead than his partner.

People close to Brown dismiss this as a caricature which is put about by Blairites. They point to Brown's last Budget of the first term, laying exactly the foundations he had promised the country would see when he entered the Treasury in 1997. They cite instances when the Prime Minister deferred to the Chancellor at important strategic moments in the government's life. Each side claims the stronger champion. To Brown's cohorts, he is the man who dominates the government and leads Blair. The Prime Minister's side instead claims to be led by a subtle operator who can play Brown's game and win the big battles cunningly, without hang-ups.

Most of the Cabinet are still trying to decide what these men are really like underneath, what drives them, and what keeps them together despite the increasing tensions and the always obvious differences in temperament.

Blair, the natural showman, has enjoyed the physical side of politics – the stage presence, the speech that moves an audience, the close encounter with an elector or another leader. Watching him with one of the audiences in the round assembled for meetings he did throughout the first term and the election campaigns was to see someone comfortable on the swivelling stool in an arena, jacket off, hands pointing, brain whirring. In the same way, he has a relish of the intimacies of contact with other leaders like Clinton.

Blair seems to be able to shake off the tremors of the office when he is at home. He'll want to talk about how he wishes most of all that he could have been a great tennis player, or about his last game against one of his bodyguards at the courts he uses at Chequers, or about how much time he's trying to spend in the gym discreetly built inside Downing Street. Political conversation is not theoretical or academic, but about people. How can so-and-so behave like that? Why can't people in the Labour Party realize what an extraordinary man David Trimble is and why he must be supported? Don't people realize that Paddy Ashdown and I moved everything forward by years? He talks about a political game of chess that takes different turnings and swings in unexpected directions. To Blair, politics is an unfolding pattern of the unexpected, a jigsaw without a picture on the box.

He also retains a feeling for his own inexperience. He'll recall his first G8 summit when Clinton, joking at the new boy's expense to

Boris Yeltsin, recommended that the Russian President, with his experience of the Chechen war, might go to Belfast to help as an intermediary in Northern Ireland – and how, to his horror, Blair watched Yeltsin listen to the translation and reply seriously that he thought it was an idea which he would take up – offering Cossacks on the Falls Road. The early days with Yeltsin were a diplomatic testing ground, in finding a way, for example, of resisting an invitation to have a summit meeting on a Russian submarine under the polar ice cap.

Even when Blair talks of public services, the obsession at the start of the second term, he enjoys the sweep of the subject and the personal anecdote rather than the painstaking argument. As a politician, he flies by his instincts and acts quite often on impulse. One visit to Cumbria during the foot and mouth crisis convinced him that the 2001 General Election should be postponed from 3 May, the date to which his team had been working for more than a year, the date to which a detailed timetable had been attached. A majority of his Cabinet colleagues thought he was wrong; the election team, led by Brown, was strongly against postponement. He wouldn't hear argument. The decision was made.

The private and public Blair are the same. His personal credo – a bit of Anglo-Catholicism, a bit of the philosophy of John Macmurray, a bit of the Koran – is applied to everything. It means that he tends to try to think the best of everyone, even in the most unlikely circumstances. He startled the Foreign Office, for example, by saying that he thought Binyamin Netanyahu, when he was Israeli Prime Minister, was deep down a peacemaker committed to a deal with the Palestinians on the kind of basis that the Americans had been negotiating for years. Robin Cook had to persuade him that perhaps he was allowing his hope to overrule his judgement. Blair, in the end, is an enthusiast.

Brown's enthusiasm is intellectual. It sustains an ambition that is unyielding but everything comes from mental effort. It is how he operates. Deep inside him is a set of attitudes and principles – about poverty, about equality of opportunity, about a society like the one his father imagined – and they sometimes seem to control everything. He thinks about politics all the time. Mandelson would say of him, when they were close, that he lived and breathed politics twenty-four hours every day. He'd never relax. Even with a glass of beer watching *Match of the Day* there would be a strategy to think through, or a phrase to be minted for a speech or a mental note to be made of a book someone mentioned that had to be read. Brown relaxes with tennis or in watching football or rugby (indeed, almost any sport can get his attention, but not quite as easily as a *Financial Times* leader) but most of his life is a self-controlled piece of concentration.

Though he laughs and jokes with friends, his public appearances often have a sombre air. In interviews he is notoriously difficult to warm up. Face to face in a studio he is more mellow, but the sound of the Chancellor announcing a three-point plan down a phone line from Brussels, or from a distant radio car, is sometimes a trial. The lists and statistics are fired out like a Gatling gun. Anyone who can't see the issue of the moment in the terms that he has already sorted out in his own mind does not deserve much consideration, he seems to imply.

Blair is capable of annoyance too, and disguises his occasional tetchiness badly, but on most occasions adopts a take-it-or-leave-it attitude, in the knowledge that interviews are ephemeral and momentary. The sun will rise tomorrow; there will be another speech or another interview; yesterday will pass away.

Since their instinctive reactions are so at odds, they have had to develop a set of unspoken rules by which they can carry out their private discussions and preserve the precious bond that has served them so well. One of the most senior members of the Cabinet says: 'I have never seen Tony take Gordon on full-frontally. I don't think it has happened. He simply won't do it. We know that they have their disputes. But Tony avoids public battles with him.' At least one of Sir Richard Wilson's senior officials who watches many Cabinet meetings and has attended on past Prime Ministers, sees this as a shortcoming. 'It means that whether or not it really is weakness, the Prime Minister's Cabinet colleagues see it as that,' he says. 'Brown is stubborn. Extraordinarily so.' Each displays strength and weakness. Blair can allow an impression of deference to Campbell or Brown to spread without flinching, although it disturbs some of his colleagues. Brown has to cope with a manner, involving a great deal of impatience, that suggests fragility – but rests on a rock of conviction which gives him his foundation. The trick of Blair and Brown's relationship is that each understands the mental architecture of the other.

It is difficult for Blair to pick up every challenge: if he did the government would proceed by means of a series of rows. When he does pick a moment he insists, usually quietly, that his mind is made up. A favourite Brown response is: 'If that's your instinct, that's it.' The reference to instinct, which each of them makes quite often, reveals the extent to which they understand that their closeness has produced a way of working that depends more on 'feel' than on structured argument.

This means that when they fall out it is often over something apparently quite trivial. The funeral of the Princess of Wales was a case in point. In the hasty arrangements made by Buckingham Palace, with Alastair Campbell drafted in from Downing Street as a tactical adviser to assist in the panic of those days, the senior members of the government who were invited to Westminster Abbey were Blair, Prescott, his ceremonial deputy, and Robin Cook, who had been given a personal invitation by the Spencer family because he had spent a great deal of time with the Princess discussing landmines and their removal, a cause to which she had become devoted.

Brown was not on the list. He was furiously offended, possibly because Cook appeared to be pulling rank. Downing Street had to douse his anger for the two days leading up to the funeral. One of those close to it says it was a row fought with a passion which Blair found puzzling. The outcome, though its origin was never publicly admitted, was an announcement from Downing Street just after the funeral in September 1997 that Brown would chair the Diana, Princess of Wales Memorial Committee charged with the responsibility of finding a suitable way of commemorating her life. It was a chairmanship which few in the Cabinet would have wanted. It was daft to burden the Chancellor with it. But it was a necessary palliative, a peace offering from Blair, and it was accepted.

The episode illustrates the confined nature of many of their arguments, which are often petty irritations that spring up and throw one of them off balance for a while, before order is restored. They have found that they cannot run government any other way. They have come to rely on direct but private negotiating channels, the habit that is partly a reflection of Blair's personality and partly the best way of preserving the working partnership with the Chancellor.

Their government has become something of a metaphor for their personalities. Blair, for all his tendency to theatricality and his relaxed style, is surprisingly remote from most of his party; he is not a gregarious Parliamentarian. MPs tend to be brought in groups to see him: he doesn't mingle naturally with them. His family is a private cocoon which is jealously guarded and which is kept, as far as possible, away from his 'working' friends. The reason the Blairs spend a great deal of time at Chequers – much more than the Majors – is that it allows them to shut out the crowd.

Brown, of course, seems to worship at the altar of privacy too. The tendency to try to conceal his emotions was endemic in the society in which he grew up. Metropolitan types are often puzzled by his reticence about his private life before his marriage, but for children of fifties' Scotland sex outside marriage would be something conducted with the vision of an aged aunt standing at the end of the bed watching disapprovingly. You were taught to draw a veil over quite a lot. It means that he finds public displays of emotion uncomfortable, unless they are channelled through politics. It was striking that on the morning after the announcement, in July 2001, of the coming birth of his child he was seen smiling for the cameras with a relaxation that looked new. 'He looks as if he feels free at last,' a close acquaintance said.

Their own characteristics dictate the personality of the throng around the throne. It comes from four people: the Prime Minister, the Chancellor, Campbell and Mandelson. Two of them are no longer there, technically, but their influence pervades Number 10 still. At the height of the government's difficulties with foot and mouth, a Labour MP rang the Prime Minister's office. He spoke to Jonathan Powell, who asked, as agile aides do, what the MP had thought of the coverage of the government on radio and television that lunchtime. How did we come across? The MP gave his answer, and got the reply: 'That's exactly what Peter thought.' This conversation took place at about 2 p.m. It was clear to the MP that Mandelson was plugged in to Blair's office as closely as ever, offering advice on the hour, every hour. He had resigned two months before but, once again, as everyone in Number 10 knew, he was a presence at the Prime Minister's side, the ghost in the machine and the political essence without which Blair seems sometimes to lack confidence in himself. Although Mandelson had been removed from Brown's side as joint coordinator of the election campaign – to the relief of staff at party headquarters who had dreaded the explosions that the arrangement would produce – he was helping to write speeches for the campaign, offering strategic advice and acting as a day-to-day sounding board for the Prime Minister who told his staff that he still depended on Mandelson's advice.

The survival of Mandelson as one of Blair's principal courtiers reveals the unchanging quality of the court. On its outer reaches, ministers come and go and rise and fall in influence. Inside, the old loyalties and rivalries dictate everything. Mandelson, despite the anger which he felt at his second resignation, cannot let go. One minister describes it in a cruel sentence: 'When you're on heroin, it's hard to get off.' The drug is influence and power, and Mandelson's attraction to the source of power hasn't waned, despite the deep resentments which disturbed him after he was removed from government for the second time. Nor has Blair's addiction to his old friend's advice.

Mandelson's principal grudge is against Jack Straw who, as Home Secretary, told Downing Street that he believed that his call to one of his junior ministers, Mike O'Brien, in support of a passport application by the Hinduja brothers was the exercise of improper pressure. Sir Richard Wilson, the Cabinet Secretary, went to some trouble to ensure that the Hammond report on the affair commissioned by the Prime Minister did not suggest that he was the principal agent of the 'resignation', but he still has a place in the Mandelsonian pantheon of villainy. These feelings, however, are separate from the intimacies of the old gang, which zing with a special passion.

As Blair and Mandelson faced the inevitability of his second resignation when they talked in the Prime Minister's study on 24 January, it was Campbell who oiled the trapdoor. Asked by journalists late that morning whether Mandelson would still be Northern Ireland Secretary by the end of the day, Campbell said he didn't know. From a Downing Street press secretary, that was a death sentence. When he said it, no decision had been taken but he knew that Blair would have to face the truth: despite his hopes of survival, harboured until that morning, Mandelson could not survive. The newspapers were rampant, the government was shivering at the thought of a pre-election financial scandal – in the Foreign Office, the Home Office and the DTI it was known that the Hindujas had been fingered by the security and intelligence services as dangerous friends who should be avoided – and for at least two days Campbell had known that resignation must come. The scene in the Prime Minister's study was simply the ritual act of preparation for parting. Campbell came in as Blair and Mandelson spoke and all but said 'get on with it'. Within a few minutes Mandelson stepped into Downing Street to say that he had decided that it would be better if he left the government.

An hour and a half later their faces in the Commons were a ravaged tapestry of despair – Blair distraught at the inevitability of losing the friend whose attraction to the dangers of politics was too great, and Mandelson whitened by the shock of a departure which he had thought only the day before that he could avoid. It looked like a family tragedy.

That Mandelson remained afterwards a trusted courtier, a friend always ready with a strategy or a piece of tactical advice, is evidence of their mutual obsession. The intensity of the relationships binding the quartet transcends the usual networks of loyalty and obligation and rivalry that always run through politics and gives Blair's Downing Street a heightened emotional air. The first four years put the relationships under the sorts of strains more usually associated with a creaky marriage but they could not be severed.

Campbell and Blair were a unique pairing of press secretary and Prime Minister. The nearest equivalent, of someone who could talk to the boss with vicious bluntness, is Joe Haines, who served Harold Wilson for much of his time in Downing Street. Towards the end, in 1975-6, Haines was able to tell Wilson that he was drinking too much, once pointing out to him in his room at the Commons that the very large brandy which he had started to need before Prime Minister's Questions had been rather too large, and his answers had been slurred. But even Haines, a laconic and sometimes acerbic man, would not have told the Prime Minister that a speech or a suggestion was 'fucking crap'. Campbell is not someone who puts on a different character when he enters the Prime Minister's study: if anything, his natural aggressiveness intensifies. Even in front of visitors he will make his boredom or his contempt or his anger quite obvious. Ministers are sometimes mystified by it. They fear Campbell because of his power, but one Blair loyalist in the Cabinet says this: 'I do not know how Tony can take it. Alastair treats him like a child sometimes.'

Blair is untroubled by the reaction to Campbell. Though he is capable of being irritated by the brutal satire of Rory Bremner (which resulted in him being banned from the campaign bus) he has never indicated any embarrassment about his closeness to Campbell or his willingness to be the recipient of blunt advice and criticism. He soaks it up, and it is a symptom of his own confidence. A less secure Prime Minister couldn't live with Campbell for a week. Blair's irritations are minor, usually about briefings which have gone wrong. But there has never been a serious breach with Campbell. He is ever-present, and even when his public role led to bad publicity for Blair his relationship, in the phrase that Mandelson used to describe his own bond with Blair, never missed a beat.

But Campbell's dealings with Brown are different. They have many similarities. Both are tall, dominating, forceful characters who use physical intimidation in argument as a natural part of their weaponry: they glower and they loom. Campbell, whose bagpipe-playing is as important to him as his support for Burnley FC, is an emotional Scot and believes he understands the churning depths inside Brown. This does not make them soulmates. It makes them suspicious of each other.

Campbell denies utterly the 'psychological flaws' remark attributed to him. Brown does not believe him and was not only angry but deeply hurt when he read it. He complained to Blair that Number 10 was getting out of control: an accusation which the Prime Minister found almost risible, because it was exactly the charge which he and his closest advisers had been laying against Brown's office. The political outcome in the Downing Street family was that relations between Brown and Campbell now had an extra layer of suspicion attached.

There is one particular problem, which disturbs Brown no less than it disturbs a number of members of the Cabinet. Campbell keeps a diary. He has taken notes since he joined Blair's staff in 1994 and there is very little of substance in the story of New Labour and the Blair government that he does not know. He has been present for every crisis and he has seen, more often than almost anyone else, the agonized arguments between Prime Minister and Chancellor. Mandelson has told friends that everyone knows Campbell will publish his diary some day, when the Downing Street days are over, and says this: 'Gordon is frightened of Alastair.' He's not the only one.

Fear is an important ingredient in the life of the quartet. Mandelson, famed as the great schemer, has a fear of the Prime Minister. He speaks of Blair and not himself as the manipulator: 'he uses me all the time'. At the height of his powers, when he was a formal courtier in the Cabinet Office next door to Number 10 in the first year of the government, the Cabinet (of which he was not yet a member) thought of him as the most powerful figure in the government apart from Blair and Brown. Mandelson saw it differently, and believed himself to be someone used by a Machiavellian Prime Minister, whose relationship with him was quite different from the one popularly portrayed. Blair, who remains deeply fond of Mandelson, was seen by his friend not as a weakling in need of sustenance from a fawning court (the caricature built up by some of Brown's friends) but as a more cunning tactician in personal dealings than Mandelson himself. One of the reasons for Mandelson's despair at both his resignations, apart from the stings of public obloquy and the simple loss of power, was that he believed his relationship with Blair was misrepresented. Far from being the dominant, manipulative half of the relationship, Mandelson thought himself to be the victim. He still does.

These are the kinds of feelings which flow around the quartet. The Hinduja affair released feelings of betrayal and anger on Blair's part, followed by ruthless decisiveness, then incredulity on Brown's, fear and bitterness on Mandelson's. Everyone was unbalanced and the feelings that lie just under the surface poured out again. Blair and Brown have been unable to escape that fate because the network trembles with deep feelings of friendship, disappointment and betrayal – an amalgam of emotions which can no longer be broken down into its constituent parts. Everything is fused. One of the reasons is that in quite different ways Blair and Brown have created a kind of personal politics which neither is able to unravel. Each relies in part on the other to preserve the relationships which brought them to power and have sustained the dominance of their government. They are trapped because of their success.

The duopoly brings together two different kinds of politics. Blair and Brown have different attitudes to loyalty, one practical and one much more emotional. Mandelson says of Blair that he sees political loyalty as a deal, in which favours are traded. This is certainly true in the Cabinet. Prescott is not especially close to Blair. They talk a good deal, but each knows that Prescott has never been a figure in the government with the clout of Brown, nor of Campbell. Blair, however, has traded loyalties with his deputy. When he became leader in 1994 he was worried about Prescott. He did not know him well, and Prescott's Labour background was one which Blair knew that he only vaguely understood. Yet Prescott has been loyal to Blair, keeping his explosions private. For all his contempt for some aspects of the government he has not destabilized the Prime Minister. In return Blair has protected him and talked up his role.

Brown's friends cannot imagine him dealing with a deputy in that way. The relationship would have to be more intense for it to survive. If Brown were in the position of appointing a deputy, he would select from the group of acolytes who have over the years demonstrated unquestioning loyalty to him. Despite his experience – half a lifetime's – in the arts of the political manoeuvre, Brown is a figure whose instincts and personality still dictate his behaviour. From his days as a student he has always operated in a close group. He still takes advice from his brothers and from a circle of friends who go back to Edinburgh days, and, in the case of Murray Elder, to nursery school. They are a trusted political family. In the Commons, his friends know that he will repay loyalty by defending them – but only if that loyalty is absolute. Ministers like Andrew Smith, Nick Brown, and Alistair Darling are utterly loyal. Others who served in the Treasury and became critics – notably Alan Milburn and Stephen Byers – are aware that there is no going back. 'With Gordon,' says a former Treasury minister, 'you know that deals are signed in blood. He won't let you down, but only if you promise the same. He's that kind of man. No mucking around. Are you for me or against me?'

Like Brown, Blair has some close friends to whom he is absolutely bound but, significantly, the two friends to whom Blair has shown complete loyalty are not from Parliament – Campbell and Anji Hunter. They are trusted in part because they cannot be corrupted by political ambition. No one outside Blair's own family understands him better than Hunter. Irvine, scarcely a politician, is still close, but Blair's other friends are outside politics. He has no gang with whom he will unwind by replaying the latest government crisis or plan. Brown does.

Because each knows that the other brings to the relationship something that it needs, they have had no choice but to stay locked together. Brown, with his night-and-day political obsession, brings a sense of drive and conviction that Blair knows is on a different level from his own. Brown also understands, although the recognition shivers with an angst dating back to the leadership capitulation, that Blair has a political skill in enticing voters into Bill Clinton's 'big tent' that surpasses his own.

Brown is well aware that Blair's achievement in the first term was to occupy so much of the political middle ground that the Conservatives found it impossible to find territory in which they could wage a successful fightback. They were squeezed out, and the arguments in the leadership election that followed demonstrated that a substantial section of the party recognized that the Blair 'project' had done what it set out to do. However much they might argue against aspects of economic policy, or the domineering tone of the government, or its confusion on Europe, they could not argue away Blair's occupation of the centre of the political battlefield. Blair has harnessed Brown's intensity which has given the government its discipline, and in return Brown has acknowledged that it is Blair who sets the political tone. They have succeeded, at least if the re-election campaign and the result are to be taken as the measure.

But the dependence on each other makes their government vulnerable, especially when the two personalities fail to back each other up. Chaos ensues when the mechanism which allows one's failings to be compensated by the other doesn't work. Appropriately enough, one of the best analogies for the failures of Blair and Brown is drawn from below the surface – the debilitating row over the financing of the London Underground.

Blair has always been fascinated by Ken Livingstone and nervous of him. When he arrived at Westminster in 1983, Livingstone was leader of the Greater London Council and the embodiment of the leftism that Blair thought was threatening to destroy Labour. Although the Bennite tide had started to recede nationally, Livingstone, to the delight of Fleet Street, was refusing to retreat. The GLC taunted the Thatcher government and the Labour opposition too. Why wouldn't Michael Foot support him, asked Livingstone. Foot had realized that although the GLC had support for some of its radical policies on transport, for example, it had been successfully caricatured as the repository of all that was known in those days as 'the loony left' and had to be distanced from the party. Foot's aides were scarcely on speaking terms with Livingstone in the period just before the 1983 election. They hated him. Foot himself, who is a kindly man by nature, was bitter about Livingstone, whom he regarded as a factionalist and a destroyer. When the Conservatives abolished the GLC, Neil Kinnock, by then the Labour leader, believed it was an act that would have been impossible to put through Parliament had it not been for Livingstone.

So Blair feared Livingstone's destructive power, hence one of his most serious political mistakes. The whole Labour Party knew that Livingstone was more interested in being the first elected Mayor of London than in remaining MP for Brent East. But Blair could not contemplate the notion of a Livingstone victory. Despite polling advice which showed Livingstone as by far the most popular candidate, he insisted that the party find another one. The result was farcical. Frank Dobson was reluctantly persuaded out of the Department of Health to challenge Livingstone and was duly installed as a candidate.

Labour used an electoral college to select their candidate even though the London minister, Nick Raynsford, had told the Commons in May 1999 that 'the Labour Party will elect its candidate on the basis of one member, one vote. That is clear.' It wasn't. Each section – Labour members, unions and affiliated societies, and MPs, MEPs and Greater London Authority candidates – had one-third of the electoral college, which was a desperate mechanism to produce the right result. Even Dobson thought it 'stupid'. He won by 51.5 to 48.5 per cent. But Livingstone had won 60 per cent of the votes of party members and 70 per cent of the union votes. Dobson's candidacy, after a period of political brutality in the London party directed from Downing Street, was a joke. It humiliated Dobson and embarrassed Number 10. Predictably, Livingstone launched his independent candidacy and won, with the Tory Steve Norris kicking Dobson into third place.

It was a re-run in technicolour of the championing of Alun Michael as first secretary in Wales despite the obvious unpopularity of a strategy run from London and in the end he had to accept the victory of Rhodri Morgan, whom he had opposed on the grounds that he had too many 'old Labour' leanings. The ploy failed, to Blair's surprise, despite the warnings given to him by Welsh MPs. London was worse.

When Livingstone challenged the government on the financing of the tube the problem was compounded. As well as Blair's instinctive opposition to Livingstone, and his fear of him, he stirred up Brown's deep antipathy.

Brown had good reason to dislike Livingstone, since as early as 1998 he had suggested publicly that the Chancellor should be sacked for running a policy that he interpreted as a surrender to the financial markets. He opposed the independence of the Bank of England and turned this into a personal campaign against Brown. The two were not on speaking terms. Brown regarded Livingstone as a party factionalist of the sort that he thought should be extirpated; Livingstone regarded Brown as a bully who wouldn't change his mind when it was made up. There was some truth on both sides. So when Blair stumbled into the mayoral mess, Brown had no interest in championing Livingstone's cause. And when Livingstone decided to oppose the Treasury's preferred public–private partnership (PPP) for the tube there was a predictable explosion.

Livingstone had undergone a metamorphosis in the Mayor's office. He was talking enthusiastically to the City and to business about how he wanted to build a partnership with them for the good of London; he seemed determined to be flexible in his thinking. GLC looniness had gone. Here was a Mayor talking about competition on the buses, cuddling up to business, operating across party lines. In re-inventing his political personality, his most dramatic stroke was in bringing in as transport commissioner Bob Kiley, an American who had revived the New York and Boston subways. Kiley thought the government's plan for a public–private partnership wouldn't work and was a safety risk, because it separated the running of the trains – by a publicly owned London Underground – from the maintenance of the track, signals and stations to three privately owned consortia. Brown had decided early in the life of the government that this was the best way to put the potential costs (and the almost inevitable overrun) on the backs of the private contractors and not on the taxpayer. Livingstone sailed into battle.

Blair met Kiley several times to try to find a way out of the impasse. Prescott was pulled in by Blair to try to change Brown's outright opposition: he failed. Kiley, Prescott announced, was going to be allowed to redraft the PPP proposals to try to devise an alternative that would satisfy both sides. The Treasury simply refused to let it happen. The Chancellor would not budge. By the time Kiley was sacked as chairman of London Transport (although he remained Livingstone's Transport Commissioner) after months of discussions with government in an effort to get a deal, Brown had still never met him.

The dispute then headed to the courts, with Livingstone hoping to turn the episode into a ground-breaking challenge to central government by one of the devolved institutions of which it boasted. He failed.

The mystery in all this was Blair, who knew that Livingstone's plan was popular with the public. All the polls carried the same message. Among London Labour MPs (who dominated the capital's politics) it was more popular than the Treasury alternative. Kiley, despite being criticized in Treasury briefings as a man whose reputation was greatly inflated and who didn't understand the British public sector, was popular too. Why not move?

The mystery deepened. Of all the disputes with Brown in the second half of the first term this was the one which appeared to give Blair the opportunity for a clean victory. Cabinet colleagues realized that he could make a popular decision and at the same time demonstrate his supremacy in government. For once he could be First Lord of the Treasury. Livingstone sent that message to him directly. But Blair would not overrule Brown. No episode in government reveals more clearly the dependence they have on each other. The political benefits were not sufficient for Blair to force the Chancellor to change his mind.

Brown's argument was simple. He held the view that money had been squandered on London Transport in the past and would disappear down a black hole once again if the Treasury surrendered control to Livingstone. He argued that his duty was to keep public money on this scale under his own control. He told Blair that this was a principle on which he would not budge. The politics of the issue would not change his mind. It was a classic Brown piece of defiance.

Kiley, a former CIA officer, who then used his skills to deal with the endlessly wily politicians of New York and Boston, was astonished. Livingstone had told him in typical style when he arrived that he would find dealing with Whitehall strange after his American experience. 'You'll find it's a bit like East Germany,' he told him, 'except that we have elections every four or five years.' After one of his efforts in Whitehall to get the government to abandon the public-private partnership, Kiley returned and told Livingstone: 'You're wrong. It's not East Germany. It's bloody North Korea.' In a splendid mixture of metaphors he linked North Korea with Kansas, because his nickname for Brown is the Wizard of Oz. Kiley came to believe that when you got to the end of the Yellow Brick Road you found that there was nothing there, only an illusion. Brown thinks exactly the same of Livingstone.

In the story of the Underground are distilled the forces that drive Blair's government. The Prime Minister's own nervousness at his party's past, epitomized by Livingstone; Brown's refusal to give way to an old enemy and his determination not to change a policy once settled in the Treasury; above all, Blair's refusal to overrule his Chancellor on an important matter of public policy even when it carries the prospect of popularity for the government and the likelihood that it will allow him to be portrayed as the Prime Minister who can't be pushed around by the Treasury. Although Blair was advised inside 10 Downing Street to challenge Brown directly and appeal for a change of heart, which he did, with the help of Prescott, Brown was resolute. Blair backed down, irritated but resigned.

This was a dispute about character and willpower. Brown was determined not to concede a financial argument. And Blair did not want to overrule him in public. The circumstances in which he has refused to let the Treasury prevail have been on issues that have not been argued out in the open. They have not involved a public repudiation of Brown, although sometimes Blair has refused to give way with a Brown-like resolve. The two had an abrupt series of exchanges about the funding of the BBC, which is a good example. In Downing Street it became the source of a great deal of anger, though little of it seeped into the public domain.

Brown was convinced that the government should impose a tougher financial regime on the BBC, involving an extra levy which the corporation would have to charge for its digital services. This had been recommended in a government report commissioned from Gavyn Davies, who was to become chairman of the BBC and the economist closest to Brown. Blair disagreed; Brown believed he had been 'got at' by the BBC. As usual, the dispute got nowhere near the Cabinet. A series of meetings took place in Blair's office to try to resolve it. Brown was adamant. 'I am having nothing to do with this,' he said at a meeting in which Blair indicated his unhappiness at the Treasury view. Blair told him directly: 'I'm sorry, I've made up my mind.' The decision was made. Brown was angry, but impotent.

Such episodes find Blair in a determined mood, ignoring what ministers claim are Brown's 'insults' – their interpretation of his broody silence when Blair argues a case with which he disagrees. But in public, as with the tube, he is deeply reluctant to be seen to be at odds with the Chancellor. On Europe, the most obvious public argument swirling back and forth between Downing Street and the Treasury, they worked together on the speech Brown would give at Mansion House just after the 2001 election to try to make sure that they could buy time with a form of words that would not open a new burst of speculation. It worked. There were some headlines the next day, but the argument over the euro then went into a quieter phase. Blair had neutered it.

At every turn, when irritation or rivalry threatens the stability of the relationship there is an effort to stabilize it. In the nature of things, that effort usually comes from the Prime Minister. He has spent his leadership in the knowledge that Brown's ambition has not gone and has to be managed. Brown, on the other hand, is aware that he is acknowledged by Blair as the government's biggest thinker and strategist, the Chancellor who, in Blair's own words, 'has sixteen times the firepower of Ken Clarke' (Brown's old opponent in the Major government). This arrangement seems to some of Blair's friends to be one that the Prime Minister should resent more than he does; to Brown's friends it is simply a recognition of his place at the centre of the government, the Chancellor who engineered economic stability in the first two years (at the cost of popularity in the Labour Party) to allow the prospect of greatly increased investment in public services in the second term.

Blair has often been exasperated by what he considers Brown's stubbornness. More seriously, he believes Brown's supporters on the backbenches, around him in the Treasury and in Fleet Street to be damaging to the government because they portray government decisions and its standing in public esteem in terms of the Chancellor's decisions or outlook or prospects of succession. He is rigorous in support of Brown in conversation with outsiders, but does hint at the difficulties they encounter day by day. He will express a degree of mystification about the tactics used by his old friend: he understands the ambition that still burns, and the political determination that drives him, but he cannot share his all-or-nothing approach to politics.

On Brown's side there is a frustration born of the passing of time. Brown had been swallowing the consequences of the Granita dinner for seven years by the time of the re-election, with no obvious end in sight. No wonder he appeared to be chewing over a somewhat indigestible future. The Chancellor turned fifty in February 2001 – no great age in politics, but a milestone nevertheless. His colleagues believed that he was finding it more difficult rather than easier to deal with Blair in government. 'Gordon will never be reconciled to Tony as leader. It's as simple as that. It's part of the furniture.' That is the judgement of one minister who has attended many meetings with them, and who believes that one of the principal reasons for Brown's dislike of collective meetings is simply that he finds it difficult to recognize Blair's supremacy in front of colleagues. Brown himself denies this: he believes that such interpretations come from people close to Blair who have an interest in putting him down. He is right in that judgement. His view of some Downing Street courtiers is a mirror image of Blair's contemptuous description of some of the Chancellor's own crew. He argues that the Prime Minister does not take such a conspiratorial view of his behaviour in government, and does not believe Brown to be as reluctant as some suggest to accept the Prime Minister's authority.

But Blair's frustration does run deep. He has told close colleagues that he believes Brown's strengths are undermined by great weaknesses – even claiming that he has 'saved' Budget speeches by working them through with Brown at Chequers on the weekend before they are delivered. In turn, Brown has often expressed to friends his doubts about Blair's grip on strategy and has indicated a degree of disbelief at Blair's distance from his party. Such gripes have gnawed at their relationship over the years.

The admiration which they profess for each other is undermined by these feelings. Blair's regular choice of Lloyd George as his historical figure with whom to compare Brown has a touch of irony, and not only because Lloyd George was the most famous Liberal of them all. It was he who coined the phrase 'there's no friendship at the top', a motto of politics which hangs inevitably over a government like Blair's. Blair and Brown can still accurately be described as friends, in the sense that there are ties of loyalty which neither wants entirely to sever, but the intensity of their dependence on each other has gone as the intensity of the rivalries at the top of government has increased.

Each is more of his own man now than he was when the government was formed. Their personal lives, away from the office, reflect it.

The birth of the Blairs' fourth child in May 2000 was, obviously, an important event for them all. Those who know the Prime Minister well are aware of how profoundly it affected his outlook. He is the father of three teenagers and a child, and theirs is a close family. Unlike some politicians, he knows his children well, and is absorbed in discussion about their future. He is married to a powerful woman – the person who, more than anyone else, drew him into politics – and his family life looms large. They spend a great deal of time at Chequers together and Blair's ability to turn his gaze from government to his family is striking to all who watch him there. He is not obsessed by the premiership.

The importance of family ties is central to Blair, as he made clear by naming his fourth child Leo, after his father. Blair's childhood and youth were affected by two traumatic events involving his parents. His father's stroke in 1964 when Blair was eleven was an event which changed everything. It was three years before Leo Blair could speak properly again. It introduced a sense of deep uncertainty in the family. Secondly, Blair's mother, Hazel, to whom he was reportedly very close, died of throat cancer at the young age of fifty-two, just after he graduated from Oxford. She was of Donegal Protestant stock and his utter absorption in Northern Ireland is thought by some of those who know him best to reflect in part a commitment to her memory. In addition his sister, Sarah, developed a form of arthritis at a young age. The Blair family was marked by a series of tragedies.

Such a history is bound to have shaped his own attitude to his children, just as the background of Cherie Booth, whose parents parted from each other, has left its own scars. Their closeness to their children, and their determined religious commitments, are a striking part of Blair's character: it is part of the reason for the self-contained image which he wears.

The equivalent in Brown's life of the birth of Leo Blair in 2000 was, of course, his marriage. His relationship with Sarah Macaulay went back to the mid-nineties after the break-up of his friendship with Sheena McDonald. The wedding was not for him the routine formalization of a long-standing relationship, but a commitment, with all the seriousness that he brings to everything. However, the public awkwardness which was displayed in the performance for the wedding photographs only seemed to evaporate properly when they announced in July 2001 that Sarah was pregnant.

Brown holds to tradition. He is close to his mother, who lives in rural Aberdeenshire, the part of Scotland where her own roots lie and where she and Brown's father moved when he retired from the ministry. His death was a blow to Brown, who had immense pride in him, and the concept of family is one that he and his brothers cherish. One inheritance which Brown was fortunate to escape was a family name on his father's side. Had Dr John Brown's middle name been passed on to his middle son, it might have caused some amusement among the Chancellor's Cabinet colleagues. His father was christened John Ebeneezer Brown, and any hard-pressed spending minister would have been happy to point out that it is a name chiefly associated these days with one figure, Dickens's Mr Scrooge. Gordon Brown's wedding has evidently not changed his determination to keep public and private lives apart. Before long, the Browns would face tragedy in their marriage but in the period before the 2001 election the settled picture was of two men who seemed to have grown out of the carefree opposition days of old, and the early days in government, to a maturity that revealed more of their individual personalities than of their closeness and shared experiences.

That distance was often awkward and in the approach to the 2001 election it sometimes seemed to be a yawning void. Blair tried to bridge it, with the inevitable help of Mandelson, and he and Brown resumed a more civilized relationship than they had had for years in planning the campaign. But Blair's hopes for a smooth approach to the election were torpedoed by events. Mandelson's resignation in February 2001 drained Blair and those around him, and the foot and mouth outbreak cut off so many areas of the country, and became such a focus of public anxiety, that the election timetable, in place since autumn 2000, was abandoned. Blair himself took the decision to postpone the poll, aware from his own awkward visits to diseased areas that the government would seem wildly out of touch if it went ahead with an April campaign. Ministry of Agriculture vets were culling cattle across the land, piles of carcasses were smouldering in mass graves, and disinfectant mats were spread on country roads and lanes. The election circus would have an odd backdrop. So they waited. One of the consequences was that the strategy went askew and by the time all the parties took to the road in May for an election on 7 June, Labour was suffering from two problems – an assumption among its workers and candidates that victory would be easy (William Hague's popularity ratings being even worse than Michael Foot's in Labour's catastrophic 1983 campaign) and a struggle between Blair and Brown for control.

With Blair spending a great deal of time on the road, and Brown manning the command centre in London, their staff were hardly surprised when each of them began to succumb to temper tantrums.

Even without the embarrassing episodes – John Prescott's punch and Blair's nervy encounter with Sharron Storer in Birmingham – the campaign was edgy. Blair felt that he was being pushed around by Brown; Brown was unhappy with some of the performances he was obliged to watch from London, stuck in Millbank. One of Blair's closest friends claims that he felt humiliated by the experience. Blair has laughed off that description, but he finds it difficult to deny that the campaign was deeply unhappy under the surface. His relief when it was over was as much a result of the feeling that he could start afresh in government as of the size of his majority.

After the counts, when Blair arrived back in London from his constituency to thank his staff, Brown had already flown down from Edinburgh and was on the stage set up outside Millbank looking over the Thames. They greeted each other with smiles, but betrayed not even a momentary hint of ecstasy. David Hill, a veteran party spokesman and arm-twister of Fleet Street's finest, had been brought back from his lobbying firm for the campaign, and was spreading extravagant words: 'All of you in the media have to understand something about this result – it's probably the most astonishing victory in British electoral history.' Looking at Blair and Brown, you might not have believed it.

Euphoria had been banned at the moment of victory. Any repeat of the '97 frolics at the Royal Festival Hall risked looking arrogant, they had decided, so there was to be no public rave. Behind the controlled façade, however, the feeling that was struggling to find a way out was not one of wild celebration: it was of deep frustration. Blair was impatient with his Cabinet and with Whitehall, and Brown was impatient with Blair.

In Number 10, all the anxiety about 'delivery' in the public services and about the need to confront the public cynicism revealed in the General Election turnout (the first to dip under 60 per cent since the arrival of universal suffrage) was focused once again on the central partnership. Only if it worked did the government seem to function, and yet it was also seen by those around Blair as a great impediment. On Europe and on relations with the Labour Party – troublesome territory for Blair – Brown was seen as a problem, the right-hand man who was pursuing his own course and taking the opportunity at every turn to indicate that he was different from the Prime Minister. The reason why the melancholy air seeped through Number 10 after re-election was the recognition that the problems in the relationship were doomed to remain. There was no known surgical procedure in politics that could remove them cleanly, because the Prime Minister was bound to his Chancellor by a promise which could not be broken without destroying the government and starting again.

Even in the Thatcher years, when the personality of the Prime Minister was the focus for every picture of Cabinet struggle or Whitehall policy dispute, politics proceeded on predictable lines. The ideological differences in the Cabinet were known, and from time to time the pendulum would change direction for a moment before swinging back. But, as in the Labour governments of the seventies and the Major governments that followed Thatcher's, hers did not have at its heart a single pulsating relationship that was apparently indispensable and unstable at the same time.

When Blair was elected in 1997 he told Mandelson that he was depressed by the persistence of the personal difficulties of opposition in government. After his re-election he had a matching frustration, in the knowledge that the problem of 'handling Gordon', which he had first identified ten years before, was still there. And he knew that on Brown's part there was a sense of impatience which beat just as strongly, and which Brown believed to be entirely justified. When he started to reshape the government and Downing Street, it was with an awareness of that unsettled business being a destabilizing force which was likely to grow more powerful as the second term went on.

His first order was an unexpected one. He told Campbell: 'We've got to pull back. Pull back.' These were words that zipped round Whitehall like an order. Everyone on the inside knew what he meant. The government had spun itself into a tangled ball. A play called *Feelgood* was filling the Garrick Theatre every night a few hundred yards from Number 10, spraying Blair and his friends with merciless satire, depicting a political world in which nothing is real, only contrived for attention and deceit, and in which no motive is pure.

For Blair, who continued to convince himself that he had high motives and had kept his personal integrity, this was painful. His relationship with Campbell was portrayed as that of the chain-swinging bully dominating the weak master. Brown was portrayed in every cartoon as a smouldering presence about to burst into flame and consume Blair. When Blair wasn't being portrayed as a weakling he appeared as a dandy, a flibbertigibbet. Blair is fairly thick-skinned, but this was wounding. Like most Prime Ministers (with Major a notable exception) he gave up reading newspapers closely after a year or two in office, concentrating on the *FT*, and leaving the rest to Campbell to summarize, but he was aware that, although he was the most powerful Prime Minister the country had seen since the Thatcher of the immediate post-Falklands era, he was being painted as a creature of feeble impulse and devotion to gesture politics.

For someone who believed his absorption in Northern Ireland over four years had been proof of statesmanship, and who revelled in his iconoclastic approach to his own party, the caricature was hurtful, more so than he let it appear in public. Hence 'pull back'. It meant something simple. With Campbell retreating, with Hunter (at first) and Powell running the three new departments in Number 10, the tone would change. Downing Street briefings would be taken over by Godric Smith, Campbell's deputy and a career civil servant, untouched by the tar brush of party spin. Campbell's move, conceived by Blair himself, was meant to make a practical difference and to send a message from Number 10 that the frenzy of control of Whitehall announcements and the effort to manipulate Fleet Street with the fingertips was over. The message was transmitted, but too late to stop the habits of the first four years from bringing the government entirely unnecessary troubles. At the beginning of 2002 the resignations of the chief information officer and Stephen Byers's political special adviser at the Department of Transport was painful evidence for Blair that his government had not learnt the lesson which he intended to absorb in the aftermath of the election. An obsession with presentation, manipulation and control still dogged ministers and their advisers. Blair glimpsed the problem at the end of the first term but failed to cure it.

Some of his friends attribute that failure to the most obvious likely cause – his lack of any experience in Whitehall before 1997. The truth is even more complicated. Labour's introverted style in government, and its belief in the power of presentation as rival to substance and strategy, was and is a reflection of its personality. All governments have characters who plot and wrestle with each other, and they all have moments of crisis when the ugly emotions of the back-room arguments spill into the open, but none has become so expert at turning inwards as Blair's. Those who work with him and with the Chancellor understand that part of the reason is the relationship at the top. It sets the tone. This is not a government that has ever learnt how to relax.

One picture from the election campaign shows how powerfully the central struggle influences everything. The war room in Millbank Tower which was the command centre for Labour's re-election campaign, was a huge space housing dozens of people, occupying the whole first floor, with only two private bolt holes to allow an escape from the throng. One was for Blair, the other for Brown. The party planners placed them in the most natural configuration, as if by instinct. Blair's was along a short corridor leading from one corner and Brown's was in the corner diagonally opposite. They could not have been further apart.

No feng shui expert is needed for the message of that geography to be understood. Though Prime Minister and Chancellor often huddled together in the course of the campaign, and made a careful point of appearing as a practised double act at a string of press conferences, their private spaces were far apart. The two sets of advisers operated in different spheres and, despite the running conversation between their principals, they seemed happiest when there was no contact and each group was absorbed separately in the business of one man. Those who remembered the 1997 campaign realized that the diagonal line from corner to corner was not only the axis along which power flowed, but the measure of a distance between the two camps that had been growing for four years, and which seemed to be lengthening before their eyes.

13
War

Blair emerged from his re-election campaign a bruised Prime Minister. He told those around him that he was determined to try to recreate a sense of freshness and resolve in a government and party that had started to seem listless and fractious. He was aware that somehow he had started to drift away from them, and they from him. But instead of finding that familiarity once again, he rediscovered something quite different – the intimacy of war.

Within a hundred days of the re-election he was thrown into a maelstrom. The Prime Minister who had tried to make Cabinet changes in June designed to make it easier for him to be re-engaged with his ministers and to find the pulse of his party once more was suddenly transformed into the war leader fated to make the big decisions alone. Blair, however, did not find this uncomfortable; nor did he resent the turn of events that shook politics. He found it as satisfying as anything he could imagine.

That is not to say that he felt unmoved by any of the shocks that began backstage at the TUC conference in Brighton just after lunch on 11 September when he first heard that one of the World Trade Center towers had been hit by a passenger jet, nor that he relished some of the military decisions that followed. But from the day of the attacks, Blair was gripped by the crisis and utterly enmeshed in its complexities and its drama. He gave no sign to anyone close to him that he wished it would all go away. Mingled with his natural horror at the news from New York and Washington was a tingling determination to plunge into this new phase of politics. One of his Cabinet ministers watching him in London on the evening of

11 September said that everyone around him realized that he had grasped the scale of the change more quickly than anyone else. 'You realized that on this kind of occasion he's always ahead of you. He'd made the leap before most of us knew what was happening.' By the time he uttered a few sentences on the stage of the conference centre to the confused and half-innocent TUC delegates and abandoned his speech to return to Downing Street he was convinced that a military campaign more dangerous than the Kosovo operation was inevitable.

American Airlines flight 11 hit the north tower at about 1.45 p.m. by the clock in Brighton. Within seventy-five minutes the south tower had also been hit, part of the Pentagon in Washington was in flames and, in New York, the north tower had collapsed in a cloud of dust and debris that enveloped Lower Manhattan. By 3.10 Blair was announcing that Britain stood 'shoulder to shoulder' with the United States and committed himself in principle to the retaliation which, even in that early hour, he knew must come.

Prime Ministers are isolated at such moments. Though war cabinets are put together, and the military planners in Whitehall set up the apparatus to turn the government into a war executive, the moments of decision are often solitary because the Prime Minister's perspective is unique. Indicative of the isolation was the fact that, after the first rush of news in the week following 11 September, Blair's most important meeting occurred without any of his officials or advisers being present.

It took place in Washington on 20 September on the evening of an extraordinary day. Blair had already visited Paris and Berlin in the previous seventy-two hours to talk to President Chirac and Chancellor Schroeder. He began in New York, visiting Ground Zero itself, and attending a service in St Thomas's Episcopal Church on Fifth Avenue where the relations of many of the British victims had gathered. As usual on such occasions, Blair was drawn naturally into the pulsing emotions of the moment, not shying away from the bear hug offered by the Mayor, Rudolph Giuliani, and spent longer than had been expected with the people whom the government had flown to New York to visit the source of their grief. But he had to fly on to Washington quickly. George Bush was due to address a special session of both houses of Congress that evening, with the Prime Minister in the audience, and Blair was to dine with him at the White House beforehand, the invitation a mark of gratitude for Britain's support in the first hours of the crisis. The visit was important for Blair – Prime Ministers spend many hours trying to manoeuvre themselves into positions of such prominence, outpacing their peers in the jostling around the centre of power – but in New York there was a slightly absurd complication. The British journalists accompanying him on the trip had to file their stories, and the television pictures, before the Prime Minister's plane took off for Washington. They had purple prose to send home, and were taking their time. Blair's staff were becoming agitated. Campbell was whipping the press corps on, but it was clear that Blair was likely to arrive late at the White House. As diplomatic stumbles go, this might turn out to be a spectacular pratfall. Bush was preparing for by far the most important speech of his life. America was waiting for it; much of the world would be watching the performance by a President whose election had been mired in farcical vote confusions in Florida and weeks of court argument, and whose international experience was nil, trips across the border to Mexico from Texas and occasional holiday forays to Europe as a young man not giving the impression of any serious immersion in foreign affairs. Blair's delay seemed invariably to be adding to the strains racking the White House.

Having finally reached Washington, the prime ministerial cavalcade sped from Andrews Air Force base to the White House in a rather nervous state. But the atmosphere changed when they were greeted formally by a President who appeared, to everyone's astonishment, to be relaxed. Blair suggested to him that he might wish to have some time alone before the speech – the Prime Minister told his staff that he'd certainly have taken the chance to compose himself – but Bush declined. The speech was finished, he'd rehearsed the night before and again that morning, and there was no more to do. Instead, he took Blair by the arm and led him away from the gaggle of staff, administration officials and ambassadors.

They disappeared into the Blue Room in the White House and talked for about twenty minutes, entirely alone. It was the most important conversation of the crisis so far.

Bush was direct. His own recollection, given to aides later, was that in describing what he intended, and asking for Blair's support he said 'full use of the US military . . . bombers coming from all directions'. Earlier that day he had been told by the director of the CIA, George Tenet, that another terrorist attack on the United States could be expected within 48 hours (it wasn't to be) and the conversation with the Prime Minister took place in an atmosphere high with the danger of the unknown. Yet Bush seemed to Blair to be surprisingly cool, a picture which stayed with him after the visit and played a considerable part in persuading him to defend Bush against his critics, and the less comfortable members of his own Cabinet. When Bush spoke to Blair in the Blue Room he knew that the first American special forces were on their way and would be inside Afghanistan on Sunday, five days later. The military campaign on the ground had already begun.

When he rejoined his companions, Blair had changed. Sir Christopher Meyer, British ambassador in Washington, told colleagues that he realized around the dinner table later that evening that Bush had confided to Blair the American plans for retaliation, as far as they had been drawn up. The Prime Minister divulged no details of the conversation that evening but appeared to his companions to be a man who had taken on a new (and perhaps surprising) calm. In the preceding ten days, Blair and Bush had spoken frequently on the telephone, but this was their first direct contact and the officials who travelled home with Blair realized that it was the moment when he and Bush jointly committed themselves to the military campaign which began publicly seventeen days later on 7 October when bombers flew over Kabul, Kandahar and Jalalabad in Afghanistan. From the moment of his White House meeting, Blair showed no reservations about American policy. There were critics of the war close to home – more than a dozen Labour MPs publicly opposed the government in the Commons and a substantial number of others grumbled quietly about the sense of rushing to war in an American slipstream – but Blair decided from the start that there would not be a querulous note from Number 10. He became Bush's strongest supporter in Europe and operated as a kind of ambassador plenipotentiary for the White House.

Between his visit to Washington and the start of the bombing, Blair visited Brussels (to brief fellow European leaders on the intimacies he had been granted in the White House) and Moscow, Islamabad and Delhi. In the week after the first raids he was in Geneva, Oman and Cairo and welcomed the PLO Chairman Yasser Arafat in Downing Street. In the next ten weeks, apart from European visits, he was in Syria, Saudi Arabia, Israel, Jordan, the United States again, India, Pakistan, Bangladesh and, finally, Afghanistan.

In this period of about four months, Blair was separated from the business of government that after the election he had assumed would preoccupy him well into the second term. The message from voters, many of whom would vote Labour anyway, had been clear. They wanted public services to perform better, and Blair duly echoed the message he had picked up when he spoke on the night of his re-election. 'Delivery' – on the railways, in the hospitals, on streets where crime was everywhere, in crowded secondary school classrooms became the purpose of government. Blair settled in to what he believed would be a practical phase of government, and nudged and poked the various think tanks and strategy groups he had assembled around Number 10. Some senior civil servants thought the performance and innovation unit, the delivery unit and the forward strategy group were puffed up outfits who seemed to produce more than they actually did, and who were rather too fond of criticizing Whitehall's way of doing things – a habit they knew would endear them further to a Prime Minister always anxious for an explanation as to why his high-flown words of 1997 had not, for example, cut street crime or removed logjams at inner-city accident and emergency units.

The government was supposed to have been refreshed by its reshaping after the election. In particular, Charles Clarke, the new party chairman, was given licence to express Blair's own doubts about the performance of his government. He took to the task

enthusiastically, and though he felt a slight chill blowing from Downing Street in the autumn, when he appeared to admit too cheerily
that the railways were in a worse state than they had been in 1997,
his was supposed to be the central message of government. They
wanted to do better. Blair was stung by the knowledge that Railtrack,
running the network, seemed as ineffective as ever (and even more
unpopular) and that the promised improvements in NHS 'delivery'
appeared slow. So, while the Conservatives concerned themselves
with internal business and unfinished battles between the factions
around the now departed William Hague, Blair told his colleagues
that public services would be the test by which they would stand
or fall. Such was the Conservative trauma after Hague resigned on
the morning after the election, that Downing Street believed there
would be a clear run. Blair's own experience told him that a new
leader would take some months to find a foothold – at least if the
novice Iain Duncan Smith was elected, as he hoped, and not the
sturdy warhorse Kenneth Clarke. Blair's hope was that he would
now have time to develop a better strategy for the public services,
and the wider domestic agenda, than the one he had taken to the
country in June. The low turn-out could be attributed to any number
of social factors, but Blair could hardly deny that his government had
failed to excite the country. So he needed to readjust his antennae.

After 11 September, such a preoccupation seemed almost quaint.
Instead Blair focused on terrorism, global alliances and war. The
most obvious symptom of his transformation was his party conference speech on 2 October, delivered on the same platform in Brighton where he had heard of the New York attacks and had seen the
first confused television reports. He decided that his subject should
be the world and nothing less. Blair, the preacher, wanted to lead
a moral debate. Some of those around him were horrified.

On Saturday, three days before the address, a draft was being
passed around. Blair had conceived the messsage himself (though
other hands played a part in the drafting) but a number of those
who would normally have been part of piecing it together had been
ignored. The usual menu of departmental promises had not been
compiled; the pasting in of catchy lines submitted by eager policy

thinkers in Downing Street was not required this time. Campbell liked Blair's text; so did Peter Mandelson, who was still sore over his enforced resignation, but could not let the conference pass without joining in. Others were less sure. Sally Morgan, then Blair's political secretary, was anxious to fill it out with domestic policy. She failed, to the delight of others around Blair, one of whom said afterwards that 'the rats tried to gnaw the speech to bits'. As delivered, it was the speech Blair wanted to give.

He turned it into a statement of moral attitude. Instead of using international affairs as a backdrop, which was the normal pattern in conference speeches, he reversed the picture. The NHS, education and other public services were turned into domestic reflections of a wider truth: community at home became a fragment of the wider interdependence he said he had long believed defined the modern world. Blair spoke as if this were the confession of something which he'd previously kept hidden, an embarrassing family secret. The truth was now revealed – his belief that a worldwide coalition of the good had to be assembled, that no compromise with the forces of evil could be contemplated, that there was a tangible threat of global chaos if the United States was not supported in its determination to fight back, that politics had once again become the business of morality. He made no concessions to those colleagues who murmured about his 'Jesus mood' and the newspapers which expressed irritation with the Prime Minister as moral tutor. If the Rwandan massacres of 1993 happened now, he said, Britain would have a moral duty to intervene, just as it had in the Balkans. And he sprang from a defence of the British operation in Sierra Leone – supporting the government there against insurgents – into a kind of hymn for Africa, saying that the developed world had to form and sustain a partnership that would address the problems of that continent that sometimes seemed insoluble – poverty, debt and civil war.

The speech was startling. Even those around the conference hall who believed he was getting carried away with the 'war against terrorism' could hardly deny that he was a Prime Minister in spectacular form. He spoke like someone possessed of a new idea, and some of his newspaper critics who a few weeks before had been deeply grudging about Blair's power to devise a second term strategy – notably Polly Toynbee and Hugo Young in the *Guardian* – were won over, writing of a Prime Minister who had found a language to pull together his ideas at home and Britain's obligations abroad. The speech was seen by Blair as a new beginning for the second term, but it was also a confession because it tried to define his premiership in terms that even he would have been embarrassed to use in time of peace but now felt to be an authentic expression of his outlook. He was more comfortable with some of the high-flown rhetoric of this text than he would be with the more mundane patchwork of a routine leader's speech, and seemed driven by the crisis. Even ministers who felt the performance was over the top knew that it wasn't a fake.

The conference therefore became the most peculiar since Margaret Thatcher had stood on the same platform in 1984 with the ruins of the Grand Hotel smouldering a few yards away. Blair was a leader who evidently expected war – 'there is no diplomacy with bin Laden or the Taliban regime' he told his party – and who was ready to stand squarely beside an American President for whom the Labour Party generally had almost no regard and spoke of as a music hall joke. His speech was a declaration of confidence in his convictions. Twenty-two days after the American attacks in Afghanistan he was celebrating his own freedom to speak in the moral terms with which he'd always been at home and which his Cabinet, almost to a man and woman, found unsettling. He might be on his own but he was enjoying it.

It was a straighforward fact that no one else in the Cabinet could have made the Brighton speech because no one else had such a sharpened sense of the moral challenge that Blair saw in the events of 11 September, and none would have found it so natural to pull together the international crisis and domestic policy. When he said 'this is a moment to seize', he meant it.

Even the joke about the government's intentions at home was crafted to play to the new persona. Picking up a reported comment from an anonymous minister, he said: 'The journey hasn't ended. The next stage for New Labour is not backwards; it is renewing ourselves again. Just after the election, an old colleague of mine said – "Come on, Tony, now we've won again, can't we drop all this New Labour and do what we believe in?" I said: "It's worse than you think. I really do believe in it."' The conference laughed, but with a degree of embarrassment and perhaps a touch of the guilt that Blair intended his audience to feel. Few of them attached the 'New' to Labour now, and many thought of the early days of Blairite evangelism as they might think of a fevered phase that was always going to pass. The conference speech, in normal circumstances a unifying message meant to bind the party together, was as much a personal statement by Blair as an attempt at inclusiveness.

The passage on Europe had a special force. Blair conjured up the picture of potential chaos round the globe, anarchy that could be prevented only by cooperation among the great powers. That was how bin Laden and the Taliban would be beaten; how the 'Partnership for Africa' would come to the aid of that continent; how the concept of community at home could be made to make more sense in the new century. But it was also, said Blair, the spur to full integration between Britain and the rest of the EU. With Brown beside him on the platform, the five tests zipped up safely in the Chancellor's pocket, Blair said that the future meant building political and economic bridges with Europe. His words could mean only one thing: no one listening to him in Brighton had any doubt that he was placing the European campaign in the context of an international commitment he had decided to turn into a political credo. Economic and social ideologies were dead, he said. Twenty-first-century politics was a matter of values, based on the notion of community between people and between countries.

Blair had planned to deliver the European message in the TUC speech abandoned on 11 September, when the plan had been to make the case for the euro more boldly than before and to talk of the benefits in jobs. Now that practical argument was turned into something rather grander, as if European integration was a natural extension of the duty to go to war in Afghanistan. But Blair could not conceal the caution and frustration that still bedevilled his European urges. 'Seize the moment' he might say about retaliation against the Taliban, but there was no seizing the nettle of the referendum on joining the euro. For all the fine words, that policy was the same as it had been for the last year or so, and some overexcited European ambassadors coming away from Brighton on that Tuesday afternoon had to calm themselves before composing their diplomatic telegrams home, knowing enough of Blair to suspect that an almost reckless boldness and a natural caution were still living side by side in him.

'The kaleidoscope has been shaken. The pieces are in flux. Soon they will settle again. Before they do, let us reorder this world around us.' These words were his own, not a speech-writer's, and they revealed to his party Blair's sense of being released on to the international stage to play the great game. He was Washington's new special friend and although the fact was accepted only grudgingly in Paris, and even in Brussels, the relationship with Bush made him the natural conduit to a continent whose leaders were virtual strangers to the President. Yet his freedom of manoeuvre in the leaders' club did not transform his premiership at home. The kaleidoscope of his own government had a pattern that was both familiar and immobile. The pieces were not in flux, but locked together.

While the world spun around him, and he sped from desert rendezvous to White House dinner, the domestic life of the government was stubbornly routine. The crisis on the railways was moving faster than most of the trains. The negotiations over Brown's pre-Budget report in November were as awkward as ever, and perhaps even more irritating to them both than before. The 'new' Cabinet felt less fresh than Blair had intended it should be when he asked before the election 'where are the people?'. But for a Prime Minister chairing a daily war cabinet such concerns can be pushed away for another day, and they were.

When that war cabinet met for the first time on 9 October, two days after the bombing in Afghanistan started, Blair was careful to avoid the political awkwardness that would have resulted from the exclusion of Robin Cook, the immediate past Foreign Secretary whose wounds were still tender, and Clare Short, the International Development Secretary, whose instincts are not warlike, at least abroad. Brown was there, of course, with the Foreign, Home and

Defence secretaries, the chief of the defence staff and the heads of MI6 and MI5, Sir Richard Dearlove and Sir Stephen Lander. This was therefore a bigger group than had been assembled by John Major for the Gulf War or by Margaret Thatcher for the Falklands. But although it was big, Blair was no more minded to submit the most important matters for collective decision than he was in his regular dealings with the Cabinet. It was his campaign.

John Major reveals in his autobiography how even the members of such groups are often excluded from operational information. When he was told by George Bush Snr on 15 January 1991 that bombing on Iraq would start the next day (the American planes using a British base on Diego Garcia in the Indian Ocean), the only other minister who was given significant advance warning was Tom King, the Defence Secretary. Douglas Hurd, the Foreign Secretary, knew only about an hour before the first bombs fell.

The Blair war cabinet's daily meetings, however, gave even those ministers and officials who were not privy to the more minute military details a vivid picture of the Prime Minister's attitude to the war. And the first three weeks or so were characterized by frustration. By the end of October the bombing appeared to have achieved little. Osama bin Laden was at large and the Taliban regime in Afghanistan, though apparently in possession of no significant weaponry to deploy effectively against American (and British) power was still in place. Though anti-war sentiment was patchy in Britain – in the early days the government was untroubled – and almost invisible in the United States, Blair was irritated with what seemed to be slow progress. October was a difficult month. Ministers were dispatched to microphones to speak of a campaign that might take many months, but found it increasingly difficult to explain how it was that a ramshackle regime, lightly armed and with rusty radar, could keep at bay a coalition of forces led by planes which were dropping hundreds of thousands of tons of bombs on Afghanistan's cities with little discernible opposition.

Blair's gloom was deepened by the embarrassing incident of the 'bad news' memorandum sent by the special adviser to Stephen Byers, Jo Moore. The leak of the memo, from a department that was to continue to cause Downing Street its most persistent political aches and pains, came at a bad moment. By mid-October, just as Blair's frustration with the difficulty of promising quick solutions in Afghanistan was bubbling up in nearly every meeting of the war cabinet, it was revealed that Moore had suggested in a departmental e-mail on the very afternoon of the World Trade Center attacks that it was a good time to 'bury' bad news if any unpopular announcements were pending. The revelation of the memo caused outrage because of the use of the word 'bury', written almost at the moment of the collapse of the Twin Towers, but the problem for Blair was more profound. In allowing Moore to stay in her job, which he did in a way that made it impossible for him to retreat later, as he might have wished to do, Blair seemed to be confirming that even if the kaleidoscope of world events was in flux, his was a government that was in the same thrall to spin as ever. From the high point of the conference speech a fortnight earlier he had dipped to a point where a number of Labour MPs were becoming restless (most of them in private) about the bombing, bin Laden was nowhere to be found, and the coalition in the Middle East was creaking. Arafat told him in Downing Street at the height of the Moore affair of his worries about relations with the Ariel Sharon government in Israel, and his inability to prevent many young Palestinians being drawn into violence against Israeli citizens. At home and abroad, troubles seemed to multiply.

It made Blair's Middle East tour at the end of October extremely awkward. He had to endure a humiliating press conference in Damascus where his talk of progress to Middle East peace was put down by Syrian President Bashar al-Assad, thought by the Foreign Office to be more congenial than his father and an English-speaking man of some sensitivity, with an unbending reassertion of the Syrian view that Israel was a terrorist state. How could you have a 'war on terrorism' and condemn Palestinians who were fighting Israel? By the time Blair returned home at the beginning of November the skies seemed to have darkened.

The clouds were not lifted by the arrival in Downing Street soon after his return of a group of European leaders. The occasion, however, had a farcical tone. Blair had stopped in Italy on his way home from the Middle East to brief the Prime Minister, Silvio Berlusconi. He was engaged in preserving Berlusconi's *amour propre* rather than having serious talks, but unfortunately let it be known that there would be a dinner in Downing Street that Sunday for one or two European partners. Berlusconi said he would be there. Jacques Chirac (with his Prime Minister Lionel Jospin) and Gerhard Schroeder were already coming, and soon the news was in every capital. José María Aznar of Spain said that he would be there. The Belgians, who held the rotating European presidency at the time, then asked Blair to invite their Prime Minister, Guy Verhofstadt, and said he would bring with him Javier Solana, the EU's foreign and defence representative. All this ensured that Romano Prodi, the European Commission president, fumed in Brussels at his own exclusion. He had already had words with Blair about a breakfast meeting in the margins of the last EU summit of the British, French and German leaders which left out other countries (and him) and when he saw television pictures of Solana arriving in Downing Street in the back of Verhofstadt's car, he exploded. But it was too late. Dinner was already being served.

Comic though the arrangements may have been, the dinner was not a jolly affair. Blair found his colleagues gloomy about the prospects of the war in Afghanistan. Little seemed to have been achieved; civilians were dying from the bombing yet no obvious military breakthrough had occurred. Chirac intervened with one melancholy thought about the coming Muslim holy month. Laying down his fork, he addressed the room gravely: 'We all know we are likely to bomb a mosque during Ramadan by mistake. What do we say then?' No one had a simple answer, and Blair, freshly bruised from his visits to Syria and Jordan, was keenly aware of the fragility of the Arab part of the coalition. As they dispersed, the message came from Number 10 that good friends had discussed the campaign in a positive manner and the Prime Minister would be able to report to President Bush that week that support was solid. The truth was more complicated. An undercurrent of alarm and gloom was running strong.

Specks of evidence appeared which pointed to the government's defensiveness. John Reid, the Northern Ireland Secretary, was sent on a tour of TV and radio stations that week to deal with the concerns expressed about civilian casualties, in particular by two Muslim Labour peers. He complained that the critics made it sound as if Afghanistan was being carpet-bombed. That was far from the truth. The land area affected was 0.0002536 per cent of the country. This remarkable figure seemed to say even more about the government's anxiety to head off opposition than about the diligence of its statisticians.

Blair therefore saw George Bush on 7 November in a mood of some impatience. His determination had not dimmed since 11 September – everyone who spent time with him found him steely eyed and single-minded – but his colleagues in the war cabinet were sensing frustration. One sign was his fondness for Lord Guthrie, the former chief of the defence staff, now Blair's favourite soldier. His successor, Admiral Sir Michael Boyce, was uncomfortably aware that a back channel was operating with Guthrie. His influence could be justified in part by a chance relationship with General Musharraf of Pakistan, whom he had known since they were both cadets at the Military Academy, Sandhurst, and whose support for the campaign and control of his own Islamic militants was a keystone of Western policy. But Blair's fondness for Guthrie went deeper. 'He's Tony's kind of general,' said one member of the war cabinet, 'an SAS man until he dies, always wanting to get stuck in, never interested in hanging around.' The genial and voluble Guthrie caught much of the spirit of Blair's war.

The Prime Minister found that although the September attacks were events of unimagined magnitude that came, literally, out of a clear blue sky the campaign that followed did not change his political character. He was not reshaped by war; it reinforced his confidence. The Blair who sat at the war cabinet table, and in the Cabinet Office briefing annexe (COBRA) deep under Downing Street with his military advisers, was the Blair that all his colleagues recognized, but somehow distilled to his essence. The war suited him. He was energized by the knowledge that Downing Street was the crossroads for the United States and Europe, that the subtlety of British intelligence from the Arab world was becoming recognized in Washington, and that he was able to speak publicly with the moral tone that, before the election, had seemed increasingly inappropriate for the workaday questions of public service 'delivery' and had irritated his Cabinet. Now he was in command.

Yet this command, though unchallenged in his party, could not produce political strength that would necessarily outlast the war. Leaving aside the possibility of military disaster, which could turn the government upside down, Blair's preoccupation with the military campaign was inevitably allowing domestic disputes to fester. Brown was taking little part in the campaign, save to assure everyone that the Treasury would pick up the bill for the campaign and would also try an attack on money-laundering which everyone knew was too late but which was hailed as one of the practical benefits to come out of the disaster of 11 September. Prescott was a member of the war cabinet, but took little public role in arguing the government's case, despite holding on to the title of deputy prime minister. Outside the bunker a tangle of domestic problems began to grow. Byers's decision to allow Railtrack to fold and go into administration in October, with no replacement company ready to take over, was one of them. Like others, it would still be there after an Afghan peace was declared.

And Blair's relationship with Bush, the centrepiece of the campaign, could never be assumed to be permanent. In the early days it was a remarkable phenomenon (American network news shows, astonishingly, devoting some minutes to Blair's party conference speech) but it was clear in Washington that, although Blair could exert some influence on policy, and could certainly act as an early warning system of trouble from Europe and some parts of the Arab world, he would be able to use his access with the President only as long as he subscribed to the thrust of American policy. A Blair who became agitated, uncertain or squeamish would not find himself such a welcome guest at Camp David, or the Bush ranch in Crawford, Texas. The bloom would fade quickly.

Blair worked hard to make sure it would not happen. Downing

Street had been frankly distraught at Al Gore's defeat in November 2000 and the election of a Republican and found it had to work hard to make up lost ground with Bush, though in the Washington embassy Sir Christopher Meyer had spent a considerable amount of time working his way into the Bush circle, with the new President himself, and particularly with Condoleezza Rice, the National-Security Adviser. With Colin Powell at the State Department regarded as a secure Atlanticist and a restraining influence on the wilder spirits in the Pentagon, Blair threw himself into the new relationship with some hope that it could be made to work smoothly. Fortunately for him, the personal chemistry with Bush was good. At its essence was informality. Blair was comfortable with Bush's jeans and flying jacket style and, though their backgrounds were markedly different, they found it fairly easy from the start to converse at the same level. Both preferred anecdotal, instinctive judgements to dry analysis. They found they suited each other.

Blair's early assessment of the President was that although his international compass was limited, and he would never talk politics with the intellectual flavour that would be expected in Europe, he was clever. He was also open to argument. This was, of course, useful to Blair who could happily conclude that it was evidence of Bush's underlying intelligence that he would come to share the view of the British Prime Minister. The example Blair cites most often is that of Vladimir Putin of whom Bush was instinctively and straight-forwardly suspicious. 'Once KGB always KGB', he said of the Russian President. Blair spent time trying to fill out the picture, and took some credit when the relationship with Washington warmed up fast and Putin sped happily off to Texas to relax on the Bush ranch.

But Bush was still unpredictable. On his 20 September flight to the US, Blair had a fifteen-minute telephone conversation with President Khatami in Iran. He mentioned it to Bush. 'You *talk* to these guys?' asked Bush. Blair said that Jack Straw was about to go to Tehran to see his counterpart, the first Foreign Secretary's visit since the fall of the Shah in 1979. Bush was astonished. It had not crossed his mind that any overtures should be made to Iran, which, despite its historic hostility to Iraq, was bracketed in American minds with Saddam Hussein's regime as a sponsor of terrorism. This was one effort to change Bush's mind which was notably unsuccessful, resulting in the President's inclusion of Iran in the 'axis of evil' of terrorism identified in his January 2002 State of the Union message, a phrase which embarrassed his own State Department and alarmed his European allies, resulting in such signals of diplomatic turmoil as Iran's grumpy refusal to accept Blair's nominee, David Reddaway, as the first British ambassador in Tehran for more than twenty years, though his credentials would have certainly made him a welcome appointment. But the Bush speech demanded that Tehran show its displeasure with the Americans and their closest friends.

From the start, Blair's conversations with Bush were peppered with surprises. For example, in discussions of military strategy Bush would express his determination to attack if particular concessions were not made by throwing his hands up in the air, looking up to the ceiling and shouting 'Ke-POW!', presumably in imitation of an explosion. The first time, Blair was unsettled.

Fortunately for him, the relationship was not put to the test during the military campaign. The days of frustration in October gave way in early November to a string of advances for the Northern Alliance, the grouping of anti-Taliban forces, and by 7 December all Afghanistan's cities seemed to have been wrested from Taliban control. Bin Laden was still uncaptured, and whether dead or alive no one seemed to know, but Blair could argue that the first phase of the 'war against terrorism' had been completed.

There remained the questions the critics had asked from the beginning. Who was to define 'terrorism'? Could Britain support a new American attack on Iraq without firm evidence of a link between the regime and 11 September? Could Britain hope to warm up relations with Iran while supporting the Americans who regarded Tehran's support for Hezbollah guerrillas against Israel as state-sponsored terrorism and who were aligned with Saddam Hussein by Bush in an 'axis of evil'? If it was indeed a war, why were the prisoners taken by the Americans in Afghanistan and transported to their base on Cuba at Guantanamo Bay not treated from the first

as prisoners-of-war? What international legal procedures were appropriate for soldiers if they weren't prisoners-of-war (because they
didn't fight for a legally constituted army)? And so on. Even without
the threat of another attack, the springing to life of an al-Queda cell
somewhere in Europe or the United States, these were questions
which, by the end of the first part of the campaign, sounded a
troubling continuo accompaniment under the satisfied noises emanating from Downing Street and the White House.

Being lifted above the throng by war was an exhilarating experience for Blair. He responded physically, sleeping even less than
before and plunging with gusto into hours of military planning
meetings and conversations with other leaders. His Cabinet thought
him leaner, hungrier, tougher. In the run-up to the election, sapped
by the indecision brought on by foot and mouth, he had often
appeared close to the wobbly Blair of caricature. Now he was more
like the obsessed power-manipulator, convinced of his mission and
impatient with the fainthearts, even if his critics found the crazed
Cyclops of Steve Bell's cartoons in the *Guardian*, with its one
whirling eyeball and flapping ears, rather unlike the real thing. Blair
was certainly in the grip of a powerful belief and although prey to
the worries that come with war was enjoying himself hugely.

The Blair that found release after 11 September, and enjoyed
behaving in a way perhaps truer to character than ever, was convinced that the war had changed his premiership irrevocably: that
nothing could be the same again. The evidence was certainly around
him. Six months after the attacks, Alastair Campbell was still having
daily conference calls with the White House and the Pentagon to
consider how the case for the 'war against terrorism' should be put
to the public, day after day. Blair's relationship with his defence
chiefs was now even closer than after Kosovo. He was the European
leader who played the principal world role, Chirac's age and experience notwithstanding. He could claim to have deployed his feeling
for Islam to good political effect. And at home his personal rating
hardly dipped. Even when his trips to India and Pakistan early in
2002, and a few weeks later to West Africa, were scorned by Iain
Duncan Smith, the new Conservative leader, as 'designer diplomacy'

he was able to look at opinion polls and Philip Gould's endless focus-group discourses and conclude that on balance, people preferred a Prime Minister who was in demand than one who was on the sidelines. All this was cheering for him.

But wars induce dream-like states, for soldiers, generals and politicians. What if the Afghan campaign of 2002 turned out to be illusory in its effects, leaving Blair not as a Prime Minister who had risen above the rest of his government and party but had become dangerously detached from them? The appearance of strength in combat can turn easily into a quality of leadership that seems remote from the lives that it seeks to direct. Blair's conference speech had an uplifting effect on many in his party, and apparently many in the country at large and in the United States, but mainly it had an uplifting effect on him. He found a means of levitation. For a few months it gave him the sense of having escaped the bonds of earth. Occasionally, however, the heroics were replaced by weird wartime pathos.

The first Afghan campaign lasted for a mere four months. From the beginning it was odd. There was no doubt in London and Washington from the first days that bin Laden's organization was behind the attacks, but it quickly became clear to the public who were being asked to prepare for a long struggle – perhaps longer than the Cold War, said Bush's defence secretary Donald Rumsfeld – that the enemy was a shadowy will-o'-the-wisp, and one that had in the past done a great deal of business with some of those who were now lined up to eradicate it. Afghanistan was a country with no infrastructure and minimal defences and yet it was said to be virtually impregnable to ground invasion. In the United States and to a lesser extent in Europe people were being asked to support a campaign that would carry them across the mountains into the unknown. They were also told that even if Afghanistan were cleansed quickly of the Taliban and its satraps there would still be danger, and they had seen enough of Islamic fundamentalism and the consequences of American policy across the Middle East to suspect that the warnings were justified. So a straightforward aim – retaliation for 11 September – turned into a mesmerizing military and political game, with no rules and no simple objective. Leaders who wanted to be able to declare a quick victory were never going to find it easy.

Blair's only visit to Afghanistan seemed to exhibit exactly that quality of the unexpected and the melodramatic. He was on his way home from Pakistan, Bangladesh and India. The trip had been planned some time before, but it was decided that it shouldn't be cancelled, despite an outburst of comment at home suggesting that Blair was spending too much time in the air and on foreign soil. Murmurings from Downing Street about the dangers of conflict between India and Pakistan, both nuclear powers, didn't stop several newspapers turning on Blair for alleged *folie de grandeur*. India might be accusing Pakistan of harbouring terrorists who attacked the Parliament in Delhi, and the two leaders might be reluctant to meet to talk peace, but still Blair was thought by some to be better off at home, perhaps assisting trolley-bound NHS patients, casualties not of war but of old age and infirmity only, to find proper hospital beds. Nonetheless he went, and it was decided to have an Afghan stopover on the way home.

The intense military campaign seemed over, although some American bombs were still falling, and special forces from Britain and the United States were still scouring the southern caves in search of bin Laden and traces of his network. An interim government under Hamid Karzai was in place in Kabul, albeit made up of warlords and factions who at one time had been considered as unappealing to the West as the Taliban who had superseded them. So Blair was to stop for a couple of hours outside the Afghan capital to meet the new leaders and become, once again, first among equals. He would be the only Western leader to have set foot in the country since 11 September. Few politicians, and certainly not Blair, would need persuading that if the symbolic step could be taken, it should.

His military plane landed at Bagram Airport just outside Kabul at dead of night. A weird scene then unfolded. Blair's staff and the reporters accompanying them were warned that the fringes of the airfield were littered with mines. The place was dangerous. A welcoming party had been assembled consisting of the interim Prime Minister, his closest colleagues and a bevy of characters whom the

Blair entourage couldn't identify, a number of them shrouded in heavy scarves. Then, as the Prime Minister's party picked its way across the field a disaster befell Alastair Campbell. He was carrying an official case, packed with papers including briefing documents for Blair, among them some of the assessments provided for Downing Street by the intelligence services on the people the Prime Minister was about to meet. Whether Campbell tripped, or whether the locks on his case snapped under the pressure of the contents, no one can be sure. But the result was dramatic. The bag sprang open as if it had been detonated and a whirlwind of paper spread over the airfield. The moment of Blair's first meeting with the interim government of the 'liberated' Afghanistan therefore took place with his closest aide chasing across a mine-strewn airfield in search of confidential documents being carried by the wind into the freezing night. Some of them may still be there. The welcoming party appeared not to notice and a brief series of conversations ensued, watched by the accompanying warlords and their shrouded protectors.

As photo opportunities go, it was an odd one. And the scene became even odder. If Blair needs to be reminded of the peculiarity of the world that had opened up for him on 11 September, and the strangeness of the events that had brought him to Afghanistan in January to declare his support for reconstruction and his commitment to peace in the region, he need only recall the circumstances of his departure, one of the strangest that a British Prime Minister has known.

An official pointed out to him that the military plane that would carry him to Oman was ill-equipped. A bucket was being provided for the travelling press should they need to relieve themselves on the flight, and there would be a curtain for decency. But perhaps the Prime Minister might care to take precautions before leaving? So Blair set off across the runway accompanied by Campbell and some British soldiers. Over in the grass, a squaddie told him, they had sunk a drainpipe in the ground, end-up, to serve as a primitive urinal. If the Prime Minister didn't mind . . ? Blair, who was probably more worried about stepping on a land mine, headed for the pipe. Somewhere in the dark, it was found. The last sight any passing Afghan might have had of the distinguished visitor was of the Liberator Blair carefully relieving himself into a drainpipe, trying his best for a straight aim, by the faint light of a torch held in the trembling hand of a British soldier.

14

No Peace

The Prime Minister's Afghan visit left him with more than a bizarre memory of war. He carried away with him through the night, on his draughty plane crossing the desert, the knowledge that Gordon Brown was facing the greatest tragedy of his life. At Bagram airfield, surrounded by soldiers and warlords, Blair was told of the death of Jennifer Jane Brown after ten days of life.

No family event of such magnitude had affected the life of the government since Blair and Brown took power. It was raw and played out in public. Blair knew how deeply the loss would affect Brown, every corner of whose character he had come to know so well, and everyone around the two men realized that the pain of the event was bound to play a part in whatever lay ahead.

Everyone had seen Brown's manifest joy after Jennifer's birth in Kirkcaldy on 28 December. He appeared outside the hospital the following day and cast away his usual reserve as he expressed the thrill of fatherhood for which, as he put it, he had waited longer than most people. 'Politics seems less important today,' he said. Not the sort of sentiment generally associated with the Chancellor. The pictures of him on that day are memorable portraits of sheer happiness. The baby had been born prematurely because of potentially dangerous problems discovered by doctors and weighed only 2 pounds 4 ounces at birth, but the prospects seemed good and the parents expected the best. Instead they had to face the horror of a tiny life cut short. On Friday 4 January Jennifer Jane suffered a brain haemorrhage and was transferred to Edinburgh Royal Infirmary.

That evening Blair and Brown spoke, while the Prime Minister was in India. Precisely what passed between them remains private, but Blair was deeply affected by the conversation, confiding to close friends how painfully he felt the distress of his old friend and his wife. On Sunday Jennifer Jane was christened in hospital by the Church of Scotland minister who had married the Browns sixteen months before, and the following morning she died in the presence of her parents. Everyone who knew them, in politics and outside, understood how shattering a moment it was for the couple, and they were the focus of a huge tide of public sympathy. At the funeral service in Kirkcaldy four days later the press contingent was sober and restrained. Yet the Browns wanted the extent of their brief happiness to be known. At least two national newspaper editors were invited to attend. In the words of the address by Gordon Brown's brother John they thought of Jennifer as 'a transforming presence'. He described her as 'a little angel who came and went and changed the lives of those she left more powerfully than her tiny size or brief life could have suggested. For ten days her presence filled their world . . .'

The Blairs, with the Prescotts and close political and family friends, attended the service and the experience moved them all. There was no effort to conceal emotion, and everyone understood how deep the wounds would be. Brown, uncharacteristically, stayed away from his Treasury desk for a couple of weeks to stay with his wife in Scotland beyond the public gaze, in the privacy they had requested.

Such moments of personal tragedy, pushing politics aside, change the mood. Brown, inevitably, appeared different when he re-emerged. In the past he had been a figure whose reserve seemed to deny him an extra degree of warmth in the public mind, except among those who were his political followers. His marriage and, especially, his daughter's birth had changed that. For a few short days, the smile seemed relaxed, the bubbling good humour after the birth was on public rather than private display, which was rare, and the public face of Brown seemed different. Now, as a result of having had to go through fire, that persona took on an extra dimension.

The personal and the public can never be separated entirely in politics, because people in power behave as individuals, driven by their characters and their backgrounds. If they try to behave like machines, they do not last. Blair and Brown survived the first term in government because their shared commitments were stronger than the personal irritations that got between them, and the disagreements and frustrations were born of closeness rather than a lack of understanding. Their rows were the rows of intimates, not of strangers. Those who watched Blair respond to Brown's tragedy recognized, even from thousands of miles away, the special wavelength to which they were both occasionally tuned at the same time. 'I know it sounds corny and soppy,' said one close friend of Blair's who was in India, and who is also close to Brown, 'but sometimes on Tony's part it's an appeal for love. He wants something back.' This was not meant either as a compliment laden with innuendo or as a piece of overdramatization, but was simply an observation about what lies beneath. The unspoken coda is that Brown has found it difficult in recent years to respond in the way that Blair would like. Blair is the boss, but in emotional terms it is he who is more often the supplicant in the relationship. A more antagonistic portrait might be painted by officials who witness the arguments, the huffiness and the cold fury which, from time to time, each displays towards the other. Sometimes that is true, but not always.

For Blair, the pain that had engulfed Brown in the New Year was made all the worse because before Christmas the two had gone through a passage that was, even by their standards, a stormy one. The background made Blair even more anxious to strip away the awkwardnesses in their relationship and restore a man-to-man level of contact which would acknowledge Brown's words on the day of Jennifer's birth: that politics seemed different now. Yet their very intimacy meant that this could not be done by some wiping of a slate: the texture of their relationship, even in this shadow, showed the rough edges of their arguments as well as their understanding of each other.

They were both tested in the New Year by the confluence of tragedy and a patch of serious political trouble whose dangerous undercurrents threatened to flow through the whole government.

In his New Year message Blair had promised that public services were his priority. A spate of hospital horror stories was flowing across the front pages, train strikes were breaking out across the country, public service unions were complaining about a government too dazzled by the private sector, and even the previously quiescent debate about the safety of the triple MMR jab for measles, mumps and rubella turned into the kind of argument that is particularly difficult for government because it appears to pit Whitehall and its 'experts' against the instincts of many individuals. In such circumstances, it is difficult for ministers to win. For Blair the debate was especially irritating because it was fuelled in part by his decision not to reveal whether he and his wife, Cherie, had decided to have Leo inoculated, which would normally have occurred some time after his first birthday. Blair took the line that there was a principle of family privacy at stake. But his refusal to reverse that position (even when a number of other ministers said they were happy to confirm whether or not their children had been given the jab) turned that simple defence, which the Blairs were determined not to abandon, into a source of trouble for the government. The medical establishment insisted that the vaccine was safe, and the government's public health advisers warned parents that waiting for three single injections put their own and others' children at risk – but an atmosphere of mild panic developed and made Blair's conviction look like a policy mistake. Having made it, there was nothing he could do. To say that Leo had been given the jab would make it seem as if the principle of privacy had never been a principle; and if he hadn't, as seemed highly unlikely, government advice would be undermined. The episode was messy and damaging and seemed to sum up the miserable politics of the New Year for Blair. The period began to feel, in Downing Street, as outside, something of a turning point for the government.

That feeling was exacerbated by the Browns' tragedy. Seven months or so after the election and at the end of an unexpected and unpredictable war – or at least its opening battles – the government found itself moving into a different phase of its life. It was as if the adolescence of the first term, with the Afghan adventure as its melodramatic climax, was turning into a weary acceptance of adulthood. Things were going wrong; forgotten problems were demanding attention; the allowances made for inexperience and freshness were now being denied. Blairism was having to grow up.

The symptoms were obvious. Ministers started making multiple mistakes. Stephen Byers, though he insisted that the unhappy coincidence of a New Year holiday in the sun while a train strike broke out at home should not be counted against him, seemed to be unable to shake off the arguments of the former chief executive of the collapsed Railtrack and passenger groups that his was a strategy without staying power. The fact that he still had Jo Moore, author of the 11 September memo, at his side did not help him, and Downing Street was not amused to see an interview given by him in the *Guardian* in January which dwelt on the usefulness of the third way in dealing with the railways, appearing to conclude that it was not much good in providing answers to such practical problems. By this time Blair was admitting that he had underestimated the importance of transport reform in 1997 – though he was given plenty of advice which he could have taken – and Prescott was having to accept that it was in his vast department that policy on the railways had languished for too long without urgent attention. With a string of disputes breaking out between the biggest transport union and some of the train operators, and no successor to Railtrack likely to be in place for a year, the vultures continued to circle above Byers.

Blair and Brown each had to accept a share of the blame for transport. Prescott was well known to hold the view that the stringent regime of the first two years, when Brown kept to Conservative spending plans, had made it impossible to take the right decision early enough. Blair, however, found the transport story developing another uncomfortable dimension, opening up the question of how his government was run.

As a result the various policy problems of the New Year, which tend to come in awkward clumps, as every Prime Minister knows, became more than a passing difficulty for the government. Because of previously suppressed anxieties in the Labour Party and the unions, exacerbated perhaps by a war during which many of the discontented felt they had to remain silent out of reluctant loyalty, Blair was thrown into an argument about his style of government. Even while he was in West Africa, making good his conference promise to launch a Partnership for Africa among the rich industrialized nations, his Cabinet and party were engaged in a more profound debate about future strategy than at any time since the start of the first term.

One of the unlikely stimulants for this argument was John Birt, now Lord Birt, the former director-general of the BBC. When *The Times* revealed what the Labour Party had not known officially – that Birt was producing a long-term report on transport strategy – the whole extended apparatus of Downing Street and Blair's groups of advisers were exposed to the glare of comment, and indeed some ridicule. Birt's management style in his latter years at the BBC had been controversial and the subject of withering mockery from his former chairman Marmaduke Hussey in his memoirs. In the midst of a railway network grinding to a halt, the arrival of Lord Birt, whose decisions were famously channelled through consultants and strategy groups, became a symbol of Blair's search for answers in the seminar room rather than round the Cabinet table. Byers did not bother to conceal his contempt. When he appeared before Gwyneth Dunwoody's transport select committee and she asked him why he thought Lord Birt of all people had been asked to engage in what was known as 'clear skies' thinking about future policy, 'It was something to keep him occupied,' replied the Transport Minister, to loud laughter in the Commons committee room. For a relatively senior Cabinet minister to make mockery of a special adviser to Blair was remarkable; for a minister whose job was hanging by a thread it seemed foolhardy to be questioning the Prime Minister's judgement for a second time, following his frank *Guardian* interview. 'He's off his head,' said a Cabinet colleague afterwards. But Byers had clearly had enough. He would accept blame for failing to get the railways right over the next six months; but he was not prepared to be humiliated by allowing it to be suggested that other people had to be employed to do his thinking for him.

In fact, Birt's task was so long term as to have little to do with Byers's immediate problems, but the fact that it caught the political imagination spoke loudly for the concerns that were developing about Blair's style. They were prevalent in the civil service – the retiring Cabinet Secretary Sir Richard Wilson was known to worry about the plethora of outside advisers milling around Downing Street – and among MPs there was a feeling that the Prime Minister listened more attentively to his panels of outside advisers than to his party.

Blair had hopes for new thinking from his forward strategy group, including Birt, though a number of its members did not take as seriously as he did the territorial struggle for access in Number 10 itself. There was the performance and innovation unit; the delivery unit; the Number 10 policy unit itself. Individuals from outside took on specific tasks, such as the former CBI director-general Adair Turner, who was looking at the health service and spending one or two days a week in the department with his team, talking to senior civil servants and Alan Milburn, the Health Secretary. The growth in these groups was remarkable towards the end of the first term, with good reason. They were Blair's answer to the power of the Treasury, the very power he had conceded to Brown before they won the 1997 election and moved into Downing Street.

To counter Brown's authority and singlemindedness, Blair had realized that Number 10 had to fight back. He had always believed that a Prime Minister's Department was inevitable and desirable. The Treasury's grip on policy through the three-year spending reviews, controlled by Brown with headmasterly rigour and a political shrewdness which was felt by Number 10 to reflect his own interests at the expense of Blair's, provided Brown with the apparatus to shape an economic policy that had begun to look like his own. Blair searched outside for advice to counterbalance that power, and in doing so found himself attracted to the presence of figures from the world outside politics who arrived with no party baggage and were under the control of Blair alone.

His development of Number 10 as an extended think tank as well as an executive office also revealed his own suspicious and distant relationship with the traditional Whitehall machine. One or two civil servants at the top of the government machine believed they saw in Blair an incomprehension about the system which was at his command, even at the beginning of the second term. He preferred to turn to outside advisers for 'independent' thinking than to make Whitehall work for him. For officials who had spent a lifetime oiling those wheels, Blair's attitude seemed irritating, even insulting. But they recognized it for what it was: an impatience with a system that seemed to have failed to deliver. More than his ministers, Blair blamed Whitehall for the failure to deliver on public service reform. Just as he was willing to infuriate the TUC by referring to 'wreckers' in the public service unions who were reluctant to embrace reform, so he was happy to challenge traditional civil service departmental thinking by bringing in outsiders.

One of his ministers, bringing together Blair's wartime style and his method of devising a second-term strategy, noted that he was behaving exactly like a French president in his tendency to stand apart from the government run by his Prime Minister (in Blair's case, Brown) and to call on great and good external advisers to stand by his side. He was not a Prime Minister absorbed in the parliamentary system, determined to make Cabinet government work, but a chief executive anxious to find the quick solution.

The character of the early part of the second term was set by this aspect of Blair's political personality, and Brown's determination to keep his grip on the direction of economic and social policy. The two frequently collided and although the Afghan campaign appeared to cause a suspension of normal political disputes it did something close to the opposite. The war helped to sharpen Blair's desire for solutions which ran counter to established party thinking – lazy thinking as he sometimes considered it – it heightened Brown's desire to shape economic policy in his own way.

The arrival of Blair the war leader led to an intensification of the old rivalry. After 11 September the common view around Westminster and Whitehall was that Blair's performance on the world stage separated him from the more mundane struggles to maintain his dominance on policy inside the Cabinet, for example on the euro. He was thought to have passed into a different kind of realm.

The natural assumption that followed was that his political power had somehow been secured: his supremacy was clearer. That was not Brown's view. It had become clear to Brown that the Prime Minister did indeed intend to serve out his second term – Blair refused invitations in general conversation between the two to suggest anything else. Equally, the Chancellor appeared determined to remind everyone, inside and outside Number 10, that he had no intention of allowing his claims to the succession to pass away by default, just because there was a war on.

Blair therefore found himself facing a series of arguments over the pre-Budget report, the familiar arguments over the euro were fanned into flames from time to time and he found himself with no obvious sidekick in the Chancellor when he ran into trouble on such disparate issues as David Blunkett's anti-terrorism bill and House of Lords reform.

Blair's references to the euro in his conference speech were sufficiently enthusiastic, cast as they were against the tapestry of a newly ordered world, to be troubling to Brown. In the late summer Ed Balls had been authorized to issue from the Chancellor's side in Washington a statement describing a report in the *Financial Times* as 'fantasy and garbage' because it suggested that Prime Minister and Chancellor had agreed on a putative date for the referendum in autumn 2002 or spring 2003, on the assumption that the five tests would be met. Brown and his team simply would not let such an assertion go unchallenged: his camp said there had been no deal. So when Blair spoke with such passion in Brighton about Britain's European destiny, from around the Chancellor there came the familiar sniffy noises. By the time Brown addressed the CBI conference in November the tone was cautious again. He warned that it would be a great mistake to 'shortcut or fudge' the assessment. Now who in government, his Cabinet colleagues wondered, might want to do that? There was only one candidate.

Downing Street briefings made in advance of Brown's speech said it represented no change in policy. From the Chancellor's team came a rather different spin before he addressed the dinner in Birmingham on the Sunday. Blair was due to talk to the conference on Tuesday and the resurgence of gossip about the differences between them angered Number 10, which was determined to say that the advantages of membership were 'plain to see'. But Blair, to his irritation, had to add a passage denying that he and his Chancellor disagreed. In the formula he had had to employ so often before, he said that despite what people were reading in the newspapers the policy hadn't altered. But Blair went back to Birmingham two weeks later to speak to the European Research Institute and this time abandoned any sign of caution. The tests would have to be met, he stated, but the task of his government was to reverse the 'failure of imagination' that had saddled Britain with a half-hearted relationship with Europe and 'an embarrassingly long history of Euroscepticism'. The thrust of his speech was clear. He was determined to have his referendum and believed that the five tests would produce no obstacle. Their Birmingham outings seemed to move the argument on.

In November Blair's attitude changed. A couple of European commissioners who visited Number 10 in the period between his two Birmingham speeches found him worryingly vague. But by early December when Romano Prodi sat down with Blair he found him more positive than before. From then on he assumed that Blair was driving the argument forward and trying to wrest it from the Treasury.

The euro argument is inseparable in this period from another dispute with Brown which, according to spending ministers caught up in it and officials who watched its duels, was possibly the most sustained argument they have yet had in government. They were trying to settle Brown's pre-Budget report. Brown thought Number 10 was being obstructive. Blair thought Brown was being needlessly prickly while he was busy trying to keep the war on track. 'Bloody, bloody, bloody' is one Downing Street description of what happened. Entwined in the unsettled argument about the euro, this clash of wills was the real story of the start of the second term, largely concealed under the cover of war.

Brown was looking ahead to his third comprehensive spending review due in July 2002, which would be his most difficult. The first had been relatively easy because it had started from the low base of the Tory spending plans which the hair-shirted Brown had maintained. The second, in 2000, was able to promise healthy spending increases on the public services up to 2003–4 because of steady growth in the economy and low inflation. But the next calculation would be more difficult. The independent Institute for Fiscal Studies calculated that even on the most optimistic growth forecast Brown would have to find an extra £5 billion a year in borrowing or higher taxes to fund the rate of spending to which the government was committed. That calculation, moreover, was made before 11 September. Though the depth of any American recession was unclear when Brown began to make his estimations, and he could be reasonably confident that his economy would weather anything but the wildest storm, he faced a difficult calculation.

Brown decided on a course which served two purposes. It would allow him to take the initiative from Number 10, always an attraction. And he could continue to develop a distinctive approach to economic and social management which was clearly his own. For the first time since coming to office he began to talk about the virtue of higher taxation if it was necessary to pay for better public services. He used a language that was discreetly but clearly at odds with the New Labour rhetoric of his Prime Minister and Labour's first term.

Brown was careful to promise to stick to the election pledge that income tax would not rise in the second term but in a series of comments before he announced the pre-Budget calculations he floated the idea of a more open debate on tax. He left the *Financial Times* in no doubt in an interview that he was willing to consider publicly the possibility of higher taxes; a week later he was telling *The Times* that, although his fondness for his old friend Prudence meant that he could avoid tax rises in his spring budget, who knew what lay ahead. By the time he made his statement on 28 November, the headlines were almost laid out in advance. 'Brown Will Raise Taxes to Revive The NHS' said *The Times* on its front page. This time there was no complaint from the Treasury.

Behind this determination of Brown to change the language of tax lay a difficult series of exchanges with Blair. Their discussion took place at a time when Blair was chairing daily war cabinets, disappearing into the Downing Street bunker with military and intelligence advisers, talking on the telephone to Bush and the principal European leaders and flying hither and thither in support of the coalition now bombing Afghanistan and looking for the elusive Osama bin Laden. While Brown was saying little in public about the war, in private he was saying a great deal about the economy.

Blair was suspicious of the Chancellor's attachment to tax credits as the best means of attacking poverty, and in particular his plans for credits for children and pensioners. Brown, for whom poverty remained at the centre of his politics, was unshakeable. He carried the battle through a number of departmental budgets and was particularly insistent about health. He could not be convinced that the Blair–Milburn plans for extra funding would deliver what the service needed without substantial internal reforms. To make his point he established a Treasury investigation to examine the likely future demands for health spending.

Such arguments went on for weeks before the report was given to the Commons at the end of November, and they appeared to be seen by both sides as a straightforward struggle for supremacy rather than a debate about the health of the public finances. Blair certainly thought that Brown was behaving badly: they were back to the grim days of the election campaign. Brown, on the other, resented Blair's cranking up of the European argument and wanted to be able to develop a social policy which would be recognizably his own. Intriguingly, their arguments became closer to a right–left argument than any dispute they had during the first term. One of the reasons was the rise of David Blunkett in the Home Office.

Brown was irritated by Blunkett. One reason why he irked the Chancellor was obvious. The new Home Secretary was already a Downing Street favourite, as he had been at the Department for Education and Employment. Although some members of the Cabinet thought that shares in Blunkett as a future leader were trading at an inflated price (talked up by what were known as sources close to the Home Office) he was nonetheless an increasingly powerful figure, probably closer to Blair than Jack Straw. He was also, in Brown's view, a voice from the right.

The Home Secretary's anti-terrorism measures were not supported by the Chancellor. There was no debate in Cabinet – nothing new there – but it was well known in Whitehall and Westminster that Blunkett would be wasting his time if he looked for support from the Treasury when the inevitable trouble came from the backbenches. Downing Street was solidly behind him, because Blair believed that new powers of imprisonment without trial were justified in the face of intelligence reports about al-Qaeda and other Muslim fundamentalist activity in Britain. Many Labour MPs were unconvinced, though most of them could be whipped into acquiescence. But in the Lords a goodly rebellion was brewing. Brown was privately contemptuous of Blunkett's dismissal of 'airy fairy' concerns for civil liberties expressed by opponents of detention without trial without the option of judicial review for terrorist suspects. When Blunkett faced the biggest Labour revolt of the Parliament – thirty-two MPs went into the opposition lobby – there were no long faces at the Treasury. His climbdown on the establishment of a new crime of religious hatred, a defeat skilfully assisted by the Conservative spokesman Oliver Letwin, was evidently hard for him to swallow – he came close to losing his temper badly in the Commons. Blunkett's difficulties led to the government having to abandon its plans for the restriction of the right to jury trials in England and Wales.

The significance of the episode for Brown went far beyond the issue of terrorists and the law. Blunkett represented the headmasterly thinking which was becoming an increasing source of discontent in the party. Illiberalism had been a charge made against Jack Straw when he had been Home Secretary; it was now becoming a concern that pulled together Blair's opponents in all parts of the party. Old lefties never reconciled to the nineties reforms, liberals who were happy to talk of the 'third way' as long as it didn't stray too far, and a smattering of others who simply did not like the Blair style were starting to stir. The liberal left press, principally the *Guardian* and the *New Statesman*, was starting from a position of opposition to the government on a number of social issues – faith schools, religious hatred as a new offence, the restriction of jury trial and, of course, the anti-terrorism bill. Blair, in turn, took the course that he had followed so happily for many years, since the days of opposition. When challenged, he made a virtue of standing firmer than ever.

This was the posture with which he felt comfortable. He was also encouraged in it by Philip Gould's focus group results, which persuaded him during and after the Afghan war that 'resolution' was the quality that voters wanted. There was no advantage in being flexible or open-minded because the charge would be that he had become a ditherer. Gould reported that the public were unconcerned about his foreign trips and, despite the efforts of some newspapers, the polls seemed to bear that out. The other, perhaps more controversial, piece of advice was that Blairism in the public mind meant a determination that did not flag or fail. Gould was preaching to the converted, of course, since Blair had always believed that Thatcherism had survived beyond its natural span by an effort of will. Faced with opposition, his instinct was to do the same.

Blunkett was made of similar stuff. Brown was not. Although his stubbornness is legendary in the Cabinet, and his refusal, for example, to consider any alternative to the public–private partnership for the London Underground seemed a spectacular piece of defiance of party and public opinion, he saw himself as ideologically quite separate from that stream of thinking inside the government. He came to believe that Blunkett was a reactionary Home Secretary. Relations were not good. Just before the pre-Budget report he went so far as to have a meeting with the Home Secretary, duly publicized by his aides, to clear the air. It had taken place only because all Westminster had learnt that Brown was expressing dismay at the proposals and the language emanating from the Home Office.

Brown's visible discomfort was a reflection of his instincts, but it was also good politics. In distancing himself from the Blunkett regime at the Home Office, he could make an obvious break with the drift of Blairism that all his party could understand. Though he and the Prime Minister might share a political style that valued 'resolution', Brown had never been drawn towards Blair's social outlook. He saw Blunkett as too authoritarian, and in a party in which Home Secretaries have almost always had to fight the accusation that office pulls them rightwards, Brown's ambitions and the unease of a substantial number of backbenchers found common cause. He didn't have to make his feelings clear in a speech; a studied silence was enough. The message was clear, without the need for Machiavellian manoeuvres: Brown was irritated by the government's tone.

The troublesome period at the end of 2001 therefore contained a clearer ideological argument than had developed inside the government before. The war diverted much attention from it, but around Blair there was building a serious intellectual challenge, with Brown at the centre of it. The argument was emerging from the very success of Blair's first term in setting a tone: there was a body of belief which was now clear enough to give everyone something to chew on. Brown was happy to subscribe to the general aim of public services with new competitive disciplines, and to an economy that operated under tight fiscal rules. But he was much less happy with Blair's social instincts. The kind of approach that had been epitomized in the first term by Chris Woodhead's reign as head of the school inspectorate in England (under Blunkett) was deeply unattractive to Brown. He enjoyed being tough – grimness was his political forte – but he took great care to stay anchored to those in his party who felt that part of that traditional credo was dissolving in front of them. Even if he disagreed with them on policy questions, he wanted to suggest that he was a source of emotional sustenance.

Vague though this might have seemed, it was important with the unions. Many of Brown's policies irritated the public service unions. Though he talked about poverty and low pay, and pushed through the minimum wage and the New Deal for the young unemployed, he supported disciplines and reforms across the public services which offended leaders like John Edmonds. But Brown maintained a channel of contact, and serviced it carefully, which allowed him to remain much closer to the union hierarchy than Blair could ever hope to be. He actually enjoyed union platforms, Fabian meetings, poverty seminars, and his office often seemed more welcoming to old union friends (even if they had come to complain) than to some ministerial colleagues.

The lines of an ideological dispute with Blair would be difficult to draw in detail, because on much policy they have found common cause. The difference is cultural. Brown has always felt uncomfortable with much that Blair finds easy – royalty, ceremonial, most of the brasher entrepreneurs of the nineties, and the Woodhead-style figures whom he sees as the antithesis of Labour culture.

The pre-Budget arguments acted as a cipher for this deeper drifting apart. The European argument has remained a struggle for control. Brown made clear in spring 2002 that he was willing to turn the debate in Brussels into a campaign for retaining more control over public spending. His principal foreign policy interest (and almost the only one he spoke of) was debt relief and, with Blair's genuinely enthusiastic support, he turned his passion into one of the main thrusts of his chancellorship.

It was therefore clearer than before in the months after the 2001 election that two new Labours were developing. One was Blair's, which involved more discipline and more recourse to the private sector for solutions. Brown, on the other hand, prepared for his third comprehensive spending review with a different agenda. He wanted to be a redistributive Chancellor, happy if necessary to tweak the tax system to provide more money for public services, while keeping the promise of no income tax rises. He would apparently stay out of foreign affairs, and say as little about the war as possible, and avoid any observations on law and order, schools or social reform that would remind anyone of Home Office policy.

Brown suffered a good deal when the autumn burst of speculation about their relations came round again, because for the first time some Cabinet colleagues noticed that the story was written as a tale of briefing from the Chancellor's men. To a greater degree than before, he was identified as the manipulator of the row. It put him on the defensive, and when he took the unusual step of going in person to the *Sun* in Wapping to 'clarify' his remarks about tax – promising the ever vigilant tabloid that its readers would not face whopping tax increases – the unusual interview was seen, rightly, at Westminster as a form of apology. He did not enjoy the reported observation of Alastair Campbell that he had become 'a colossus out of control' nor the whispers from around Blair that the Prime Minister's patience was close to snapping.

Under the pressure of the war these worries and disputes were apparently distressing them both. Blair would put down the telephone on Bush, only to find Brown complaining about another piece of resistance from Milburn, or Hoon or Estelle Morris to the Treasury. Then Brown would wake up to a story which reported that Number 10 was fed up with subterranean briefing from the Treasury about the euro and would stomp into Blair's office to complain. Back and forth they went, stalking around a boxing ring which both by now knew so well and wondering whether the cuts to the brow and the ugly bruises would turn into something even more wounding.

Neither wanted to throw the final punch. Brown would never confirm, and his friends sought to deny, that he demanded of Blair in the summer that the Prime Minister tell him how long he wanted to stay in office. Blair, as far as can be judged, has never thought seriously that Brown should be removed from the Cabinet (though there are Number 10 advisers who have told him that he should). Each time one gets close to the point of taking the fatal step, he seems to retreat.

Just before the pre-Budget report, Brown gave an interview to *The Times* in which he decided to talk frankly about the relationship – or as frankly as was safe. Philip Webster and Peter Riddell reported that he looked 'uneasy, shifting in his chair and almost blushing' but was 'unusually direct and explicit'. He said twice: 'Tony Blair is the best friend I've had in politics. We have worked together for many, many years.'

And then, after the war, came Brown's own tragedy. The old values reasserted themselves and tears were shed on both sides. For a time the roughness of their trade was smoothed over. But the two personalities whose politics were shaped together had begun to diverge more seriously than before and behind the closeness which enveloped them after Jennifer Jane Brown's death they were both aware of sharpening divisions.

The very pace that the Afghan campaign gave to politics, after a weary, nitpicking election campaign and the disappearance of the Conservative opposition into its tent for the leadership election, meant that their instincts began to pull them apart once more. Blair found energy and purpose in the war, and felt more strongly than ever that his most natural political posture in politics was as the man who doesn't blink, Blair the Resolute. Brown, by contrast, was reminded of his lack of enthusiasm for the world of diplomacy and discovered that some of the domestic consequences of the war were unwelcome. Even more than in their first term in government, Blair and Brown were beginning to operate in their own spheres, more content with their own friends and their own priorities than with each other.

A hidden camera in Downing Street would have captured a lingering intimacy in Blair's office. The business of government was still distilled in their personal dealings. But each was looking more often over the other's shoulder at what lay ahead. Blair was finding fulfilment in his (surprising) relationship with Washington, while Brown's interest appeared increasingly to lie in sketching a future path for Labour that didn't take the third way. They weren't publicly in dispute about anything the government did (though their protestations of euro-unity were becoming threadbare) but their instincts and attitudes were becoming easier for everyone to separate. Blair was moved by the war; Brown was disturbed. The difference gnawed at their relationship.

Labour, having been a party led by two rivals, was becoming a party of two cultures.

15

A History of the Future

The moment when the rumble of the 'war against terrorism' began to give way to a clamour closer to home was signalled by a familiar and intimate sound – the ringing of Peter Mandelson's telephone. Soon after the New Year, the old relationship was rekindled. Blair needed him and their breakfast-time conversations became once again a regular start to the Prime Minister's day. They were evidence that, war or no war, the second term might not be as different from the first as Blair had hoped, and that in dealing with the kind of political difficulty which Brown might prefer to let the Prime Minister handle alone, there was only one place to turn.

Mandelson's reappearance at the Prime Minister's shoulder was spectral. He could not be seen. He did not slip in and out of the offices outside the Cabinet Room as he used to in the old days. But he was there. After the troubles of the autumn, and with mistakes and embarrassments piling up in the New Year, Blair reached out instinctively for his courtier and cup-bearer, the grand vizier who had once been privy to every strategy and every decision. Mandelson still nursed the hurt of his second resignation, and had been agonizing with friends about his future in politics, but now found himself in favour again. He enjoyed Blair's admission that he was needed: that even the whispering and the jealousy that his influence brought with it in its wake was better than life without Peter.

And in restoring one relationship, Blair allowed distance to develop in the other with Brown. To Mandelson it felt as if Blair was coming home. To Brown, the picture looked different and darker. Blair and he seemed more and more to inhabit their own worlds, each with his own preoccupations and friends, each with his own strategy for the future. Their lives would overlap, then move apart again. A negotiation – over a Whitehall spending bid, or a sensitive announcement, or even a euro speech – would bring them together, but never for long. Each seemed to be leading a different kind of life.

Brown's commitment to his debt relief programme and his determination to use tax credits to attack poverty at home became even more obviously the centre of gravity of his politics. Many of his predecessors in the Treasury had used the position to become all-purpose participants in the business of government, commenting on the whole sweep of politics. Reversing the usual pattern, as his time as Chancellor moved on he became less anxious to be seen to be involved in every prime ministerial move, and more concerned to make his own case, and make it distinct.

He had deliberately avoided any important speeches about the war, and kept well away from Blunkett's territory into which he had no desire to step. Pressed to praise Cabinet colleagues he would find the words, but there always had to be a reason. Around Whitehall he was known to be convinced that some of them – particularly those with the bigger budgets – were weak. His defence of Stephen Byers, for example, after the decision to force Railtrack into the hands of administrators, rang hollow in the ears of civil servants who had heard his private views on the conduct of affairs in the Department of Transport.

Most of all Brown had become the Chancellor who was evidently out of sympathy with the Prime Minister's style. Blair's instinct for the concerns of the *Daily Mail* reader was a strength which had confounded his opponents and helped Labour to its big majorities, but Brown's private dislike of the 'middle England' agenda was well known. He was perfectly capable of buttering up Fleet Street editors whom he privately disliked, and kept his links with the Murdoch machine particularly well oiled, but the Brown style in the second term was to be the Chancellor who was his own man.

A year or so after the election he would have served longer at the Treasury than Denis Healey, the Chancellor who dominated the grim seventies for five years, and by 2003 would overtake Nigel Lawson, Margaret Thatcher's favourite, as the longest-serving since the Second World War. He was immovable, unless by a sacking that would be so perilous for Blair that it was assumed it would not ever happen. He had become a figure dominating his own territory, staked out carefully over the years with jagged defences designed to repel any invader, including the Prime Minister. Downing Street advisers wondering about the latest thinking on the euro in the Treasury were kept in ignorance: unthrifty ministers making their bids for special treatment in the next comprehensive spending review found him unrelenting in his pursuit of his own strategy; Blair's hopes that Brown's relations with Prescott, Cook and Blunkett might warm up were left unfulfilled.

The Chancellor was a mirror image of the Prime Minister, becoming a more intense version of himself as time passed. Blair was surer than ever that his premiership was best sustained by a Thatcher-like resistance to pressure, and a determination to sound like an outsider in his own government. Brown's entrenched role was as the social engineer who was redistributing wealth, who was willing to talk about extra tax to pay for health, the reformer who still couched his speeches in Labour language. After five years in power they were not interested in submerging their differences in outlook, but in making an exhibition of them.

Brown worked hard at nurturing the backbenches, and doing so on his own terms. It is no exaggeration to say that no one can remember him uttering the words 'third way' and, although his support for the Prime Minister was always restated when required, he was never caught in an unguarded moment of enthusiasm for a Blair speech or a Campbell strategy. Distance was maintained. And from Number 10 came muttering about Brown's friends and bag-carriers, with particular head shaking for his old attendant muckers Charlie Whelan and Paul Routledge, considered in the Blair circle to be evidence of the Chancellor's funny judgement about the company he kept. The Chancellor's men snorted with matching derision at Blair's advisers and friends.

The more trouble there was, the more Brown's distance was

resented. On reform of the House of Lords, for example, he had almost nothing to say. The policy was a disaster for Derry Irvine. A majority in the Cabinet, with Prescott the most vocal, was deeply unhappy about a reform that would produce a second chamber that was in competition with the Commons by being largely elected. The alternative, which Irvine duly cobbled together, was worse. A chamber with 20 per cent of its members elected, as he proposed, simply emphasized the undemocratic nature of the 80 per cent. When Irvine presented his ideas to the Parliamentary Labour Party behind closed doors he was nearly shouted down, with Lord Williams of Mostyn, Leader of the Lords, having to try to rescue the Lord Chancellor's dignity in the face of something near collective contempt.

Robin Cook, as Leader of the Commons, could not resist the pleasure of pointing up Irvine's embarrassment and implying that he would be able to sort out the mess, but the damage was painfully exploited by Iain Duncan Smith who came up with a Tory plan for an 80 per cent-elected Lords, which managed neatly to suggest that the Tories were casting off old prejudices in the cause of modernizing while Blair was resorting to government by fix and cronyism. There seemed to be plenty of supporting evidence.

John Birt and the other advisers and strategists crowding round Downing Street were caricatured as an unelected shadow government. The charge had a sting. Blair was the leader who had always been comfortable with outsiders. He had made his leadership a study in distancing, from the challenges to Labour orthodoxy in opposition to the rhetoric of the third way in government. The war helped to reinforce the image of the Prime Minister who stood alone, away from the throng. He had always enjoyed the feeling and in the same way as Margaret Thatcher relished being a Prime Minister, always pushing and prodding her party and sometimes appearing as a one-woman opposition to her own government, Blair took some pleasure in his role as a figure who stood apart. He was turning Downing Street into more of a Prime Minister's Department, a chief executive's office rather than the engine of a collective government, and he was listening to outsiders whom he thought might bring him the solutions that his own government – to his evident mystification – had failed to produce.

But Blair's belief in that style as a strength was challenged, and undermined, by the Byers affair in early 2002. The storm blew up from nowhere, raged around his head, and appeared to subside quickly. But it left a trail of damage, and the debris could not easily be cleared away. The Prime Minister himself showed the scars of the experience, and they did not fade.

The ingredients were familiar: Jo Moore, author of the notorious 11 September e-mail and political fixer; Stephen Byers, accident prone Transport Secretary; the hulk of Prescott's old Environment, Transport and the Regions Department now stripped of the environment and dominated by its transport responsibilities; the civil service information officers who had been engaged in guerrilla combat with some ministerial special advisers since 1997; the press, which scented blood at last.

The performance had an overture in the Mittal embarrassment, which served to expose one of Blair's old weaknesses, his tendency to be dazzled by the rich. On Foreign Office advice, he had written a letter to the Romanian Prime Minister commending a 'British' company which was doing a good bit of business in buying up that country's privatized steel industry. Such letters flow regularly from Downing Street and the Department of Trade and Industry in any administration, but Blair was embarrassed when the company was revealed to be employing only a hundred or so workers in Britain, to be registered in a tax haven in the Dutch Antilles, and to be run by a millionaire who had given £125,000 to Labour not long before the Blair letter was signed. Despite the government's protestations that this could be revealed only by its own rules on transparency of campaign contributions, and Blair's own description of the furore as 'garbagegate' (a classic Campbellism), the political effect was to turn attention again on the issue which had troubled Blair in his dealings with the tarnished ministers Geoffrey Robinson and Keith Vaz. Could this government be trusted?

Byers then took the stage. The bizarre cause of the trouble was the death on 9 February of Princess Margaret. Two days later, at the Monday meeting of Byers's officials, his head of information, Martin Sixsmith, suggested that it would be a mistake to issue a set of rail passenger figures which were considered 'bad news' by the department on the coming Friday, as Jo Moore had suggested, because it would look as if Byers was trying to slip them out on a quiet news day. Sixsmith had arrived in his post after the row about the 11 September e-mail and was anxious that nothing similar should happen again. Later in the day, when he realized that Princess Margaret's funeral was going to be held on Friday he became alarmed and e-mailed Byers (with a copy to Moore) saying that no 'bad news' should be issued on that day, because it would be assumed to be a repeat of Moore's September mistake. He was firing a warning shot, because he had no evidence that Moore was planning to use the funeral in that way. His Whitehall experience, however, suggested that it would be sensible to take precautions.

All this would have been a routine piece of departmental fixing, but for a leak of the e-mail to two newspapers. When Sixsmith confirmed its existence (though not its precise wording) the ingredients were in place for a spicy story. Moore, who had been saved by Byers after the September fiasco, was being accused of trying once more to manipulate the flow of news. The civil service, in the form of Sixsmith, was in torment at Labour's obsession with 'spin'. Byers was apparently unable to stop a feud in his own office. For Blair the affair was dangerous for the reason that it contained, in one delicious cocktail, a distillation of what his opponents considered his greatest weaknesses – an obsession with news management, an inability to understand the nature of a non-political civil service, and a Cabinet consisting of ministers who found it difficult to keep a grip on their own departments. The story therefore exploded across the front pages.

For nearly a week the fine points of the exchanges inside the department became a talking point for people who would find it hard to tell the difference between a ministerial special adviser (Moore), a civil service head of information (Sixsmith) and a permanent secretary (Sir Richard Mottram). But when Sir Richard was quoted as saying of his department 'We're all fucked', and when Sixsmith said that he heard the announcement of his own 'resignation' while he was at a hospital appointment (before he was aware that he had agreed to go), the issue became the most dangerous in politics: who isn't telling the truth? It was obvious to anyone, Whitehall-wise or not, that someone was not. Byers told Jonathan Dimbleby on ITV on 24 February that he did not involve himself in personnel matters – and therefore, by implication, had no part in Sir Richard's request for Sixsmith's resignation. But Sixsmith broke cover on the *Today* programme two days later to say that Sir Richard had told him directly of a discussion he had with Byers in which the secretary of state had said that if Jo Moore had to go, so must Sixsmith. That afternoon, Byers had to go to the Commons and apologize for his misleading remarks in his television interview. Blair was not there to hear him – in case he was drawn into a collective humiliation for the government in front of the Commons and the TV cameras – but Byers survived by rallying backbenchers to his side (using his Railtrack decision of the autumn as evidence of his credentials as the man who was trying to undo Tory privatization of the railways) and with the help of a notably weak Conservative attack from the opposition front bench.

The affair died. But the wounds were deep. Once again, the government's alleged strength – its skill at news management – had proved to be a spectacular weakness. A secretary of state who had all but admitted lying several times about the conduct of affairs in his department was cheered at a meeting of the Parliamentary Labour Party for surviving what Downing Street called 'the media feeding frenzy'. Blair, who said before 1997 that he would not keep in his Cabinet a minister who told a lie, had to defend Byers. Civil servants, unsettled for years about the blurring of the lines between their advice to ministers and the activities of the political advisers sitting at the ministers' doors, saw the episode as a glimpse into the darker side of Blairism.

For the Prime Minister, Byers's narrow escape was a warning. Despite the monthly MORI poll in *The Times* at the end of February suggesting that the affair hadn't helped the Conservatives (stuck on 28 per cent of the vote) and that his government was still commanding the support of an overall majority in the country (51 per cent), the spectacle had been ugly. Blair seemed a Prime Minister unable to sort out family squabbles in his ministers' offices and unconcerned that a member of his Cabinet had made a series of misleading statements about his own role. Above all, it seemed to mark a return of the old politics, with its disputes and wrangles, its deceits and jealousies. The high-flown words of the conference speech were a long way in the past. Within weeks the polls began to fall.

This was the preliminary to a vital phase of the second term. Brown was preparing a Budget, and a comprehensive spending review three months later, which would lay out the government's tax and spending plans for the rest of the Parliament. In May there would be local elections – notably in London – which were going to be a difficult test of the government's standing. The first two months of 2002 were Blair's most uncomfortable in office, and once again Brown seemed to be standing apart from the trouble.

The loudest noise coming from the Treasury while the Byers affair dominated politics was not the sound of the Chancellor leaping to the defence of Blair or the Transport Secretary, but of his chief economic adviser, Ed Balls, wading into the euro debate. In the last week of February he made a speech warning of the dangers of entering the euro at the wrong time – pointing out that it wasn't necessarily true that membership would automatically benefit the British economy. He sounded unenthusiastic about an early referendum, and found the *Sun* ready to interpret his words as a 'veto' on a vote in 2003, a front-page story which infuriated Downing Street. Since Peter Hain, the Europe minister in the Foreign Office, had given an interview a few days before to *Le Figaro* in Paris which had been notably enthusiastic about the euro, Balls's speech was taken as the resumption of the old *pas-de-deux* between the departments, evidence of a government that still wobbled on the issue that Blair had identified as the great challenge of the first years of the century.

The Byers mess and the euro exchanges were reminders of the chaotic muddles of the Major administration when the government seemed to have lost its nerve and sense of balance at the top. Blair needed to find coolness and a sense of strategy, and Brown let him get on with it alone. He'd give as much advice as was asked for in private, and would certainly not undermine Blair in public, but it was a measure of the Cabinet's understanding of the relationship at this juncture in the second term that they would regard as far-fetched the notion that the Chancellor might take to the streets to appear as the Prime Minister's friend in time of need. It was no longer the way they worked.

The paradox of the period that began at the end of the Afghan campaign was that it appeared to be a moment of change, yet Blair and Brown were ever more imprisoned in their own characters and their styles. Emboldened by the loneliness and dark drama of war, Blair was the Prime Minister who would challenge his party and the unions and Whitehall to reform. He and the 'wreckers' would fight it out, come what may. Brown would have no part in that. As someone who had always believed that the 'third way' was a meander rather than a true path, he reached more confidently than before for an old language. Preparing his justification for Labour's taxation plan to pay for public service improvements, in the spring of 2002, he was in effect writing his own credo for New Labour, and one that would be different from Blair's.

The balance of power between them was also becoming more difficult to read.

For example, was Anji Hunter's departure good or bad for Blair? When she left his side at the start of 2002 to join BP, Brown's friends were delighted. Although the Chancellor's own relationship with her went back far enough to retain some warmth, he regarded her straightforwardly as a figure so well attuned to the angst of the English middle class that in his book she scarcely qualified as a member of the Labour tribe. She had also had huge influence on Blair's daily thinking (she was even in attendance at the war cabinet). But her relationship with Cherie Blair had chilled, and Sally Morgan – now a peer – was a rival for Downing Street status, so she found it more pleasant to think of a lucrative, less stressful life outside than to stay on in 'Peyton Place', as she put it to a friend. She was just old enough to remember *Peyton Place* as a progenitor of the modern soap opera, an America populated by flaky and grasping characters prone to spectacular self-centredness, perpetual intrigue and hysteria. Off she went. It was not surprising to Blair's intimates that as she disappeared the Prime Minister's telephone calls to Mandelson became more frequent and even longer. But her absence seemed to change little in Blair's style or outlook. After nearly five years in Number 10, he was a personality who had found himself. As in the Thatcher years, a Blair-watcher could predict with confidence how he would respond to an event, even what he was likely to say. The days of surprise were over.

Even a year earlier, Hunter's departure would have precipitated a period of serious imbalance in Downing Street. Now it seemed a more natural development, more evidence of the passing of the government into a new phase of its life. The Prime Minister knew that he was now engaged on an effort, over two or even three years, to make good the promises that mattered most. He was convinced that he would stand or fall by the delivery of his promises on the public services, and appeared to acknowledge how that objective had been undermined by his lack of understanding early in the first term of the depth of the transport crisis and the political effort that would be needed to escape from it. When the recurrent mini-crises of some Whitehall spin scandal had passed, or another rich friend of Lord Levy's had come and gone, it was on that ground that Blair would be tested.

He also believed that despite the problems that rained down – from the humiliation of Keith Vaz for his treatment of a Commons investigation into his finances, to the internal chaos at the Department of Transport, to the controversies that dogged some Labour donors – he had been strengthened by war. Frank Field, the maverick MP, was typically undiplomatic in a television interview in December 2001: 'When you've been a megastar on the international stage twice, like Tony Blair has, I don't think the Prime Minister is going to come back to play number two to Gordon Brown for that much longer.' Although the anti-Blair press now had a spring in its step, pillorying the Prime Minister who wanted a 'whiter than white' government and found himself explaining away his relationship with fund-raisers, and lampooning the travel-weary statesman who spoke of African revolutions but could not make the trains run on time, his own instincts were sharper than ever, and his determination absolute.

Blair in such a mood was a source of deep frustration for Brown. As time went on Blair seemed even less likely to consider early retirement than at the end of the first term, and, perhaps even more seriously, he was willing in private to challenge Brown's political weight. He had one particularly useful weight to put on his own side of the scales – Scotland.

The Edinburgh Parliament had not turned out to be the story of progress and success that Brown had hoped. When Henry McLeish had to step down as First Minister over strange rent arrangements for his constituency office, and for misleading the Commons authorities as a result, Brown's friend Wendy Alexander (sister of Douglas, Labour MP and a Chancellor loyalist) was expected to stand. She did not, but before her withdrawal there was trouble for Brown in the Scottish press, usually friendly towards him. The message was simple: keep out of Scotland. If the Chancellor was playing an active role in choosing McLeish's successor, he should not be. Worse was to come for Brown. The election of Jack McConnell was unwelcome, because he and Brown had fallen out years before over the leadership. McConnell had been secretary of the Scottish party but, to Brown's dismay, had become a Blair supporter after John Smith's death.

The wider problem for the Chancellor was that the Edinburgh Parliament had lost its shine. McConnell himself had to make public a messy extramarital affair before his election, and from London the place looked unstable and unpredictable. With much of the Scottish press in cynical and rough mood, the project which had been so dear to Brown for a generation was not a subject about which he could boast. Blair seemed to hope that it could just be whisked away, like the House of Lords.

So each man had his weaknesses. Brown was still seen by many in the Commons as the brilliant strategist flawed by his obsession with leadership; Blair was becoming a figure more distant from the foot soldiers who had to take their orders and vote for Blunkett's latest bill, many of them with unease. And around them the Cabinet wondered if, in the transition from a government with all the confidence of youth to a wearier and more troubled outfit, they might be able to see at last through the twin spheres of Blair and Brown, each turning independently on its own axis, and glimpse a world beyond.

Some of them certainly began to behave with the touch of arrogance that you need as you grip the greasy pole. Charles Clarke, named as chairman by Blair in a typical piece of defiance of party tradition (there being an elected post of chairman on the national executive, which Blair ignored), began to beat his breast in a remarkable way. As if to contrast with the spin culture which had come to characterize the government, he made a series of admissions about first-term failures which he presented as grown-up politics. His voice has become important at the Cabinet table.

Alongside him is his old colleague from their days in Neil Kinnock's office as leader of the opposition, Patricia Hewitt. At the Department of Trade and Industry she dug herself into an important strategic battle station, from where she managed the notable feat of keeping good relations with Number 10 and the Treasury at the same time, an act of some skill which had eluded her predecessor, Stephen Byers. In her dreamier moments she was wondering when the Labour Party might turn to a woman as leader. Alan Milburn at Health did not have as good a relationship with Brown, but he too was beginning to think of a future at the top. Despite having to say the unthinkable, and challenge the party and the trade unions to contemplate radical reform in the funding of the NHS, he had the politician's pleasure of knowing that the great issue of the day was in his hands. If Blair made a success of Health, it would be to Milburn's ultimate credit.

With Blunkett secure in the Home Office as perhaps Blair's new best friend these four began to emerge six months or so after the election as the centre of gravity of the Cabinet. With Alistair Darling at Work and Pensions, Estelle Morris at Education, Geoff Hoon at Defence and John Reid in Northern Ireland the unspectacular but steady performers, Blair could at last wonder seriously if he had a Cabinet with weight. For the first time it was not difficult for him to imagine that one of the leading quartet might become, in time, a natural successor.

But he also knew the truth – that the government was still essentially seen as a collaboration, and sometimes a struggle, between two men. The public understood it accurately. Each time a flurry of briefings and corrections whizzed back and forth between Number 10 and Number 11 everyone recognized that the daily struggle for control and supremacy had once more broken to the surface and become visible for a moment. They knew, too, that it would continue unseen when the moment passed.

A Prime Minister can hope that the knowledge that he has a restless and ambitious colleague snapping at his heels is likely to evoke some sympathy. The image of the patient Blair, soaking up the complaints and grumbles of his Chancellor, is one which Downing Street has managed to project with some success. Brown, on the other hand, can hope that he is seen as the ideological pulse of the government – worrying about poverty and debt, the young unemployed and social exclusion and never getting himself too close to dodgy fund-raising, international jet-setting or war. Each is a caricature, but pins down something of the struggle of the second term.

In part it will indeed be ideological. The Afghan campaign stirred feelings in the party which reminded some MPs of the days when it was easy to know who stood where on every issue: this was a question on which some people broke with Blair completely, and when more than 100 MPs expressed 'deep unease' at any British support for an American attack on Iraq, it was a serious chorus of descent. With the unions' public fury at the 'wreckers' speech and Blair's determination to open up the public services debate to consider new ways of raising private funds, the arguments were beginning to divide the party on clearer lines. Blair, full of confidence and defiance in the face of the critics, has chosen the language of battle. He may get one.

In the Commons, there are signs of life even among some of the backbenchers renowned for their obsequiousness (specializing in what Tony Benn called 'vomit-making' questions to the Prime Minister designed to ingratiate themselves). Robin Cook, an activist Leader of the House, is pushing reform and does not worry about upsetting Downing Street; his move from the Foreign Office left feelings of hurt that will never pass away entirely. Blair's task is going to be made more difficult by a party that is minded to be less quiescent.

Benn, retired but still a Commons presence thanks to the Speaker's decision to give him access to the precincts in recognition of his fifty years as an MP, catches the flavour of the malcontents in a typically elegant way:

The third way was invented to provide some sort of an ideological cover for the strategy of abandoning the trade unions and the historic commitment to a socialist society. It never had any base in public support and with the low turnout in 2001 the Labour vote is lower than it was in 1992.

New Labour is probably the smallest political party in the history of British politics, but because they are all in the Cabinet it seems very strong. For the first time in my life the public seems to be to the left of a Labour government.

Blair's task is to prove him wrong. Brown hopes he can prove him half-right. That is the difference between them.

Brown is appealing to his party for a kind of ideological loyalty, trying to exhibit enough of the characteristics of a 'Labour man' – as a redistributive Chancellor, a figure with a sense of party history who'd find ways of never calling trade unionists 'wreckers' – to be a focus for hope. Blair, by contrast, does not try to draw from that well. His appeal is based on his untouchability as leader and that dashing confidence which he enjoyed displaying in the Afghan campaign. It was a confidence he found it much more difficult to muster when faced with the Byers muddle, and it's what his friends and advisers have been trying to restore to his domestic performance. Without it, the Blair phenomenon loses power quickly.

Blair believes that his strength is his ability to stir up unease in the hope of provoking creativity and political boldness. It is for that reason that he has felt it right to take on the unions rhetorically, in a way that Brown simply would not do. John Monks, general secretary of the TUC, who was infuriated by the 'wreckers' speech, which he saw as a crude insult and an impediment to his own efforts to work with the government on public service reform, put it directly to Blair like this: 'the trade unions and the party are like Ernie Wise and you're Eric Morecambe. When you're in trouble and you need a cheer from the upper gallery – that's where the *Daily Mail* and the rest of middle England are sitting – you give us a good hard slap on both cheeks. We're your prop.' Blair gave him a wry grin. He could hardly deny the telling accuracy of the observation. Monks gives him a message that is heavy with alarm. 'We're all very, very apprehensive in the unions. We will try to find a way through and we will try not to put you up against the wall but it is going to be difficult.' He fears rampant apathy among trade unionists who will lose their sense of kinship with 'their' government.

But that alarm will encourage Blair rather than depress him. He believes, with the faith of the traveller on the 'third way', that the transition can be made and, in its maturity, his government can rethink the public service formula, preserving the ethos of a service for all but drawing on the private sector for new vigour and some money. The public service unions do not believe it for a moment. For Blair this is another hairpin bend that must be taken with the screeching of tyres – the kind of noise he likes. For Monks it is recklessness and evidence of a desire to abandon the familiar just because of its familiarity. He has his arguments with Brown about the flow of money, but the Chancellor's commitment to the minimum wage and the New Deal for the young unemployed, together with his cultural contentment with the unions and his shared unease about Blairite rigour, make him an ally.

The challenge to Blair is profound. After the election, Brown could claim credit for an economy which would produce the money for him to present himself as the successor to Labour Chancellors of the past. The difference is that, even after the shocks of 11 September, he has the money to pay for his objectives. Prescott puts it like this to other ministers: 'It's the long game. Gordon's been saving the money. He's played the long game from the start.' Prescott's assumption, like those of many of his Cabinet colleagues, is that Brown expects to appear in the course of the second term as the unchallengeable successor who is ready to take his place in Number 10 if the Blair bloom fades and the Prime Minister becomes that most unsaleable commodity, the politician who has become a bore.

'Succession' is the word that hangs over the second term like a raincloud about to burst. Blair and Brown have worked together and maintained their civility in public, and remnants of the old intimacy survive in private. Their relationship withstood the burden of the emotional intensity of the first term to remain the centrifugal force in the government and after re-election it was still the command mechanism. But politics is not static, and Brown sees the sands passing through the hourglass.

He is restless and ambitious. The evidence is in his demeanour. He is still uncomfortable in rooms where the Prime Minister is in command. One of his senior colleagues, who sits close to him in Cabinet, says this: 'For goodness sake, why doesn't he enjoy it? He's the most redistributive Chancellor since 1945. The most progressive Chancellor since Dalton. He's probably the most powerful Chancellor there's ever been. Why doesn't he enjoy it? It's extraordinary.' In fact it is extraordinary only if you ignore the emotional history with Blair, and the sense of unfulfilled ambition that lurks under the solid armour of Brown's public face. And entwined with it must be the fear that the brilliant shooting star – the student radical, party intellectual, dominating Chancellor – will never streak across the sky in its full glory.

Brown believes, much of the time, that he will still be Prime Minister. But he cannot be sure. He wants it. He has wanted it since he arrived in Parliament. He believes he should have had it already, which makes him want it more. And he believes that Blair has gone as far as any Prime Minister can go in promising it to him. Brown's tragedy is that he also knows that such promises are undeliverable. A Prime Minister who fixes a moment for departure is a rare bird indeed. Departures are almost always difficult and dangerous. Even the most obvious of all in the modern era, Churchill's handover to his annointed successor Eden in 1955, was mismanaged with such gaucheness and apparent selfishness that it engendered bitterness and moments of hatred between the old friends. How much more difficult it is for these two, each convinced that his way is best, and tending as time goes by to diverge rather than to come together. Brown knows that the prize may never be his. For him, that would make any successes as Chancellor hollow triumphs and the possibility condemns Blair's government to a strange life for the rest of its days.

Some members of the Cabinet believe that it will, in the end, be Brown. Irvine, who sits beside the Chancellor across the table from Blair, is one. Alistair Darling and Margaret Beckett are others. But it remained true even during Blair's winter 2001 troubles that a majority of the Cabinet would not be ready to walk into a curtained polling booth and put a cross against Brown's name. There is too much resentment at the Treasury, and at Brown's control of their departments, for that to seem the most desirable succession. No other yet seems likely, and ministers still accept that the baton may be passed on in the way that the rivals envisaged vaguely in 1994. But they are far from sure, and a majority believe that the relationship between the two is more likely to end in tears.

Brown will continue to be the Iron Chancellor. He will try to deliver the social benefits for which he wants to be remembered above all, even though to some of his colleagues he will continue in the process to illustrate the truth of P. G. Wodehouse's immortal observation, that it is not difficult to tell the difference between a Scotsman bearing a grievance and a ray of sunshine. But as time goes on he will have to confront the fact of Blair's determination.

He has made up his mind to fight the next election as Prime Minister. Any hope Brown may have of Blair's voluntary retirement rests on one unlikely premise, a euro referendum in the course of the second term that Blair loses. It is an outcome that the Prime Minister is determined to avoid, and even if he succumbed to the consequence of a fatal error of political judgement it is hard to see how Brown – whose five tests would have triggered the referendum and who would be compelled to be by the Prime Minister's side throughout – could be the beneficiary.

No one close to Blair doubts his two objectives. One is to take Britain into the single currency, to build the last span of the bridge to Europe. The other is to be elected to serve a third term. Blair sees in the European decision the opportunity to gain that place in history which second-term Prime Ministers naturally crave. Northern Ireland, once the repository of some of that hope, no longer shines with promise. Making the trains run on time and delivering public investment to public services in ways that bring visible dividends are second-term obsessions in Whitehall but they don't have the lustre of the national statement that a referendum result would give. Blair wants to ride the tide that will carry him across the English Channel. His ambition is fraught with fears, of course, although after the launch of the euro on 1 January 2002, there was enough movement in the polls to suggest that scepticism might be less entrenched than before. By Easter, those around Blair believed that they might well be ready for spring 2003. They waited, as ever, for Brown.

A referendum victory would propel Blair into a third election with his blood up. And for Brown the future would seem melancholy. A two-term Chancellor, even one who could claim to be the architect of such achievements as the government could muster, would look like an ageing pretender, a Prince of Wales doomed never to be king. But the most likely political outcome is that Blair will decide early in a third term – with an eye on Margaret Thatcher's eleven-year record as Prime Minister – to step down in his own time. Any earlier decision seems to depend on an Act of God, a runaway No. 24 bus in Whitehall or a sudden change of heart on Blair's part which would astonish those who know him best.

The politics and the personalities are pushing against each other. Blair's political judgement carries him down a path which will make it more difficult for Brown to succeed. The warm words of hope which Blair gave Brown in 1994, meant to preserve the relationship, seem part of another age. When Brown left Granita on that Tuesday night in May 1994, wanting to believe that he had struck a deal, and decided to rejoin his friends Balls, Whelan and Nick Brown to eat steak and chips it was perhaps an implicit acknowledgement not only that New Labour food and the Islington ambience were not for him, but that there was an illusory aspect to the whole experience.

Blair still says that he hopes Brown will succeed him, but the transition is spoken of in Number 10 as an event that may be slipping from sight. The second term is meant, with luck, to have its climax in the referendum and not in Blair's retirement. A Prime Minister who won that campaign would not be one who could resist the prospect of a third election victory which it would certainly make more likely. Brown could hardly choose that moment to mount a *coup d'état* and would have to decide whether he wanted to be Chancellor of the Exchequer for a third time (the first person to harbour that desire since the nineteenth century) or to step away from government altogether. The thought of him as Foreign Secretary is odd – the lack of executive power would frustrate him mightily – and any other job would be subordinate to the new Chancellor. Brown would not be able to bear it. Would he go?

He is a political animal from head to toe. But intriguing thoughts are often passed round his circle. The International Monetary Fund is a possibility. The World Bank? Even the European Central Bank cannot be ruled out for Brown, though it is hard to see France and Germany accepting a British president. The last time the top IMF job came round Brown was not seriously interested but took the trouble to talk it over with some fellow finance ministers around Europe, spreading the message that he was not someone who necessarily saw himself spending the rest of his life in Whitehall.

At some moment in the future, if Blair is settling into a third term, and other ministers are flexing their leadership muscles, which are already twitching, Brown might have to decide to make the break. He has friends in America and Europe who would encourage him, and some have already suggested that he should begin to think seriously about an international financial role.

These are distant thoughts for both men. But they will be distilled in the politics of the referendum, which will settle the timing. Blair will test his hope against public opinion. He will also work on

Rupert Murdoch, purveyor to date of a pure stream of Euroscepticism. When Blair first attended a conference of Murdoch's News Corporation on Hayman Island in Australia in 1995, Murdoch introduced him by saying that if they were going to have an affair, as people had been suggesting they might, they would do it as porcupines make love. Very slowly. Blair has been careful with him ever since and will weigh the passions of the *Sun* and *The Times* (to the despair of many in his party). In timing the referendum, that will be as important as the Treasury assessment of the five tests.

Not until then will the patterns in the sand start to settle and give Brown an opportunity to study the lie of the land. He has support in the unions and in the party – new MPs elected in 2001 received invitations to Number 11 in the first week, just as the 1997 intake had – and though his Cabinet allies are in the minority his political authority is immense. Blair himself says he is Labour's most formidable force, and the party acknowledges that he stands, like Blair himself, above the rest of the Cabinet.

But Brown is the challenger who can do little to advance his chances of inheriting the crown. He cannot precipitate Blair's departure without a charge of disloyalty that would make his succession improbable. The partnership which took them into government and which has made their administration work cannot be broken without consequences which would almost certainly be politically fatal for both of them.

Blair is well aware of the pain this conundrum causes. Roy Jenkins told him once about his own relationship with his old student friend Anthony Crosland. They were young blades together, ambitious MPs, and they were two of the principal intellectual forces in the Labour Party of the Gaitskell era. Jenkins leapt ahead. On the ministerial merry-go-round he was Home Secretary while Crosland was stuck at Education, Chancellor when Crosland was at Environment. Then in 1976 he progressed from Home Secretary to be the first British president of the European Commission, just as Crosland reached the Foreign Office for the last eight months of his life. Jenkins explained to Blair the difficulty this caused in their relationship, which was to both of them the most important they had, apart from that with their wives. Crosland was the older by a couple of years (exactly the same gap as that which divides Brown and Blair) and, according to Jenkins had a better brain. Blair often says that he knows, too, that Brown has a sharper intellect. Yet Crosland did not quite make it, and Jenkins did. Now and again when Jenkins and Blair meet, the Prime Minister gives a smile and says: 'Tell me the Crosland story again.'

Blair and Brown know that their partnership cannot last for ever. It has delivered them and their party an extraordinary period of untrammelled power and a capacity to influence their era in a way that few governments have an opportunity to do in their short time in the sun. Yet it has also given the two of them a sharpened sense of the melancholy undercurrent of politics, the understanding that every agreement brings in its wake the chance of failure, disappointment and personal tragedy. Their partnership is also their struggle.

Each knows now that the long years of apprenticeship and the achievement have taken them to a zenith from which they may well now be fated to begin their descent. They will start that journey together, but they know they will end it as they began – as friends whose rivalry is inescapable. They are bound together, until the life they have chosen to lead drives them apart.

'He loves me not!'

Chronology of Events

Date	Blair	Brown	Date	Events
6 May 53	Born in Edinburgh			
		Born in Giffnock		
20 Feb 51				
1961–6	The Chorister School, Durham			
1966–71	Fettes College, Edinburgh			
1961–7		Kirkcaldy High School		
1967–73		Edinburgh University		
			10 Jan 57	Macmillan PM
			15 Oct 64	Labour elected. Wilson PM
			31 Mar 66	Wilson re-elected
			18 June 70	Labour defeated. Edward Heath PM
			28 Oct 71	Jenkins rebellion
1972–5	St John's College, Oxford	Rector, Edinburgh University	1 Jan 73	Britain joins EEC
28 June 75	Mother dies		28 Feb 74	Labour elected. Wilson PM
			10 Oct 74	Wilson re-elected
1975		Publishes *Red Paper on Scotland*	5 June 75	Referendum on continued EEC membership
1976	Trainee barrister in Irvine's chambers		5 Apr 76	Wilson resigns. Callaghan PM
1978		Chairman, Labour Devolution Committee	1978	Scotland Act passed
			1 Mar 79	Devolution referendum
3 May 79		Contests Edinburgh South	3 May 79	Labour defeated. Thatcher PM
29 Mar 80	Marries Cherie Booth		3 Nov 80	Foot elected Labour leader
			Mar 81	SDP formed

Blair	Brown	Events
		Sep 81 — Healey defeats Benn for Labour deputy leadership
		25 Mar 82 — Jenkins wins Glasgow Hillhead for SDP
27 May 82 — Contests Beaconsfield by-election		
		2 Apr 82 — Argentina invades Falklands
	1983–4 — Chairman of Scottish Labour Party	
20 May 83 — Selected for Sedgefield	16 May 83 — Selected for Dunfermline East	
9 June 83 — Elected MP for Sedgefield	9 June 83 — Elected MP for Dunfermline East	9 June 83 — Thatcher re-elected
	Oct 83 — Publishes *Scotland: The Real Divide* with Cook	2 Oct 83 — Kinnock elected Labour leader
7 Nov 84 — Junior Treasury spokesman		8 Mar 84 — Miners' strike begins
		5 Mar 85 — Miners return to work
		24 Sep 85 — Mandelson appointed director of communications
	Nov 85 — Trade and Industry spokesman	
	1986 — Publishes biography of James Maxton	
8 July 87 — City and Consumer Affairs spokesman	8 July 87 — Shadow Chief Secretary to the Treasury	11 June 87 — Thatcher re-elected
Nov 88 — Shadow Energy Secretary		Oct 88 — Smith suffers heart attack
		26 Oct 89 — Lawson resigns

	Nov 89		Nov 89		
Nov 89	Shadow Employment Secretary		Shadow Trade and Industry Secretary	11 Feb 90	Mandela released
				8 Oct 90	UK joins ERM
				1 Nov 90	Howe resigns
				28 Nov 90	Thatcher resigns. Major PM
				9 Apr 92	Major re-elected
				13 Apr 92	Neil Kinnock resigns
				18 July 92	Smith elected Labour leader
23 July 92	Shadow Home Secretary	23 July 92	Shadow Chancellor	16 Sep 92	Black Wednesday – Britain leaves ERM
Jan 93	Visits Washington, DC	Jan 93	Visits Washington, DC	12 May 94	Smith dies
31 May 94	Dinner at Granita	31 May 94	Dinner at Granita		
		1 July 94	Announces he won't stand for leader. Backs Blair		
21 July 94	Elected Labour leader			31 Aug 94	IRA announce ceasefire
4 Oct 94	Announces review of Clause IV			29 Apr 95	Special Labour conference approves new Clause IV
				22 June 95	Major resigns
				4 July 95	Major re-elected
				9 Feb 96	IRA break ceasefire – Docklands bomb
				29 Oct 96	Cook–Maclennan talks announced

Blair	Brown	Events
Government 1997–2001		5 Mar 97 — Cook–Maclennan talks reported
2 May 97 — Prime Minister	2 May 97 — Chancellor	1 May 97 — Labour elected. Blair PM
8 May 97 — First Cabinet meeting: 'Call me Tony'	6 May 97 — Independence of Bank of England	
		9 May 97 — Format of PMQs changed to one thirty-minute session a week
		14 May 97 — Queen's Speech
		29 May 97 — Clinton addresses Cabinet
		19 June 97 — Hague becomes Conservative leader
		30 June 97 — Hong Kong returns to China
	2 July 97 — First Budget: windfall tax on private utilities, new tax on pensions	
		20 July 97 — IRA ceasefire restored
		22 July 97 — LibDems join Cabinet Consultative Committee
	7 Sep 97 — Appointed Chairman of Diana, Princess of Wales Memorial Committee	6 Sep 97 — Funeral of Diana, Princess of Wales
		11 Sep 97 — Referendum on Scottish Parliament
		17 Sep 97 — First meeting of Lib–Lab Cabinet Committee

18 Sep 97	Referendum on Welsh Assembly
29 Sep 97	Livingstone beats Mandelson in NEC election
30 Sep 97	First Labour Party conference speech as Prime Minister
13 Oct 97	Meets Gerry Adams at Stormont
16 Oct 97	Meets Bernie Ecclestone at Downing Street
18 Oct 97	*The Times* headlines interview: 'Brown rules out single currency for lifetime of this Parliament'
27 Oct 97	Tells Commons that UK will not join the launch of euro in 1999
11 Nov 97	Ecclestone admits £1 million donation to Labour
16 Nov 97	Apologizes for handling of decision to exempt Formula 1 from proposed ban on tobacco advertising. Denies any wrong-doing
29 Nov 97	Geoffrey Robinson admits £12 million offshore trust
1 Dec 97	Jenkins Commission established
10 Dec 97	Forty-seven Labour MPs rebel against lone-parent benefit cut
11 Dec 97	Adams becomes first Republican leader since Michael Collins to meet Prime Minister at Downing Street

Blair

5 Jan 98	Launches British Euro presidency at Waterloo
4–7 Feb 98	First official visit to United States as Prime Minister
24 Mar 98	Address to French National Assembly
11 June 98	With Paddy Ashdown, releases joint declaration for constitutional reform
27 July 98	First Cabinet reshuffle – Peter Mandelson in; Harriet Harman and Frank Field out; Nick Brown demoted

Brown

17 Mar 98	Budget: introduction of Working Families' Tax Credit
18 June 98	Announcement of national minimum wage £3.60/hour
14 July 98	Comprehensive Spending Review: triple-counting of public spending plans

Events

18 Jan 98	Source close to Blair despairs of Brown's 'psychological flaws'
20 Jan 98	Robinson rebuked by Parliamentary Standards Commissioner for not declaring offshore trust
10 Apr 98	Good Friday Agreement signed
22 May 98	Voters in Northern Ireland and Irish Republic back Good Friday Agreement

15 Aug 98	Real IRA bomb in Omagh kills twenty-nine
21 Sep 98	Third Way seminar in New York with Clinton
29 Oct 98	Jenkins Commission recommends 'alternative vote plus'
18 Nov 98	Standards and Privileges Committee publish report recommending Robinson makes an apology to the Commons
16 Dec 98	US and UK military forces launch cruise missile and air attacks on targets in Iraq
22 Dec 98	*Guardian* reveals that Mandelson kept £373,000 loan from Robinson secret
23 Dec 98	Mandelson resigns as DTI Secretary. Robinson resigns as Paymaster General
1 Jan 99	Launch of the euro in eleven EU countries
4 Jan 99	Charlie Whelan announces he is to give up his job 'as soon as an appropriate opportunity becomes available'
20 Jan 99	Ashdown announces intention to retire as LibDem leader

Blair	Brown	Events
23 Feb 99 — Launches National Changeover Plan to prepare UK for the changeover to the euro		
	9 Mar 99 — Budget: introduction of new 10p income tax rate and 1p reduction in basic rate to 22p	
		24 Mar 99 — NATO airstrikes launched against targets in Yugoslavia
3 May 99 — Visits refugee camps on Kosovo–Macedonia border		
		6 May 99 — Elections for Scottish Parliament and Welsh Assembly
		20 May 99 — Biggest backbench rebellion in first term – sixty-five Labour MPs vote against government's proposals for reform of incapacity benefit
		10 June 99 — Yugoslav generals sign peace deal with NATO ending Kosovo war
	14 June 99 — Ian Austin's appointment as special adviser announced	
		9 Aug 99 — Kennedy elected LibDem leader
11 Oct 99 — Cabinet reshuffle – Mandelson back as Northern Ireland Secretary		
		14 Oct 99 — Launch of Britain in Europe

26 Oct 99	Deal between government and opposition peers ends the right of most hereditary peers to sit in the Lords
4 Nov 99	Blairs are the guests of honour of the Hindujas at the Indian Festival of Light event in London
18 Nov 99	Cherie Blair's pregnancy announced
1 Jan 00	Millennium Dome opening fiasco
16 Jan 00	Pledges NHS spending will be brought up to the European average
20 Jan 00	Wakeham Commission recommends a partially elected second chamber
10 Feb 00	Welsh First Secretary Alun Michael resigns before a vote of no confidence
15 Feb 00	Welsh Assembly appoints Rhodri Morgan as new First Secretary
20 Feb 00	Frank Dobson defeats Livingstone to become Labour's candidate for London Mayor
6 Mar 00	Livingstone announces intention to stand as an independent
11 Mar 00	Travels to Russia. Becomes first EC leader to meet Acting President Vladimir Putin
21 Mar 00	Budget: extra funding for the NHS

	Blair	Brown	Events
19 Apr 00			Mandelson makes positive speech on the euro
4 May 00			Livingstone elected Mayor of London
16 May 00			Mandelson speech about the damage to Britain if it stays outside the euro
20 May 00	Cherie Blair gives birth to baby boy, Leo		
26 May 00		Criticizes Oxford University for elitism over Laura Spence	
7 June 00	Heckled at Women's Institute conference, Wembley Arena		
30 June 00	Proposes £100 fines for drunken or antisocial behaviour		
6 July 00	Euan Blair arrested in Leicester Square for being drunk and incapable		
17 July 00	Sun and The Times publish leaked memo written by Blair saying the government is perceived to be 'out of touch' with gut British instincts		
18 July 00		Comprehensive Spending Review: extra £43 billion for public services from 2001–4	
3 Aug 00		Marries Sarah Macaulay at his home in North Queensferry	

8 Sep 00		Blockades of petrol refineries begin
14 Sep 00		Fuel protests called off
26 Sep 00	Admits mistakes over pensions and the Dome at Labour Party conference	
27 Sep 00		Leadership defeated at conference after delegates back motion calling for restoration of link between earnings and pensions
11 Oct 00		Donald Dewar dies
17 Oct 00		Labour and LibDems in Welsh Assembly agree to form coalition
26 Oct 00		Henry McLeish appointed new Scottish First Minister
8 Nov 00	Pre-Budget report: rise in pensions and cut in motoring costs	
2 Jan 01		Lord Hamlyn revealed as mystery £2 million donor to Labour
4 Jan 01		Labour announce further £4 million in donations from Lord Sainsbury and Christopher Ondaatje
24 Jan 01		Mandelson resigns from Cabinet for the second time
20 Feb 01		Britain's first case of foot and mouth for twenty years found in Essex
23 Feb 01	Becomes first European leader to meet President Bush	

	Blair	Brown	Events
5 Mar 01			Increase in minimum wage to £4.10/hour
7 Mar 01		Budget: more money for health and education. Increased children's tax credit	
9 Mar 01			Hammond Report published. Clears Mandelson of acting dishonestly
2 Apr 01	Announces delay in local elections until 7 June		
26 Apr 01			Phoenix the calf saved from slaughter
8 May 01	Announces General Election in a speech at St Saviour's & St Olave's Church of England School in Southwark		
16 May 01	Heckled by Sharron Storer, disgruntled partner of an NHS cancer patient		Labour launch manifesto *Ambitions for Britain* in Birmingham. John Prescott punches protester in Rhyl after being hit by an egg
17 May 01	Tells morning press conference 'John is John'		
22 May 01			Margaret McDonagh alleges broadcasters colluding with protesters

Government 2001–

8 June 01   Cabinet reshuffle – Cook from Foreign Office to Leader of House of Commons; Straw becomes Foreign Secretary; Blunkett becomes Home Secretary

20 June 01   Mansion House speech – euro referendum unlikely to be called before 2003 and might not be held at all during the lifetime of this Parliament

18 July 01   Sarah Macaulay's pregnancy announced

9 Aug 01   Announces establishment of inquiries into foot and mouth outbreak

11 Sep 01   Leaves TUC Conference in Brighton and returns to Downing St

12 Sep 01   Announces recall of Parliament

7 June 01   Blair re-elected

16 July 01   Government defeated in the Commons. One hundred and twenty Labour MPs rebel over membership of Select Committees

11 Sep 01   Terrorist attacks in New York and Washington

	Blair	Brown	Events
13 Sep 01			Iain Duncan Smith defeats Kenneth Clarke in Conservative leadership contest
19 Sep 01	Visits Germany for talks with Chancellor Schroeder		
20 Sep 01	Visits Paris for talks with President Chirac		Lib–Lab Cabinet Committee suspended
20 Sep 01	Visits New York. Has dinner with President Bush in Washington		
21 Sep 01	Visits Brussels for emergency EU summit		
2 Oct 01	Addresses Labour Party Conference		
4 Oct 01	Visits Russia for talks with President Putin		
5 Oct 01	Visits Islamabad for talks with President Musharraf		
6 Oct 01	Visits Delhi for talks with PM Vajpayee		
7 Oct 01			US and UK launch raids on Kabul, Kandahar and Jalalabad
7 Oct 01			Railtrack placed under administration
8 Oct 01	War cabinet meets for the first time		

9 Oct 01	Visits Geneva				9 Oct 01	Jo Moore 'burying bad news' e-mail revealed
10 Oct 01	Visits Oman					
11 Oct 01	Visits Cairo					
15 Oct 01	Meets PLO Chairman Yasser Arafat at Downing St		15 Oct 01	Announces anti-laundering measures to crack down on terrorist finances	16 Oct 01	Jo Moore apologizes publicly for her e-mail
					23 Oct 01	IRA announce implementation of decommissioning scheme
31 Oct 01	Visits Syria and Saudi Arabia					
1 Nov 01	Visits Jordan, Israel and Gaza					
7 Nov 01	Visits Washington				7 Nov 01	White Paper on second stage of Lords reform published
8 Nov 01	Special Assistant, Anji Hunter, announces she is to leave government to become Director of Communications for BP					
					13 Nov 01	Kabul falls to Northern Alliance
					17 Nov 01	Mo Mowlam hits out at damage done to government by rivalry between Brown and Blair
22 Nov 01	In *Times* interview, describes Blair as 'the best friend I've had in politics'					

	Blair		Brown	Events
		27 Nov 01	Pre-Budget Report: £1 bn extra for NHS	
		2 Dec 01	On *Breakfast with Frost* refuses to deny that a deal existed with Blair on the leadership succession	
				5 Dec 01 — Parliamentary Standards Commissioner Elizabeth Filkin alleges that pressure brought to bear on her during inquiries and criticizes watering-down of her post
		17 Dec 01	Outlines plans for a twenty-first-century 'Marshall Plan' for the developing world	
		28 Dec 01	Daughter, Jennifer Jane Brown, born	
1 Jan 02	In New Year message warns of a year of 'unprecedented' changes throughout public services and 'unsettling' reforms			
3 Jan 02	Starts tour of South Asian countries. Meets leaders of Bangladesh, India and Pakistan			
		7 Jan 02	Jennifer Jane Brown dies after brain haemorrhage	

8 Jan 02   First Western leader to enter
Afghanistan since the fall of the
Taliban. Photo opportunity at
Bagram Airport with Hamid Karzai

11 Jan 02   Funeral of Jennifer Jane Brown

3 Feb 02   Told Labour's Spring Conference
that government would not back
down in its drive to modernize public
services despite the efforts of 'wreckers'

6 Feb 02   Hints that his son Leo has had the
MMR jab

11 Feb 02   Criticized for writing a letter in support
of Lakshmi Mittal's takeover bid for
Romania's steel industry, Sidex

15 Feb 02   Spin doctor Jo Moore and Martin
Sixsmith, head of communications at
Dept of Transport, leave their jobs

Bibliography and Illustration Credits

Ashdown, Paddy, *The Ashdown Diaries, Vol. 1, 1988–1997*, Allen Lane, 2000
—, *The Ashdown Diaries, Vol. 2, 1997–1999*, Allen Lane, 2001
Brown, Colin, *Fighting Talk: The Biography of John Prescott*, Simon & Schuster, 1997
Brown, Gordon (ed.), *The Red Paper on Scotland*, Edinburgh Student Pubs, 1975
—, *James Maxton*, Mainstream, 1986
Gould, Philip, *The Unfinished Revolution: How the Modernisers Saved the Labour Party*, Little, Brown, 1998
Hennessy, Peter, *Cabinet*, Blackwell, 1986
—, *The Prime Minister: The Office and Its Holders Since 1945*, Penguin Books, 2000
Jenkins, Roy, *The Chancellors*, Macmillan, 1998
Kampfner, John, *Robin Cook: The Biography*, Phoenix (revised edn), 1999
Kavanagh, Dennis, and Seldon, Anthony, *The Powers Behind the Prime Minister: The Hidden Influence of Number Ten*, HarperCollins, 2000
Langdon, Julia, *Mo Mowlam*, Little, Brown, 2000
Lawson, Nigel, *The View from No. 11*, Bantam, 1992
Macintyre, Donald, *Mandelson and the Making of New Labour*, HarperCollins, 1999
Major, John, *John Major: The Autobiography*, HarperCollins, 1999
Mandelson, Peter, and Liddle, Roger, *The Blair Revolution: Can New Labour Deliver?*, Faber & Faber, 1996
McSmith, Andy, *John Smith: Playing the Long Game*, Verso, 1993
Oborne, Peter, *Alastair Campbell: New Labour and the Rise of the Media Class*, Aurum Press, 1999
O'Farrell, John, *Things Can Only Get Better*, Doubleday, 1998

Pimlott, Ben, *Harold Wilson*, HarperCollins, 1992

Rawnsley, Andrew, *Servants of the People: The Inside Story of New Labour*, Hamish Hamilton, 2000

Rentoul, John, *Tony Blair: Prime Minister*, Little, Brown, 2000

Riddell, Peter, *Honest Opportunism*, Gollancz, 1995

—, *Parliament Under Pressure*, Gollancz, 1998

Routledge, Paul, *Gordon Brown: The Biography*, Simon & Schuster, 1998

—, *Mandy*, Simon & Schuster, 1999

Seldon, Anthony (ed.), *The Blair Effect: The Blair Government 1997–2001*, Little, Brown, 2001

Sopel, Jon, *Tony Blair: The Moderniser*, Michael Joseph, 1995

Stephens, Philip, *Politics and the Pound*, Macmillan, 1996

Woodward, Bob, *Maestro: Greenspan's Fed and the American Boom*, Simon & Schuster, 2000

Young, Hugo, *One of Us*, Macmillan, 1989

—, *This Blessed Plot: Britain and Europe from Churchill to Blair*, Macmillan, 1998

plate section

1 Portrait of James Maxton by John Lavery © Scottish National Portrait Gallery

Brown as student © The Scotsman Publ. Ltd. Edinburgh

2 Tony Blair with Michael Foot © PA Photos

3 Brown congratulates Blair © Graham Turner/The Guardian

4 Blair and Clinton in silhouette © PA Photos

5 Tony Blair giving a speech to the WI © PA Photos

6 Campbell and Blair © PA Photos

Gordon Brown © Martin Argles/The Guardian

7 Tony Blair and Gordon Brown at Millbank © PA Photos

8 The Blairs in India, 2002 © Popperfoto

cartoons

Page xii © Chris Riddell (first published in the *Observer*)

Page 1 © Richard Wilson (first published in *The Times*)

Page 77 © Charles Griffin (first published in the *Express*)

Page 127 © Peter Brookes (first published in *The Times*)

Page 231 © Dave Brown (first published in the *Sunday Times*)

Page 371 © Nicholas Garland (first published in the *Daily Telegraph*)

Index

'GB' indicates Gordon Brown and 'TB' Tony Blair.